seamlessly. I was moved to tears of sadness and frustration but also tears of joy! Well done indeed."

—Michael Berenbaum, Distinguished Professor of Jewish Studies, American Jewish University, Los Angeles, CA

"Dr. Wolf's book breaks new ground in describing Soviet postwar rule in Hungary, with its forbidden zones, secret files, seizures of property, and paranoia which favored only the privileged party elites. ... *Not A Real Enemy* merits a worthy place in recalling the Jewish people's darkest night and its ongoing thirst for rebirth and renewal."

—Monty Noam Penkower, Yom Yerushalayim 5782, Professor Emeritus of Jewish History at the Machon Lander Graduate School of Jewish Studies (Jerusalem), is the prize-winning author of many books on the Holocaust, on American Jewry, and on the rise of the State of Israel in the years 1933-1948.

ADVANCE PRAISE

"Robert Wolf deftly combines his father's testimony and his own research into a riveting historical narrative to recreate a sensitive and sophisticated portrayal of Jewish life in Hungary before, during, and after the Holocaust. It is a profoundly moving account of the Wolf family's dignity, courage, and resilience in the face of implacable hatred. It is a story of loss, but more importantly of survival and the strength of the human spirit in the face of overwhelming odds."

—Edward B. Westermann, Regents Professor of History, Texas A&M University-San Antonio and author of *Drunk on Genocide: Alcohol and Mass Murder in Nazi Germany.*

"*Not a Real Enemy* is a powerful tribute and compelling narrative that begins at the turn of the twentieth century and takes us through the turmoil of World War I and the build up to the Holocaust. It then brings us into the death camp of Auschwitz Birkenau and into the slave labor camps of Hungary and also to life under communism and the daring escape into the free world. The writing is crisp, the story complex but the author weaves the narrative strands together

NOT A REAL ENEMY

THE TRUE STORY OF A HUNGARIAN JEWISH MAN'S FIGHT FOR FREEDOM

ROBERT WOLF

JANICE HARPER

ap

ISBN 9789493276741 (ebook)

ISBN 9789493276727 (paperback)

ISBN 9789493276734 (hardcover)

Publisher: Amsterdam Publishers, The Netherlands

info@amsterdampublishers.com

Not a Real Enemy is part of the series Holocaust True Survivor Stories

Copyright © Robert Wolf, 2022

Robert@RobertJWolfMD.com

Winner of the Silver Nautilus Award Historical Fiction 2023.

Winner of the National Indie Excellence Award 2023.

Cover image: Alexander von Ness of www.nessgraphica.com

All Rights Reserved. No part of this publication may be reproduced or transmitted in any form or by any means, electronic or mechanical, including photocopy, recording or any other information storage and retrieval system, without prior permission in writing from the publisher.

CONTENTS

Author's Note	vii

PART I
FAMILY

Goodbye	3
Hope and Prayer	9
Induction	23
Fresh Start	33
Sheep Farm	45
Private Practice	54
Fortunate Son	63
Winter	75
A Gilded Life	86
In the Company of Guards	97
Downtown	103
Home	117
Unwanted	129
Return to Camp	142
Occupation	152
Alone	158
Twenty-five Kilos	161

PART II
IT'S BETTER NOT TO KNOW

Retreat	177
Marching On	189
Escape	199
On the Run	208
Hunting Season	221
Under the Bed	227
Captured	235
Pink Robe	241
Mathiasfold	247
And They Marched On	260
Homecoming	267

PART III
FROM YELLOW STAR

Sheets of Gold	285
Quick Escape	297
Under the Dark Skies	304
Judit	319
Two Weddings	329
Dark and Getting Darker	334
A Broken Man	341
Revolution	347
Not a Real Enemy	356
Second Thoughts	364
Stranger on a Train	376
Freedom	387
Epilogue	397
Acknowledgments	401
Amsterdam Publishers Holocaust Library	403

AUTHOR'S NOTE

This is a true story, or as true to history and the life of Ervin Wolf as the author could tell it. All names have been changed other than the author's own family and public figures. The events and characters depicted are real, though in some cases, names have been changed. Viktor Kroonenberg is a character of the imagination but based on a real person. Guards' names and certain details are imagined, based on the account of Ervin Wolf, and accounts from other Hungarian conscripts in the Labor Service at that time. Dialogue is imagined, while the events themselves are based on the notes and memories of Ervin Wolf as told to his son, Robert.

PART I
FAMILY

GOODBYE
OCTOBER 1943

The house was dark and quiet. Ervin stepped into his parents' bedroom, knowing that despite the early morning hour, his father would want to say goodbye. A part of him wanted to just leave, not face him. Not see once more the creeping fear that day by day had etched itself deeper into his father's face so that now his fright was unmistakable.

At 21, Ervin had never left home, and he had certainly never imagined his departure from his family would be anything like this. How could anyone imagine such a thing? But here it was. And here he was. The time had come.

Ervin's father, Joseph, was awake and sitting in his bed in the dark. As he heard his son enter the room, he reached across the nightstand and switched on the gooseneck lamp. The light illuminated his face as if it were the work of an old master, a renaissance portrait painted in strokes of pain and love. Ervin realized, in that moment, that he had never examined his father's face so closely before. He noted the unrepaired broken nose that did not fit well on his face. At first sight, his nose looked distorted, but at second glance, Ervin saw not the nose, but the warm eyes, already wet with tears he dare not let fall. The face symmetric, the skin, unblemished. All framed with fine, textured hair graying at the temples. The misshapen nose, Ervin noted, added to his father's beauty, rather than detracted from it. The nose, like the tear-filled eyes, spoke of a hurting life. A life that had endured. A life in need of repair.

Ervin stepped closer and sat on the edge of the bed. "It's time to say goodbye, Father," he said, his voice cracking. He would not permit himself to cry. He raised his head higher, as if by posing himself erect, he might grow stronger.

The elder man took Ervin's hand in his own and held it tightly, then leaned over and kissed his son's head. "Good luck, son," he said. "Be strong. I hope we will see you again soon, God willing." Then his eyes slid away, his face and posture stiffened, and Joseph showed no further emotion.

Ervin's own gaze fell upon his father's nightstand and as it did, he noted each familiar object, as if by memorizing their existence, their shape, their placement, he might fix them there forever, as if he might will his return to this home, this room, this moment alone with his father, by the force of his own mind. The pile of change emptied each night from his father's pockets onto the small porcelain tray his grandmother had so carefully painted. His father's favorite jackknife, with mother-of-pearl handle yellowed from age, the blade always razor sharp. Joseph did not keep the knife for self-defense. He had no need for that. No desire to injure. It was the knife he used to peel and cut his favorite Golden Reinette apples, spiraling the peel in one long, unbroken piece that he would toss to young Ervin, who marveled at the coil of golden bronze skin before being offered a wedge of the sweet fruit. Joseph never went anywhere without that knife, finding it a practical yet comforting tool to always have on hand. Ervin called it his father's teddy bear, a term that always brought Joseph to smile.

Beside the knife was Joseph's prized possession, his gold pocket watch with double covers, hanging from a golden chain like an amulet. Inside one of the watch's covers was a blurry picture of Ervin's mother, a photo so old and tattered that Ervin could not imagine she had ever lived so long ago, had ever looked so young. Inside the other cover was a photo of Joseph's own mother, centuries old Ervin imagined, as he had never met her. She had died from a heart condition at a young age, leaving six children, of which Joseph was the middle child. Ervin couldn't imagine not having had a mother.

Ervin raised his gaze from the table to his father, stood and bowed slightly before leaving the room. Stepping outside the bedroom, he noticed a light coming from the front room. As he walked down the hallway one last time, he saw the entryway softly illuminated by the glow of a single sconce. He thought of the many guests who had been welcomed into their home over the years he had grown up there. Would there ever again be a knock at the door, a ringing of the bell, that brought not fear, but happy expectation? Would the voices that came through the door ever again be heard aloud, chattering unrestrained, or would they forever be hushed and worried? Would Ervin ever see again another evening gathering of his parents' friends and colleagues, dressed in their most elegant attire, the classical music of Liszt or Brahms playing on the phonograph as their joyful laughter rang through the apartment, unconcerned about the future? Would he ever again be fascinated by the sparkling champagne and amber Tokay they drank from crystal glasses as he had been as a small boy? By the time he reached the end of the long hallway, he knew, somehow, that those magical days were now his memories.

His mother was standing at their doorstep wearing an old coat she used to wear to the market. She appeared tired, her eyes swollen, and she turned her head away to hide her tears.

"I packed some walnut crescents in your bag," she said, "and a few pierogis. They will be cold, but perhaps you can warm them somehow."

Ervin smiled. She would have been up all night baking the cookies, rolling the pierogi dough, and filling each dumpling with mashed potatoes and cheese. "They will be delicious cold," he assured her, heaving his bag onto his back.

"*Yevorechecho Hashem Ve'Yishmerecho,*" she murmured, resting her hand upon his head. May God bless and shield you from harm.

They looked at each other for a mere moment before he nodded, turned the latch, and left his home. Walking down the staircase to the foyer below, he let his hand pass along the white tiled border, noting the simple blue tulips on the tiles that had so delighted him as a child. When they reached the foyer, he opened the outer door, gesturing for his mother to precede him. It was still dark outside, the streets empty. He and his mother walked together in silence, the only sound an occasional bicycle or the wheels of the milk cart as it made its rounds from house to house. Slowly, he heard the singing. His mind so aloud with his thoughts, he had barely discerned the sounds, but as the voices pierced his reverie, their song grew deafening. The trees were full of sparrows calling to each other in their high-pitched chirping. Ervin shuddered at the sound, so foreboding in its innocence.

It was a cold, foggy morning in early fall, and though the walk to the railway station was not far, Ervin found his backpack to be very heavy and difficult to carry. As he walked he wondered what he could discard from it and yet, he knew that to discard anything might mean the difference between his survival and demise. Ervin was determined to survive.

The commuter train was already waiting on the ramp when they reached the station. His friends, at least a dozen, were ready to go. All wore the same look of pride and worry on their faces, all looked less like men and more like children as they huddled in their wool coats, seeking to comfort as much as warm themselves.

Their recruiting station was in Komárom, a town in Hungary bordering Slovakia and approximately 64 kilometers from Győr, the place of their departure. Ervin's home. What would be expected of them when they reached Komárom was anybody's guess. No one really knew the fate of the young Jewish men drafted into the Auxiliary Labor Service, one only knew that Jews were not permitted to join the German-allied Hungarian military. Instead, they were conscripted into forced labor and sent, unarmed and poorly equipped, to Ukraine and the most remote regions of Hungary, their parents left with no knowledge of what their children were enduring, other than the occasional letters that arrived, no doubt opened and reviewed by government agents. These parents would do their best to read between the lines to guess at what their sons were really made to do, how they were really doing. They knew only that the work was hard, the conditions brutal, the boys hungry. They knew some labored in the harsh cold, cutting trees and carrying the heavy logs back and forth all day, all night. Some dug graves and buried bodies. So many bodies. Some were forced to cross the mine fields, human mine detectors. So far, none had returned home to tell what really happened.

Ervin, the only child of Dr. Joseph and Kamilla Wolf, had never known labor of any kind, much less hard labor. He had, if anything, been coddled by his parents, spoiled with every toy and sweet and privilege a child of wealth might enjoy. True, his father could be a stern disciplinarian and Ervin knew too well the whack of a stick or the sting of a belt for misbehaving or worse, for being late. But his father was neither cruel nor cold, and Ervin never doubted for a moment the love both his parents felt for him. If anything, he understood his father's discipline was less a correction of Ervin than it was a correction of himself, for Joseph's own childhood had been a punishing one, one he had devoted his life to undoing.

Ervin nodded toward his friends, set his backpack down, and turned to his mother. "Thank you, mother, for everything," he said, referring not to the cookies and pierogis he knew he would treasure with every bite, but for his life, for his joy, for all she had brought to the world in the half century she'd lived. He knew that if he lingered, he would break down, blubbering in her arms, and that he could not do, not in front of his friends. Not in front of the soldiers already watching them.

"I love you, Ervin," she said, her face flickering through her efforts to control it. "Be strong. Have faith. And promise me you'll write home about whatever is happening. Tell me everything." She kissed his cheek, then hugged him tightly to her chest, holding him closely until he pulled himself away.

"I promise, Mama, I will," he said, giving her a final kiss goodbye. Then he walked toward his friends, as if he were leaving for holiday. Before he could greet them, the train whistle sounded and the soldiers herded and pushed the boys into the trains, cursing them to move faster. Ervin struggled with his backpack, barely able to climb aboard it was so heavy, but he managed just as the train slowly started moving. As he walked down the aisle, he looked out the window and saw his mother, who stood like a sentinel, unmoving, except to lift her hand and wave to Ervin. He slipped into a seat as he watched her standing there, alone on the platform, until at last, his mother was completely out of sight.

HOPE AND PRAYER

Joseph listened to the click of the door as his wife and son walked into the cold, desolate street for what he feared might be their last walk together. He shaved and dressed, carefully buttoning his collar and adjusting his silk tie, as he did every morning, before slipping on one of his tailored, monogrammed suits, now beginning to fray. Though he continued to see his patients, many could no longer pay and, as a Jew, his access to supplies was limited. But his mind was not on his dwindling resources this morning. All he could think about was the danger his son was heading toward, and the danger that was coming closer to their home with each new day.

Joseph had known few years without danger, and never took for granted the prosperous life he had established. Born in the city of Alba Julia, then the capital of the Eastern Hungarian Province in Transylvania, he had grown up the middle of six children from a well-to-do family in one of the region's oldest Jewish settlements. Being Jewish at that time, and in that place, was a marker of belonging. Virtually every family he knew was Jewish, and to be Jewish was as respected in the Kingdom as to be Christian. He was as much a Jew as he was Hungarian, as he was a boy, which is to say, the normal state of things, unchanging, unremarkable.

After his mother died when he was still a child, however, the happy life he had known came to a harsh and sudden end. His father remarried and little love was shared between the children and their new stepmother. She ran the household efficiently but lacked the maternal instincts a natural mother might have for her children. The children were, at most, to be fed, bathed, and tolerated until such time as they left home, the sooner the better. As for Joseph's father, he was equally distant, a stern disciplinarian, and was at loss as to how to make sense of the sensitive boy his second son was proving to be. He had no use for the boy's playful laughter, much less his tears. He wanted only that the boy behaves and not embarrass him. When he failed at the former or succeeded at the latter, corrective measures were taken to shape him into something for his future as a man. Thus, Joseph found that the most sensible path to a peaceful coexistence in the household was to conceal his feelings and avoid making mistakes.

Toward that end, he kept his focus on his schoolwork, where he found a comforting fit for his intellectual curiosity. He had an innate affinity for mathematics, where numbers and equations were never messy, never ambiguous. Mathematics, and later science, were the closest he would ever come to achieving perfection, he felt, and so he buried himself in these studies where his passion had found a home.

Not everything about schooling came with ease, however. Being a short lad, and a motherless one at that, he found the social life in the schoolyard to be fraught with battles as he defended himself daily from the torment of older, taller, and meaner boys. An anger swelled inside him, fueled by the persecution from the boys at school and the abuse his father inflicted at home. He wanted to strike back, but more than that, he wanted these people—his family, his schoolmates—to care about him. Yet they didn't. At home, he could stave off the abuse by avoiding any missteps, and thus, he learned to be obedient, polite, and ever punctual. If he gave no cause for punishment, he could endure the indifference his father and stepmother offered. At school, however, avoiding error was, if anything, cause for further abuse. There was nothing he could change about himself to stop the torment—he could only change how he reacted. The torment finally came to an end at the cost of a broken nose during one especially brutal fight, branding him with a disfigurement that he wore with pride as that was the last time the boys went at him. They learned that he would no longer cower at their cruelty but would withstand their blows with a determination and will that their own malice could not match.

Joseph was listening intently to the BBC on his shortwave radio when his wife returned from the train station. Though as a Jew, he was forbidden from even owning a radio, like so many prohibitions, he had learned to defy the law with discretion—a discretion that was paramount since being caught could lead to his arrest, and that was a consequence he dare not suffer for it would mean the loss of their home and income—and thus, Kamilla's destitution. But survival also meant paying close attention to troop movements and any reports that might signal what was to come, so he kept the volume as low as possible and the radio itself hidden away when not in use. Every night he'd pull it out to listen to the BBC news from London, broadcasting in Hungarian through so much static he had to push his ear up against the speaker to hear it.

The war had been raging for four years now, since 1939, and with every passing year, he prayed that Germany would lose the war, but instead, the fate of the Jews across Europe had only worsened. Though it had been thought the Jews were being deported to labor camps, many now believed the Jews were being killed as part of an extermination program, what they termed the *judenrein*—the complete "cleansing" of the Jews. If true, the real aim of the Germans was not segregation as they claimed. It was annihilation. And so it was that he paid close attention to the news, gleaning as much information as he could, as their lives changed daily now.

It was October of 1943. America and their European allies had demanded the German's unconditional surrender, and just a few days before, the troops had freed Naples from German occupation. Soviet troops were advancing as well, forcing Germany to retreat. While this was welcomed news, it also signaled danger. The weakening of the Nazi forces was met with their increasing determination to accelerate their attacks on Jews not only in Germany, but also in its allied countries, which included Hungary. So far, Hungary had not succumbed to the worst of the acts against the Jews. While there was a quota of how many Jews could be employed, or even self-employed for that matter, they weren't entirely banned from working in Hungary. But the removal of Jews from their homes and businesses was well underway throughout Europe and Joseph feared it was only a matter of time before they reached Győr. For that matter, they already had, given that he'd just said goodbye to his son, knowing he might not return, knowing he might be beaten, starved, tortured. Even killed. And Joseph was helpless to do anything to stop his son's conscription to Labor Service. What he could do was carry on. He could continue to live as normally as possible with Kamilla, praying for his son's protection and safe return. And paying close attention to every news report, every speech, even every rumor.

The rumors were terrifying, if true. Though the conscription of young Jewish males was presented as just another form of military service, there were rumors they were in fact being killed, just as there were rumors that the Jews who were being shipped away were being sent to death camps. One rumor he dared not believe was that some boys sent to work in the Labor Service in Ukraine had been burned alive. He had done his best to protect Ervin from the worst of these rumors, for he knew it would only weaken him with fear. Ervin was so young and, though strong of character, he had never known hard work, much less a hard life. That was one of the reasons Joseph had been so heavy with the switch when Ervin misbehaved, and while he had often been too hard on the boy as his own temper flared, he had been motivated as much by a desire to toughen the boy as a desire to punish him. Yet now, having said goodbye to his son, perhaps for the first and last time, he wondered if he and Kamilla had erred in coddling him as they did, spoiling him even. Perhaps he should have been even harder on the boy to prepare him for survival. He could only pray Ervin would survive the Labor Service. He could only pray he and Kamilla would, as well.

"He's gone," Kamilla said, taking off her coat and hanging it on the brass coatrack by the door. "I packed him some walnut crescents and pierogis. I hope I packed enough. He looked so thin." Joseph turned toward his wife and seeing her strip off the coat like a thick layer of skin, he wondered what the last few years had done to his beautiful wife. Though not yet 50, the once lively face lit with fire was now gaunt and sagging, as if drained of life beyond her years. Her beautiful dark hair was unwashed and, though cut short, it had been months since she'd had it styled. Such simple things once taken for granted had become extravagances they'd been compelled to forego. Her whole body sagged under the weight of the ominous Hungarian sky, and he wanted to fling that sky off her and save her from its suffocating pressure.

Instead, he rose and said, "You rest. Let me bring you breakfast. I don't have patients for another two hours." He walked over to Kamilla and wrapped his arms around his dear wife and let her fall upon him sobbing.

When Joseph had grown and left his father's home in Transylvania, it was not to be shipped to Labor Service. He had left, instead, to attend Pázmány Péter University in Budapest. It was the most prestigious medical school in Hungary, but he had little money beyond what his father paid for tuition. When his older sister, Berta, and her wealthy husband Kálmán, offered Joseph room and board in their spacious home, he was delighted. Berta and Kálmán owned an elegant haberdashery in downtown Budapest in the most fashionable part of the city. But when Joseph arrived, rather than the lovely guest bedroom of his imagination, he was shown to a small, sparsely furnished room near the rear stairs where the coal was delivered and stored. The dim light made it difficult to read and write, and his studies were often interrupted by the cacophony of the many servicemen who passed up and down the hallway, calling to each other, moving and unloading heavy carts and deliveries. Added to his isolation and stress was the raucous noise Berta's children made as they raced through the house, uncontrolled and undisciplined. He had never known such loneliness as those years, and his self-pity was compounded by the attentions lavished on the unruly children, while his own existence seemed to feel at times as insignificant as that of any stranger bringing coal.

Despite Joseph's isolation in the home, his brother-in-law, Kálmán, found him to be useful. Rarely at the haberdashery, where

Berta worked daily, Kálmán frequently enlisted Joseph's services in securing rentals of horse-drawn carriages in which he would take a series of lady friends on promenade. Other times Kálmán would have Joseph arrange appointments for him at fashionable spas where he took frequent thermal baths and remained for weeks at time, gambling, dining, and entertaining the ladies as his wife managed the store for him. Joseph detested playing the conspirator in these dalliances by having secured such shameful amenities for his brother-in-law behind his sister's back, and yet he knew that to decline the requests would mean he would ultimately have no home —and hence, risk having to drop out of medical school. Instead, Joseph learned the art and utility of silence.

It was just before graduating from medical school in 1911 that Joseph met Kamilla. He was working in a hospital in Budapest when he noticed a beautiful young Jewish woman, modestly dressed in the orthodox tradition, yet demonstrating such an outgoing nature and strong will that he couldn't help but be intrigued. She was the daughter of a successful tailor from Újvidék and had brought her mother to Budapest for medical care, where Joseph was one of the doctors on her mother's medical team. Joseph was flattered when she sought him out frequently to ask about her mother's care. He was struck by her beauty and charm, as well as by her intellect and, he had to admit, the interest she showed in him.

They began courting, and he learned that, despite her love for her mother, she yearned to break free from her family. Their conservative religious views demanded that she ascribe to an ultra-orthodox life more suited to the 1800s than the modern era the new 20th century heralded. In the new century, women enjoyed public lives, hugged their sons and brothers without shame, and dressed in the latest fashions rather than cover themselves from chin to toe in dark and dreary dress more befitting of mourning than of living. Kamilla was clearly sensible and devout, but at the same time, joyous and even a bit flirtatious. She longed to start her own life on her own terms, and now that she was in Budapest, where she was introduced to a world she'd never known, she was even more determined to make that happen. That was fine with Joseph, for his own family had been the source of such disappointment and indifference. Together, he was certain, he and Kamilla could indeed start a new life, their own family, and on their own terms.

Shortly after Joseph graduated from medical school, he and Kamilla wed, but no sooner had they done so than World War I erupted, and Joseph offered his medical skills to the war effort. He was initially assigned to a military hospital in Aussig, a small city in the Austrian Empire about 600 kilometers northwest of Budapest. He and Kamilla were happy together, enjoying long talks of all that was happening in the world. They spoke of literature and the arts, and when Joseph had a rare day off, they went to museums, walked through the parks, and in the evening, enjoyed classical music and operas.

Kamilla was proud of her new husband, so handsome in his military uniform, and so knowledgeable on such a range of topics. Through Joseph, Kamilla was learning so much about the world that had been closed off to her as a girl growing up cloistered in such a conservative tradition. Her mind and spirit blossomed, yet she found it difficult to settle into their new community, knowing that Joseph could be sent far away at any time. The prospect of being alone in a new city was further complicated by a growing chill as the war provoked a new wave of political sentiment that the couple found disturbing. Aussig was a diverse city comprised of Germans, Jews, Slovaks, and Hungarians, yet a rising tide of suspicion and distrust among the groups was developing, so as newcomers—and among a small minority—not much more than a dozen—Hungarians, Joseph and Kamilla did their best to find a place in the city they knew was only a temporary stop on the long road of happiness ahead of them.

In the meantime, neither Joseph nor Kamilla were in a hurry to start a family—they knew that once they did so, their lives would be changed forever, and with Joseph having to serve the country, it wasn't a good time.

"The best course of action," Joseph told his wife, "would be to save our money for now. We shall have a small family, but we must be prepared financially before we do so, don't you agree?"

"Yes, of course, Joseph," Kamilla agreed, though she knew well that children often came long before one was ready. She knew, as well, that there was no point in discussing the topic further with her husband, for it risked turning into an argument over a topic on which they agreed. She yearned to be a mother but was barely past her own childhood herself. She could wait and, in the meantime, Joseph offered wise counsel on matters of their future security. "But I do think we could do with a small puppy for now, don't you agree?"

Joseph laughed at the prospect. A puppy was a small indulgence he was confident they could both afford and enjoy. "Why, yes, my love, if it's a puppy you want, it's a puppy you shall have."

Not one week later, Joseph came home from work with a large cardboard box that he could barely hold onto.

"My goodness!" Kamilla cried. "What on earth have you got inside that box?" She could hear a faint whimpering and scratching and could barely contain her excitement.

Joseph, as well, could hardly hide his own joy as he set the box down in the doorway of their small apartment and after closing the door, opened the box. Inside was a small brown and white terrier with giant, happy eyes.

Kamilla threw her hands to her face and gasped in delight, then bent down and picked up the tiny creature. "He's adorable! Where on earth did you get him?"

"There was a posting in the press for terrier puppies," Joseph said, "and I hurried across town after work so I could bring one home to you. Do you like him?"

"Like him? Why I adore him!" Kamilla cuddled the small pup in her arms, but it was eager to explore its new home. She set him down and let him run about, and both she and Joseph laughed with delight as he barked each time a neighbor passed through the hallway of their building.

"What do you think of a name?" Joseph asked her.

"Why I've no idea," she responded. "What do you think?"

"How about Sandor?" he suggested. "Guardian of men."

"I don't believe this little pup could guard so much as a meaty bone, much less a man such as yourself!" Kamilla teased as she picked up Sandor and cuddled him once again in her arms. He immediately settled down and snuggled into her caress.

"As long as Sandor guards your heart with his charms, I am a happy man," Joseph replied, delighted with his new little family, such as it was. The political climate of war may have turned the world upside down, but together they could shut out that world, until such time as it was once again turned upright.

Kamilla enjoyed setting up her new home, spending time with Joseph, taking Sandor for long walks, and meeting her neighbors. But just as she'd feared, no sooner had they settled into their new city, than Joseph was assigned to a Red Cross ship stationed in the Black Sea. Alone in Aussig, Kamilla missed him immensely and worried for his safety. But she wasn't alone in her longing for her husband—nearly every young woman she knew had become a war widow, and together they formed a tight community of women who got together to discuss a range of topics, from how to cook a proper strudel or perfectly seasoned *gulyás*, to sharing the latest news from the warfront or, too often, the home front. The Germans were becoming increasingly vocal in their view that the war was less a war to protect the interests of the Austrian Empire in Serbia and more an effort to bring an end to the Constitutional Monarchy of Germany. As much as she enjoyed these conversations, however, she missed the cultural outings she'd shared with Joseph and longed for his return. She thirsted for greater mental stimulation. She also missed her family. True, they had frustrated her to no end with their conservative views. But she loved her parents and siblings—a sister and two brothers—and had barely had any communication with them since she and Joseph had married. He was so determined that they had no need of their families of origin—for his own was far from loving—that he could not see how she might miss hers. If anything, he discouraged her from even speaking of them, showing little interest, and reminding her that their own love was love enough for two. So she said nothing to him of her longing to see her family, instead, writing to them and telling them of her happy life. And she didn't want to burden Joseph with her inconsequential problems being a lone woman in Aussig, however, for he was risking his life daily, as well as saving lives daily. Instead, she wrote to him of the simple pleasures she found in her new solitary married life.

October 1914

Dearest Joseph,

How I miss you, my love. I think of you throughout the day, as I go to market and buy cabbages to stuff for dinner, or a bit of meat to make a stew, and wish so much that I could share these meals with you. I content myself with the company of the other wives nearby, and we often commiserate about the husbands we so love and worry for. I do hope that you are safe, and that you are keeping busy with your work, for I know how you love it.

In the evenings I miss you even more, and keep my mind busy studying the Torah, or reading whatever books I can find at the library. I find reading the holy texts gives me courage to endure this difficult time. It inspires me to have faith in God, and in your safe return, as I pray for every night.

Sandor continues to delight me as he begs for my attention, and just yesterday he pulled out all my yarns from my knitting basket in an effort to find his favorite ball, which had ended up in there somehow. When he found it, he picked up each ball of yarn and dropped them one by one back into the basket where they belong! He is such a funny little dog and such wonderful company. I know he misses you, because each time we pass the train station where we saw you off, he stops and watches, as if waiting for you to return. I half expect to see you there myself.

The Germans continue to press for radical change, which I find distressing, particularly as they increasingly present Jews as the source of their grief for some inexplicable reason. After all, are we not allies in the war's effort? And among the wives who get together are both Germans and Hungarians, Jews and Christians, and we have no trouble getting along. It appears that it is the men who must always find cause for dispute!

I find that in addition to the Torah, by reading books of poetry and novels, I can escape to a world where anything is possible, and God's mysteries revealed. When you return, I want to read some of these works *with you, to share with you all that there is to discover in this amazing world that God has gifted us.*

In the meantime, I am learning how to be a better cook and budget our money as frugally as possible, for the krone is near worthless these days and inflation has made it all the more difficult to get by. What once bought a whole cabbage now buys but a leaf, and even that is rationed. But rest assured that I spend not a bit more than you have been able to send to me for I am eager to do my part in building our future together when you return. Be safe, my love, be safe, and know that my prayers for you are endless.

With all my love,
Your Kamilla

Kamilla did not have to write of her worries to Joseph, who in just the few years they had been together had studied his bride well. It was her keen mind and lively spirit that had entranced him, matched by her devotion to God and, dare he say it, to him. For in Kamilla he had found a true partner, someone who truly cared for him and saw in him so much more than his family had ever discerned. With Kamilla, he had a future, one of great reward and potential, for she spurred him to be the best man he could be.

In reading her letters, however, he worried about her. He knew she was doing her best to get along among her new neighbors, but he also knew she was no doubt feeling overly worried by this rising tide of German nationalist sentiment. Joseph was well acquainted with the antisemitism that had long plagued the Jews throughout the Empire. In centuries past, Jews had been persecuted and expelled from the region and not permitted to own land, but Joseph was confident that those days were behind them. Since the Dual Monarchy had been established in 1867, Jews had become equal subjects of the Habsburg Emperor under law. They were as entitled to own land, enter the civil service, serve the military, or run for public office, as any citizen. Jews now comprised a sizable minority in the Empire, and because they had been forbidden from owning land for so long, and thus could not support themselves through farming, many had become well established in local businesses and banking.

They also comprised a good portion of the doctors, teachers, and lawyers in the country. In short, they were needed. And it wasn't as if being Jewish came with a required way of thinking. Yes, he was Jewish, but his life had mostly been a secular one. His Jewish ancestry may well have been fundamental to his identity, but he believed in the Hungarian Kingdom more so than anything else and Kamilla was little different. Perhaps she was more devout than he, but she, too, was Hungarian first and foremost. The Germans making so much noise would soon fade away as no one would take them seriously. He wanted to assure Kamilla that while he understood her worries, she was right to focus on the common ground she shared with her new friends.

November 1914

My beloved Kamilla,

It warms my heart to hear from you and I am pleased to hear that you have found community in your friendships with the local women. They will provide you with much needed entertainment in these troubling times. How I miss the simple life we had just commenced to live when the brutalities of war drew me away from you. I will not bore you with the tedium of my days toiling on the ship, for war is not a subject any woman, much less a woman as sensitive and lovely as you, my dear, should pollute her mind with. But rest assured my love that I am safe and working hard.

At times, the hardest work is holding my temper, which I find flaring far too easily these days as the desperation of our situation calls for constant vigilance and focus. When some of my staff become distracted, I must chastise them in order that they attend to our duties of care. How I miss your calming influence on me, as I know my frustration is not with my staff as much as it is with this war itself and the hellish conditions in which it has placed us.

So many men have lost their lives or been so savagely wounded that they pray for death, that I wonder at times what God's plan for mankind might be that he would subject us to such horrors.

But I am comforted knowing that soon it shall be over and we will be reunited.

Until that time, I encourage you, my dear wife, to be patient and know that our future together will be a grand one. True, we must be frugal now, but our frugality will plant the seeds for a prosperous future if only we restrain our desires a little bit longer. As for your concerns about the Germans, I would not worry. There are always loudmouth young men in need of an audience and these groups are just that. They will soon busy themselves with the more mundane concerns of life, such as earning a living and raising a family. Pay them no mind.

Enjoy your new friends among the wives, for it is best to rest your mind during these difficult times—if for no better reason than to sharpen it for my return. In due course, we will once again enjoy the theater, the opera, and especially, each other's sweet caress.

With all my love,
Your Joseph

Kamilla's heart warmed at Joseph's letters, yet in truth, she was more restless than patient. Her life in Aussig provided her with security, yet she still missed all she'd once had—her family, despite their stifling lifestyle—Joseph, and the excitement of Budapest. She had thrived in the intellectual community she had found there among the diverse community, where Jews and Christians lived and worked side by side. Still, the pressure from her family to bear children—as many as possible—and ascribe to the orthodox tenets she'd been raised in—had tempered her joy in that city and persuaded her that Joseph was probably right, she was better off keeping her distance from them. Even in Aussig, the pressure to have a large family and content herself with a life of domesticity was great. Knowing that whatever turmoil she was going through would soon pass, she did as Joseph had advised and did not dwell on her worries for the political tides nor her personal desires to see her family or enjoy a more stimulating life. It would come in due time. Patience, she well understood, would be her closest friend.

As for Joseph, every letter he received from his wife had become a treasure, and each one had delighted him more than the last. Fortunately for him, his work had occupied his time and mind nearly around the clock, so he had been able to push away any melancholy or self-pity, a skill he'd mastered in childhood after the death of his mother. The skill came in handy as he worked in primitive conditions with few supplies and was regularly faced with the difficult decisions of medical triage when he had to choose in an instant which men could probably be saved and which men probably could not. In the latter, probabilities became certainties when they received no care, and their deaths gnawed at the back of Joseph's mind as if he were haunted by their ghosts. Not even the medical staff were spared. Viral infections spread through the ships with no care for who they took down, whether a nurse, a doctor, a chaplain, or a rabbi, regardless of how few staff they had. The morale could sink so low that fights broke out, some took to drink, and far too many became despondent, and their work suffered for it as a result. Added to all this stress, hospital ships constantly risked being sunk from mines, torpedoes, or enemy attack.

Yet Joseph didn't flinch. Just as he'd withstood the pain of a broken nose to defeat his childhood enemies, he withstood the pains of war to defeat his nation's enemies. Despite his own small role in that effort, however, the Austro-Hungarian State he defended was ultimately defeated. Joseph returned to his bride a decorated hero in a war that had been lost. He accepted a position as a country doctor in a rural area in Transylvania just outside of Alba Julia, the place of his birth. Thus, he and Kamilla happily departed Aussig for a more tranquil, peaceful life among the vineyards and pastures. There, they would start their life anew.

INDUCTION

"Identification!"

Ervin turned from the train's window to see a tall young man in uniform, no older than himself, glaring at him, his hand outstretched for his identification papers. Ervin obediently presented them and, once satisfied that they had the right Jew on board, the man turned to the next young man seated on the train and repeated his demand.

It was a packed train and Ervin was thankful he'd even gotten a seat. It seemed as if everyone was shouting and shoving, and while the train itself moved slowly, it lurched and stopped so often and so abruptly on its journey that every few minutes the passengers were thrown back and forth like dominoes knocking the others down. Ervin felt nauseous from the jerky movement, but he was in no hurry to reach their destination. Once there, his life would change in ways he couldn't imagine. Until then, he tried to lighten the mood by joking with his friends. They all felt that strange sensation of dread and delight. Dread at what was up ahead, delight at being together for the adventure.

Nearly two hours later, the morning light now bright, the train pulled into the station in Komárom. Just as they'd been pushed and shoved into the train, they were pushed and shoved out of it, where Hungarian gendarmes were swarming. These were the *csendőrség*—

easily identified by the large rooster feathers affixed to their bowler hats. Though reputed to be well trained enforcers of the law, they were as known for their cruelty as their skill. Ervin's heart raced, but the *csendōrs* merely handed them off to a few soldiers waiting to escort the young men to their destiny. It was in that instant that Ervin realized he had lost his humanity in the eyes of these uniformed soldiers. No longer was he even looked down upon as a Jew. He was, in that moment and into the unforeseeable future, an animal to be herded and put into service. A jolt of terror shot through him as the realization hit him and he was flooded with fear. But he knew better than to let them see his fear, for if they did, he was certain they would maximize the terrifying effect they had on him. Instead, he stood taller, shoulders back (not an easy task, given the weight of his backpack that once again pulled on his spine), and chin high. He compelled his face to reveal nothing of his inner thoughts and emotions. If they were determined to view him as nothing, then his survival would depend upon maintaining that illusion. He would do nothing to attract their attention, while expressing only respect for those he least respected. How much he'd aged in that short train ride, when just two hours before, he had been a boy walking with his mother.

The soldiers ordered the men to march and they did so in silence. Once again, Ervin cursed his heavy backpack. He half-cursed his parents as well, for it was they who had insisted he have the heaviest clothes they could find, and not just for winter. They insisted he have proper clothing for all four seasons. Just finding the clothes was no easy task. They'd had to find everything on the black market and pay sky-high prices. His father had recruited all his patients and friends in the specialty trades, calling on a furrier, a shoemaker, a tailor, even a shirt designer, to make everything Ervin would need. His mother knitted him a warm wool pullover, several pairs of socks, and a pair of long gloves using an expensive water-repellent lambswool yarn. They even had custom-made flannel shirts and underwear made for him, and his father had given him a pair of double-soled, tall boots made of cowhide and a lambskin jacket, both of which he was already wearing. On the jacket's arm was the yellow band, marking him as a

Jew, as did the obligatory cap upon his head that announced his inferior position as a conscripted laborer unfit to serve the Royal Army. It was those small but demeaning markers of his unworthiness that the gifts from Ervin's father did so much to obscure to both the outer social world and Ervin's inner private world. Though cursedly heavy, the gifts reminded Ervin of his worth when lesser souls sought to tell him otherwise.

Ervin's father had also surprised him with two practical items—a collapsible rubber wash table and an unbreakable stainless steel mirror, both of which he'd been able to purchase from Hammacher Schlemmer, one of the finest department stores in Hungary. As well, they gave him a small gold pocket watch to mark his entry into adulthood. Knowing the watch would be stolen or confiscated—likely by the guards themselves—Ervin was grateful he could conceal the watch in his pocket. He'd felt lucky that his parents were able to afford so much and had been so generous with him, but when he'd hoisted all the little luxuries on his back, he wished they hadn't been so generous.

He had never carried so much weight upon his vertebrae before and wondered with every step how many hours he would have to do so. His pain was relieved after nearly an hour when they reached the village of Szőny, where they were escorted to a grassy area. There he saw a long, windowless concrete building, its rounded roof covered in moss. In place of windows were a series of small gun turret holes that faced them ominously. He recognized the building as part of the fortification of the Czech border, having been built starting in 1935 in a futile effort to defend against the Nazis. Hungary, however, had succeeded in reclaiming all the land across the entire Czech Maginot line, so that by the time Ervin had joined the Labor Service in 1943, these fortifications ironically had come under control of German-allied soldiers. Just as Ervin became aware of where they were, the heavy iron gate clanged shut behind them, the sound startling him into another realization of his imprisoned status.

"Move!" a soldier ordered, and again, they were herded into a flowing line of frightened young men, mere boys really, pushed past the concrete building toward a large courtyard lined with long wooden troughs. Beyond the troughs was a stable, where horses or pigs had once been kept. This stable, Ervin realized as the soldiers ordered them inside, was their destination. This stable built for animals was now his new home.

And yet his first emotion was one of relief, not horror. He was so desperately relieved he would soon be able to take off his backpack. He would gladly have slept with the pigs had that been required, if only it meant he no longer had to have that heavy weight pulling at his spine. His back would surely hurt even more in the morning, he was certain, given the sharp pains that were already shooting through him with even the slightest movement.

But once inside the stable and relieved of his pack, the reality of his situation hit him. His new home was dark, damp, and dirty, and on top of it all, crowded. Thin, soiled blankets were piled in a corner, but there were no beds or pillows in sight. Ervin had never slept in anything other than the finest sheets on soft mattresses in beautiful rooms. His new home was the stuff of nightmares, that was sure, but it was not one he could awaken from. He wanted to be back home. He wanted his mother and father to burst through the opened door and take him out of there. And he wanted to relieve himself, but there was not a bathroom in sight. Again, like animals, they would relieve themselves outside, where not even an outhouse would provide them neither privacy nor the most minimal comfort.

Ervin had just settled down to eat a few of his mother's cold pierogis when an officer appeared in the doorway.

"You!" he barked, pointing to a scared young man. "You!" he said, pointing to another, then another, then another. "You!" he shouted, jabbing his finger straight at Ervin, then again, and again, and again, randomly pointing to this boy and that. Ervin hurried to put his food away lest they take it and, as he did so, he saw that his hands were shaking as visibly as if they were powered by batteries. He was terrified.

"Let's go!" The officer's face was stern, but not angry. Not kind, though, that was clear. Ervin had no idea what was happening, but he took comfort in the fact that he was accompanied by some familiar faces among the boys who had been selected. Like the other boys, Ervin started to grab his heavy backpack, his spine twitching at the thought, but the officer ordered them to leave the bags there. "You work."

Ervin's back was already throbbing, but he didn't dare say a word. He joined the group of boys as they were marched to a distant field and ordered to haul rocks from the field and stack them in a pile. They were given dull pickaxes and wheelbarrows, some with broken wheels, and told to fill them up, take them to the pile, unload them, then return, prying the rocks from the gripping soil with the pickaxes if need be. Ervin took one look at the task and concluded it was impossible. He could barely imagine bending over, he was so sore, much less hauling the heavy weight. He had never in his life done such work. For that matter, he had never even done so much as make his own bed. The housekeepers, cook, or nanny had seen to such things, and when the Wolfs were forced to let them go, his mother took care of everything. Work, for Ervin, meant the mental discipline of his schoolwork, not physical labor.

While some of the boys went right at it, Ervin made up his mind to take it easy. No sense wearing himself out too soon. He scanned the ground for the lightest rocks and tossed them into a wheelbarrow as if he were pitching balls. As he did so, he joked with his friends about his masterful aim but soon realized few were laughing. Nearly everyone was focused on lifting and moving the rocks, and Ervin's lighthearted efforts weren't winning him any applause. At best, he was ignored. Others glared.

"Hey, rich kid," one acquaintance yelled, "if that's the best you can do, maybe you'd better call your mama to come help you!" At that, some did laugh.

He began to feel even more alone, as it came to him that his predicament was dire. He was hungry. His back was hurting. He wanted to go home. And he had to lift the heavy rocks and hoist them into the wheelbarrow, whether he wanted to or not. Whether it hurt him or not. Whether he could or not. For the first time in his life, Ervin had to put his body, not his mind, to work. To do so, he realized it was the power of his mind that could save him.

Ervin willed himself to ignore his hunger, his throbbing torso, and his intensifying fear. He concentrated on his pain and discomfort not as indicators of the horrifying situation he was in, but as signs he was growing stronger. His growling stomach strengthened him. His hurting back was growing stronger. His fear was an enemy he would vanquish. And as he concentrated on these signs of his increasing strength, he willed himself to swing the axe and lift, swing the axe and lift, placing the heavy rocks in the nearest wheelbarrow, again and again in the biting cold as his frigid fingers bled from the repetitious effort of lifting or prying the rocks from the ground, again and again and again. For someone else to cart away. After all, there was only so far his mind could take him on this first day of his new life.

By the end of the workday, having had neither breaks nor bread, the boys were given some crackers and small chunks of cheese, and allowed to pass a bucket of water to drink from. It was the worst meal Ervin had ever tasted, and yet, he ate it with relish having been so famished from all the heavy labor and nothing but a few bites of pierogi all day. He could not wait to return to the stable where he would sleep not like a lamb, but at least, like a horse.

Once back "home," however, he was hit with another blow. "Looks like we're leaving you," a friend said.

"Yeah, we're either the lucky ones or you are," another said. "They're moving us out to a new place tomorrow. Looks like you'll be staying here."

"Me?" Ervin asked. "Why me?"

"You and half the others," the first friend said. "They announced the names of everyone who's getting transferred closer to Győr. You weren't on the list. Maybe that's a good thing, maybe not. Hard to tell. What did you do all day anyway? They kept us here all day, doing nothing. At least you got to go somewhere."

Ervin sure didn't feel lucky. He would have paid dearly to do nothing. And now his friends would be leaving. And they'd get to be stationed closer to home. What had he done for God to single him out like that?

"Hey, it's not so bad," he heard a familiar voice call out from a few stalls down. "You'll have me to keep you company, how's that?"

Ervin stood—his vertebral column searing with pain as he did so—to see if his ears weren't deceiving him. Sure enough, looking past several stalls, there in the darkness he could barely make out the face of his friend, Frank. He couldn't believe his good fortune on such an unfortunate day. Ervin had always admired Frank, who had been one of the best students in high school. Sadly, despite his sharp wit and good grades, like so many Jewish students, Frank had been rejected from university, so instead he'd stayed home raising angora rabbits and helping his father with their lumberyard business. Yet another broken career, Ervin had thought, when he'd learned of Frank's misfortune, but Frank sure hadn't let it embitter him.

Frank and Ervin were near opposites in both looks and personality, and Ervin admired those qualities in his friend that he himself lacked. Frank was tall and muscular, Ervin short and thin. Frank's fair complexion was a contrast to Ervin's dark hair and olive skin. Frank was a cool and levelheaded guy, not emotional like Ervin. He was also independent and much more decisive than Ervin, with a much stronger personality, though Ervin had a clever wit and underlying charm that served him well. Nonetheless, Ervin's charm masked his insecurities. He feared venturing out on his own, doubting his ability to get on in the world, despite his parents' encouragement that he could be anything he wanted to be. If anything, his parents held too exaggerated an assessment of Ervin's potential, he felt, and didn't see how much he doubted himself. Now he was indeed out in the world but, rather than being able to be anything he wanted to be, he had to become whatever it was these soldiers wanted him to be—which is to say, a workhorse. His parents sure hadn't prepared him for that.

Thank God for Frank, Ervin thought. He had never needed anyone like he felt he needed Frank at that moment. Frank would not just be a familiar face amid this horrible ordeal. His common sense and leadership were just the thing Ervin needed now that he was under the control of these brutes. A friend like Frank could help him get through it, he was certain. The question was, what did he have to offer Frank besides mere friendship? He prayed he'd find the answer, because in that flicker of a second in which he recognized Frank's face through the stable's darkness, the intensity of his need for just such a friend swept over him.

"I'll be damned," Ervin called out to his old friend. "Frank More. Come here. I've got something for you."

And with that, he unwrapped all he had to offer. A few crescent cookies and some cold pierogis. It wasn't much, but in that cold and lonely moment in a stable built for livestock, it was the most generous gift Ervin could provide to the friend who gave him more than mere comradery—having Frank beside him gave him hope he would survive.

In the days and weeks that followed, Ervin and Frank grew as close as brothers. Ervin felt comfortable around Frank and Frank found Ervin's clowning around just the diversion he needed. Whether washing up in the pig trough on a cold morning or going to sleep on the floor of the stable at night, Ervin was the first to make light of their discomfort and turn the humiliation into a joke.

"Mmm-hmm, this pig water sure does wonders for the skin," he'd say, dunking Frank's head in the trough, knowing Frank would do the same to him when he least expected it.

"Here, Ervin, let me help you with that acne of yours," Frank would say, in kind, laughing at the wet mess the two of them made. Whether stealing each other's blankets when they were ready to sink into a coveted sleep or covering each other when a blanket came off in the night, the two boys provided each other with comfort, humor, and solace.

"What do you miss most about home?" Frank whispered as he and Ervin lay on the cold, hard floor of the stable after another rough day of work.

"Oh, that's easy," Ervin answered. "I miss my bed. How about you?"

"I miss my dog," Frank said. "Jankó. He's a mutt, but smart as a whip. Sure wish he was here."

"Your parents taking care of him?"

"Yeah, for now. But I know he misses me. I'll tell you what I don't miss."

"What's that?"

"Those damned rabbits."

As time passed and they settled into this new normal, Ervin's moods and thoughts improved, as did his back and his strength. The first week or so had been the most difficult, with his back so injured he moved in agony, but as time passed, the pain subsided and he found his body really was growing stronger, though not nearly as strong as most of the other boys. Of course, he still resisted the work altogether, but Frank was quick to give him the kick in the butt he needed.

"Come on, Erv, you can do better than that. The way you're holding that shovel you'll be lucky if you can dig your own grave. You need to stand with your legs wider apart," he'd say, "like this."

During such lessons, Ervin would sit back and watch Frank demonstrate, hoping to trick his friend into doing the job for him. Of course, he knew Frank wouldn't fall for it, but the routine they'd established provided a regular source of banter between them.

"Okay, and then what? How do I dig the hole deeper?"

"You put your weight on your front foot like this, see? And then you push with your leg like this." Frank demonstrated by hoisting a big load of dirt onto the blade of the rusty shovel. "You want to keep the load close to your body," and with that, Frank tossed the big pile of dirt straight at Ervin, laughing at having beat his friend at his own game.

The truth was, Ervin was beyond grateful for Frank's good humor and guidance. It really did make a difference to know how to lift a weight, use a shovel properly, and push a heavy load. He knew he'd never be as strong as Frank and most of the others, but if he could get through a single motion, a single task, a single hour, a single day, he knew he was surviving. In turn, he discovered he was gifted with the ability to assess a situation—or a guard—quickly and decisively, a skill that benefited both him and Frank as they applied their wits to mitigating the tortuous circumstances in which they'd unexpectedly found themselves. This officer was insecure and thus could be flattered. That officer was cruel and hence would escalate his cruelty if he discerned the least adverse response. This soldier was easily fooled. That soldier was seeking favor from his superiors. The more they watched and witnessed the behavior of those who ruled them, the more they understood the motives and desires of each. Such information, they soon discovered, served them well as each day brought new discomforts and ordeals, and each day brought new opportunities to minimize them. Still, there was no predicting the next surprise, but one thing they knew for sure, there was always a next surprise.

FRESH START

"What shall we do?" Kamilla asked Joseph, as she poured him and herself each a small glass of Tokaji, the sweet white wine of Hungary that they enjoyed sipping occasionally when they sat by the fire and talked. Though they were living amid the wine-growing region of Transylvania, Kamilla and Joseph preferred the luscious, amber-colored wine of their homeland to the fruity local wines.

"Well," Joseph replied, savoring his first sip with a thoughtful gaze into the glass, "our life here can be a good one. We're close enough to Alba Julia that we can visit regularly, yet we're far enough outside the city that we can enjoy the country life."

"It is nice here," Kamilla agreed, though her spirit didn't match her words. "But do you really want to stay?" They had just settled into their new life in Transylvania, and Joseph enjoyed his new position as country doctor. But having lost the war, they discovered they faced even greater conflict at home. The Austro-Hungarian Monarchy had been destroyed by the war, and with the signing of the Trianon Treaty, its lands divvied up among the victors, with the Kingdom of Romania claiming Transylvania for itself, and Kamilla's own homeland of Újvidék annexed to the Kingdom of Serbs, Croats, and Slovenes, and known as the South Slav Kingdom. The Kingdom of Hungary thus lost two-thirds of its population, and these Hungarians

—which included most of Hungary's Jewish citizens—found themselves living as minorities in other nations. They had become, in effect, foreigners on their own soil.

Of even greater concern, Hungary had invaded Romania in a failed attempt at regaining Transylvania and the two nations were at war. The communist leader Béla Kun, a Jewish prisoner of war incarcerated in Russia, aligned with his captors and, when they released him in 1918, he seized power in Budapest. Though Kun promised he could restore Hungary to its former glory, he instead formed the Hungarian Soviet Republic and established a series of land reforms that further divided the nation. What had followed was anything but glorified as the land reforms and a series of economic reforms failed and the communists rapidly lost control of all but the police force. Reports of a "Red Terror" sweeping the countryside were chilling as these law enforcement officials sought to beat the populace into accepting the new society. Anyone suspected of counter-revolutionary tendencies was beaten in the streets, arrested, persecuted, some were even killed. Neither Kamilla nor Joseph was eager to live under such rule. Yet continuing to live in Romania, as both Hungarians and Jews, put them at risk as outsiders.

The young couple had a choice to make. They could remain in Alba Julia and live their lives as Hungarians under Romany rule, risking the social tides turning against them, or they could move westward, where they could live their lives as proud Hungarians once again, even if it meant being surrounded by turmoil and violence.

"I've received an offer from the Romany authorities," Joseph revealed. Kamilla's raised brow prompted him to continue. "They would like me to stay on. They've offered a more generous salary, and I dare say it is tempting."

"Ought we yield to such temptation," Kamilla asked, "if it means forsaking our duty to our nation?"

Joseph smiled as he looked past his glass and into the eyes of his loving wife. He realized many wives would have expected him to accept any financial incentive that came his way, regardless of its cost. Yet Kamilla instinctively understood his reticence to accept the offer.

"My thoughts exactly," he agreed, "for Jews have long been

persecuted and it may only be a matter of time before we find ourselves targeted by the Romanies, if not for our heritage, then for our nationality. Already I feel the glare of hatred from some when they discern my Hungarian accent."

Kamilla nodded but said nothing. She was all too familiar with the snide remarks and sideways glances she was increasingly feeling since they'd settled in the area. A part of her desired to leave. Nonetheless, she was equally convinced that such sentiments would pass once the political climate died down, and she longed to start her family. She knew, too, that as Joseph's wife, she could perhaps influence her husband's decision, but it would be his decision to make, not hers.

"On the other hand," he mused, choosing his words carefully, "should we return to Hungary, we will find that it has changed. They say this Red Terror is unlike anything Hungary has ever seen. I fear we may find ourselves living amongst even greater conflict than we face here."

"Surely it cannot be that bad," Kamilla said. "The news does tend to be sensationalized, and it is hard distinguishing what is fact from what is fiction."

"True," Joseph agreed, unconvinced himself that there was anything to fear. "I have heard that the violence is largely limited to the countryside. And it appears to be dying down. If we were to settle in a city, I think we'd be fine. The Hungarian leadership will change and once that happens, they'll get it under control."

"Yes, I'm sure of it," she agreed. "After all, you're a doctor. They won't come after us. It's the troublemakers they're going after, I've heard. The scoundrels and thieves. It's here we stand out as foreigners. In Hungary, we'll be back home."

Joseph nodded. The violence in Hungary was real, but mostly a rural concern. Kun's goons were targeting counterrevolutionaries, not Jews, whereas to remain in Transylvania as foreigners posed a greater risk, he felt. There was one other concern. Joseph's sister, Berta, as well as his father, felt that Joseph had a responsibility to his family of origin that his marriage to Kamilla ought not preclude. After all, had they not cared for him when he had nothing? Now that he was poised to earn a steady income, surely he would help them? Joseph sighed heavily, his obligations to his wife, his family, and his nation pulling him in so many directions.

"But there is also the matter of my family," he observed after a few moments of thoughtful silence. "They are urging me to stay put."

Now it was Kamilla's turn to sigh. She had barely met Joseph's family, yet she already discerned the turmoil they brought to her husband. "The family that has all but ignored you until now, now that you are a doctor and will be earning good money wherever you go?" Kamilla's words were strong, but her voice soft and playful. She sympathized with her husband's ambivalence toward his family, for she knew how much she loved and missed her own. But she was married now and learning to adapt to a new life with Joseph. Since marrying, her mother had recovered from the illness for which she'd been hospitalized, but Kamilla's father had died shortly after. Once widowed, her mother had settled into a life of mourning, dressing in long black gowns accessorized only with simple black chokers. She rarely smiled and had little to say, having retreated into a silent world of her own imaginings. Kamilla's sister, Gizella, had married a wealthy gentleman who owned a lumberyard and seemed happy enough, as well as secure, but the two women were not close. Her younger brother, Oscar, was a coal miner in Sudetenland and had little to do with the family, while her older brother, Tivadar, lived somewhere in Hungary, but his whereabouts never discussed. Her family had shattered into a multitude of shards since the war, just as her country had. The family of her childhood was no more. She wasn't sure she was ready to accept that loss, but she wasn't sure how much choice she had in the matter. After all, she was married now and her obligation was to her husband.

Joseph was also hesitant to abandon his family, yet Kamilla was right. They had always kept him at a distance. Now that he was married to a woman he adored, and now that he had endured a war and witnessed atrocities no human ought to witness, he had little patience for asking for a love he wouldn't receive from those who had withheld their affections from him for so long. He was determined that the life he'd share with Kamilla would be a life made on their own terms, not on the dictates or desires of others. They could cherish their families from afar without obliging them their demands. And while he knew Kamilla loved her family, she certainly would accept that they no longer had need of her, nor her of them. Joseph was prepared to cut ties with his family, even if it pained him to do so. And Kamilla would discover, he was certain, that moving further away would enable her to break free of her own family's yoke upon her, he reasoned. As long as they had each other, they would be fine. Joseph reached for Kamilla's hand and held it in silence as he savored another sip of the Tokaji.

At long last, he finished his drink and spoke. "I believe the answer can be found in this glass of wine."

Kamilla looked at him with curiosity. Joseph wasn't one to be cryptic. If anything, he was as practical a man as she'd ever met. Then it struck her. He was being as clear as ever. Just as the wine they preferred had grown from Hungarian soil, so too, had they. Their roots were with their land. They would never be Romanies. They had always been devoted and patriotic Hungarians. They would live as Hungarians, even if it meant packing everything up, bidding their families goodbye, and leaving once again. It was a decision that at the time seemed to be unmistakably the right choice. And yet it was a decision that would forever seal their fate in ways they never could have foreseen.

Kamilla and Joseph settled in the city of Győr as voluntary refugees in early 1920. They'd had few funds to make such a move and arrived destitute but optimistic. The cost of traveling had been so great that they left all their belongings behind, though doing so was a small sacrifice for they had acquired little in the few short years they'd been married, as Joseph had spent most of those years serving the Empire during the war. But they were happy, in love, and thrilled to return to Hungary, even if they did so amidst considerable violence and unrest.

As they'd suspected, the Red Terror was subsiding and had never been a great problem in Győr. The Kun regime had collapsed the previous summer nearly as quickly as it had been established, with

Kun fleeing to Austria. Trials of the worst of the Red Militia had begun and it looked like peace would finally prevail.

They quite liked Győr, an industrial city between Vienna and Budapest in northwestern Hungary. They were attracted to the city's Baroque architecture and idyllic setting, with three rivers—the Danube, Rába, and Rábca—providing a lacework of calming waters flowing through the city, with small islands scattered along the rivers providing recreational opportunities for afternoon visits and picnics. The charming streets meandered through ancient buildings with flowering balconies, majestic domes, twisting columns, and brilliant sculptures that told of the region's history and achievements. The heart of the city was the downtown area with its long and busy street through the business district, showcasing elegant stores with beautiful displays of the latest fashions in their windows. There were also several pubs, inns, ice cream parlors, confectionaries, and coffee houses along the streets, offering a variety of late afternoon indulgences. After five o'clock and on holidays, cars and carriages were prohibited and the street transformed into a promenade of pedestrians dressed in their finest clothing. This pleasant setting was not without its dark side, however, as the outer perimeter of Győr was otherwise industrialized with factories marked by a series of tall, slender chimneys constantly polluting the whole area with foul-smelling, pitch-dark clouds of soot. But neither Kamilla nor Joseph were concerned about the pollution and noise from industry, which they saw as the necessary cost of a growing economy.

"With so much art and culture here," Kamilla noted with enthusiasm when they first arrived, "we can raise a family of our own and never grow bored. Imagine our children growing up here. They will have so many opportunities." She took hold of Joseph's arm and leaned against him as they walked along the streets of their new home. They had found housing in a downtown hostel, while Joseph searched for work so that they could afford to secure something more permanent.

"The music alone is reason to settle here," Joseph agreed. "Once I'm established, we can attend operas and classical concerts every week, my dear, and you can get lost in the libraries while I'm at work." He leaned over and kissed his wife, feeling a sense of hope and excitement for their future he hadn't felt since they'd first met. "And I can establish a good practice here. Plus, we can always escape to Vienna or Budapest if we get restless. It's only a two-hour train ride."

Kamilla smiled. "I don't think we'll need to worry about growing restless here, Joseph. We can finally settle down and stop being uprooted. But yes, let's occasionally enjoy the big cities as well." She was at peace. They'd come home.

After applying for several medical positions, however, Joseph began to feel discouraged. While he had not initially perceived that there'd been any pattern to the rejections for employment, by the fifth time he was told there was no position open for him—when in fact a position had been posted—he knew. The chill in the air became unmistakable. With the fall of the Red Terror, a new enemy had been identified, and this one was an old enemy—it was Jews who were unemployable in the new Hungary. In place of the Red Terror, a White Terror had been gaining power, and this one was reaching the cities and striking back forcefully against anyone perceived as sympathetic to the communists—which of course meant the intellectuals, the artists, the teachers. Even the doctors. And given that Jews were such a strong presence in these circles, to be Jewish came to mean one was perceived as inherently sympathetic to the communists and socialists.

Joseph tried to keep his spirits up around Kamilla, for he didn't want to admit to her what he feared he would soon have to admit to himself. Perhaps he had erred in leaving Alba Julia. The very reason he had felt they ought to leave—to avoid persecution—appeared to be the very social tides that were turning against them in Hungary. But now that they were there, returning to Romania was not an option. They were indeed proud Hungarians, so they would live as proud Hungarians. They would not turn back in the face of the nation's problems—problems that would surely pass.

At long last, after weeks of rejection and with no income to support them, an opportunity was presented to Joseph and he accepted a position in dentistry with the Hungarian government, since doctors were considered qualified to practice dentistry. Having seen enough trauma in wartime, he welcomed the shift to oral healthcare, which suited him well as working with teeth required both keen attention to detail and a certain artistic gift. What's more, there was little competition other than the occasional untrained self-appointed "dentist" who specialized in pulling out perfectly good teeth. Joseph had no use for such charlatans and now, with secure employment, he was determined to become the most skilled and sought-after doctor of dentistry in the region.

Although he now had a good job, it did not pay well, so Joseph and Kamilla were unable to find an adequate and affordable apartment downtown, as they'd planned. Instead, they rented a modest room in the industrial area that cost little and thus offered few comforts. They were housed on a fifth-floor walkup with a toilet on the third floor shared with several others. The room itself included a single sink, but no kitchen and barely enough room for their bed. Rather than overlooking the lovely panoramic view of the rivers and islands, as they'd envisioned, their view was of smokestacks and blackened roofs. As for entertainment, while they were able to take walks in the downtown area on occasion, the walks near their home were neither pleasant nor safe. Thieves were rampant and all it took was for one young man to shout, "Jew!" and in a flash, a mob could be upon them stripping them of their valuables and leaving them with a good pounding. Joseph and Kamilla had yet to endure such attacks but had heard enough to know how common they were becoming. Thus, they contented themselves with quiet evenings at home, reading aloud from the classics or listening to the radio.

"Shhh!" Joseph snapped, turning the knob on the radio to catch the latest news report. Kamilla had been chattering nonstop since he'd come home and all he wanted to do was listen to the news. While the war may have ended abroad and the Red Terror of the countryside had been quashed, it was clear that a new form of violence had been resurrected in the streets of every city in Hungary, the White Terror that was branding patriotic citizens like Joseph and Kamilla as enemies of the state. The idyllic life they'd planned was turning into anything but idyllic, and tensions were drifting from the streets into their home. Kamilla left Joseph to his radio and began chopping cabbage and onions for a simple stew she'd make on their hotplate. Her thoughts were lost in memories of her former joys and the family she'd left behind, as Joseph listened intently.

"The National Assembly of Hungary, whose Parliament has elected Admiral Horthy as Regent of the Kingdom of Hungary, hereby announces that the great leader has accepted the position," the newscast reported, announcing not just the ascension of the conservative leader, but also the restoration of the Kingdom itself. "The decorated wartime Admiral of the Austro-Hungarian Navy and leader of the opposition party who defeated the communists, will lead the Kingdom into a new dawn. His Serene Highness of the Regent of the Kingdom of Hungary will enjoy the general prerogatives of the king and command our armed forces."

Kamilla turned from her task, the announcement catching her ear. "What does that mean, Joseph? Is this nightmare finally over?"

"I do hope so," he said, as the news turned to state-sponsored commentary for which he cared little. He had closely followed the rise of Horthy and was well versed on the implications of his ascension. "He held out for great power and Parliament seems to have granted it. Now he can do something about this chaos, assuming he wants to."

"Let's hope he does," Kamilla said, turning back to her cooking. "I just want to get back to a normal life," she opined.

"We all do," Joseph said, shutting off the radio. "I just hope he does the right thing. Horthy hasn't been sympathetic to Jews since this White Terror began. But he's got a keen political sense and knows how to restore order. He may not be my first choice, but I think he'll do the right thing. He's a patriot and a leader and that's what we need right now. Let's just give him time."

Kamilla looked over her shoulder to her husband and smiled. He brought her such comfort. Finally, the Kingdom would be restored, Hungary would thrive once again, and she and Joseph could settle into a better life and start their family.

The region did indeed stabilize under Horthy's rule, but he

proved no friend to the Jewish communities as he associated Jews with labor unions and social democrats. Thus, although the violence had subsided, the antisemitism intensified and Joseph and Kamilla faced another difficult choice.

"Joseph, you know how happy I am with you here," Joseph's supervisor began. Joseph immediately sensed something was wrong. Though he'd only just begun working as a federal employee, he'd never had any complaints about his work and, if anything, his patients were quite happy with him. But his supervisor, an otherwise meek, officious little man who seemed more comfortable with his accounting ledgers than his employees, was now avoiding any eye contact with Joseph. He never had been one to look him in the eye, for that matter he never had been one to say much of anything to Joseph other than, "Good day," "good work," and "good evening." But now, he was visibly shifting, as if trying to position his body in the safest possible posture for whatever words were about to come out of his mouth.

"Yes, so you've said," Joseph replied, "and I am quite content with my position. Is there something on your mind?"

"Well, it's this new government, you see," he said, picking up a pencil and nervously tapping it on his desk. "It seems they've issued yet another decree and I'm afraid this one affects you."

"How so?" Joseph asked, the dread already washing over him.

"I'm afraid permanent federal appointments are now limited to Christians, and as you know, your position would fall under those guidelines..." His voice trailed away, as he turned his gaze first out the window, then at last, to Joseph as he dropped his pencil and concluded. "I'm afraid that I will have to convert your appointment from a permanent one to a temporary one, which means you will no longer qualify for a pension and, should a Christian apply, I will have to let you go within a few months. I do hope you understand. My hands are tied, you see."

Joseph did see. There was nothing the man could do, as the rulings were coming from a much higher office, though at the same time he sensed that the man cared little whether Jews had work or not. He returned home that evening, despondent and discouraged.

The life he had offered Kamilla was turning into a life of disappointments. How much longer would it go on like this before he could enjoy a life of his own making?

And then it hit him. It was within his control to make himself over if need be. And it appeared it need be.

"What shall we do?" Kamilla asked when Joseph had returned home from work and told her of these recent developments.

"There is a possible solution," Joseph proposed, "although you may not like it."

"You mean return to Romania? Oh, Joseph, I am so tired of relocating every few months. Surely if we stay things will get better eventually, and there is no assurance that things will be any better in Romania. It is only a matter of time before even greater problems arise there."

"I agree," he said, "but my proposal is one which will enable us to stay. What do you say to our converting to Christianity?"

"Convert!" Kamilla gasped. "You mean, forsake our Jewish heritage? Become Christians? That would just kill my mother." Kamilla threw her hands to her face in near horror at the suggestion.

"I know, I know," Joseph said, reaching for his wife and taking her in his arms. "But what does it really matter if we call ourselves Jewish or Christian, so long as we are Hungarians? After all, we do not practice our religion. And as for our families, they need never know. But converting will free us of this damnable stigma that has so thwarted our slightest efforts to lead decent lives. It would mean nothing in the eyes of God, for God will watch over us whether we call ourselves Christians or Jews. But it would mean freedom here in our homeland. We could walk the streets without fear of being taunted or assaulted. I could continue with my work, and we could move out of this wretched hovel to a more pleasant home and start our family. Won't you at least consider it, for our safety here on earth?"

Kamilla saw her husband's point of view and could not contradict it. It was true that although she was a faithful Jew, she now lived a secular life. And God did want her to be safe from persecution, of that she was certain. If they did convert, it wouldn't be long before the antisemitic sentiments that had grown so bold were quashed. It was just yet another reaction to the nation's loss of so much land and so many of its citizens. Calm would return in time.

"Alright," she said after thinking it over for a few days. "If you think we should, let's convert. And once this is all over, we can convert back. Just as long as my mother never finds out."

Joseph nodded. It was a decision that did not bring him joy, but it was a judicious conclusion, and he was grateful his wife was both pragmatic and supportive of his suggestion. The next day, he contacted a local priest and he and Kamilla began Bible study, reading the New Testament and learning to express their devotion to Jesus Christ, a mythical figure in their view, but one who would protect them, if in an unintended way. At home, they carefully put away any signs of their devotion to the Old Testament and their Jewish identities. It seemed a small price to pay for their security during such a tumultuous postwar era, an era that would surely pass in time. After all, it was the 1920s, the Golden Age. Good times were ahead.

SHEEP FARM

If Ervin thought that sleeping in a stable and washing up in a pig trough was dreadful, his next residence was far worse. They'd only been there a couple of weeks before a guard woke them before dawn and told them to start hiking again. By that point, Ervin's paraspinal musculature had grown strong enough that the backpack that once weighed him down as if filled with rocks now felt immensely lighter. But the hike itself seemed endless as they marched far across the countryside, not reaching their destination until the sun had nearly set. Tired, famished, and his throat as dry as kindling, Ervin wanted only to quench his thirst and feed his body. He was thankful they were forbidden from talking, as to do so would only hurt his parched throat all the more. Still, he managed to croak out a few words when they were ordered to halt.

"Where the hell are we? It's just a bunch of hills."

"Look over there," Frank said, pointing in the distance where a large flock of sheep were grazing. "Looks like they've brought us to a sheep farm."

"Think they plan to slaughter us?" Ervin asked, half seriously.

"We'll find out," Frank said, as he fixed his gaze on the soldiers who'd escorted them. One of them, a mean-eyed hoodlum who spit a lot, glared at the young men.

"You'll sleep here for the next few nights. There's a creek about a half kilometer that way," he said, nodding toward the east then spitting on the ground as if to make his point. "You can wash up there. Don't piss in it. That's your drinking water. You'll get some dinner when it's ready. Don't expect much."

The men looked around and at each other. No one dared ask the question, "Where will we sleep?" But the soldier noted their confusion and, with a slight smile, he added, "You'll sleep in there. Don't get too comfortable."

"There" was an open-air shack made of ancient rotting wood. It had no walls and the roof was sagging under the weight of moss and vines. It appeared to have been a storage area for wood or equipment, as it was too dilapidated to provide shelter even for sheep. No one budged toward it until another soldier started hitting the men with the butt of his rifle, pushing them toward the decrepit shack. "Move!" he ordered, and the men reflexively obeyed, too horrified to say a word.

Inside the hut, if it could even be called that, they were immediately surrounded by thousands of flies, no doubt attracted to the stench of feces that lingered from animals past. Ervin's stomach turned queasy when he saw the filth they were expected to sleep in, but he had already learned to shut down in such moments of dread. How far away his warm and comfortable home felt to him now that his life had turned, overnight, into a series of horrors. By shrinking his environment from that which surrounded him to the limits of his own body, he could view his body not as something that was being abused and assaulted, but as something that came between him and his horrifying surroundings. His flesh became a barrier that would protect him from the stench and filth and the repulsive sights and sounds of swarms of flies that enveloped them like demonic clouds of darkness. Indeed, it was a metaphorical cloud of darkness that had shrouded Europe these last few years for some inexplicable reason. Perhaps he could make sense of the current situation intellectually, but not morally. There was no making sense of the horror, only accepting that it was a horror he must pass through to survive. His small body would blanket his soul, protect it from the disgusting conditions that no shepherd would have sought for shelter. Better to be struck by lightning, Ervin thought, as he crawled deeper into his own soul, waiting for this terrible moment to pass.

Once they'd set their packs down on the filthy earth of the shack, Ervin and his friends hurried to the creek to find water. It was already growing dark, but fortunately the rising moon was nearly full and provided them with a faint light as the sky darkened. Few spoke, and what words were muttered were nearly inaudible. Everyone was exhausted. Everyone was hungry and thirsty beyond endurance. And everyone was horrified and longing to be home. Not even Ervin could crack a joke about this nightmare.

By the time they returned, a pot of boiled cabbage had been set outside the shack alongside a pile of stale, molding bread. Ervin had to restrain his urge to jostle his way to the front of the line he was so hungry, but at last, he reached the lukewarm slop and had wolfed down almost all of it before he'd even sat down. Once sated, he returned to the creek where he washed his aluminum bowl with a fistful of sand. He thanked God, almost sarcastically, that his mother couldn't see her son living in such conditions. The life she had given him and the future she'd envisioned for him were a far cry from the life he was now living, as if he'd been reduced to a caveman without so much as a cave.

He was thankful for the long johns his parents had given him, though it pained him to soil them by sleeping on the wet earth. Still, they kept him warm, and he shared his extra pair with Frank, who had only a thin nightshirt which failed to keep him warm.

"Thanks, pal," Frank said, giving him a friendly slap on the back. "Really. I appreciate it."

"It's nothing," Ervin said. But both boys knew the gift was more than nothing. To sleep through the wretched night, warm and dry, was a gift they both appreciated as such small comforts made the unbearable slightly more bearable.

"There's breakfast. Get it now while you can." A new guard, a round-bellied guy with an ugly face by the name of János, called out in an almost friendly tone. He didn't bark at them like the other guards, but instead, spoke to them as if he were just one of the guys.

Ervin shook Frank awake and they grabbed their bowls and cups and headed outside—at least, if it could be called that, as their shelter wasn't exactly inside.

The grassy fragrance of the fields mingled with something cooking nearby and Ervin nearly forgot the nightmare of sleeping in such filth.

"Smells good," Ervin said, surprised to smell something other than the foul cabbage they were so used to.

"Almost too good," Frank replied, his caution on alert, but his hunger drawing him toward the delicious aroma.

"I got you some sausages," János announced, as the boys all gathered around a makeshift table near an open fire where sausages and eggs were frying. János seemed to be enjoying himself as he served the hot breakfast to the hungry men, the first meat they'd had since arriving. Spit-a-Lot was nowhere to be seen and only one other guard, off in the distance enjoying a cigarette, was keeping watch.

Along with the sausages and eggs, they were served some sheep's milk cheese and chunks of stale bread, a veritable banquet unlike any they'd been served, and all washed down with milky hot tea. János seemed pleased to hear the boys grumble their thanks, and Ervin was hopeful he'd cook for them every day, but that dream was short lived as János set them straight.

"Don't think you'll eat like this tomorrow, fellas, but it's All Saints Day, and even you people deserve a holiday once in a while." His face was kind, yet the stab of his words stung like a papercut to Ervin, who knew that "you people" meant Jews, and not in a kind way. They were a different kind of people. And bad things happened to different kinds of people.

They remained at the sheep farm for several days, blessed with having no work to perform, though János was true to his word and there were no other morning banquets. But he wasn't bad for a guard. Apart from that unexpected breakfast, he'd proved neither kind nor cruel and pretty much left the boys alone. Ervin concluded that the breakfast hadn't been so much for them as for himself. János liked food. He liked eating it and no doubt liked preparing it. And fortunately for Ervin and his mates, he'd at least prepared it for them once—probably because Spit-a-Lot had the holiday off and wasn't around to put a stop to it.

But all in all, the sheep farm, wretched as it was, wasn't entirely bad. True, the nights were dreadful. But the days were fine. It was the first time since Ervin had arrived for his service that he'd had a moment of rest and he used the time to hang out with Frank and his new friends, sharing pranks, stories, and dreams, and at long last, to write to his parents.

Dear Mother and Father,

I hope that this letter reaches you and that you are both well. I have been kept busy with a variety of chores and have learned to use a shovel quite well. Who would ever have imagined that such a bookworm as me could grow strong as an ox turning the earth upside down? You will be pleased to know that my old high school chum, Frank More, is here and we make quite a team. I am so happy to have a kindred spirit. We joke and laugh a great deal and I delight in pranking him, and he me. It makes the time pass, as there are often long stretches of tedium, even when hard at work.

The guards are, for the most part, decent fellows. It is just that they have been placed in a situation that calls on them to be stern. Some, of course, are more stern than others, but so far, I haven't had many troubles.

I do so miss you both, and Mother, I would give anything to taste your cooking once again! The food is, as you can imagine, rather wretched, but as long as it passes my tongue rapidly, I can avoid tasting the miserable gruel.

We are currently resting at a sheep farm somewhere far away. I have lost my sense of direction so I'm not quite sure where we are, but I look forward to moving on soon. The countryside is glorious and the sky vast. At night I look up to the veil of stars and wish for these days to pass soon so that I might see you both once again. Until then, do not worry about me, as I am strong in mind and body (you would be surprised to see how strong I have already become!) and trust in God that these difficult days will soon pass.

Your loving son,
Ervin

"You think it'll ever reach 'em?" Frank asked, his own letter to his parents sticking out of his shirt pocket.

Ervin shrugged. "Probably not. But if we don't write anything, we know they'll never see it."

"That's what I figure, as well. You tell them the truth?" Frank's face was that of a sad-eyed clown—a big smile for laughs, but the eyes fallen and near tear-filled. Ervin felt for his friend, knowing how painful it was to maintain the spirit when so much crushed it every day.

"Of course not," Ervin said. "I can't let them worry. If I told them the truth, my letter would be one big word—*HELP!*" They both laughed as the truth of their predicament had been spoken aloud.

"I told mine that God sent me here to keep you alive," Frank half-joked, though they both knew there was a kernel of truth to the statement.

"And I told mine that God sent me here to keep you out of trouble," Ervin retorted.

"You tell 'em you're so soft you can't lift your own backpack?"

"Nope. Told them I'm strong as an ox. You tell yours you're so scared you need me to hold your hand?"

"Nope. Told 'em I've got the courage of a five-star general and this whole thing is a breeze!"

Both boys laughed and gave each other a playful shove. They were both scared, Ervin far more than Frank. Both barely able to keep up with the back-breaking work (though there was no doubt that Frank was a lot tougher than Ervin in that regard).

"Think they'll mail our letters?" Ervin asked Frank, repeating Frank's own concern.

Frank shrugged. "Don't know if they'll send them, but at least we know one thing."

"What's that?" Ervin asked.

"They'll read them."

After three days of idling at the sheep farm, enjoying the respite but not the shack, Spit-a-Lot burst through the door, spitting on the earthen floor as he did so. It was not yet dawn and not even the birds were awake.

"Vacation's over! Get moving!" He marched up and down the rows of sleeping young men, kicking each one whether awake or asleep.

Everyone scrambled to get their things together as fast as they could. His tone made it clear that whatever was up ahead, it wasn't going to be pleasant.

"Come on, get pissing and moving!" he commanded. "Got bread outside, eat it before the crows get it."

A rush of scared young men poured from the shack and into the darkness, scattering to pee and hurry back to snatch up whatever stale bread they could grab. They knew it might be the only meal they'd get until the day came to an end, and no telling what that day had in store.

By the time the sun rose they'd been marching for over an hour. Ervin found his backpack had grown heavier after just three days of lifting nothing heavier than a fork of wilted cabbage. As much as he had boasted to his parents of his growing strength—and half convinced himself of his impressive muscles—he knew he was still the weakest man among them, and for that he felt an embarrassment he did his best to conceal by keeping the group entertained with his clowning around. If he could get a boy to laugh, not only did he lessen that boy's misery, if only for a moment, but he lessened the chance they'd tease and torment him for his weakness. And to be honest, for his sloth, because Ervin could study 20 hours straight without so much as taking a break, but physical labor remained a punishment he could not bear. Yet his only value to these soldiers was what physical labor he could perform, an irony that chilled him as he realized with each marching step toward their unknown destination that if he failed to perform, they might kill him.

It was during these long hikes, or while working from sunup to sundown in the cold autumn air, that Ervin felt both immensely grateful for the warm clothing his parents had given him and sympathetic for the other boys. Few had proper clothing and as they worked so much harder than he, he noted their threadbare coats, gloveless hands, and boots so badly torn they were near pointless. While all wore the requisite army caps—uniforms and, of course, rifles, denied them—they provided no warmth. Ervin's privilege was striking against this ragtag battalion of discarded young men, men displaced not by their loving parents, but by the very nation they now labored for, the very nation they'd lived in since birth, sworn allegiance to, and honored with pride.

It was no longer pride that Ervin felt, but sympathy and gratitude. Sympathy for all the other men who had so much less than he, and gratitude that even in such a frightening and brutal situation, he was fortunate. He thought back to that first day, a lifetime ago, but barely a couple of weeks, when he'd first set out cursing his parents for weighing down his pack with such heavy clothing. Now that heavy clothing was keeping him warm while others shivered. Ervin still hated carrying the pack, but his displeasure was matched by the humility it brought him. He was a most fortunate son in a most unfortunate situation. He just hoped the other men didn't resent him his good fortune, though he knew far too many did so. He saw it in their glares, felt it in their kicks when he wasn't moving fast enough, heard it in their muttered comments. Were it not for Frank looking out for him, Ervin couldn't imagine how they might treat him. While Frank had his back, he might not be protected from the guards, but he'd surely be protected from his workmates.

After hiking all day, being served a bit more bread and thankfully some cold beans, they camped under the stars, then resumed their hike in the morning. As they hiked further with no knowledge of where or why they were going, a subtle dread crept upon him. He could tell, as well, that Frank shared his fear, as he'd fallen silent, his face pale and eyes fixed at his own boots as they marched on. Frank was the one who had it all together, the one who couldn't be scared. Yet he was, and that realization progressively unsettled Ervin. But he knew he had to ignore his fears. His fear would defeat him more surely than any external enemy. Pushing aside his fear, Ervin marched on, Frank close behind. Eventually, the terrain was becoming familiar, and Ervin realized they were heading back toward the train station where they'd first disembarked.

Hours later, his feet blistered, back aching, and stomach growling, Ervin saw that he'd been correct as the train station came into view. He felt a touch of pride at being right, though it was over such a small matter. Still, everything about his life had become uncertain—where he was, where he was going, what he would have to do, whether his parents received his letters, how they were doing, how long this nightmare would continue—that just having guessed they were heading toward the train station lessened the strain. It was the uncertainty, he was coming to realize, that was so tortuous.

Ervin glanced over to Frank and saw that he had taken a few steps back, as if to bolt at any moment rather than get on that train. "Come on," he said, gesturing for Frank to step up. "They won't hurt you, Frank, you've got the back of a workhorse! They're putting us to work."

Frank took a few steps toward Ervin, relaxing his posture as he did so, putting on a show of cool indifference, but it was only a show. "Yeah, you're probably right. But just getting on that train scares the hell out of me. Where are they taking us next?" Frank's voice faded, but his words did not. They lingered in the air, as one by one, they boarded the train.

PRIVATE PRACTICE

Kamilla had thought that converting to Christianity would be a mere formality that wouldn't change her in any way. Yet once she had done so, she felt a deep sense of shame, as if she had somehow denounced her own family and her past. Taking the Bible lessons became an even greater indignity and, although she read the teachings of Christ with a certain respect for the humanity and wisdom they reflected, she also felt it cruel that she was compelled to read the texts. The very fact that she had to conceal her identity and denounce her own religion and heritage just to be able to participate in society seemed contrary to everything she was reading in this New Testament about forgiveness and compassion. Where were these attributes among these Christians casting them out?

"I understand," Joseph said, as weary as she at the masquerade they were made to perform. "But what matters is what's in our hearts. After all, neither of us are practicing Jews, so if this is what we need to do for me to continue working, then it is not such a great price to pay."

"I wonder if it might be," Kamilla said, "if it means living our lives as imposters, for that is how I feel."

Joseph pulled his wife to him and held her close. "It won't be for long, my dear. There are always tides that will turn against us, but the tides always recede. Soon enough we will be free to be whatever we want to be, you shall see." He kissed the top of her head and lifted her chin so that he could kiss her tender lips. He knew his wife was right, but he felt powerless to do anything other than comply with the demands made on him to not be Jewish. He also felt torn, having fought and risked his life for the very nation that now demanded he denounce his Jewish identity or starve. Was that what he had risked his life to preserve? He couldn't fathom it. Surely, the social climate would soon change.

And yet, Joseph returned to work one day to be told he was no longer needed. Converting to Christianity, it seemed, had been insufficient. His very blood was Jewish, and no amount of Bible lessons or crucifixes displayed around his home and office could change that fact.

"I wish I didn't have to let you go," his supervisor said, clearly more uncomfortable with the conversation than the act itself. Joseph knew there was another man ready to take his place, a man whose Christian heritage would offer no cause for moral quandary, regardless of his beliefs. "But it's not my decision to make, I do hope you understand."

"Yes, of course, sir," Joseph lied. "No doubt you've been put in a very difficult position. I'm so sorry."

His supervisor heaved a sigh of relief, relaxing his shoulders as if freed of a pressing weight. He'd been absolved of guilt.

Joseph returned home having been the one to apologize despite being the one who had been wronged. *Why had he apologized?* he wondered, as he carried his medical bag through the streets, the streetlights already lighting up as darkness descended. It was a lovely summer night and, as he walked home, later than usual for he'd had many patients to attend to, he wondered how much of that summer he and Kamilla would be able to enjoy if he could no longer provide for his wife. With no job, they'd have no money, and with no money, they'd have no food. All that he had promised his bride was vanishing and he feared destitution if he didn't do something to turn things around. Not being one to give up, Joseph knew what he had to do. His salvation was in his own hands, quite literally. If he had a medical bag and a medical degree and could pass himself off as Christian, he and Kamilla would survive. When he returned home that evening, he told Kamilla he had lost his job but not to worry. He would open his own practice.

But Kamilla *was* worried. They no longer had an income. And she was expecting.

After much searching, Joseph couldn't believe his luck when he found two rooms on the main street of Győr at 6 Baross Street. The neighborhood was just what he and Kamilla had imagined when they first thought of moving to the city. Its brick streets, busy markets, and nearby parks offered all the charm and amenities of city life, and they were confident the location would draw patients and offer a safe environment for raising their new family. The rooms themselves were modest and only a simple curtain separated his office from their living quarters, but Joseph was confident that if he could attract a few patients to start off, word of mouth would quickly spread and over time he'd prosper. Still, he knew it would be a struggle the first few years and despite his efforts to assure Kamilla there was nothing to worry about, he was indeed worried. What little equipment he had was inadequate for a functioning dental office and he had no funds to buy more. The office itself needed improvement, as the wallpaper was old and peeling, the windows barely opened, and the curtain would be insufficient once a crying baby arrived. As for plumbing, most rooms in Hungary lacked private toilets in the 1920s, though a small sink provided Joseph with some running water and a drain, provided Kamilla didn't use it during the day.

"We can't continue to live like this once the baby arrives," Kamilla told Joseph. She wanted to be supportive and knew her husband was trying his very best to make do with what he had, but it just wasn't practical to have no access to running water during the day and how in the world would she keep the baby from wailing? After all, that's what babies do, she reasoned, and no one would want to see a dentist under such conditions.

"I know we can't live like this," Joseph snapped. "Don't you think I'm doing everything I possibly can? Just this morning I had a new patient, but I couldn't treat him because I didn't have an X-ray machine to give him a proper diagnosis. We need money and I'm in the damnable position of not being able to make enough money because I have no money!" He was at his wit's end, knowing he had a wife and soon a baby to support, but having no idea how to do that if no one would hire him. His enthusiasm for starting his own practice had faded as quickly as it had appeared now that he realized all that he lacked to treat his patients.

Kamilla knew there was no reasoning with Joseph when he was in such high temper. She put a kettle of water on the hotplate to make tea and let him stew in his own juices while she focused on coming up with a solution. Surely there was someone who could help them, provide them a small loan until Joseph's practice was established. She had great confidence in Joseph's skill and work ethic, but his hot temper was not helping any. By the time she'd prepared the tea, she had a solution to suggest.

"Didn't you say you had a distant cousin here in Győr?" she asked him as she poured his tea and offered it to him. "Someone quite well off?"

"Oh, yes, my great grandfather's brother's grandson or something like that. Viktor Kroonenberg. But I have never met him. The only reason I even know about him is because Berta told me he became quite wealthy during the war by selling army supplies. He wouldn't know me at all." Joseph sipped his tea, his temper calming with every sip. He hadn't meant to snap at Kamilla like that, but he did wish she wouldn't press him anymore than he was already pressuring himself. Nonetheless, she was right. They couldn't continue to live as they were.

"Still, you're family. It wouldn't hurt to contact him and introduce yourself. The worst he could do is show you to the door."

She was right, of course, Joseph thought, still fuming at the impossible task before him. Why should it be so difficult just to earn a living when he was educated, experienced, and so willing to work? Must he now grovel for alms?

"Joseph, please," she said, reaching for his hand. "At least look him up and ask if he can help you with a small loan. Would it be better to be unable to pay the rent and we find ourselves evicted?"

Joseph set down his teacup and smiled softly. "Alright, my love, I will try. He may not even see me, but I will at least ask for a meeting. But if he refuses me, either the meeting or the money, I am not sure what we shall do."

"God will answer our prayers," Kamilla said, picking up her knitting basket and resuming her work on a small blanket for her coming child. "Put your trust in God, and in yourself, and we'll get through this."

"That is, assuming God doesn't smite us for converting," Joseph laughed. But inside, his soul was weeping. He hoped and prayed Kamilla was right.

Joseph sent a letter to Mr. Kroonenberg introducing himself, noting their family connections, and asking if he might visit. He explained that he had served in the war and moved to Győr with his wife and recently begun a dental practice. He was doubtful he'd even receive a reply but was happily surprised when the following week a letter arrived in the mail inviting him for drinks the following Thursday. Donning his finest clothes, meticulously cared for as he couldn't afford to replace or expand his wardrobe, Joseph arrived as punctually as he demanded of others. He did not want to keep his relative waiting and feared the slightest misstep would lead to disastrous results. Kroonenberg was his only hope, and it was a longshot.

When he arrived promptly as scheduled, he saw that Kroonenberg's home was an impressive one, and there was no doubt that Berta's gossip of his wealth had not been overstated. His home comprised the entire five floors of a stately building in an upscale neighborhood and, as Joseph was ushered in by a domestic servant, he marveled at the luxurious entryway of marble floors and gilded wallpaper that was larger than both of Joseph and Kamilla's rooms combined. A crystal chandelier sparkled above a round table large enough for an entire family to feast at, and yet it held only a floral centerpiece and porcelain dish for calling cards. Joseph set his card in the dish as he awaited the arrival of his distant cousin, wondering if he'd impress this man who shared his blood, or if he might be received as yet another peasant begging for charity.

He hadn't waited long before a short yet elegant man with strong features and the same burning eyes as all the Wolfs opened wide the sliding doors to the drawing room and introduced himself.

"So lovely to meet you, Joseph. I am delighted to know I have kin in Győr to visit me now that you are here. Come, let's have a drink and get to know each other."

Joseph immediately felt at ease and his whole posture relaxed as he greeted the cousin he'd never met and followed him into the drawing room.

"Shall we have a glass of port? I have a magnificent 1900 that is anxiously awaiting a good pour into a couple of glasses." Before Joseph could say a word, his cousin was pouring a rich, red wine into small crystal glasses, its amber edges showing the fortified wine's maturing age.

"A toast to our blood and ancestry," Kroonenberg declared, raising his glass.

Joseph did the same and, after the first sip, he knew that even if he walked away empty-handed, he would at least have tasted the most magical elixir that had ever passed across his tongue.

"Why, this is marvelous," Joseph exclaimed. "How have I ever missed such a drink?"

"Oh, this is not the drink for common man," his host replied, smacking his lips and admiring the drink he held up to the late afternoon light pouring in from the windows. The room itself was richly appointed, with book-lined mahogany paneled walls and a massive fireplace in which a warm fire burned. Even the chairs were opulent, upholstered in the richest green velvet Joseph had ever touched. "It's a fortified wine from Portugal, the House of Cockburn, and to be honest, it is to be enjoyed after dinner, but I say why wait? It is far too delicious to delay another moment!"

Joseph smiled. This new relative was quite the character, but he couldn't deny that he was thoroughly enjoying himself. After a bit of small talk about the city and the distant relatives they shared, and another small glass of the delicious wine served with a plate of blue cheese, biscuits, and a few nuts, Joseph told his story. He began with his service during the war, then followed with being exiled from

Transylvania, hired in Győr, then converting to Christianity in a failed effort at keeping his job before starting his own practice.

"Of course, even as a Christian, I am finding it difficult to make a living as we arrived in Győr with little but the clothes on our bodies, and now with a new baby on the way, I fear we may leave the city as penniless as we'd arrived." Joseph took another sip of the port, thankful that the spirits were giving him the courage to say what he had to say next. "Which brings me to the purpose of my visit. I know that as a man of means, you are not frivolous with your investments. But if you might consider investing in a struggling dentist such as myself so that I might purchase the medical equipment I need to make a go of it, I would assure you I will repay you every forint, and with interest." Joseph had made his case and bowed his head ever so slightly in respect to his new cousin and hopeful benefactor. Then he awaited the kick out the door.

In reply, Kroonenberg sat silently, his mind clearly at work calculating the costs and benefits of considering this latest plea for monetary assistance. He sipped the last of his port and then said, "Joseph, you are my kin and I can see that you are a good man. And I have no doubt that should I invest in your practice, you would indeed repay me."

Joseph could hear the reticence in his voice and awaited his kindly rejection. He was already composing his apology in his head when Kroonenberg said, "I'll tell you what, good man. I will give you all the money you need to start your practice under one condition—and it is a serious one, one that I insist upon if I am to help you out."

Joseph's heart pumped faster at the possibility of salvation and his fear of just what that condition might be. After all, he knew nothing of his new relative, but what he did know was that great wealth was often accompanied by great secrets. What if this man were to ask him to commit a crime? With Joseph's access to gold, mercury, and medications, he was a prime target for the unscrupulous. Was his newfound cousin such a man?

"Yes, Viktor," Joseph said, hoping to conceal his nerves. "Anything. What would you like for me to do? I'll surely pay you whatever interest rate you require."

"You are family," Kroonenberg said, dismissing the suggestion with a wave of his hand. "I have no desire to make a profit from you, and I trust you to repay me as you're able. I ask only that you put an end to this ridiculous charade of yours and that you and your wife convert back to Judaism and stop living as Christians. Why, it's simply ludicrous!"

Joseph had never been so relieved. Indeed, he desperately wanted to stop the charade of pretending to be Christian, and reclaiming his Jewish heritage was a small price to pay in order to succeed. Of course, doing so came with risks, he well knew. To revert to Judaism posed a risk should the social climate worsen. Nonetheless, Kamilla would be happy to hear of it. Joseph knew she was unhappy with their conversion. But what choice did he have? To decline Kroonenberg's provision would mean destitution. He couldn't build a practice without the proper equipment. How could he possibly take such a risk, launching his practice with what little he had, all because of a possible alternative risk? Joseph realized that there was no escaping who he was. He was a Jew. And if Christians had no interest in having their teeth treated by a Jew, there were certainly plenty of Jews in Győr who had need of a good dentist. They would come. Besides, Joseph rationalized, the stigma that branded Jews as undesirables would never take hold. Soon the social climate would warm and they would live together again, Christians and Jews, as neighbors and friends. It was only a matter of time.

When he'd returned home and told Kamilla of his fruitful meeting with his new kin, Kamilla was thrilled to hear the news that her suggestion had been a wise one and, even better, that she would no longer have to wear a crucifix around her neck. She immediately took it off and went about the house removing the crucifix that hung over the front door, the one above the mantel, the New Testament on the table, and the portrait of Jesus that hung on the wall. As much as she'd come to view herself as a secularist with more interest in libraries than houses of worship, having lived as a Christian was more difficult than having lived as an orthodox Jew in her family home. If anything, the pretense had pushed her closer to her Jewish roots and filled her with a sympathy for her mother's orthodox ways.

The rituals that she'd abandoned had played a purpose that she hadn't even realized until it had all been stripped away from her and replaced with the rituals of an entirely different religion. Now, she was finally free to raise her child as Jewish, not as Christian, and her husband would no longer worry that his business wouldn't succeed. With the funds from Viktor Kroonenberg, Joseph could invest in the most modern dental equipment—and thus provide a level of skill and service no other dentist in the area could provide.

Joseph did purchase the most modern dental equipment, including an X-ray machine and dental sink, which his landlord permitted him to install at Joseph's expense. He was able to buy a proper dental chair, as well as better tools and materials, so that he could treat cavities, gum disease, and broken teeth. He could even build dentures for his patients. Within weeks of setting up his new practice, the word had spread and just as he'd expected—no doubt, in part, from a bit of Viktor's nudging of his friends and associates—Joseph had more patients than he'd ever imagined.

His rush of business came just in the nick of time, for in the spring of 1922, with the help of a midwife named Mrs. Gold, Kamilla gave birth to a healthy baby boy right there in the dental chair in Joseph's office. Both she and Joseph immediately fell in love with the little newborn they named Ervin.

"He shall be the luckiest little boy in all of Hungary," Kamilla declared, looking into her baby's tiny eyes and holding him to her breast.

"That he shall be," his proud papa agreed. "We shall give him the world."

FORTUNATE SON

Ervin could not have known the struggles his parents had endured in the early years of their marriage, for it wasn't long after his birth that his father's practice did indeed prosper and at last the Wolfs could enjoy the Golden Age the 1920's promised. Their baby boy was loved and spoiled from the moment he was born and neither Joseph nor Kamilla could have been happier. Even the prejudice against them seemed to be easing, just as Joseph had been confident it would. True, the antisemitism remained, but as Joseph's practice grew, so did his reputation, and the respect he received far offset the occasional snubs he encountered in public.

Within two years, they were able to move from the cramped, two-room apartment to a much nicer two-story building with large windows, high ceilings, and spacious rooms, all opening to a lovely Baroque courtyard. Every apartment of the building offered a circular, open porch on every floor, permitting the residents to relax and socialize together. Kamilla no longer felt isolated from the world as she had in the last apartment. She made friends with the other mothers in the building, as well as those she met in the nearby park where she would take her baby boy for strolls in his carriage. Few could have known the poverty and hardship they'd suffered, other than those just like them who had their own stories to tell. But they seldom spoke of these hardships as they prepared for a new more peaceful and tolerant era.

For Ervin, the world he'd been born into was one of love and safety. He was adored by his parents and spoiled from the start. His father built him his first toy, made from a simple spool, its edges cut to create a cogwheel with a rubber string around it and a toothpick to roll it up. That toy worked like a tank and had required a clever imagination to design. His father also taught him his first trick, by placing a lit match on a water filled plate and covering it with a glass. As the flame went out, the water disappeared from the plate, appearing in the glass, as if by magic. Ervin was fascinated with the trick and asked his father to show him again and again and again. While just small gifts and moments, Ervin treasured the presents from his father who clearly adored him. His mother also showered him with attention and affection and spent most of her day caring for her darling boy.

Joseph wanted to raise Ervin as the respected son of a successful man, and Kamilla wanted her son to have all the treasures life had to offer. Of course, neither intended to raise a child without good character, kindness, and morals, so these qualities were instilled in him from the start. But at the same time, Ervin was lavished with love, attention, and more than his fair share of toys and treats.

Győr had wonderful parks, all beautifully maintained with shade trees and fragrant flowers. When the weather was nice, Kamilla would take young Ervin to the neighboring park from early morning until dinnertime. She stayed busy with her knitting and chatted with the other mothers at the park. But it was there that Ervin had his first encounter with a terrible man. The groundskeeper was an old, grouchy man who snarled at the children and glared at the mothers. He wore an armband on his uniform with the town's symbol and carried a big cane. Ervin hated that cane, and the armband especially disturbed him, as it wasn't like anything other grownups wore. It looked as if his arm would fall off if that band was removed.

The grouchy man seemed to always have his eyes on the children and would bully them to stay off the lawn. "Get out!" he'd shout in a voice as deep as a scary bear's. "Scram!"

The mothers would instantly gather the children closer, and Ervin could tell the mothers were rather frightened of him as well. What frightened Ervin the most, though, more than the armband and more than the reaction of the mothers, was the way the scary man would point his cane as if it were a sword or a gun or a stick he could use to beat the children. The cane may have been the only symbol of power the grumpy old man had, but it was indeed effective, as the children quickly learned not to step on the grass.

But the park was otherwise the ideal spot, and Ervin had great fun playing with the other children. And it was there that he met his first playmate, a cute little girl named Luca who lived in the building across the street. Luca had large chestnut brown eyes and dimples in her cheeks that seemed perfectly fitted to her sweet disposition. She adored Ervin and he her, and they played together as closely as if they had been brother and sister. Luca lived with her mother and aunt and, though they were not well off financially, their generosity of spirit endeared them to Kamilla. Luca's mother gave Ervin his first doll, a rubber Mickey Mouse. The Disney character was brand new at the time, but already in Budapest the animated shorts introducing the beloved cartoon mouse—a new version of Steamboat Willy—had become quite popular. Ervin adored his rubber mouse and played with it night and day.

Ervin and Luca became inseparable, and the children's mothers often cared for the other's child when errands needed to be run or one of the mothers just needed some rest. Kamilla came to think of Luca almost as one of her own and, rather than find caring for the little girl an extra burden, she delighted in her company and Ervin's joy whenever Luca came to visit, or he visited her.

One day, however, Luca couldn't come play. "She's very sick," his mother told him, "and must stay in bed." Ervin was upset, so he made her a pretty get-well card and asked his mother to give it to her. He couldn't understand why his mother seemed so sad about the matter, for he knew once Luca saw the card, she would get better and they could play again.

But Luca didn't get better and a few days later, he found his mother crying. She called him to her and, pulling Ervin onto her lap, she said, "I'm so sorry, honey, but I have sad news. Luca was very sick and the doctors couldn't make her better. She became so ill that she died and went to Heaven. We won't see her anymore." Ervin didn't understand what his mother was trying to tell him, but he was scared by her tears and he ran crying to his room, throwing himself on his bed and sobbing as he never had before. But what came after confused him even more.

He watched from his window as an ugly horse-drawn carriage, as black and frightening as the night, came to Luca's building and took her away. Nor could he understand the meaning of the huge red tag with a label he couldn't read that was glued to her family's front door. Even more confusing, for the next six weeks, Ervin was not allowed to play with any of his friends. He couldn't even leave his apartment and he missed Luca terribly. He just knew she'd come back. But why he was being punished by being kept inside, he had no idea.

What Ervin couldn't have understood at that young age was that his little friend had succumbed to diphtheria, an infectious disease for which there was no effective treatment at the time and, given his playtime with Luca, he may have been exposed himself. All he understood was that his friend was gone while he was being punished. Alone in his room and apartment, he safeguarded his Mickey Mouse, holding it close and not letting it out of his sight for fear it would be taken away as well.

It was Ervin's first experience with loss and the painful memory seared itself in his mind. He knew he could never bear to experience such a loss ever again, and clung even closer to his parents, knowing they, at least, would never be gone.

During the summers, Kamilla would rise early to get to the market so that she could have her choice of the freshest produce. Before Ervin had been born, she always waited until the vendors were just about to shut down their stalls, so that she could bargain for the best prices on whatever was leftover. Now, with her little boy by her side and a bit of money in her wallet, she finally felt as if she'd made it. How funny, she thought, that it was a beautiful bushel of beets or the tiniest new potatoes that instilled in her that sense of pride that comes with adulthood, rather than any fine carriage or gown. Of course, she'd been an adult for several years by that point, a married woman, but the struggles of poverty and exile she and Joseph had faced had acted like a closed door to that adulthood, as if she weren't quite ready to take her part in public life. Kamilla was indeed ready, and with Ervin by her side as she selected the finest vegetables, the best cuts of meat, and the freshest wild mushrooms, she had the confidence of a noblewoman.

She had, as well, the frugality of a housewife, for she knew how precarious her new lifestyle was and if she and Joseph were to grow more prosperous, she would be wise not to be wasteful with what money they did have. Not trusting the vendors, she carried a pocket-sized spring scale so that once her purchase was weighed and a price quoted, she would weigh it herself to confirm the cost. Sure enough, nine times out of ten she would demonstrate to the vendor that his own scale had inexplicably exaggerated the weight. It wasn't long before the vendors learned not to put their thumb on the scale when Kamilla Wolf came along.

Ervin found his mother's ways rather curious at the market, and every shopping trip became an instructive lesson in shopping, cooking, or healthy living. "You see these balls of cottage cheese?" she would whisper to Ervin as they walked down the narrow corridor of the local dairy market, Kamilla nodding her head toward the hand-rolled balls of curds displayed on the huge green leaves in which they'd be wrapped. "We don't want those. They aren't hygienic. They might have disease."

Ervin learned early on the importance of hygiene and the dreaded fear of disease coming from anything less than hygienic—which at his young age, he took to mean very, very clean. Even the fresh milk that was delivered to their home daily by the milkman posed a danger. He wasn't allowed to touch it until his mother had boiled it thoroughly to kill any possible bacteria. The threat of contamination was constant.

His mother had a similar concern for any precut poultry as it, too, might be infected. The new practice of cutting off the heads and feet of poultry was every bit as risky as rolling the poor bird in dung, as far as Kamilla was concerned. She wanted only the freshest meat or poultry, and the least processed. To ensure that a bird was to her liking, Ervin would watch with bewilderment as she thrust her hand into its viscera or peered inside to give the freshly killed fowl a complete abdominal examination.

"Mommy, what are you doing?"

"I'm checking for fat," she'd explain. "We want a nice, fatty bird and this one here is a goose, so it's important we get a good-sized goose liver."

Once satisfied with her purchase, Kamilla would take the liver to a local export store where she would sell it for such a good price that the remainder of the goose cost her next to nothing, and the family could enjoy the bird for the next several days. The fat itself was saved for cooking and in the winter, Kamilla would save an especially big goose liver for themselves, preserving it in a thick layer of goose fat that she'd scrape off when it was time to serve the liver.

Joseph admired Kamilla's frugality, as it eased the pressure on him. But even more, Kamilla was turning into quite an accomplished cook, and he looked forward to each evening's meal. Joseph reveled in the new life his growing practice was bringing. By no means wealthy, as he was still building his practice and repaying the generous loan Viktor Kroonenberg had provided that made it all possible, he could at least enjoy his family, knowing he was able to provide for them. He had never seen Kamilla happier and, though he worked long hours, when he did have time off, he thoroughly enjoyed spending time with his family. But the energy of a small boy was at times trying on his patience, especially given that his dental office was still adjacent to his apartment and consequently, he had little tolerance for the screeches and squeals of little children.

"Please, Kamilla, I'm trying to work! My patients are anxious enough when they see a dentist. Can't you keep that boy quiet?"

Kamilla had learned to avoid her husband's temper before it grew too great. Though he had never struck a blow in her direction nor spoken with any cruelty, his lack of emotional control could at times be more than she could bear. Of course, she knew when she married him that she would be wedded to a man of passion. Indeed, it was his passion and sensitivity that had endeared him to her. But with that sensitivity came the whole gamut of emotion, and now that they had a little boy running around the apartment, there were days she wanted nothing more than to tell them both to grow up.

Instead, she'd take little Ervin out to play, finding adventure wherever the sun was shining. One of their favorite adventures, weather permitting, was spending the day at the local beach along the River Tisza. It was a long walk to get there, and Ervin was especially frightened by the long wooden bridge they had to cross, especially as the passing horse-drawn carts made loud noises and shook the bridge. He was terrified the whole bridge would collapse and they'd plunge into the river, though they never did. Once across the bridge, however, a whole world of fun and joy awaited. The beach itself was primitive and muddy with no toilets, showers, or changing rooms. But Ervin couldn't have cared less. He loved the hot sunshine on his bare skin and each summer he seemed to turn even darker than the summer before.

"Go have fun," Kamilla would say as she helped him strip down to his swim trunks. "But don't go into the water without me!" Ervin didn't yet know how to swim, but he loved dipping his toes in the water and playing with the other children, splashing each other endlessly.

They ate sumptuous lunches at the beach, with fresh raw eggs always a part of the day's menu. Kamilla had read that raw eggs were essential for a healthy diet, a popular belief after the bodybuilder Charles Atlas swore by them, so she made sure her son always had one with his lunch. Her picnic basket was forever filled with delicious delights—marinated fish or cold slices of smoked meat, sweet butter biscuits with homemade gooseberry jelly, colorful peppers sometimes stuffed with *Körözött,* a curd cheese spiced with paprika and caraway, and for dessert, something sweet like walnut cakes or cookies. Ervin loved those outdoor feasts as much as Kamilla enjoyed making them. Nobody on the beach ate a finer lunch, of that, little Ervin was certain.

Though Kamilla always brought a bit of cold tea, there was no running water nearby when Ervin got thirsty, which he always did as the tea usually disappeared early. Though there was a freestanding artesian water fountain about half a mile away, Ervin didn't like to go there. The fountain was swarming with hundreds of thirsty bees and the water itself had a metallic odor that he found disgusting.

"Don't drink too much," Kamilla would caution as he took quick short gulps to quench his thirst with as little discomfort as possible. Ervin wasn't accustomed to discomfort. "It will make your neck grow big," she'd explain, a concept the little boy found as comical as he did frightening.

"Hurry up, my chocolate-covered boy!" Kamilla would say when she saw that Ervin had had enough of the foul water. She feared that whatever chemicals were in the water, they could cause a disfiguring goiter at best, perhaps sickness at worst. But there was only so much water she could carry with her, and she knew it would be a long walk home with a thirsty child.

"My, don't you have the most beautiful suntan in all of Győr!" his mother said as she helped him back into his street clothes and gave him a giant hug and a kiss, delighting in her little boy's summer fun. She enjoyed the long walk back, even if Ervin grew tired and cranky and begged her to carry him all the way home. While her small son might be irritable, she always felt confident that by the time she returned home from a long day at the beach, Ervin would be ready for sleep, and any bad mood Joseph may have nurtured would be long gone following a day of peace and quiet.

Later, when Ervin was in grade school, the town had improved the beach significantly, complete with large floating cabanas for changing clothes. In the middle of the raft was a large pool with a porous bottom that let the fresh river water in, but kept the children secure from the river's flow. The first summer the pool had been built, Ervin took swimming lessons there. The swimming instructor was a young, tanned, and athletic man with a ceremonial demeanor that was so formal, Ervin was afraid to so much as smile. The instructor fastened a heavy cork belt around Ervin's waist, which was attached to a long rope affixed to a long, heavy rod. As Ervin floated, kicked, and splashed in the water, the instructor walked around the slippery planks of the pool, announcing his instructions like a butler announcing dinner was ready to be served.

"Take a deep breath, master Ervin. Yes, that's right. Now put your face in the water and blow."

"Point your toes out like a ballerina. Keep your legs straight. No, sir, not like a frog, like a soldier."

"Kick your legs, master Ervin. Come, my good man, kick!"

"You're doing a splendid job, young man, splendid indeed. One more time."

As time went on, Ervin grew less frightened of the strange instructor and more humored by his ceremonial pretense. His comfort was aided by his rising self-confidence as he learned first to float, then to tread water, and eventually to swim. He couldn't wait to show his father all he had learned.

"Why, that's impressive, indeed, my son!" Joseph exclaimed, seeing his little boy swim back and forth, the heavy cork belt no longer needed.

"Come swim with me!" Ervin pleaded.

But Joseph only shook his head. "I'm sorry, son, but I'm afraid I can't join you."

"Why not, father? Didn't you bring your swimming suit?"

"I'm afraid I cannot swim with you, son, because I never learned to swim. You see, when I was growing up, there were no rivers or places to swim, so I just never learned."

"You can learn now, father!" Ervin said, his eyes large and sympathetic. "Won't you, please, so you can join me?"

Joseph looked at his small son, so earnest and longing for his father's company. "You know something?" he said at long last, "You're right, Ervin. I can indeed."

For the next several weeks, Joseph did just that, taking swimming lessons right alongside Ervin. While the big man seemingly looked rather ridiculous with the cork belt tied around his waist as the instructor commanded him to blow bubbles and kick, none of the other children teased him and Ervin felt so proud of his father for having the courage to learn like a child. More importantly, he loved to swim alongside his father and share the discovery of moving their bodies through water, as if flying through silk.

They were wonderful seasons packed with adventures, traditions, and warm memories. When the summers at the beach came to an end, there would be the autumn harvest of fallen chestnuts in the parks. Yet even there, Ervin learned the risks of poor hygiene, as the elderly men rolled and smoked their cigarettes openly, filling the air with the foul odor of cheap tobacco and cigars. But there was a payoff to the pollution. Ervin would collect their discarded wood matches, which he'd use to pierce the soft chestnuts, peeling away their thick hairy skin to make miniature animals, dolls, and monsters. He loved creating new little worlds from nature, and there was no better time to do so than in the fall when the chestnuts plummeted freely and the leaves turned shades of orange and red, landing at his feet as if a gift from the trees.

Those same men with their tobacco and matches had another habit that rattled Ervin. They would spit on the ground, making a terrible noise when they did, and Lord help them if any small child got in the line of fire. Getting sick was scary. The mothers would swoop up their children and hurry away whenever they heard a bad cough. Ervin became terrified of those dirty men and their puddles of saliva, as they caused diseases, he was told, like whooping cough, tuberculosis, or the diphtheria that had killed his dear friend Luca. But how he loved the park anyway. His world was secure, his family close and happy, and the only worry he'd ever known was the risk of becoming ill.

Until one day, shortly before he was to start school, his mother and father sat him down and said they had something to tell him.

"I'm afraid we have to move to a new home, Ervin," his father said in a tone that Ervin hadn't heard before. His father seemed to be hurt. He had never seen his father like that and couldn't imagine what was happening.

"But why, father? I don't want to move!"

"It's only for a little while," his mother said, her own voice sounding as sad. "We just need to move to where other Jewish families live."

Ervin couldn't understand it at all. Why did they have to move to where the Jewish families lived? There were other Jewish families right there in their own neighborhood. Ervin went to sleep that night overcome with anguish. Why did he have to leave his home and what would this new home look like? His life had been so secure, so perfect. And now, in an instant, it was shattered.

Hearing his son cry that night, Joseph told Kamilla not to worry, he would see to the boy. He stepped into his son's room quietly, the moonlight illuminating little Ervin's face, wet with tears. Joseph sat on the edge of the bed and resting his hand on Ervin's head, he said, "Remember when you wanted me to learn to swim?"

Ervin was confused. What did swimming have to do with moving to a new house? His father didn't understand. He wanted his mother to come in and hold him in her arms. But his mother wasn't there, so he answered his father. "Yes."

"What I didn't tell you was that I was scared. I was afraid I might be too old to learn. I was afraid people might laugh at me."

"You were?" Ervin couldn't imagine his father afraid of anything, and he surely hadn't seemed the least bit concerned with what others had thought of him.

"Yes, I was. But I knew if I thought about how afraid I was, then I'd never learn to swim. And if I never learned to swim, I could never swim with you, or play with you in the water, or save you if you swam too far out. So I told myself that it was okay to be afraid, but it was not okay to let my fears grow bigger than they already were. I had to be bigger than my fears."

"And you weren't scared anymore?" Ervin asked through the darkness.

"A little bit. But I knew I'd be okay. And I was. Once I started taking swimming lessons, I saw that I was safe in the water. I knew I could do it. Then my fear went away." He paused, brushing his hand across little Ervin's soft hair. "I know you're afraid to move to a new house, son, but I promise, you will be fine. Your mother and I will take care of you and make sure you have a nice home and a nice room all your own."

"You promise?"

"I promise."

"And I won't be afraid?"

"You might be. But you're bigger than your fears, so they will go away if you don't think about them. When you get scared, just remember you're only scared because you don't know what's going to happen. But once you see your new home, you'll be fine. I promise."

"Okay, Daddy," he said. "I'm not scared anymore."

"I love you, son," Joseph said, kissing his son's forehead and tucking the blankets around him.

"I love you, *Apu*," Ervin said, using the Hungarian endearment for father, as he heard his father creep out the door. Ervin fell asleep that night a little less scared of what was up ahead.

What Ervin could not understand at such a young age was that just as his father's practice was growing, the country had slipped into an economic depression that would soon sweep across the globe. Joseph faced a dilemma. He felt he could not continue his practice at his present location for too many of his patients could no longer pay—he had no choice but to reduce his own living expenses, just as most everyone in Hungary was doing.

"We shall overcome this setback as we have the others," he assured Kamilla. "It will only be for a short while. And by living among other Jews, my business won't suffer. But if we stay here, I fear the costs will exceed my income."

Kamilla nodded. She wasn't happy about moving, but she knew that Joseph was right. "We'll get through this, sweetheart," she said, resting her head on her husband's shoulder. "We'll get through this..."

WINTER

When Ervin and Frank disembarked from the train along with the other young men in their unit, they saw that they had come to a town about 322 kilometers east of their last posting and about 48 kilometers from Sárospatak, an industrial town near the Czechoslovakian border. The place was cold and desolate, but once they'd reached their barracks, Ervin was relieved to see they had at last been assigned to proper housing. Though uninsulated, the wooden barracks contained triple bunkbeds that lined both sides of the room. Within minutes of assessing the situation, however, the men realized there were not nearly enough beds for everyone. They'd be doubling up.

"Can't say that I'm keen on these accommodations," Frank said to Ervin, "but sharing a bunk with you sure beats sleeping in the mud."

"I don't know," Ervin replied. "I've heard you snore."

The boys bantered back and forth as they staked out a set of bunks to claim. There weren't enough bunks for the men, much less for their belongings and, while the beds were wide enough to accommodate two men, there was little space between bunks, so sitting up in bed to read or write was out of the question. They were cramped quarters indeed. But they were beds. Real beds. With blankets and pillows. Ervin couldn't have been happier in that moment.

"Hey, Wolf!"

Ervin froze. He knew that voice and it curdled his soul. His heart pounding, he looked across the barracks and sure enough, he recognized a familiar face. Then another. And another. Each one hard as stone. It was István Halász and his pack of thugs. They were a rough bunch known for provoking fights, looting, and bullying back in Győr, and Ervin had been the target of their abuse more times than he'd care to recall. Though they were all Jewish, his parents had forbidden him from having anything to do with them, and that was one prohibition that was as pointless as telling him not to play with rabid rats—he was not about to spend any time with these bullies. But here they were, staring right at him.

"István," Ervin said, nodding to acknowledge their leader's presence. István was tall and wide and made of pure muscle, everything Ervin was not. "Hello," he added, nodding as well to the others while doing his best to conceal his concern. As if his ordeal was not bad enough, now he'd be dealing with these guys.

"Take the bottom bunk. You'll have more space to stash your stuff underneath."

"Yeah, and if you have to take a piss in the night, it's a lot faster," added another one, a kid Ervin only knew as Kovács. Kovács was a short, stocky kid with a face peppered in acne and eyes that looked more dead than alive. He'd always scared Ervin.

The two walked over to Frank and Ervin and István slapped Ervin on the back as if they were old friends. "Welcome to Hell," he said, laughing. "You'll get used to it, kid. We've been here for damn near a year now and still waiting for a hot shower. This place is no hotel, but once you get to know the guards, they aren't so bad." István held out a packet of walnuts as an offering. Hungry and confused, Ervin held out his hand and István poured a generous helping of nuts into his palm, then offered the same to Frank.

"Here, have some dessert," Kovács said, reaching into the pockets of his bulky coat and tossing Frank and Ervin each an apple. "You'll need your vitamins." The thugs laughed, but it wasn't the mean laugh

Ervin remembered from his encounters with them at school or in the neighborhood. There was a softness, a sadness even, to their laugh that Ervin immediately knew to be kind.

He recalled when he first got to know them as children and how confused he'd been by them then, as well, but for other reasons. Every Jewish holiday, these mean little bullies would receive new clothes, as well as gifts of food, giant bags of peanuts, candies, oranges, figs, and other treats. Though Ervin had bountiful gifts of his own at home, he didn't receive any such gifts at school and to see these brutes be feted so generously just burned him with jealousy. It was only later, when he was older, that he realized how poor they were. He learned that it was Mrs. Kohn, the president of the local women's auxiliary and a hyperactive, goodhearted widow who was distributing the gifts. He also realized that every synagogue worldwide probably had someone like Győr's Mrs. Kohn.

Now here they were, after all those years, sharing their treats with him at last. How grateful he was for their kindness, and for the small but meaningful act that their gesture became as it resolved those early years of envy in such a powerful way. Of course, he told them none of that, but the fear he'd felt when first hearing István call out his name had vanished. In its place was a strange mix of gratitude and humility. These boys had been there a year. Ervin couldn't imagine remaining there that long, yet he knew his service would continue beyond that, maybe even until his death. Indeed, he had no idea when he would be able to go home. But he knew, too, that he would depend upon these boys he once feared to now keep him safe from harm. He sat down on the lower bunk and munched on the walnuts and apple as if enjoying a full course meal. He was, for now, safe and sated.

Sleeping in the tight quarters was far from ideal, but it sure beat sleeping in the filth they'd left behind. It also kept them warm. The nights had become bone chilling and the blankets did little to help. Frank and Ervin learned to synchronize their tossing and turning so that when one rolled to the right or to the left, the other rolled right along with him. In the bunk above were a couple of other guys, and another couple in the bunk over them, but it was one of them, a friendly guy named Mike who shared the middle bunk, that soon attached himself to Ervin and Frank and the pair became a trio. Mike, with his angelic round face and curly dark hair, was the third shipwreck as Ervin called them. Like Frank, Mike didn't have much and his dream was to one day attend a technical college and gain an employable skill.

"Like an electrician," he said, "but a really good one. Someone who can wire a whole building, a skyscraper even. Yeah, that's what I'd like to be able to do. Get a skill like that and I've always got a job."

Ervin nodded. He liked Mike but had a hard time grasping what it must be like to dream of work just for the sake of employment. Ervin wanted to go to medical school like his father, not because there'd be work in it, but because there was so much personal reward in healing people and saving their lives. He could barely remember when his family had lived in the Jewish neighborhood and struggled financially. His memories had been formed much later when material wealth was a given. Only after losing it all had he suffered. Still, he viewed his future much as he had his past—one of comfort, with intellectual and emotional reward. For guys like Frank and Mike, he was beginning to see the intellectual and emotional rewards of work were nearly unimaginable.

But Mike grew on him as quickly as a naughty pup. He was such a friendly fellow who didn't seem at all put out by being trapped in forced labor. He worked hard and laughed harder, easing Ervin's stress day by day. The three shipwrecks worked together, ate together, and slept together, soon getting to know the best and worst of each other as no one had before. More importantly, despite the worst in each that flared up every now and then, they cared about each other.

They were charged with building a military airport. For someone who had never built anything more elaborate than the occasional fort made of snow when he was a kid, the task seemed insurmountable to Ervin. It was already late October and the early mornings were growing progressively colder, bitterly so, and snowing on some days. They had to flatten acres of land for the planned airport. It was strenuous work as they had to break up, dig, and move mounds of heavy, frozen soil throughout the day, from early morning to nightfall. Ervin was not at all prepared for such labor, either physically or mentally. They'd might as well have asked him to hoist the whole earth onto his shoulders, the task was so impossible. One brigade would break up the rock-hard dirt with their spades and pickaxes, while the other brigade would load the loosened soil onto cast iron lorries to be rolled away on the local train tracks. Ervin, Frank, and Mike, the three shipwrecks, were assigned to push the lorries, while István and his gang were hard at work swinging the spades and pickaxes as if they were light as brooms.

Ervin marveled at their strength and, though still a bit leery of their intentions, he had to admit he was grateful for their presence. It seemed as if they had channeled all their aggression into the work before them, tearing up and moving the earth with the same deliberation and energy they'd once applied to tormenting little schoolkids. Now they were the ones being tormented, not by kids, but by soldiers and guards. Though Ervin was impressed by the way these guys handled the guards—never defying them, always flattering and complying—and getting their way more often than not. Ervin watched, saying nothing, noting everything, from István's obsequiousness to Kovács' feigned respect. They were con artists, that's what they were, and damn good at it. Ervin just hoped he wasn't one of their marks.

In any event, he enjoyed their newfound cooperative nature. "We got this," Kovács said, "you kids are too soft for this end. We'll load the lorries, you push 'em."

While not nearly as strenuous as digging and loading, pushing the lorries was a difficult job as, once loaded, the cast iron carts were as heavy as tanks. Ervin tried with all his might to get them to budge and, once he saw how futile the effort, he did what he did best—he clowned around. Pushing the lorry with his finger, the swirling snow falling heavily now, he dreamt about the comforts of home. Escaping into his imagination took him away from the reality he was living, as if he weren't really a prisoner spending the day laboring like a beast. Instead, he was back in his beautiful home in Győr, before everything was taken away, before everything turned dark and terrifying.

"Maybe this is where the term freeloader came from, you think?"

Ervin quipped, one hand on his hip, the other pushing the cart as if he were a mime creating the illusion of moving the cart that Frank and Mike were pushing with all their might.

"Knock it off, Ervin!" Mike snapped, "You're the freeloader here. We're doing twice as much work covering for you. Get to work!"

"Yeah, come on, Erv," Frank agreed. "Do your part."

Ervin saw he was letting his friends down and feared they might turn on him if he didn't help more. But the truth was, he couldn't help more. The only muscles he'd ever developed were mental ones and if he pushed as hard as Frank and Mike were pushing, he'd strain what feeble strands of strength he did have.

"Sorry guys, you're right," he admitted. "But this cart's got crooked wheels and it's hard as hell to push. We need to be smarter about the carts we select in the morning. Have you noticed some are harder to push than others?"

"Erv's right," Frank said. "These wheels aren't helping at all." Frank kept his focus on the cart he was pushing, as if the more he kept his gaze straight on the cart, the faster and easier it might move.

"They aren't taking care of them," Ervin said, pushing with both his hands, though still with little effort. "They're just letting them sit out here in the rain and snow and rust to hell. That cart we had yesterday wasn't so bad, but some of them have uneven wheels, bad axles. We need to get smarter about the carts we grab in the morning."

"Yeah, but how are we going to do that?" Mike asked, groaning as he pushed the heavy cart, though his tone had softened. He seemed genuinely curious now. "We don't know until we start using them which ones are decent and which ones aren't."

"They've got numbers," Ervin said. "Right here." He pointed to the faded black numbers on the side of the lorry, almost imperceptible from the rust and dust that had accumulated over the years. "We memorize the good ones and nab those."

"Only if we get to them first," Mike said.

"You mean only if *you* get to them first," Ervin said.

Mike glared. "Me? Why me?"

"Because I've seen you run. You run faster than any of us. You can run to the front of the line each morning and grab us a good cart."

Mike looked at Frank and Frank looked at both Ervin and Mike.

"Told you he's as clever as he is lazy," Frank said to Mike. "Why do you think I keep him around?"

Mike nodded, his smile growing. "Alright. But until then, get off your ass Ervin and push for a while!" And with that, Mike stopped pushing, Frank joining him, and the two watched their weak little friend with the much stronger mind do his best to push a cast iron lorry loaded with dirt even a mere inch. Shaking their heads and laughing, they returned to the task at hand, unimpressed with his effort, but rather impressed with his solution to easing their daily turmoil.

Over the next few days, as they pushed a series of different lorries, they noted which ones were easier than others and assigned Ervin the task of memorizing the numbers. But the work remained grueling, and Ervin was the weakest of the bunch. Pushing even the best of the dilapidated wagons was near impossible, and when he wasn't pushing them, he was helping István and his men load them—a backbreaking task he dreaded like death itself.

In the evenings, once fed and back in the barracks, he barely had the strength to crawl into bed. And each morning, he awoke with so much pain he could barely get out of his bunk until, after a couple of weeks, he realized he was less and less sore and the carts easier and easier to push.

It also helped that just as they'd planned, after receiving their orders to start their workday each morning, Mike would sprint to the head of the line and pick out one of the lorries Ervin had assured him were in the best working condition. It was key to their success that no one realize what they were doing, so Mike was careful not to call attention to his scrutiny of the numbers, seemingly pointing random to the first cart that caught his eye.

The work was still grueling, but thankfully, the impossible had become possible.

The commander in charge of the camp was an old career military man named Matus who'd been recalled from his retirement.

Matus had an old, misshapen face that looked like it had been chewed up and spit out, and he clearly wasn't too happy about having to go back to work. Fortunately, his own fate made him easier to deal with as he could empathize with the peril of the young men who labored against their will. He also seemed to bear no ill will toward Jews, never cursing them, never taunting them with antisemitic slurs, or blaming them for the death of Jesus. The lower-ranking guards, in contrast, who had been reared as peasant boys and used as watchdogs, were primitive and rough. "Get moving, you stinking Jews," they'd order, or "Get your hands off that, you filthy Jew."

For these reptilian-brained brutes, the men they were guarding were not men at all, but subhuman creatures to be blamed and punished for all the world's problems. Most of these guards were assigned the labor force because they were judged mentally unfit for duty or, in many cases, they were merely illiterate. Uneducated and unexposed to the professional world, culture, or the life of the mind, they had found solace in ruling over those deemed even lesser than they. Powerless in their former lives, they had been newly empowered over strangers they'd been told were the cause of their own misery. Thus, their insecurity, fear, and anger had a visible target they could torment. Not only were they permitted to abuse the Jews in their charge, but they were also rewarded by their colleagues for doing so. The result was a near constant torrent of physical and mental abuse, at least if Matus wasn't around to intervene. Fortunately, Matus had his eye on them most of the time and didn't hesitate to curb their appetites for aggression.

"You didn't work hard enough to be fed any supper," one of them announced, as Ervin held out his metal plate for the evening's slop. As bad as the nutrition was, by the time they were given food, no one complained about the taste, they were so starved for calories. While the guard wasn't speaking directly to Ervin—they never did speak to them, only at them, and never looked them in the eyes—there was no mistaking he meant Ervin, as he refused to fill his plate. "We don't reward lazy Jews. Jews who don't work don't eat!"

Ervin wanted to burst into tears. He knew he was lazy when it came to physical labor. But he'd never worked harder, and every inch of his body hurt from 12 hours of heavy labor. He *was* working.

And he *was* Jewish. No matter how many times he heard it, every time he was scorned for his Jewishness, Ervin felt inferior, even to the fools who held their power over him. There was no easing the pain of that deeply personal insult, the degrading of his very nature as undeserving of basic human dignity. And now even to be fed was considered a privilege he had to earn. Not even dogs were treated as badly.

"Please, sir," Ervin began, the plate in his hand shaking from his hunger and nerves. He was prepared to beg for his supper, no matter the further humiliation. He couldn't carry or move as much weight as others, he didn't have their strength. But he was growing stronger, he was working harder, and he was so hungry.

"Every man will be fed!" Matus commanded, his deep voice cracking the air. Ervin hadn't even seen the commander approach but, like a guardian angel, there he was, standing at least a foot taller than the guard and glaring at his underling with disgust. "No man in my unit will go hungry, ever," he said, remaining still as he watched the guard drop the slop onto Ervin's plate. "More," he ordered, as the guard heaped the food onto Ervin's plate, compelled to give him a more generous helping than he'd ever received.

Ervin looked up to Matus and nodded his appreciation and respect to his commander and, though Matus's face didn't move, Ervin saw compassion in his eyes and knew this commander would not subject the men to some of the brutalities he'd heard of. Since coming to the camps, tales had circulated of guards who beat the men, forced them to clear minefields without protection, gleefully tortured them for hours, and marched them for days. Just being imprisoned and forced to endure heavy labor 12 hours a day, seven days a week was unimaginably hard, especially now that the snow was falling. Ervin couldn't conceive of his situation worsening and feared that he was just one transfer away from that fate.

Perhaps one reason the camp, however horrid, was better than most was explained by the yellow and white armbands. Ervin had noticed that the men he bunked with bore more white armbands than yellow ones. The white armbands were worn by the men who'd converted to Christianity, which wasn't that uncommon as both the Catholic and Protestant churches promised they'd protect anyone who converted. Many Jewish families had allowed their children to convert to Christianity to protect them, just as Ervin's parents had once done so for their own protection. But they would not consider converting again, because they'd seen too many of such families deny their Jewish heritage altogether, even going so far as refusing to socialize with Jews once "Christianized." Ervin shared their concern, though now he was a minority among minorities, wearing the yellow armband marking him as an unconverted Jew, the worst of the worst. Even his good pal Frank wore the less stigmatized white armband, since his family became Christian. The distinction between the white and yellow bands was indeed a meaningful one, as those who wore the white band received fewer punishments and beatings from the guards. Yet even they were not free, nor were they safe. Jewish by birth, many regarded them as inherently inferior, if not inhuman. Still, the distinction divided the young men. As far as Ervin was concerned, however, he and Frank were as close as brothers and no armband could sever their connection. They were in this together. More importantly, thanks to all those white armbands, he was in a safer camp.

But when Matus wasn't around and the guards started drinking, the captive men had a taste of that cruelty. The guards would start out festive at first, more focused on the spirits before them than the men in their charge. But a few drinks in and they'd become moody and cruel, waking the men from their much-deserved sleep, kicking and beating them, forcing them to shine the guards' boots or clean the latrines in the dark of night, or order them outside to do pushups and planks in the freezing night until they collapsed. Ervin and his friends were powerless against these men. If they said a word to Matus, they'd be brutalized even more the first chance the guards had. And if they reacted at all to the cruelties, intended to provoke as much as torment them, the mistreatment would only escalate. All they could do was survive moment to moment, certain of only one thing. The guards would eventually tire of the entertainment or pass out from their own inebriation. Until they could go at it again.

Yet not all who wore the yellow armbands were badly treated. It was clear that István and his gang of misfits had a better relationship with the guards than the younger men. One of the biggest concerns Ervin and his friends shared was that the older men might entice the guards to make the younger men's lives miserable as a sort of revenge against the "rich kids." But as time passed, it became clear that they had no such intentions. On the contrary, they took on the roles of protectors to their younger workmates, proving to be quite helpful and cooperative, more like big brothers. It seemed their common fate had erased their divisions and brought them together as a united team against a far graver enemy, their captors.

While technically they weren't considered captives, they were instead considered fulfilling their patriotic duty to their country through the Auxiliary Labor Service. But there was no mistaking the fact that these young Jewish men were prohibited from true military service. They were enslaved labor—compelled to toil in service to a nation aligning with Germany's Third Reich—the fascists who wanted the world to be *judenrein*—free of Jews. The very airport they were helping to build would bring troops and weapons to aid that goal in Hungary. They were imprisoned, there was no mistaking that fact. The guards who fed and housed them were most definitely their captors, not their leaders.

Ervin just wanted to go home.

A GILDED LIFE

"Can't you settle that boy down?" Joseph snapped at Kamilla. "I am trying to study!"

Kamilla said not a word but quickly ushered Ervin to his room and diverted his attention to his bedroom toys. While Joseph had never been concerned about their son's impossible temper at the age of two, now that the boy was growing older, it seemed fatherhood had become even more difficult for Joseph, who had never had a strong fatherly presence in his own life. Joseph's father, while present, had been an emotionally distant brute, so Kamilla understood her husband's temperament. If anything, he was too emotional, which she well knew was one of the many qualities that had endeared him to her. Besides, they were living in much more crowded quarters and the boxes still needed unpacking. His temper would subside.

Ervin was just starting elementary school when his family moved to Győrsziget, a Jewish suburb in Győr. He hated it from the moment they arrived. This new place was shabbier than his old home and he could not understand his parents' concerns with money. They had always had money, hadn't they? After all, he'd never wanted for anything. All he knew was that whatever the reason they'd had to move, they didn't belong in this new place.

Their new apartment was in a relatively poor neighborhood

marked by cobblestone streets, old homes with big doors and spacious courtyards, and lots of Orthodox Jews. Ervin would watch them through his back window, marveling at the men dressed all in black who prayed all day long. He couldn't imagine why it should take so long for God to listen to their prayers. Each day he watched the long row of men, their heads bowing like bobblehead toys and long payot braids hanging like tassels from their wide-brimmed hats, their melodic voices nearly hypnotic. He wasn't sure if he was calmed by them or frightened. He knew only two things. He couldn't look away. And he hated this new home.

Living in this new place planted in Ervin the first seeds of rebellion, as he recoiled both from the Orthodox Jews who filled the streets like pitch black silhouettes of centuries past, and the Christian teachings he was compelled to memorize in kindergarten. He did not belong to either of these worlds and dreamt throughout the day of escaping to his old home—or the new one downtown that his parents assured him they would one day find and move to.

It was during this time that Ervin learned with delight that he could win the hearts and smiles of adults with his mischievous pranks and precocious charm. A forbidden sugary treat, stolen in plain sight, inevitably led to permission granted to consume the treat with no more than a half-hearted scolding. Mimicking the praying men or preaching Christians brought waves of gentle laughter from his parents and their friends. And refusing to memorize the Christian prayers brought, at times, harsh words from his teacher but exempted him from the mental labor required to master the confusing words. He was Jewish after all, and he preferred to devote his time in school to learning how to read and play with numbers, both of which he did with ease.

When he was six, Ervin's misery abated when he was sent to the local Jewish school near his home, and he was no longer pushed to be a Christian. The walk to school was a bit further than the Christian school, so his mother, father, or Nora, the family housekeeper, would accompany him. Though there had been some talk of letting her go when they'd moved to the new apartment, somehow his parents had found a way to keep her on. Ervin was happy they had done so for, while Nora wasn't nearly as loving and close as his mother, she was cheerful and reliable, and he felt safe in her company. On their walks, they would pass a chocolate factory and the sweet aroma intoxicated him with desire for a bite of shiny milk chocolate. Happily, on Fridays, big paper bags filled with the broken, leftover chocolate cookies were sold at a significant discount, and he was always permitted to buy a big bag to share with the other children.

Ervin didn't have many friends in his new neighborhood so he came to treasure those Friday afternoons when he could share his cookies. It wasn't from want of trying to make friends that he was so lonely. His parents didn't want him playing with the children in this new neighborhood.

"We won't be staying here long," his mother explained, "and you'll only have to say goodbye to them."

But it seemed to Ervin that they were staying in the new neighborhood so long that it was no longer new. He wished for friends his own age but felt happy he at least had Nora.

On Saturday afternoons, a local governess who cared for some of the wealthier children in the neighborhood would walk with him to Island Park. Vera wasn't as friendly as Nora, and far more strict, but she had a caring demeanor. Ervin enjoyed the park, which had a beautiful white glass building that reminded him of a palace. It had an elegant casino and coffee house usually filled with adults and, in the summer afternoons, salon music would play string quartets and operettas on a grand and beautiful terrace. Sometimes in the evenings, his parents would take him to the park where dance music played. Ervin thought the whole park was as enchanting as a dream, especially when the sun began to set, and the sparkling lights came on turning the whole park into a magical wonderland.

He especially loved the times his mother would accompany him to the park, where she would meet with her friends for five o'clock coffee. He was permitted to dress up in his finest clothes and join the women, which reminded him of the comfortable world he'd left behind. The waiters wore white jackets, held white napkins over their arms, and provided impeccable service as smoothly and quietly as if they were kind and gentle spirits sent to comfort and provide. The coffee was gorgeously presented in a silver pot served on a silver tray, with small silver dishes, white porcelain cups, and silver bowls filled with whipped cream. The berries and desserts were always served with a dusting of confectioner's sugar that looked like newly fallen snow. Ervin wanted everything he ate to be served with such ceremony and elegance. Not having such reward, he was content to have his mother's permission to serve the whipped cream to her friends, then enjoy whatever was left over for himself.

When the dinners ended, Ervin especially liked to watch the headwaiter, dressed in an exquisite dark smoking jacket, bring the final bill tucked in a black leather book, which he delivered with such a ceremonial flair that Ervin laughed every time.

These dinners were too infrequent in Ervin's mind, but they occurred often enough that he looked forward to them when his mother would announce another one approaching. In between such fine dinners, though, life at home was not the same. His father, while loving most of the time, now scolded him easily. Whether for playing too loudly or getting into something he wasn't supposed to be curious about, or breaking an object he didn't mean to break, it seemed not an evening went by that his father wasn't getting after him for one thing or another. He just wanted to go home. And this new place wasn't home.

On warm and sunny days, however, his mother and father would sometimes take him to the park where his parents would pay an old lady with a frightening hunchback a small fee for admission. Then they would sit together enjoying a simple picnic of smoked meats and cheeses, while watching the crowds of people playing on the beach. At the back of the park was a small, nearly hidden, white picket gate that served as the entrance to the exclusive boat club. Ervin was fascinated by the gate, imagining it opened to a luxurious world.

"There used to be a sign on that gate," his father told him one day. "It said the entrance was forbidden to Jews and dogs."

Ervin couldn't imagine why he and his family should be banned like dogs from passing through that gate. "Why *Apu*? Why couldn't we go in?"

"Because some people fear us," he answered, trying his best to explain the inexplicable. "They don't know us, so they fear us."

Ervin pondered that statement and concluded that if he was friendly, people would get to know him, and then they wouldn't fear them.

"But I'll let you in on a secret," Joseph added with a hint of mischief in his eyes.

"What, *Apu*?!" Ervin begged. "Tell me the secret!"

"I know a doctor who was a member of that club and what he never told anyone was that he was as Jewish as we are!" As Ervin laughed at the secret he'd just been let in on, even if he didn't quite understand it, Joseph played along as if it were a happy secret. Yet as he did so, he recalled the well-known local internist who had not only converted from Judaism but also had concealed his past as a Jew and joined the antisemitic club. He didn't respect the man for his shame but, at the same time, he delighted in knowing that every time he passed that gate, the antisemites on the other side of it didn't even recognize a Jew among them.

Those were the happiest days for Ervin when the whole family went to the park. His father would also be happy, smiling, laughing, and holding hands with his mother. Those afternoons reminded him of the park in his former home, where he so longed to return.

The new Jewish school was next to the synagogue and sometimes their courtyard would be alive with spectacular wedding festivities. The glamor of the nuptials amazed Ervin and one day he had the good fortune to be invited to attend one. The son of his mother's best friend was getting married, and Ervin was delighted to join his mother once again for a shopping spree. Since moving to the new house, and shortly before, his mother had taken him shopping less and less, but now with a wedding to attend, she seemed unconcerned about the money troubles she and his father so often discussed of late. This time they took the train to Budapest, though rather than sit in the comfortable first class, they sat upon the hard wooden benches in second class, where the stench of poor, unwashed workers, chickens, and sometimes even a goat, filled the air. Ervin so wanted to sit in the nicer seats but knew better than to complain. But once they'd reached Budapest, he forgot all about the miserable train ride, for at last he was once again shopping in the city's finest department store for black patent-leather shoes with new white socks, a fluffy white shirt, and a navy-blue suit very much like his father's own suits.

Ervin was so excited to dress up in his beautiful new clothes and join one of the synagogue's lively wedding parties, but his excitement was tempered by his nervousness. Since moving to the new apartment, despite the trips to the park, he'd felt so alone. He didn't understand why he couldn't have friends and he wrestled with an inner sense of unworthiness as if somehow, he and his family were not good enough for the fine residence and wealthy neighborhood they'd been forced to leave.

"Mama," he asked as they rode back from Budapest to Győr on the train, again in second class, "what if they don't want us at the wedding? What if they think we don't belong there?"

"Ervin!" she said, visibly disturbed. "What makes you say that? Of course we belong. They are our dear friends."

"But we had dear friends in our old home and still we had to leave," he said.

"My dear, we left only because times are difficult right now. There is a global depression and everyone must cut back. We'll return to downtown very soon, I promise."

Ervin trusted his mother's word, and yet, he feared something he could not quite name. He was, after all, a very young child, though a bright and sensitive one, who knew that something was not quite right. Why had they been sent to the Jewish neighborhood and what did that mean, anyway?

When the day of the wedding arrived, Ervin awoke with an unbearable rash across his body. It itched something horribly and his mother was both worried and heartbroken to not be able to attend the event. As much as the little boy wanted his mother to stay and care for him, however, he couldn't bear to feel that he was keeping her at home.

"It's fine, Mama," he told her. "Nora can watch over me."

"No, honey," his mother replied, "I must keep an eye on you myself in case it is rubella or rheumatic fever. It could be contagious."

Ervin was terrified of this disease, rubella, fearing it might be like the illness that had killed his dear friend, Luca. Though his mother assured him that it was nothing so serious as that, he prayed as he never had before that he be healed. The next morning, the rash had miraculously disappeared, and he was as healthy and happy as ever. And truth be told, deep inside he felt a relief that he hadn't had to go to the wedding. As much as the prospect of attending a fun party had excited him, he couldn't have borne it if they'd been told they didn't belong.

Ervin knew only one thing. He belonged with his mother and father. Beyond that, he wasn't sure where he belonged. Only that it seemed that they weren't wanted.

Kamilla did her best to maintain a respectable lifestyle befitting a doctor's household once they'd left downtown and settled into the new apartment. While her heart ached at the move, she understood Joseph's reasoning. Had they remained where they'd been living, the cost of rent for both their home and Joseph's office would have left them with much less money, given how many patients Joseph had to treat for free. The depression was sweeping the globe and she understood that everyone was making sacrifices, and those that she and her family had to make were minimal in comparison to others. Still, she knew what it was to stretch every pengő so that there would be enough to eat through the week. While those days of insufficient food were behind them now that Joseph had established his own practice with the help of his kind relative, she was thankful she'd retained her cautious spending habits. Doing so enabled her to enjoy occasional luxuries. And Joseph's rising success had made it possible to employ Nora. If they'd had to let her go, Nora would have been penniless. Both Joseph and Kamilla felt that having taken her into their home and employing her, they had a responsibility to do what they could to keep her on. They certainly couldn't have done that had they stayed in the more expensive apartment. More importantly, it was paramount to them both that Ervin receive the best possible education and, though he couldn't attend the Jewish school until first grade, they were determined he would do so, which meant saving even more to pay for the private school tuition.

Kamilla was also grateful for the occasions when she could meet her old friends at the park and enjoy an occasional dinner out. Though each was struggling themselves, they saved their pengős so that they might enjoy a bit of luxury. But the new neighborhood was a difficult one to adjust to as its orthodox lifestyle felt stifling to Kamilla, even more so as it reminded her of her upbringing where few freedoms were permitted women. And not being orthodox, many of the children were not permitted to play with Ervin. It broke her heart to know her little boy was shunned for not being sufficiently Jewish in the eyes of some, while elsewhere he would be shunned for being Jewish at all, yet that was the way of the world they were living in. But Kamilla was confident that soon the depression would lift, they could return to downtown, and the animosity toward Jews would diminish while the pressure from the Orthodox Jews would lessen. They just had to get through a few rough years.

Joseph, too, was confident the tides would turn and soon they'd return to their former neighborhood. But he was a bit less optimistic than Kamilla, fearing that things would worsen before they got better. The move to the Orthodox Jewish neighborhood had been a drastic one, in his view, but a pragmatic one that in the long run would ensure their economic prosperity once the depression had passed. The reduction in rent and cutting back on unnecessary expenses had enabled him and Kamilla to save when others were going broke, as well as continue to treat those patients who could no longer afford to pay. Soon he hoped to be able to buy a fine apartment in the downtown area. It would just take time and economic sacrifice for now, and besides, it was better to be where they were, among other Jewish families. The world beyond was growing darker.

He did his best to maintain a sense of normalcy throughout those trying times. He stuck to his daily routine just as he had before the move. He woke early, shaved at his desk in his office, then went for a walk where he would inevitably run into acquaintances and say a few *shaloms*. Often, he'd drop by the apothecary for a casual chat with a pharmacist friend and occasionally, on a weekend, he might meet up with his dental colleagues and friends for more serious discussions on the state of the country and the economic stress the world was enduring. But by nine o'clock each weekday morning, he would be back in his office ready to work.

Yet it was one of his more lighthearted habits that meant the most to Joseph. A few times each week he would go downtown, where he would stop at one of the candy stores, Stühmer or Cadeau, and purchase a selection of praline or nougat. The candies, which were elegantly wrapped as if fine crystals, were a real delicacy unaffordable to most, yet Joseph always found the funds to purchase a few for Ervin, whose delight in receiving the sweets was a cherished moment for Joseph. He knew he'd been hard on the boy of late, snapping at him for being too loud or too wild or just too much of a little boy. The candies had become not just a treat, but also a small gesture to let Ervin know that at the end of the day, he was loved and treasured.

Joseph stored the candies in a locked cupboard and each evening as Ervin stood by in delighted expectation, he would unlock the cupboard ceremoniously, doling one or two of the candies. It was a ritual both father and son treasured as if the sweets were bestowed but once a year, rather than but once each night.

On the shelf next to the sweets were several liquor bottles nobody ever touched, except when Joseph would occasionally offer some of the liquor to the local handyman who sometimes helped around the house, or on those rare occasions when Viktor dropped by.

"I'm quite impressed with the choices you have made," Viktor confided to Joseph early one evening as they sipped from a particularly fine brandy Joseph had reserved for his epicurean relative. "You clearly respect the value of a pengő and while maintaining a respectable lifestyle, you haven't squandered your money."

"I've done my best," Joseph replied, "and yet, I do wonder how much longer this depression will continue and whether I might set stricter limits on Kamilla's spending. She does manage the household budget well, but it seems she hasn't quite abandoned certain luxuries."

Viktor laughed gently as he held out his snifter for another pour of the luscious brandy that Joseph offered. "You are just now discovering that a beautiful woman's needs are rather expensive, my friend, and that is as it should be. For it is your desire to meet those needs that will motivate you to earn as much as you possibly can!"

Viktor's ease with Kamilla's spending relaxed Joseph, as he feared that not having yet repaid Viktor the full sum that he had borrowed, the elder patron might have had a differing reaction. Yet Joseph had been steadily repaying his debt and, in doing so, had never met any pressure from the once-unknown relative who had now become like a second father.

Joseph joined Viktor in his laughter, as well as in a second glass of brandy. "Perhaps you're right, Viktor," he said, "as I've never worked harder in my life. Still, so many of my patients have nothing, yet their teeth do not seem to care and demand as much attention in destitution as in prosperity. Fortunately, I have been saving and hope that we can leave here soon and return to the downtown area. But I do fear the depression will worsen and I must be cautious."

"Do it now, Joseph," Viktor said, "for we do not know what the future holds. If you must hold off on repaying me, then do so, but this is not the area for you, nor is it the neighborhood for growing your business. Return to downtown, and relish life while you can, for I cannot share your optimistic nature. I fear the future looms darkly over our lives. This Nazi party in Germany seems to be growing ever stronger."

"Do you honestly think they stand a chance?" Joseph asked, surprised at his cousin's concerns.

"In '28 they took 12 seats in the last election," Viktor said.

"But over a year has passed and they still have less than three percent of the vote. Surely, they'll never get further than that. They are far too extreme, and Germany is an educated country. The Germans won't stand for such madness."

"I fear you are underestimating the contagion of madness, particularly when it is wedded to hatred," Viktor said, sighing as he set down his now empty glass. "I do hope you are right, but I sense something sinister afoot. We must be ever vigilant. And we must grasp every day that we do have, for our joy may soon be extinguished."

"Viktor," Joseph laughed, "your cynical nature is endearing, but I am ever the optimist. These are dark days, but better days are before us. We must be patient."

"As we shall be," Viktor said, rising to depart. He placed a firm but gentle hand on Joseph's shoulder. "But in the meantime, get the hell out of this dismal place and find a grander home in a finer neighborhood for your family. Should you need funds, I will help you."

"No, no," Joseph said, shaking his head, "I cannot take any more money from you, my kind cousin. As I've said, I have saved some money by moving here."

"Good. Then now is the time for you to leave," he answered. "And I'm afraid it is time for me to leave as I am not as resilient as I once was and do require an early night's rest. I'll be in touch with some possible apartments that should suit you. Just promise me you'll get out of this neighborhood once and for all."

"I will certainly give your suggestion some thought," Joseph said, summoning Nora to bring Viktor's coat. "I know it would certainly make Kamilla and Ervin much happier were we to leave."

"Happiness," Viktor said, easing into his coat and donning his hat, "is ours for the taking today. Do seize it, for it may not be ours tomorrow."

And with that, Viktor departed, leaving Joseph to ponder his benevolent cousin's strange words.

IN THE COMPANY OF GUARDS

December 1943

Dear Mother and Father,

Thank you so much for the basket of food you sent. I cannot tell you how much it meant to me to enjoy goose liver and fresh fruit once again. The food here is barely edible, yet after a long day working, I hunger for every bite. Do not worry about me, however, as I am growing stronger every day and have a good group of friends who keep my spirits up. We share our gift baskets from home and everyone agrees that yours, mother, is the best of all.

I do miss you both so terribly much and look forward to returning home and being together once again. I probably worry more for you than you do me, as I know that life is difficult for all of us right now, but I am confident brighter days are up ahead. Are you still seeing patients, father? I do hope your practice is not in jeopardy, despite the restrictions on treating gentiles. It is funny, but now that I am living among so many Jewish boys, I find it is not the gentiles who resent us as much as it is the strict Orthodox Jews who most dislike us. They keep to themselves and will not even speak to us, much less eat with us, treating us no differently than the worst of the gentiles outside the camps. I must confess, they bewilder me, for we are all in this together and one would think they'd regard us as their brethren, yet that is not the case. In some ways I am reminded of those early days in the Jewish neighborhood when the Orthodox children were forbidden from playing with me. Although you protected me from the truth at the time, now that I am older and have a better understanding of why I felt so lonely there. I now see that whether Christian or Orthodox, there are always those who so fear others unlike themselves that, rather than recognize us all as God's children, they feel safer in their ignorance of our hearts and common humanity. It is so unfortunate that they cloak their fear and hatred in the guise of religion, when it is religion that teaches us to love one another.

In any event, I have forged close friendships with my old pal Frank and our new friend Mike, as well as many others who are in the same unhappy fate as I. Even some of the brutish bullies from our old neighborhood have extended their friendship and abandoned their old ways in favor of our mutual survival. While I cannot wait to return home and be together once again, as well as start medical school, I will forever be thankful for the community we've forged here in the camps under such formidable circumstances.

Well, I must sign off now as I am writing by candlelight and must preserve these candle stumps, for they are precious commodities. I love you both and hope you are well and trust that we all shall be reunited very soon.

Your loving son,
Ervin

Knowing that the guards would read any correspondence he sent or received, Ervin refrained from disclosing too much detail in his letter. He could not tell them of the harsh treatment from the guards, many of whom were cruel and unrelenting, nor did he disclose that the Orthodox boys would not even share word of outside food sources. Indeed, while everyone else shared their baskets of food sent from home, or rumors of generous neighbors from the nearby farms, the Orthodox boys shared nothing outside their small circle. To be shunned like that from others in their shared plight, other young Jewish men, cut Ervin far more deeply than the animosity of the Christian antisemites, or even the abuse from guards. Yet he had been long enough in the camps by this point that he knew it futile to hope for any change of heart on their parts, and so Ervin kept his distance and regarded them not as brethren but almost as foes.

Ervin also withheld from his parents the depths of his hunger. The food they were served was not only revolting, but also so paltry that he was losing a great deal of weight, which made it even more difficult to build up his strength. True, his muscles had developed and he was far less fearful of work—he'd long since given up the antics he'd initially employed to escape the unpleasant labor—but he suffered from headaches and dizziness throughout the day, as he just wasn't consuming enough protein and calories to stay alive. For that reason, the generous baskets of food were not just exciting gifts from home, they'd also become essential to their very survival—which was why so much had to be shared. To withhold food meant to be cut off from food when others had it.

Ervin's mother did indeed pack the very best food packages, full of goose liver and fruit, as well as cakes, cookies, and salamis. He made sure to equally divide the food among the other laborers, as they did with him. No one ever cheated the other members of the group, and they always ate together. On occasion, Ervin would be accused of withholding food, but when he did so, it was to provide for the next day's rations. As they grew hungrier, it became harder to withhold the food, but Ervin knew that if they consumed all they had and desired, they would suffer for it the next day when it was gone. Before long, the wisdom of his restraint had persuaded the group to entrust him to distribute the small rations provided by the guards, as well. All knew that Ervin's integrity could be counted on to be fair and trustworthy with the most coveted of treasures—food they needed to survive.

Every two weeks, the boys were permitted to go on leave to bathe in the neighboring town, where a local Jewish community bath was available for their use. The walk each way took two hours, and while the two-hour walk to the baths was always a victorious walk as each step took them closer to freedom—and the luxury of warm water washing away the soil, grime, and stench of two weeks' hard labor—the return walk took them closer to servitude and misery with every step. On those walks back they savored each step as if by doing so they might prolong their freedom. But they knew the truth. They had no freedom. They were captives, compelled to participate in their captivity with every step back to their confinement. So far, the only thing keeping them from raging at the injustice of their fate was not only the knowledge that to do so would mean certain punishment, but also because as miserable as their servitude was, they were not forced to dig up live mines, as some were, only to be killed or maimed in the inevitable explosions. They were not lashed to posts in rushing rivers so that they might build bridges—if they weren't killed from hypothermia or drowning—as so many were throughout Hungary. They weren't randomly singled out for public hanging to keep them in line, as they'd heard happened regularly at other camps. They weren't deliberately starved and worked to death as others were at more brutal camps. They were the lucky ones. They were merely worked to exhaustion, fed just enough to keep them alive but no more, and viciously beaten only occasionally. But none had yet been killed. None had yet died of starvation. None had yet been forced to slip on a noose and step up to the gallows, thankful that their suffering would soon come to an end.

Between those walks to town, after washing up, Ervin, Frank, and Mike would walk the streets aimlessly, as any free young men might do upon a trip to town. But the armbands marked them for who and what they were, as did the army caps they were forced to wear bearing the distinguishing insignia of the "unreliable" Jewish paramilitary labor brigade. The caps, along with the armbands, communicated a certain disrespected status that no joy could wash away. But as with so much they'd been subjected to, they, and most people in town, had learned to normalize their lowered status, to forget the caps and arm bands, except in those moments when the occasional glare stopped them short, or worse, when a pretty woman turned away at the sight of them. Those were the moments when, like a horrid scar or deformity, their fleeting joy was quashed by the sharp stab of their reality.

Frank had a relative in town who had extended a standing invitation for him to join their family for dinner whenever he was in town. Unfortunately, their invitation didn't extend to Mike and Ervin, who would patiently wait for him while he dined. While waiting, the two would wander around, trying their best to strike up conversations with some of the attractive ladies. Their uniforms did not mark them as desirable servicemen, however, but as undesirable prisoners, and with each failed attempt to converse with females of their own age, they were compelled to accept that though they were promising young men, romance was even more outside their reach than a decent hot meal.

It was during one of these evenings when Mike and Ervin were waiting for Frank that the two men were walking down the street enjoying a taste of freedom. "What do you say, Erv, shall we dine on a cheap ale this evening, or do you think we've enough for a few pierogis?" Mike asked. Their stomachs were rumbling but they had so little money between them that all they could hope for was to somehow return to their barracks with empty pockets but full bellies.

"Frank will probably bring us something," Ervin began, "so why don't we—" But before he could finish his thought, his arm was yanked so hard he spun around in pain, only to see the seething face of a Hungarian officer glaring down on him in fury.

"You failed to salute me, you filthy Jew!" the officer screamed.

Ervin was stunned into silence, stammering his protests in fragments. "I didn't, I mean, I never..." He wanted to say he hadn't seen the officer, but the man's anger was intensifying so rapidly and Ervin's shock and fear so great that he could no longer speak in words.

"You're coming with me, Jew!" the officer said, pulling Ervin toward him. He practically dragged Ervin down the street as Mike watched helplessly, the street crowded with onlookers sneering in disgust, some at the cruel officer, others at the hapless Jew whose fate was as uncertain as it was unenviable.

Ervin was pushed and shoved up the steps of the military police command, as if he had no feet of his own. Once inside, the officer barked, "This dirty Jew failed to respect an officer of the Royal Army. His labor camp must be notified so that he be severely punished as deserved." Then, as instantly as he'd appeared, he vanished, leaving

Ervin alone with the military police commander. Ervin was certain he would be hung. Or worse.

He was brought into a back office and ordered to sit, where for the next several hours he was interrogated as to why he was in town, who he had spoken to, what books he had read, who his family was. Ervin answered every question honestly, for he had nothing to hide, yet with every answer, he felt his fate seal more tightly and irrevocably. He was weak with thirst and hunger, yet not so much as a glass of tepid water had been offered him as his mouth, dry as much with fear as with thirst, struggled to form whole syllables and words.

"Dismissed!" the commander at last said and Ervin was told to return to his camp and not be apprehended again or further action would be taken. Ervin stumbled out into the street, the sky now dark, his friends nowhere to be found.

By the time he reached camp once again, having to explain his late arrival to the guards who neither pitied nor punished him, he fell into his bed as if it were the safest place on earth. Before the sun rose, he was again awake, prepared to work for the next 15 hours on nothing more than whatever thin gruel was served as breakfast. Ervin no longer felt like a man. He'd been transformed to flesh and bone and strips of muscle. A living, breathing instrument of labor, no different than the pickaxe he swung or the lorry he struggled to push each day. And, like that tool and battered cart, he was to be put away at the end of the day, brought out again the following day, put back, brought out, again and again until one day he'd just break down.

DOWNTOWN

Joseph had weighed Viktor's advice with care. While he appreciated his cousin's perspective on seizing life while he could, he was at the same time cautious. True, he had taken a tumble with the Great Depression, with many patients unable to pay. But in just a couple of years his income was rising again, and he had managed to save a respectable sum by moving to more affordable quarters. Were he to stay put, he had no doubt he'd save even more. Yet he saw how unhappy Kamilla was to live so far from her friends, and Ervin, while young and resilient, was no longer the happy and sociable little boy he'd once been. Perhaps Viktor was right. Maybe it was time to move back to the downtown area and begin again to enjoy the life they'd once had, albeit with a touch more restraint. He posed his dilemma to Kamilla.

"If we stay here, we'll save even more money and in another five years, have a tidy nest egg," he suggested.

"That would be wise," Kamilla agreed, "and yet, I fear I am not the only one who has been unhappy in this new home."

"Ervin's young, children adapt. I'm not making my decision based on the desires of a six-year-old."

"I'm not speaking of Ervin," Kamilla said.

Joseph raised an eyebrow in response and Kamilla continued.

"I fear you're resigning yourself to a status you long ago transcended. You go through the motions, yet you no longer have the joy and drive you once did." She laid a hand gently on his knee, hoping to communicate to her husband how much she cared for him.

"But no one has the drive they once had," he protested. "This is a global depression. We are all struggling just to stay afloat."

"But you continue to work and we are doing well," she countered. "I suspect that were you to find yourself working again downtown that you would attract a clientele that can well afford to pay you. Indeed, you have many prosperous patients already."

Joseph grunted his agreement but said nothing.

"Whichever you choose," she told him, "God will provide for us, as He has until now. But I fear if we stay here another five years that, though we shall continue to adjust, your spirit will continue to fade. You are not one for giving up, Joseph, yet I sense the beginnings of surrender in you. Your eyes have lost their brightness since coming here, and Ervin, too, is so unhappy."

Joseph cut his wife short and stood up, his anger rising. "I told you I will not be dictated to by a six-year-old! I have made this move for you and our son, and now you act as though I have punished you!"

"My dear, that is not what I said, nor feel," Kamilla protested. "I was simply—"

"You were simply assigning me the unhappiness you so clearly feel," he barked. "I shall make a decision shortly."

Joseph retreated to his study where he buried himself in a book, though after reading several pages, he realized he'd absorbed not a word. He was fuming, not because Kamilla was wrong, but because her words had cut so close to the truth. He was indeed resigning himself to a life below his means. He had made the move in haste, fearful of losing the few assets he had once the economy had turned so dark. And there was something else, something he'd never dared even speak to Kamilla for fear of frightening her. Viktor had spotted it as well. Hungary remained crippled from the war, and the social climate he'd returned to following his service was a more bitter one than the one that he had left. Though subtle, there was an unmistakable rise in antisemitism that Joseph was sensing from all corners. He detected it in his practice, which only seemed to attract fellow Jews and few gentiles. He discerned it in the increasing glances and sneers he encountered on the streets. And he recognized it in the news he heard on the radio or read in the newspaper. The nationalism that was rising in Germany and Poland was gaining fresh interest in postwar Hungary, which had lost so much territory with its defeat. Now, to counter that loss, it seemed as though some were recalling a mythic past, one in which Jews were faulted for the sufferings of gentiles. Though most dismissed these antisemitic sentiments as inconsequential, Joseph was more reticent. He was confident the social tide would pass, as such things always did. Nonetheless, he knew as well that a prosperous Jew could attract unwanted attention from those looking for a scapegoat to blame for their own lack of prosperity. That was the true reason he had fled to Győrsziget. It was not to save money, as he'd told Kamilla and others. Indeed, as he'd told himself most of the time. He was earning good money. He had moved to the Jewish suburb to be closer to other Jews, even if Orthodox, where he felt safer. But now he realized that the move had been a folly. His wife and son were unhappy. He was unhappy. And he was running from his fears—something he'd never imagined he would do, and yet, that is what he had done.

Joseph wasn't angry with Kamilla. He was angry with himself. He set down his unread book and returned to the drawing room where Kamilla was knitting in unsmiling silence.

Her thoughts were not on her knitting. Kamilla felt as helpless in having any say in her own life as she'd felt when she'd lived with her parents. She had followed her husband wherever his life took him and she had no regrets for having done so. Yet this last move seemed to have exhausted their spirit and, in place of the loving, joyful husband she had married, she was now having to bury her own unhappiness to pacify Joseph's moods and assure him of his wisdom in having made the move. Yet he was increasingly quick to anger and, while he may not have noticed the change in his own temperament since moving to Győrsziget, she had. He worried about money when they were far from broke. He clamored at little Ervin over the most innocent of mistakes. He didn't seem to want to make new friends in the neighborhood and was gradually isolating himself from society. He also seemed increasingly guarded, reading the newspaper as if it contained some mysterious code he sought to decipher, and he was spending more and more time listening to the radio, as if awaiting some breaking story at any moment. This wasn't at all like Joseph, who no longer even discussed political and current events with Kamilla as they had so enjoyed for years. Kamilla wanted more than anything to return to the happy home they'd shared when living downtown. But it wasn't the role of the wife to make such decisions, so the best that Kamilla could hope for was that her gentle influence might guide her troubled husband toward a course of action that would restore him to his genuine nature and not this brooding one he'd worn so frequently of late.

Hearing Joseph step into the room, Kamilla glanced up, prepared for a lecture on finances that would only serve to harden her heart and fix her fate for the next half decade or so. Instead, her eyes fell upon the gentle soul she'd all but lost. Joseph's face had softened, and his arms were already reaching out to her.

"You are right," he confessed. "This is not where we belong. Let us return to our old neighborhood."

Kamilla was unable to conceal her joy. She set down her knitting and asked, "Are you sure? If we cannot afford the higher cost of housing, then I am prepared to stay here." How quickly she had reversed her stance, she thought at the same moment she uttered the words. For she meant every bit of it. She would give anything, make any sacrifice, for their happiness and security, and now that Joseph was presenting her with a choice and not a directive, her sentiments about Győrsziget had softened. She would stay if that was what he desired, for she wanted only for her husband to worry less.

"No, darling," he said, pulling her to him and wrapping his arms around the woman he so loved. "I wanted to come here to save money, it is true. But I realize now that I also wanted to come here to be closer to our faith. Yet I feel no closer to our faith here, where we don't fit in with the Orthodox lifestyle, than I did downtown."

"I do feel the same," Kamilla agreed. "But if we must save money, we should stay."

"No, my love, we mustn't stay. I feared the rising antisemitism would make life more difficult downtown, but I was wrong. And as much as I am loath to admit it, Cousin Viktor was right. If the tides of antisemitism do worsen, we must live our life to the fullest now, while we can. But I will no longer flee from social persecution. I intend to face this ugliness head on and defeat it." He kissed Kamilla's forehead, and she pulled his mouth to hers. After a long and tender kiss, she stepped back, still holding his hands.

"I sensed there was more to your decision than our finances," she told him. "And I know we shall be both happy and secure downtown among our friends."

"That we will," he assured her. "That we will."

The new home they'd purchased downtown was even more grand than the home they had left. It was filled with light and had high ceilings that made the rooms feel spacious. Joseph had secured a surprisingly affordable price on the home, though he realized his savings had come at the cost of the nation's economy, for the depression had caused real estate prices to plunge. Nonetheless, while he knew he had to be careful with his money, he rejoiced at the savings he'd accumulated over the past two years which had enabled him to buy such a luxurious place—and he hadn't even needed to take up Viktor on his generous offer.

Ervin was enthralled with the new home and was so happy to return to his old neighborhood and the life they'd left behind. Every night at dinner, a large oak table in the living room was set with a white tablecloth, glistening silver, crystal, and china, with a glass pitcher so heavy with cold water he couldn't lift it himself. Above the table hung a beautiful chandelier and beneath it was set a small bell that his mother would ring to summon Nora. His mother never had need to leave the table during dinner, though once the meal was finished, she would clear away the dishes and leftovers and assist Nora in the kitchen while his father took a nap before rising to take a walk, returning home to study his books and newspapers late into the night.

His mother and father were much happier in the new place as

well, though his father's temper continued to be short. His father often punished him with a spanking and Ervin felt that he spent as much time hiding under the oak table as dining at it. Ervin was so confused by his father's frequent explosions, because in all other regards, he had no doubt of his father's love. Thus, he learned how to keep his father's anger at bay through good humor and playing the clown, for as long as he was laughing, he was not chasing Ervin to deliver a paddling.

Ervin's humor was further sharpened each summer when the circus came to town. Overnight the mammoth tent would appear as if by magic, with thousands of lights brightening the night sky and with it, the little boy's heart and imagination. He especially loved watching the clowns who, though feared by some of his more timid friends, brought gales of laughter from Ervin who delighted in their prattles and pranks and learned to mimic them to bring delight to his family and friends. He also enjoyed the big circus band with its funny melodies and colorful drums. The musicians wore colorful costumes that reminded Ervin of fairytale generals from Wonderland. To his young ear, the band sounded like the best orchestra in the world, and he would listen, transfixed, in the same way his mother and father listened to opera recordings on the phonograph. During intermissions, he would take his mother and father by the hand and guide them to the menagerie of exotic animals, which, despite their foul smells, fascinated Ervin. He felt as if he had been transported to a faraway jungle as he looked into the eyes of such ferocious beasts and listened to their roars, cackles, and cries.

But it was watching the people that most captivated Ervin. Like the animals in cages, people were exhibited on stage in every conceivable shape, size, and color. Dressed in grass skirts or colorful costumes, with rings through their noses or stacked round their long necks, these exotic people in all shades of brown amazed Ervin.

"These are Bedouins," Joseph explained to his son. "They are walking with the camels because they live in the deserts of North Africa where there is little water. The camels carry their gear, so that they can cross the desert in search of food."

"And those people?" Ervin asked, pointing to some lighter

skinned people in brightly colored costumes and wearing funny cone-shaped hats.

"Those are Chinese. They live on the other side of the world and their hats protect them from the sun."

"And those?" Ervin pointed to some very dark-skinned people who were no bigger than he was but looked like grownups.

"Those are Pygmies," his father said. "They live in another part of Africa."

"Why are they so small?"

"Because that is how God made them."

"Why are they so dark?"

"Because that is how God made them."

Ervin considered what his father had told him. God had created other types of people who looked nothing like the people he knew, and his father didn't seem to fear them at all. Like Zoli, the circus dwarf who Ervin thought was the funniest clown in all the circus. Zoli wore a big top hat and fancy tuxedo as he climbed tiny ladders, stumbled, rolled, and sprang back up, and ran back and forth like a comical child. But he was far from childlike in some of the skits he performed chasing beautiful girls and such, which Ervin didn't understand but his parents found hilarious. He even did acrobatics, which scared Ervin who feared his favorite clown might plunge to his death. But he never did, and Ervin always marveled at what big laughs the little man provoked.

"Do they have families?" Ervin asked his father as they strolled from stage to stage admiring the exotic people—though Zoli wasn't among them, as he was a performer, not a spectacle, unlike the people from Africa, India, and China.

"Of course, they do," his father answered.

"And mamas and papas?"

"Yes, just like you," his father said. "They are people just like we are, but they live in different parts of the world, which means they have different types of houses and different types of clothes. But they are the same in mind and heart."

Little Ervin pondered this new information. If the same, then someone like them—and even Zoli—could be his friend.

"One day I'm going to go to different parts of the world," he told his father. "If I meet different kinds of people, they can be my friends."

"I think that's a marvelous idea, my son," Joseph said, smiling with pride at his boy. Indeed, Joseph himself had made friends with those quite unlike himself for, in the war, he had learned that all men were fighting the same enemies, regardless of where they'd come from and what they looked like. It was only in returning home that he'd found that he himself was regarded as the one so different.

Every summer from May to October, the Italians came to town and brought their ice cream. Ervin loved the ice cream shop and was never happier than when he watched the Italian vendors churn their frozen delicacy in the front of their shop. The bowl they used was the biggest one he had ever seen, big enough to fit a child, and the machine they used was as loud as any truck. And the ice cream they made was the best he'd ever tasted, with all kinds of unusual flavors like rum raisin, wild raspberry whipped cream, coconut, and almost every fruit imaginable. He especially loved eating his prized dessert in the sugar cones, which he got to watch them make. The most expensive treat of all was a waffle shell that came with three scoops of ice cream, but he never got to eat one because his parents told him it was too much sugar—a concept Ervin couldn't even imagine, so he begrudgingly accepted that he'd have to wait until he was grown up to have such a delicious treat. But no matter. Going to the Italian shop was almost as magical as a trip to the circus, but even better because his father took him every evening in the summer. He was only allowed one scoop per evening, but on hot summer nights, his father always shared his portion with Ervin after the little boy had finished his cone. Once the ice cream was all gone, Ervin's imagination got busy wondering what the next night's flavor might be.

As Ervin grew, he found great delight in his studies, as reading and mathematics came naturally to him. The loneliness he'd felt living in the Jewish suburb had lifted and he once again had many friends, though he always put his studies first. After dinner he would study for his classes, often with the help of his mother who would quiz him on how much he had memorized. If she wasn't happy with his response, he would be compelled to study until he got it right, no matter how late he had to stay up to do so. His father assisted as well, quizzing him on his mathematics and written compositions. As a result of these efforts, Ervin remained at the top of his class and, with every good grade, he felt more confident and proud.

After he had finished his homework, his mother and father would take him for a nightly stroll on the main street. Ervin loved these walks because there was always something going on, and his parents were greeted with such fondness that it was clear they were both popular and respected.

Every evening the walk ended with a stop at the nearby newspaper vendor, who would hand Joseph a neatly rolled evening paper and if it was a cold winter's evening, Joseph would buy Ervin a paper-wrapped cone of warm chestnuts from the Greek vendor who sold them in a kiosk next to the newspaper stand. Once they got home, Joseph would unroll the paper, toss out the sports and business sections, which did not interest him in the least, then read the remaining pages with great interest before retiring for the evening. Meanwhile, Ervin had to review his homework once again, and then go straight to bed, as his father insisted that doing so would give him better retention of the material. But Ervin longed to stay up with his father, discussing the day's events, the latest subjects he was studying, or just sitting beside him. He couldn't wait to become a teenager so that he and his parents could all share the late evenings together. But he knew better than to protest the early bedtime, as it was important to do well in his studies.

His family had rapidly risen in social rank since returning to the downtown area where Ervin and Kamilla seemed to blossom being so close to their friends. Joseph remained more reserved, but his practice grew despite the economic setback of the times. Even though he continued to treat patients for free, his respect in the community brought him many wealthy patients who could well afford his rates. Again, Viktor no doubt had played a role in this regard, as he often dropped by in the evening to introduce Joseph to some important man or invited Joseph to come by for a drink and meet whatever wealthy acquaintance he felt Joseph should know. But for the most part, Joseph was as much a loner as Kamilla was sociable, seeming to prefer the company of his family, and sometimes Viktor Kroonenberg, over developing social connections with wealthy men in the city or hosting dinner parties.

Kamilla, however, wanted more from life and missed the world of ideas that had once so fascinated her. While she kept her friendships mostly to herself, joining her friends at the park or for tea or occasional dinners out, she did delight in hosting lavish parties at least once a year, with live music, dancing, and exquisite food and wines. Joseph was uncomfortable at these events, but he played the gentleman host with no hint of the discomfort Ervin and Kamilla knew he felt to have so many people in his home.

"What is the point in working so hard to enjoy a life of wealth if we do not share our home with our friends and celebrate our prosperity?" Kamilla would remind him when she prepared for such an event.

"My, I am so grateful that is over," Joseph would inevitably announce to no one in particular after the last of the guests had left their parties.

The life Ervin had known as a small child was long past him and he felt comfortable surrounded by material and social comforts. It was as if he'd never known loneliness and uncertainty, as if his life had always been quite perfect.

And yet, there remained a darkness that marked these wonderous days. Ervin's father was a serious but loving man, but not even returning to downtown, nor his rising success, had seemed to quell his temperament. He was damnably stubborn, at times overly strict, and often lost his temper over innocuous failings. It appeared to Ervin that his father's flaring rage and rigid rules seemed to coalesce around a single issue—Ervin's education. No matter how studious Ervin was, no matter how high his grades, his father's fears of Ervin's failure were inexplicable—and provoked both the best and worst in Joseph. He was committed to Ervin's future success and delighted in helping his son with his homework. But at the same time, he was a strict disciplinarian who had no patience for poor work habits— which included enforcing strict rules regarding punctuality. Until he was in his early teens, if Ervin ever returned home even just ten minutes late, his father would beat him with a stick. The beatings were so painful that Ervin would flee in fear whenever his father lost control, sometimes hiding behind his mother who did her best to rescue the small boy. During the worst of the rages, Ervin would lock himself in the bathroom for the entire evening until his father's rage abated. Yet he loved his father and had no doubt of his father's love for him. Many of his friends had fathers who paid little attention to their sons, something Ervin could not imagine—and they, too, suffered beatings with switches and sticks. It seemed that every child feared their father. Nonetheless, Ervin knew that his father was a tough man with a tender heart, a loner who had suffered a difficult life as a young child himself and demanded nothing of Ervin that he did not demand of himself. Still, Ervin hated those beatings.

Kamilla wished that just once Joseph could let himself freely enjoy his position as a gentleman of high standing, yet she knew that something ate away at him, something that kept people at bay. She'd compromised so much in marrying him and she didn't regret her decision a bit as she did love her husband, but it was her love for him that caused her heart to ache when she saw him pull away from friends as he did, as if he was locking himself away in his luxurious home, imprisoning himself in his fears, which seemed to grow ever greater the more he concentrated on national affairs and political troubles.

But it was his temper, which he rarely directed at her but so often directed at their son, that brought Kamilla true despair. Sometimes he hit Ervin so hard it left welts, and usually over the merest offense. She feared for how he might react once Ervin reached his teens, when boys begin to rebel against their fathers, just as girls do their mothers. Kamilla was at a loss for how to reach Joseph's heart, which she knew to be so kind and loving. But his heart was no match for the inner rage that gnawed at him relentlessly, an anger clearly borne in childhood, which no maturing could evict.

Joseph had retreated to his study once again, still fuming over Ervin's lax behavior. The boy, already 13 years old, could not for the life of him be prompt. This time, he had gone out to play with his friends and had not returned home until nearly a half hour past his curfew, protesting that he had forgotten to wear his watch and lost track of time. Joseph had given the boy an expensive watch for just that purpose and wondered if Ervin had truly forgotten to wear it, or chosen not to, preferring to challenge his father's rules of punctuality.

Ervin's future depended upon being reliable and trustworthy, and one of the markers of a trustworthy man was his showing up on time. Those who failed to do so did not go far professionally, even more so as Germany continued to rise in power in Europe, suggesting to Joseph that adhering to the German educational system would be necessary for those who wanted to succeed. Of course, there was much about Germany's ascension that troubled Joseph to no end, but he was confident that for all the stress it was causing him now, the antisemitic sentiments of the current government would give way to the more practical aspects the German economy was advancing. The new Chancellor of Germany, Adolf Hitler, was acting so swiftly and so forcefully that there was no question he would not remain in power long. He had just banned any non-Nazi party from participation in government—of even existing for that matter—and was abolishing the power of the states in his drive to rule by sheer autocratic force. He was a terrifying fool, but a fool he was, and while his xenophobia and antisemitism were extreme, Joseph was confident that it was his very extremism that would bring Germany—and with it, the rest of Europe—back to the center, where the folly of such prejudice would at long last be impossible to deny, and social order and harmony would be restored.

If only his own folly would subside as well. He knew with every explosive rage he aimed at poor Ervin that it wasn't his son he was raging against, but himself—if not against the family that had raised him with such neglect and indifference. For he saw in Ervin his younger self, and his fears for his son's future haunted him with the same persistence as did his fears for his own future. Yes, he was a successful man by any measure, yet he had so internalized the messages he'd received as a boy—that he did not belong, that he did not matter, that he was not seen—that for all his success, he continued to see himself as an outsider in his own life.

And there was another thing, something he dared not ever mention to Kamilla, though she no doubt knew in her heart. The war had ravaged him in a way not even his own unfortunate childhood had. As a physician, he saw the worst of the war's savagery. Living bodies, maimed, crushed, ripped open, were his to repair. But no matter how gifted he was, man after man could not be saved, and those he did save often returned home blinded, crippled, disabled, and all too often half mad from the insanity of combat against other humans. It was Joseph who too often had to triage which ones could possibly be saved and which ones probably could not. Trained to save lives, he was haunted by those he condemned to death by prioritizing other young men's horrid wounds. As the war waged, he was so busy sorting and saving these lives that he had little time for reflection. But once home, the nightmares began, the incessant thoughts, the nervous reactions to any loud noise his sweet son might make, indeed, anything that brought those memories back. That was the true reason he'd chosen dentistry as his specialty—it was safe, it was unrelated to the wounds of war, and it was rewarding to salvage someone's teeth. And working on teeth—the hardest substance of the human body—called on his skills and artistry. Dentistry kept him sane, but it could not keep the nightmares, the guilt, nor the memories at bay for long, as they swept over him when he least expected it. It might be something as innocuous as his son not returning home when expected that opened wide the gates to his fear and brought back the memories of young men's lives lost to human violence. Those were the moments when his anger gained mastery over his soul. Those were the moments when he roared at his innocent son, snatched him up, and paddled his bare buttocks with a stick until it bruised. Those were the moments that ended with his greatest shame.

He knew he shouldn't be so hard on Ervin, but in the long run, he pushed away that shame and reasoned that such discipline would serve him well for he would develop the good habits necessary for success. The boy was too soft, and he worried he would not be prepared for the future. Further, Ervin was such a little comic and prankster that as much as his clever wit and mischievous antics brought a smile to his parents' faces, Joseph wanted to be sure the boy took life—and his studies—seriously, for Ervin had an innate intelligence that needed direction and guidance. Still, he wished he hadn't been so hard on him. It was as if his anger had a life of its own once provoked, and Joseph had no choice but to let it loose on the son he loved more than life itself.

He knew, too, that when Kamilla came to bed she would be cold and silent. How ashamed he felt in those moments of silent rebuke. Her love for him gave him true meaning, far more than even his work. He wished he could reach into her soul and share with her the broken pieces of a childhood spent erased, persuade her of his sincere intent and desire to be only good, only kind. He wished, as well, that he could share with her the turmoil he felt as he watched Hitler rise to power and those surrounding him applaud—indeed, the praise of German citizens toward this charismatic leader was so great and adulating that Joseph marveled at their naiveté and culpability. While he did discuss these concerns with Viktor, he didn't feel it wise to be so open with Kamilla on matters of the state, for it would only trouble her and women ought to be protected from the world of politics, not invited into it. The modern world was a world on the precipice of change, a change he knew would be great and monumental, for science was evolving so rapidly—and exponentially—that it was only a matter of time before the world itself was transformed.

But with such change comes fear, and right now that fear was sweeping Europe—and taking aim, as it had throughout history, at the Jews who century after century had been scapegoated and exiled by those who held more power.

Joseph felt himself split in half by all his worries and had no idea how to heal himself. He glanced at his pocket watch and saw that it was already late. Kamilla had not yet come to their bed, so she was as angry in her silence as he'd been in his rage. He wished that he could weep but the tears had long ago been drained from him.

Instead, he readied for bed and the silence of the woman who would lay down by his side.

HOME

Their first winter in the camps was a cruel one, the temperatures below freezing every day, the snow falling gently some days, slashing the sky like knives the next. On those days, it was blinding and, despite his warm clothes, Ervin's fingers burned with cold. Each day became more difficult and more uncomfortable as they fought the frozen ground, doing their best to unearth the rocks that remained tightly gripped by the earth that didn't want to give up its buried treasures. The rusted train tracks the lorries traveled across were so coated in thick ice that it was as if they were tasked with moving not a loaded lorry, but a stationary house built of solid rock. Like Sisyphus, condemned to perpetually roll a rock uphill for no other purpose than the punishment itself, Ervin felt as if he were living for no purpose at all other than to freeze outside in the bitter cold so that he might push, again and again, that unmovable lorry frozen on the tracks.

The only thing that spared them from dying was the vulnerability of the guards themselves, who refused to linger outside and keep watch, as well as the recognition that should one man die, like a canary in a coal mine, they would all perish—and then, the work would be delayed until another set of Jews could replace them. Thus, on the most brutal days they were confined to their barracks where they struggled to keep a small wood-burning stove alive, though even crowded together, their body heat just barely kept their blood flowing. Ervin had never known such misery, yet dressed more warmly than any of his workmates, he said not a word.

As Christmas neared, Ervin felt a glimmer of hope. Never had he celebrated the Christian holiday, but he surely did so when it was announced that the men would be given furloughs home for that holiday. The first group to be granted leave were those who wore white armbands, of course, and while Ervin was disappointed not to be among the first to go home, he was happy for Frank. Fortunately, both he and Mike were among the second group sent home, and no gift had ever been as welcomed as the gift of two weeks' furlough. Ervin's father sent him enough money to buy a second-class train ticket back to Győr, and every bump he felt through the wooden bench was one bump closer to freedom. He would have gladly been tied down upon the train's roof if that would have brought him back to his parents even one minute sooner.

His mother was waiting for him at the railway station, standing in the very spot he'd last seen her, as if she'd never moved. Even her coat was the same. But this time, instead of standing like a sentinel, shrouded in grief, she was nearly jumping up and down with excitement, like a schoolgirl awaiting her first crush. Ervin practically flew from the train, he was so happy to see his mother, and the two hugged and kissed as never before.

"My son!" Kamilla exclaimed, holding Ervin at arm's length to better see him, then grasping him to her breast. "My dear son..."

"Mama!" Ervin cried, feeling once again as if he were a small boy in desperate need of his mother. "I'm so happy to see you, so happy..."

They walked back home side by side, each in a state of disbelief that they could finally see and speak to each other like any normal mother and son. Yet something had changed. Large posters with big black letters warned Christians against helping Jews in any way. People passing by who once would have exchanged a smile and greeting now turned their heads as if they couldn't bear to set eyes upon the pair, their identities as Jews unmistakable given the yellow armbands. Ervin glared at those who did so, while his mother seemed to take no notice, having by now become accustomed to her own invisibility. Her eyes were only upon the son she was so happy to be walking beside.

When they reached home and Ervin stepped inside the apartment, his father was seated in his chair and stood to rise. Ervin saw at once the love and relief that swept across his father's face as the elder man came toward his son, restrained by a lifetime of learning that a man's emotions were to be tempered, never revealed. But Joseph couldn't suppress the joy he felt to hug his son once again and, as he did so, he held Ervin close as if his greatest treasure had been returned to him and he dared not ever let go.

"Welcome home, son," he said at last, releasing his breath as if a heavy weight had been lifted, for it had. Having Ervin back home was indeed a wondrous gift.

Ervin gazed about the room, half expecting it to be changed. Though he'd only been gone less than three months, they were the longest three months he'd ever endured, and a lifetime seemed to have passed as he'd matured from boy to man in barely a season. Yet during those days and brief moments, before crashing into a deep and all-too-short sleep, Ervin had imagined this moment so often and with such vivid detail that now that the moment had come, he could hardly grasp that he was not just imagining himself back home. His gaze fell upon every chair, every table, every painting or knickknack, willing himself to memorize the contents of his home so that he might hold it in his mind's eye when the painful day came to leave again.

At last, his gaze fell upon the joyful faces of his parents, and he saw that, while their home had not changed, they certainly had. They seemed to have aged years, with new lines carved deeply into their flesh, their eyes weighted down with sadness, their hair much grayer than before. What ravages have they endured? Ervin wondered, as he realized he knew nothing of their sufferings since he had left. He realized that they were indeed facing the escalating persecution that seemed to grow more frightening every day. Yet he knew better than to discuss such a topic right away. He would, for now, relish this gift of just being together again, safe, and happy, at least for now.

"You must be starving," Kamilla said, grabbing Ervin by the arm and escorting him into the dining room, not letting go as if to do so would cause him to vanish into thin air. "Sit down, sit down, let me bring you something." Once her son was seated, Kamilla slipped into the kitchen, Nora and all help having been let go since Jews could no longer employ Christians. Ervin gazed in amazement at the sight he'd taken for granted over the years—a table set with fine china and laden with baskets and tiered stands of breads and sweet biscuits, something he hadn't seen in such a long time. At long last, he would eat a truly fine meal. As Kamilla returned to the dining room with a large tray crowded with smoked meats, pierogis, fresh fruit, and hot coffee, Ervin was convinced he was living a dream, from the very first bite to the last an hour later.

As the days passed, Ervin noted with concern that his father saw few patients, but he never complained, and Ervin sensed that it was best not to bring up the topic. The anti-Jewish laws of the last few years had made it next to impossible for most Jews to work, as the employment of Jews could not exceed 12 percent of an employer's staff and only six percent of physicians could be Jewish—whether his father was even permitted to practice was something Ervin dare not ask in the event that even those few patients were prohibited.

Ervin thoroughly enjoyed his visit, his concerns notwithstanding. He had never thought of his family home as a luxurious retreat, but that is what it had become since being conscripted into the Labor Service. Now what had once been his normal life felt almost magical, a sanctuary from the cruelty and brutality he had been enduring—and he knew he would endure again when the time came to return. Until that time, he treasured his long talks with his father, the loving way his mother fussed over him, and the thrill of falling asleep in a soft, warm bed with his parents sleeping nearby.

In the evenings, however, rather than the leisurely strolls they once took, he and his father retreated to the studio where Joseph pulled out the radio he kept hidden in a false cupboard. The two men huddled together, pressing their ears close to the speaker to listen to the BBC broadcasts on the lowest possible volume, lest Joseph be caught owning a radio. From these prohibited broadcasts they learned that across Europe new restrictions were being implemented against the Jews daily. The world had descended into utter madness and there was no sign of normalcy or sanity returning anytime soon.

As Ervin listened to these broadcasts along with his father, he felt more demoralized each evening. His incomparable joy at being back home and with his parents was balanced with the pressing weight of the world outside their doors, which grew increasingly hostile and dark. While Ervin knew he had only a fortnight to spend at home, he hadn't quite been prepared for the reality those two weeks would present. In the Labor Service, news of the outside world came only in bits and pieces. But now back home with his father, who had access to better sources and thus, much to tell him, and listening with him to the news of the war from the BBC, the seriousness of their situation could neither be avoided nor denied. It was early in the second week of his homecoming that this truth hit him as hard as any guard ever had.

Ervin had found peace in walking in the neighborhood as he once had and, though bitterly cold, the chance encounters with neighbors and acquaintances were such a delight, and the freedom to just walk at will was such a liberation, that he did so regularly. The neighbors were all friendly, and as long as he didn't venture far from the neighborhood where he was known, he didn't encounter the angry glances and turned heads he'd noted that first day back on his walk home from the train station with his mother.

Thus, it was with utter shock that he opened the mailbox one afternoon to find a hateful antisemitic newspaper had been delivered to the Wolfs.

Ervin's first inclination was to dispose of the paper right away, to never tell his parents such a thing had been placed in their mailbox. But he knew that to conceal such information might not be helpful, as his father had a right to know the extent of any threats against them. So, with a heavy heart, he walked inside and at once his father knew something was wrong.

"What is it son? What's that?" he said, gesturing to the folded newspaper Ervin held in his hands, his face a grim testament to something bad had happened.

"It was in the mailbox," he said, handing it to his father just as Kamilla stepped into the room.

"What is it?" she asked, seeing that something disturbing was clearly being discussed.

As Joseph opened the paper, Kamilla came to his side and peered over his shoulder. Within seconds, she gasped and stepped back, just as Joseph crumpled the paper in both his hands as if strangling the author himself. He stormed out of the house, dumped the paper in the bin, and then returned quietly.

That evening, dinner was eaten in near silence, their conversation for the first time stilted and forced. Though it had been nothing more than paper and newsprint, it had felt as if the evil hand of Nazi Germany had slithered over their threshold and into their sacred home. Ervin wanted more than anything to lighten the mood and did his best to tell the most amusing stories he could recall of his bunking with Frank and their synchronized turning at night so that neither fell out of bed, or his efforts to fudge pushing the lorries by securing the easiest ones to move.

But no tales he told could lift the spirits of his parents, nor of himself for that matter and, at best, he was rewarded with a polite smile or gentle chuckle before the silence fell again.

After their usual attention to the BBC broadcast, Joseph called for Ervin to join him in his studio. Once there and seated, as nervous as if he were being summoned for a whipping, Ervin awaited whatever grave words his father had to share. He knew, of course, that no more lashings would ever be suffered from his father, but the seriousness of the moment was enough to set his heart beating as fast as it ever had.

"There's something I want you to memorize," his father began.

"Yes, father, if it is a prayer or a poem, I can assure you—" but his father cut him off before he could finish.

"No, it's not. I have hidden some things of value should the police or the government come. There are reports that they are seizing the valuables of Jews, so I want to safeguard what I can." Joseph's face was as solemn as Ervin had ever seen it, and he fell silent, taking in each word as if being told an ancient spell.

"I'm going to show you where I've concealed these things, and I want you to memorize each place, as well as the names of some Christian friends who have taken some things into safekeeping."

"Okay, father," Ervin said softly, his mouth dry with fear. The ominous tone in his father's voice signaled to Ervin that his father was prepared for the worst, and Ervin couldn't possibly imagine what that worst might be. Adding, "but surely it won't come to that," Ervin awaited his father's reassurance that it wouldn't.

Joseph said nothing in reply but stood up and walked room to room with Ervin, pointing to the control box that concealed his dental drill beneath a false bottom, the hollow rolling window shades inside which important papers had been rolled and tucked discreetly away. They walked up to the attic and down to the basement, and in each were a bewildering array of ingenious spaces where Joseph had hidden his tools, their papers, Kamilla's jewelry, family photos, and memorabilia.

When they were done, he poured Ervin a glass of brandy and as he sipped it, reflecting on his father's overly cautious behavior, Joseph pulled a slip of paper from yet another hiding spot beneath the floorboards. Handing it to Ervin, he explained, "These are the rest of our belongings, and these are the people who have them. Memorize this list for we must destroy it once you do. If ever they are discovered for having helped us, they could be imprisoned or killed. They are risking their lives to help us, so we must depend on your memory and not this list. We must never mention these matters in our correspondence, you do understand?"

"Yes, father," Ervin said.

"If something must be said, we shall refer to 'our favorite flowers,' such as, 'I have planted our favorite flowers near the southern window.' Understand?"

Ervin nodded.

"Good. Now let's go over it."

For the next hour, the two men discussed the list, the friends, where they lived, and what Ervin had to do if Joseph and Kamilla were not there when Ervin came home. At one point, Joseph raised the possibility that Ervin himself might need help.

"Do you remember when we went to synagogue when you were small and you used to ask about the two Jewish men in uniform who always sat up front?"

"Oh, yes, I'd forgotten all about them," Ervin said, wondering what his father knew about them. As he grew up, he would sometimes see the same men in the streets, mingling with local gentile dignitaries. "Wasn't one a fire chief?"

"Yes, one was. And the other one—"

"The one with the captain's uniform and shiny sword," Ervin cut in. The memory was coming back to him, and he recalled how fascinated he had been by the big shiny sword and how regally the man carried himself. He had often thought the man was a gentile though he knew he wasn't, as he went regularly to synagogue and with his big nose, he looked very much like he was Jewish, Ervin thought. But he played the gentile well, so well, in fact, that Ervin consistently forgot the man was Jewish at all, while at the same time, he had been proud to see such a high-ranking officer visit the synagogue. Whenever Ervin heard the term "gentle Jew," he thought of that gentile Jewish captain and his big shiny sword.

"Yes, his name is Captain Kemeny, and he was a professional soldier for most of his life. But he was forced into retirement a few years ago because he was Jewish." Joseph paused as if to honor the pain Captain Kemeny must have suffered when forced out, and then he continued. "He still wears the uniform; I can't imagine him without it. He was a highly decorated hero during the war," he said, referring to the First World War, the one that Joseph himself had served in heroically. "He was so highly decorated that he's been exempt from most of the anti-Jewish restrictions. He has much better access to resources than any of us and he has free rein. He can go anywhere. But most of all, he has excellent connections. He's quite well respected, even among the antisemites. They love him."

"Is he one of those Jews who betray us?" Ervin asked, referring to those rare but dishonorable men and women who, though of Jewish faith and birth, exposed Jews to the local authorities for money or other benefits. Some, it was rumored, even stole money they'd promised to safeguard. Ervin couldn't imagine Captain Kemeny being such a man—his memory of him was one of such great respect that to hear he was dishonorable would have been yet one more heartbreak in heartbreaking times.

"No, no, nothing of the sort," Joseph responded. "Quite the contrary. He has been immensely helpful to our people. He is quite wealthy, and he's used his uniform and influence unselfishly to help any Jew who needs help. I want you to memorize his name and address and, if anything should happen and you need help, I want you to contact him. He will help you."

Ervin was overwhelmed by all that his father was telling him. He had hidden his dental tools, the family keepsakes, money. Making him memorize names and addresses, silly codes like "favorite flowers." Clearly, his father was being overly cautious, Ervin reasoned. But what if not? Ervin could barely fathom what was happening.

That night, despite the luxury of the soft bed with warm blankets and the comfort of having his parents in the next room, Ervin didn't sleep well at all. How in the world could it possibly come to that, to having to memorize hiding spots and friendly conspirators as if they were hiding not birth certificates and dental drills, but stolen art or counterfeit bank notes? Surely his father was taking things too far. Surely. Wasn't he?

Ervin had hoped that the topic would not be raised again, but the following evening, after listening to the BBC report, Joseph gestured for Ervin to follow him once again to the studio. He poured his son a brandy, the expensive wines and ports long gone, and without preamble, came straight to the point.

"If your mother or I are tortured or forced to endure undue suffering—" he began, and Ervin cut him off right away.

"*Apu*! No! Don't say that!" he protested. But Joseph continued, his face serious and lacking any sign of sympathy or sadness.

"If that should happen, we are prepared. We shall always carry ampules of cyanide with us, which would end our suffering quickly and relatively painlessly. I want you to know that if that should happen, we are at peace with our decision."

Ervin leapt from his chair and confronted his father. "Father, you can't be serious! Don't talk like this. You are listening to that radio too much and talking with the wrong people. They have convinced you that there is no hope, that things are much worse than they are. We will get through these times, father, you know that. The Jews have always been persecuted and we've always survived!"

"These times are different, I'm afraid, son," Joseph said, this time with unmistakable sadness. "I hope you are right, but we must prepare for the worst should it come."

Ervin shook his head, pacing back and forth as his father had done so many times when his mind was sorting out a problem. Joseph said nothing for a moment, then commanded, "Sit back down, Ervin."

Obediently, Ervin complied, but defiantly poured himself a rare second brandy. If he was going to be subjected to such talk, he would have to take it like a man and, as a man, he had every right—if not an uncharacteristic need—for that second drink. How could his father speak of such things? Was his mother aware of such talk? She had to be for his father referred not to I, but to "we." What did she think of such madness?

"And mother's alright with this?" he said at last. "You've discussed it with her?"

"Yes," Joseph nodded. "We're in agreement."

Ervin couldn't imagine his mother agreeing to such a plan. She must know that it would never come to that and that his father was being overly concerned. Yet he could not raise the matter with her. Clearly when they were at last reunited after Ervin's Labor Service had ended, such talk would die away. But the possibility, remote as it was, that his father was not mad, not unreasonable in his concerns but acting in accordance with the real risk they faced, why that possibility was too horrifying to contemplate.

"What about Cousin Viktor? Is he planning on doing the same? Maybe he has another idea." Ervin had always found Viktor a rather comical figure but respected his business acumen and the counsel he provided Ervin's father. Surely, he would talk some sense into Joseph.

"Viktor is in America," Joseph told him. "He left shortly after you left for the Labor Service. He is convinced that he will be safe there, but I am not so sure. The antisemitism there is growing and, as much as I believe we must take every possible precaution and prepare for the worst, I do not want to run away. I do not want to be a coward. And I do believe that you're correct, son, that this shall all pass and we will return to living normally once again. I don't doubt that for a minute. But at the same time, what's happening in Poland is very disturbing. Jews are being rounded up en masse and we don't even know what's happening to them in Germany. This is something new, it's not like anything we've seen before. We must be prepared."

Ervin released a deep breath of relief to hear his father concede that all would be well once again. He was just being cautious. One day they would likely laugh over these extreme precautions, and Cousin Viktor would return to Hungary, having wasted thousands on relocating to America for no good reason. Yes, his father was right to stay and not run away. Everything would be fine.

Then again, Viktor had an uncanny knack for estimating human follies and desires. It was what had made him rich in business. Might he know or sense something others hadn't? Should Ervin's parents flee to America and join him?

No, no, they couldn't do that. Ervin would be all alone if they did. No, not America, not so far away. No, he mustn't even suggest it. Not that they would be persuaded by his urging if he did. He could not in good conscience suggest they leave. His father was not one to run away and his mother oughtn't be uprooted from her home based on mere fear of the unknown.

Ervin finished his brandy and bid his father goodnight, assured that his father was overly worried but wisely vigilant, and any talk of ampules of deadly medicaments was mere nonsense.

Despite the disturbing conversations and sleepless nights they had brought him, the visit was more wonderful than he'd even imagined as he ate the marvelous meals his mother had cooked for him, reminisced over dinner about his childhood and happy family memories, and listened to the news with his father in what became a fraternal ritual. The two weeks flew, and Ervin was even more reluctant to leave than he'd been the first time he'd been called up. And just as he had that time, his father loaded him down with warm clothes to make it through the coming winter, while his mother once again stayed up all night baking and cooking so that he could return with plenty to snack on. This time, however, his mother cried as they walked together to the train station, no longer stoic, but now openly grieving as if she'd never see him again.

"I'll see you again soon, mother," he said as he hugged and kissed her goodbye. "Don't worry. We'll get through this." It seemed as though their roles had been reversed and it was now up to him to comfort the mother who had always comforted him, but his assurances did nothing to lessen his own unease at his parents' grave demeanor. He had never known them to be so serious, nor dramatic; they were no longer the same. They had aged so rapidly, so drastically, and though only in midlife, they seemed to have embraced a funereal attitude toward the current social problems of Europe. It was wartime, after all, ought everyone be concerned? And ought everyone be assured that peace would come again?

Ervin rode back on the train torn between his joy at having seen his family and concern for leaving them alone in such a state. And more than anything, anxiety about what fresh hell he was returning to.

UNWANTED

By the time Ervin had finished elementary school, he had already made up his mind that he wanted to follow in his father's footsteps and pursue a career in medicine. For Ervin, the decision was the most natural one he'd ever made. Watching his father care for patients had imprinted upon him the nobility of medical care, and he had never forgotten the warnings of his childhood about infectious disease—and the tragic death of his dear friend Luca—so it seemed as if he had always been preparing for a career in science and healing. And yet, as the social tensions against Jews escalated, his prospects of entry into a good program were increasingly jeopardized, until Ervin realized that he faced overwhelming odds against him.

Just getting into gymnasium, the secondary school for young men where he would prepare for university—similar to what is now called high school—proved to be a challenge. The gymnasium in Győr belonged to the powerful Benedictine Catholic order, and they admitted only a few Jewish students each year under their quota system. But Joseph encouraged Ervin to apply for admission despite the probabilities of rejection.

"Don't let anyone ever tell you who you are or what you can or cannot do," he advised Ervin. "As long as you have faith in yourself, and I the financial means, we shall find a way to get you into medical school. But you will need every possible advantage, so you must work twice as hard and three times as expertly as anyone else. But you can do it, son, and I will do everything I can to help you get there."

Ervin knew his father was right about working harder than others. But he had confidence in himself because he was a hard worker when it came to his studies and he had a sharp mind. He would do whatever it took to prove that he had the skill and compassion to make an outstanding physician. So he and his father set to the task of getting him there.

On his part, Joseph did indeed do all he could to help Ervin succeed. In addition to aiding him nightly with his homework and preparatory studies, he appealed to one of his patients, a priest and friend, for assistance. The kind priest assured Dr. Wolf that he would do all he could to facilitate the process, while it was up to Ervin to learn Latin while mastering his other subjects. Ervin proved up to the task and studied diligently, while Joseph enrolled him in private Latin lessons, which kept Ervin occupied through two summers. Nonetheless, he twice failed the required examination for admission, to his and his family's shock.

"I assure you, father, that I did my best, and I have no idea how I could fail, and twice at that. I was so certain I knew the material; I simply don't know what more to do." Ervin sensed that he hadn't failed and was instead being excluded for no other reason than being Jewish, but he knew that if he would say as much aloud, he would sound as if he was making excuses for his poor performance. Yet he couldn't shake the feeling that he was being discriminated against, even though he looked no different than the other students, spoke fluent Hungarian as well as everyone else, and was as devoted a patriot to his country as anyone. Still, he had grown up in a world that had come to regard him as suspicious and undesirable, and he sensed that it was those sentiments, more than his test scores, that kept him out of the best schools.

"I believe you, son," Joseph assured him, disappointed and troubled. He had quizzed Ervin often enough on all his subjects that he was confident he had mastered the material and he knew that Ervin was not one to panic during a test. Not wanting to say anything without more knowledge, however, Joseph took his concerns to his friend and patient who had offered to watch over the process.

"I did my best, Joseph," the priest said, his head cast ever so slightly down. "But there was nothing more I could do. They simply do not want to admit Jewish students, no matter how well they perform in the exams. Even those who are admitted are the sons of very wealthy patrons who have close connections to the school's leaders going back years. Their admission has nothing to do with their test scores, which aren't as strong as Ervin's, I am sorry to say. I fear if you try again another year, the result will be the same. It is unfair to Ervin, I know, but I've discovered my influence in getting him into the school is not as great as the social prejudice that keeps him out."

"I understand, my good friend," Joseph said, accepting that no matter how gifted his son, no matter how hard he worked, he would not be judged on his merits, but on his birth. Still, he was not about to teach his son to give up. He would instead encourage him to persevere and reach his goal another way. And that meant another school.

Thus, Ervin applied to the local engineering school, Realgymnasium, which unfortunately was a preparatory school for future engineers, rather than medical doctors. "It is alright, father, I can go into engineering. My skills in mathematics will serve me well there."

Joseph and Kamilla were heartbroken for their son to forsake his dream, but they admired his willingness to accept an alternative path. Nonetheless, while he applied and was accepted to the school, they did not give up hope that an alternate path would show itself. While Joseph continued to contact his professional networks in hopes that someone could assist in Ervin gaining admission to the Catholic school, Kamilla turned to prayer.

"If our people cannot help us," she explained to Joseph, "then God shall."

And sure enough, God answered her prayers when a local Jewish parochial school was nationalized. The loss of another Jewish school was an inauspicious sign, yet the conversion served them well, because students of mixed religions would be admitted. Just as Ervin was set to start engineering school, he was accepted to this new school—and he was once again on his path to medical school.

The new school was a stark contrast to the slammed doors he had encountered in his efforts to advance academically. The teachers there were humane and objective, and Ervin felt no hatred or prejudice against him. There were, of course, some prejudiced people at the institution, but they were outnumbered and thus reluctant to openly voice their odious views. And while most of the students were Catholic, there were enough students from other religions that there was no discernible resentment toward any one religion, and most students got along well.

During the summer, it wasn't uncommon for the students to socialize at the beach, where Ervin loved to spend the whole day swimming in the beautiful Olympic-sized swimming pool that had been built by the town and opened to much fanfare. He had become an accomplished swimmer over the years and was on the regional junior swim team, so he devoted as much attention to his swimming skills as he did his studies. Each morning he would head to the beach and swim for several hours. Around midday, Nora would arrive with a basket filled with a freshly made three-course dinner, complete with polished silverware, fine china, crystal glassware, a pressed linen napkin, and fresh tablecloth. Dried and dressed in a fine linen robe, Ervin would feast like a spoiled prince, entirely unaware that this daily summertime routine was the least bit unusual. He had become so accustomed to a life of luxury where he was served whatever he wanted and provided every comfort, that to be treated like a royal as he trained in the community pool seemed every bit as natural as swimming itself.

After finishing his delicious meal, he would place everything in the basket, and then take it to Nora, who would be waiting at the gate.

"Thank you, Nora," he would say, ever the gentleman, then he would return to his friends who had likewise grown accustomed to the regal dining ritual their friend enjoyed each day while they dined far more humbly. Yet never did a cross word stain their friendships with Ervin over the luxurious lifestyle he lived, and never did he disdain those who came from humbler homes. In swimming, all that counted was one's physical power and team spirit, and both were something Ervin had in abundance.

Then one day, in his third year of high school, he arrived for practice just as he had every other day and received an unexpected notice from the swim captain. It seemed that Ervin could no longer swim with the team.

"But why?" he asked, stunned.

The captain just shook his head. "These are just the rules," he said, avoiding Ervin's eyes. "I don't make them. I'm sorry. It's nothing personal. These are political decisions."

Ervin had a close friend on the team who was standing nearby when this happened. The friend, a good-hearted Catholic who visited Ervin's home nearly every day, merely shrugged when Ervin approached him. "I like you so much, Ervin," he said. "It's just too bad you're Jewish."

The words hit Ervin hard, as he saw, for the first time, the glint of prejudice in the boy's eyes. Never had he so much as hinted that Ervin's Jewishness was the least bit relevant to their friendship, yet the tone in which he'd said these words spoke not so much to the boy's disappointment in the social animosity toward Jews as to his belief that Ervin was likable despite being inferior.

Ervin returned home crushed. He could not understand why he could no longer swim with the team. And he realized, with every step he took toward home, that he had also lost a friend. When he told his parents of the turn of events, Joseph confirmed his worst fears.

"Damn them!" he cried, slamming his fist on the table. "They cast us out from nearly everything. Not even the waters they swim in can be polluted by Jews!"

Joseph's temper had not been as hot in ages, yet Ervin saw now that he was as angry as he'd ever been, though this time, he was not aiming his wrath at Ervin. For all their battles over the years, he had never doubted his father's love and support and in recent years his father's anger had subsided. The two continued to clash, as did all fathers and sons as the latter grew increasingly independent and the former remained his protector, but Joseph no longer chased Ervin under the oak table, nor whipped him with a switch or belt. Both were becoming more mature and in control of their emotions, while for her part, Kamilla had made it clear to Joseph that his anger was his greatest weakness, and she would not tolerate it any further. A sense of peace had seemed to pervade the Wolf household, even as tensions outside their home intensified. Joseph's worries had shifted from his son's punctuality to the continent's security, and this latest act against them had brought the hostilities outside their door into their very home.

In 1938, when Ervin was 16, Austria had been annexed by Nazi Germany, a grave act that brought the horrifying prospect of war much closer to home, as Austria was but a stone's throw from Győr. Antisemitic graffiti was now the norm, with bridges, walls, and pillars regularly defiled with hateful commentary, curses, and threats, which, like a thousand papercuts, bled their souls ever so slowly and painfully. Not only were Jews fleeing Nazi persecution, but so too were Christian professors, authors, journalists, and anyone who spoke out against the Nazis. While most of these refugees fled to neighboring European countries, some fled to Hungary.

Many were captured and sent back, where they would meet certain death, while Joseph and Kamilla welcomed some of these refugees into their home, hiding them from the authorities and instructing Ervin to not mention a word. Ervin, of course, complied, for even in Győr, the prospect of Nazis gaining power was not entirely outside the realm of possibility, for antisemitic speeches were increasingly common in the public squares, and the first of such "official" speeches had already taken place in Győr itself. In an especially nasty and provocative speech, a minister of the Conservative Party, to the great surprise and chagrin of the city's many Jewish members and supporters, openly condemned Jews as a blight on the nation and a threat to national security. These sentiments trickled downward and many in the general population began to openly flirt with the idea of a victorious Hitler, while expressing agreement with the hateful propaganda that blamed Jews, the universities, and the press for all of Germany's problems. The days were growing darker, yet life carried on.

As the time grew closer for Ervin's applications to medical schools, there was no question that he would receive the best possible preparation for his collegiate studies. Just as he'd done when preparing to enter gymnasium, he set his mind to getting into the best medical school he could. He studied late into the evening every night and gathered all the information needed to commence the application process. There were four possible medical schools in Hungary, and, with his father's help, Ervin began the laborious task of filling out each application by hand, being sure not to deviate in the least from the detailed requirements that could be used to automatically disqualify an otherwise excellent applicant—using the proper margins, paper color, type of ink, and type of pen. Even the way he folded the application had to be exactly as specified or it would not be unfolded. Ervin made sure he followed these instructions exactly, writing the most reasoned and eloquent personal letter he could, and obtaining excellent letters of reference from some of Győr's most respected citizens. His grades being among the top of his class, Ervin crossed his fingers that at least one of these schools would admit him.

Every school rejected him. The letters of rejection were written in polite rhetoric stating that they were sorry, but all available seats had been filled. It was clear, as he and his Jewish friends were discovering, that one's religion mattered far more than one's qualifications. Ervin felt, for the first time in his life, completely defeated. He was not yet 20, but it seemed as though his future had already been determined by those who didn't know him. Because he was Jewish, he was regarded as fit only for menial work, not for work of the mind, and not for work of any social significance. With only a year left in high school, he had been cast off before he'd even come of age.

"We shall get you into medical school," his father told him one evening at dinner. "I still have some connections I haven't drawn on, but now is the time to do so. I know some influential attorneys in high positions and though they will require substantial remuneration for their efforts, they will get you into school. Don't worry, son."

"No, father," Ervin said, letting his silver fall to the porcelain plate with a sharp ring. He was at wit's end and felt so defeated and frustrated. But he could not allow his parents to pay what he knew would be nearly all their savings, for such bribes were well known to be so costly that only the wealthiest could afford them. "You mustn't do that," he protested. "I won't accept it."

"But Ervin," Kamilla interjected, "your father is only trying to help. And please be careful with that silver before you break the china."

"I'm sorry, mother, but I just can't let you do this. The cost is too high and you and father will need all you have for retirement, especially as it looks as though war will soon break out with Russia. You must look to your own security first. I will find another way."

"Very well, son," Joseph replied. "But should you change your mind, the offer still stands. Your security is as much our concern as our own."

As the family continued to enjoy their meal, the silence that descended grew audible. Ervin so appreciated all the support he received from his family, but he could not let them take any risks on his behalf. As he finished his dinner amid the sounds of clinking crystal and cutlery, he reflected on another reason that he was reluctant to accept his parents' financial help—he wasn't sure he would graduate. Not that he lacked confidence in his intellectual skills and discipline, but Ervin had heard many stories of an antisemitic youth organization that was springing up in universities. This group, known as the Turul, terrorized Jewish students by throwing blankets over them and beating them until they understood beyond any doubt that they were unwanted and would endure further beatings until they left. Knowing the probability that he would be subjected to such beatings himself if he were admitted to a good school, Ervin couldn't risk his parents investing in his future, only to be chased out of school with no degree.

There was only one possibility Ervin could foresee and that was finding an entirely new direction. A pivot. A new vector.

He did not need to be a doctor, as much as he wanted to be one. He could pursue a more pedestrian occupation, one with respectability and a steady income. He was, after all, an optimist by nature. His good humor would see him through whatever fate had in store for him, provided his parents weren't brought to destitution in their efforts to assist him.

When Ervin began his final year of high school, Germany invaded Poland and just two days later, France and the United Kingdom declared war on Germany. The world's second war had been set in motion—a war that would be fought over the fate of Europe's Jews, as well as restraining Germany's global reach which, under Chancellor Adolf Hitler, was proving to be aggressive. Joseph received the news with despair. Viktor had been right all along. The contagion of madness was indeed greater than Joseph had ever anticipated, for the party of the buffoon who had led a failed *coup d'état* in 1923 had received 43.9 percent of the vote ten years later, with Hitler being appointed Chancellor by the German President, Paul von Hindenburg, as a result. Now well established in power, Hitler was dispensing with any pretense of democracy—or human decency for that matter—and he was determined to bring all of Europe under his control. While Joseph was confident that the global leaders of most of the world's nations would not stand for such aggression, he was coming to see that Viktor's cynical view of human nature was not as nihilistic as he'd imagined. One only had to walk through the streets of Győr now to feel the unmistakable resentment against the Jews—and the intensifying propaganda that seemed to be turning once kind, gentile souls into primal beasts who genuinely feared and increasingly loathed their Jewish neighbors.

"You must understand," Viktor explained to Joseph as they walked through the streets of Győr one chilly autumn day in 1939, "we comprise less than ten percent of the city's population, but within that minority, we have held unique and powerful positions in commerce, education, and the law. To be powerful in one respect but vulnerable in another is always a dangerous position in which to find oneself. We are simultaneously a threat, as successful competitors for these positions of power and influence, and a target, as minorities among the greater population."

The wind picked up and rain began to fall like slivers of glass, causing Joseph to pull his woolen coat tighter against his chest, as if he were both huddling from the coming storm and from the advancing Germans. After a moment of silence as the two men walked more rapidly to escape the unexpected rainfall, Joseph at last spoke, nearly shouting above the roar of the wind picking up.

"For the love of God, Viktor, our people have been persecuted for thousands of years! Surely, we shall drive out these damnable Nazis, minorities or not!"

In response, Viktor merely chuckled, then slapped Joseph on the back and said, "We shall do our best, shan't we? Now what say you we slip into this club just up ahead and have ourselves a glass of tokay?"

Joseph smiled and nodded, though he didn't have it in him to join his cousin in laughter. He nearly doubted his own words more than he did Viktor's, for he had seen just in trying to get his son a proper education that the stigma against Jews was growing daily, not diminishing. His own business was still good, but the future Ervin was facing was fast becoming a bleak one. As much as he wanted to scoff at Viktor's grim outlook, he couldn't help but acknowledge that he was probably right.

They ducked into a dark and dry gentleman's club where Viktor was immediately recognized and treated like an esteemed client of high standing, which of course he was. How refreshing, Joseph thought as they were seated in stately wingback chairs with leather as soft as a baby's skin, to be so respected within these walls, while outside them they were taunted and ridiculed as if Romany "Gypsies."

Ervin had made up his mind. If he was to be excluded from medical schools upon graduation, he would find some form of manual labor that would require a good mind, but not so manual that it would demand of him strength he did not have. And he knew just what that position would be—he could work as a dental assistant, where he might not be a doctor, but he would be providing healthcare and keeping his mind and hands busy throughout the day. With many of his friends forced to work in factories, a tedium he couldn't imagine, work as a dental assistant would be far more agreeable and he knew just the person to help him in this regard.

Ervin's father employed an excellent, well-trained dental technician who had learned his trade in Germany. Ervin discussed his interest in apprenticing with him and he readily agreed. Like his father, Ervin appreciated the artistic side of dentistry, and gaining skills as an apprentice would provide him the opportunity to refine his own artistic skills. Thus, Ervin spent the last year of high school engaged in his studies as the war intensified and, when he graduated in 1940, with the blessings of his parents, he started his apprenticeship and went to work.

That first year on the job, he cleaned the laboratory, worked with plaster, and cleaned up after the doctors had worked on their patients. By the second year, however, the war growing ever more heated with Hungary declaring war against Russia, he was able to observe and learn all the technical skills his father's colleague possessed. At the same time, he completed vocational school, something usually reserved for high school dropouts, but his country was at war, and he was coming to learn his place in this new wartime environment. As a Jew, he could no longer be a doctor, but he could find a place in society if he kept his head down, challenged no one, and focused on his work. By the end of his second year, he passed the official dental technician examination, became a master at his trade, and found steady work in several dental labs. He was still living at home, but making good money, though his parents never accepted any of it from him. They were more concerned that he save his money and establish himself as best he could.

It was at this same time, in 1942, that Ervin met a cute girl from Budapest while vacationing at a resort on Lake Balaton. He thought he might pursue a serious romance with this charming girl, with whom he corresponded once he returned home, but that dream was not to be. In the winter of 1942, at Voronezh, by the Don River, the second Hungarian army was destroyed, and 200,000 soldiers were killed. Not long after, the Hungarian army massacred 3,300 Jews in Újvidék, Novi Sad, not far from where Ervin's mother Kamilla had grown up. The threat to Ervin and his family was growing closer and more personal, a threat that turned stark and terrifying as rumor circulated that Jews were being purged throughout Europe. Just what that purge entailed remained the stuff of rumor, but there was no question, life as they'd known it was about to change.

Yet through it all, Ervin remained protected. Joseph and Kamilla, themselves dependent on rumor and clandestine news from the BBC, kept as much as they could from him. He was, for the most part, unaware of all that was happening, as Jews, no longer permitted to have radios nor to congregate, lived isolated lives. Ervin himself was focused on his work and, though the romance he had hoped would blossom had faded before its time given the limits on Jewish movement through the country, he contented himself with the knowledge that he was secure, and wars had forever been fought throughout Europe only for the continent to return to peace eventually. He continued to work and nobody bothered him. Outside of work he lived a simple life. He joined a nondenominational rowing club where he spent part of the summer. In the winter, he and his friends played cards and went to the movies. Their neighbors remained polite. Politics simply were not discussed and, as for antisemitism, though it was audible outside their doors, many Christian patients remained loyal to his father's practice and continued to use his services. As for his mother, Kamilla continued to do her shopping as usual and was never refused services or treated with any discrimination. Though there were items that were rationed to Christians and difficult to find, such as coffee, chocolate, and sugar, her Christian friends helped her to obtain those and more so that the Wolfs always had good, fresh food on the table, albeit no meat.

But by the spring of 1943, when Ervin turned 21, he received notice that he was to enlist in military service through the Hungarian Labor Service System. He was less concerned with serving his country than he was the "unreliable" designation he received as a Jewish man—the designation hurt him deeply, as he was patriotic and loyal to his country. To be declared unreliable was a humiliation far greater than being rejected from high school, medical school, and even the swim team. The designation officially defined him as both unwanted, and now, unreliable. He fumed at the injustice.

For Joseph, however, the notice to enlist was far more serious than a temporary injustice. He received, through his connected patients and friends, reports of what happened to the young men sent into the Labor Service. 50,000 Jewish men—closer to boys than to men—had been sent to a forced labor camp in Russia and another 5,000 had been sent to the death mine in Bor, Yugoslavia, where they were subjected to abuse, torture, and beatings by guards. Many of them were used as human mine detectors, forced to cross fields riddled with live mines, rarely surviving the ordeal. That was the future awaiting his son and while Joseph wanted to prepare Ervin for what lay ahead, at the same time he knew that he should not terrify him.

Instead, he set about preparing Ervin for the psychological ordeal and working through his networks to obtain all that his son would need to stay warm through the brutal winters ahead. As Kamilla knitted Ervin a thick, warm pullover, Joseph readied his son for war.

RETURN TO CAMP

Ervin had long realized that the uncertainty of his fate was among the most painful aspects of enduring it. Yet following his furlough and knowing just what was in store for him, returning to camp was in many respects far more difficult than his first arrival. Then he had had no idea what to expect and the uncertainty had brought immense anxiety. But now that he knew just how horrible Labor Service was, he was even more distressed. He had so enjoyed his visit back home, so loved seeing his parents again, and so worried to have to leave them, that every mile on the train was a mile closer to misery and he loathed every moment of the journey. He found, however, that by reliving his visit in his memory, he could keep the misery at bay, if only in his imagination.

Thus, once back, he reveled in his daydreams while he toiled in the brutal cold. He was glad he still had Mike and Frank to work and bunk with, but his spirits were sinking daily. Adding to his misery, the labor worsened. The ground had frozen so solid that the work for the airport had to be suspended and with that suspension came a whole new routine. Each morning, after awakening at dawn, they would wash and dress, though the latter was often unnecessary as it had become so cold that they slept in their clothes all night. Once dressed, they marched across the snow-covered fields for several kilometers before they were fed a breakfast of black coffee, half a loaf of bread, and a pasty marmalade that bore no resemblance to any Ervin had ever known. It tasted more like sour sugar paste than fruit, but he ate every bit of it because he knew he wouldn't have anything more until the end of the day. Sometimes, however, they received sausage or bacon, which always brightened up the dreary day ahead.

Fifteen minutes later, whether finished eating or not, their march resumed for another five kilometers to the headquarters of the defense command. With every step, Ervin felt they were viewed more like animals than men.

"I see the pigs are here," one commander announced each morning, sneering at them as if they were subhuman. "Well, what are you waiting for? Get to work!" Dismissing the men with a wave of his hand, the commander was replaced with another equally arrogant officer who would divide the group into four-man teams. They were never the same team, so Ervin never knew if he'd be assigned to a good crew or a bad one, and he missed the camaraderie he'd found in working with Frank and Mike. But no matter who he was matched with, they were all in the same miserable state, compelled to work like pack animals for fools whose only power was derived from their birth.

After gathering their tools for the day's work, the men hiked for another hour escorted by armed guards, carrying the heavy hammers, pickaxes, ladders, spades, rope, and dynamite to their work site. The hatred the guards aimed at them was so great that Ervin realized the guards could massacre them all in a single burst of rage and no one would bother to pick up their bodies. They were viewed as so unhuman, so inconsequential and replaceable, that even dead, the only concern the guards would have would be retrieving the tools the men carried and losing a day's labor until the next crew could be put to work.

Ervin was determined not to give them the satisfaction of his death, no matter how restful eternity might be.

Their new job in the mountains involved digging holes eight feet deep and three feet in diameter where explosives would be buried. This work was even more difficult than preparing the field for the airport and required digging into the rocky, stone-covered soil that was so frozen, they often had to use dynamite to make any progress. By the end of the arduous day, without so much as a break, they hiked back to return the tools, reaching their barracks in the darkness where they were so exhausted, they barely knew what they were eating, which was probably just as well. Sometimes Ervin was too tired to even lift a spoon and went straight to bed, unaware of his surroundings, unaware even of his own name.

Their efficiency at work slowly improved with each passing day. They became experts at the careful use of dynamite, rapidly jumping from the deep wells the moment a fuse was lit. They also learned how to rub their shoes with grease to waterproof them, which helped them avoid the frostbite that had cost more than one man some toes. But not even the grease could do much to help with the rising water that accumulated in some of the deep wells they dug, so they were allotted pails that they attached to long ropes, with one man filling them and another standing outside the hole pulling it up to dump the contents into the closest brook. Hauling the small buckets of water one at a time until, at last, the holes were dry enough to light a fuse, but not so dry as to ward off the chill that would set in for whatever man was unfortunate enough to be assigned the bottom of the hole, the men raced to finish the task before the water rose any higher.

Ervin hated being posted at the bottom of a well and did everything he could to talk his way into the coveted spot outside it. It was one such day when he was tossing the water into the brook that the pail went flying along with the water, landing in the rapidly flowing stream where the current quickly took it away. Knowing he'd be beaten or worse if he failed to return the pail—since the pail had greater value than his life—fear shot through him like a bullet. He raced down the steep, snow-covered hillside, the brambles slashing his bare face as he bore straight through them. When he spotted the pail snagged on a branch, he jumped into the icy water as if it were a small child he had to rescue rather than a rusty old pail.

The frigid water enveloped him like a coat of ice, and he struggled to breathe, gasping uncontrollably, while swimming straight for the bobbing pail. In all the swim meets and races he'd competed in, he'd never swam as fast and powerfully as he did now. He had to get the pail. He had to survive. He could not drown—his parents couldn't bear it if he did. Gasping for breath as he raced for the pail before it sailed away again, he finally snatched it between his fingers and swam for the closest bank. While only a matter of feet, those last few strokes felt Olympian. At last, he made it to the bank, pail in hand, climbing out of the water covered in wet leaves and looking like some terrifying swamp creature that had sprung from the murky waters.

Triumphant, Ervin marched back through the deep snow, colder than he'd ever known cold, returning to his worksite hoisting the beat-up old pail like a golden trophy he'd just won.

An applause greeted him as if he'd crossed the English Channel, and it wasn't until he was back to work that he even realized he was soaking wet. He worked the rest of the day in the bitter cold and wet clothes, but as miserable as he was in the flesh, he was deliriously happy in spirit. For the first time, Ervin truly felt victorious. Even better, he felt strong. He may have started out the weakling of the unit, but he had something inside him that he now knew was more powerful than brute strength. He had an inner strength and fury that no guard could ever stamp out.

And all those swimming lessons hadn't hurt either.

It wasn't long before they received word they'd be transferred again. This time they would be moved to the Carpathian Mountains where they would be working under the defense command to enforce the border. The train took them to Nagyberezna, a beautiful small town in northwestern Hungary, surrounded by magnificent snow-covered mountains. Even better, rather than the cramped barracks they'd been sharing, the men were assigned to private homes where they were provided warm shelter and real beds. Though these beds were in the homes of peasants who had barely anything themselves, Ervin felt blessed to have such lodgings, and he was even more comforted to discover that there was a small Jewish community nearby with a modest synagogue. It felt nearly normal, as if he truly had been assigned to military service and not the indentured labor that had left him feeling like a branded criminal.

The work, however, was nearly as rough as what they'd been doing before. No longer tasked with tearing up and relocating the earth to build an airport, or digging deep wells in the frozen ground, now they were charged with working in a cold, unheated church where they constructed huge concrete tubes to serve as some form of underground drain system. Ervin's team worked in pairs pressing down on the newly poured cement to make the tubes as strong and compact as possible. Each tube took the two men eight hours of heavy labor to complete, but at the end of those eight hours, their shift thankfully ended. After the last post, the work at Nagyberezna was a blessed relief. Still, Ervin was hungry and exhausted at the end of each day.

Unfortunately, the comfort of a warm bed did not last long, for no sooner had they settled into the peasants' homes than they were relocated. This time, they were sent to another barracks in the countryside. There, in place of comfortable beds, they slept on a hard concrete floor. While cold and rough, it was at least dry, and Ervin was adapting, however unhappily, to his new way of living. Constantly moving, constantly hungry, constantly tired, and under the watchful eye of guards who were more cruel than humane, each moment of his new existence became a moment he knew would pass. In time, this nightmare would be behind him, he told himself, he had only to endure a single moment at a time. But the moments mounted, and the never-ending constancy of misery was forever taunting him as he struggled to survive.

Every morning they awoke and walked to a nearby brook, broke up the ice that had sealed it in the night, and washed themselves in the icy water. Then they'd eat breakfast, which this time required no lengthy morning hike and, after eight hours of hard labor with no more food or rest, they'd eat supper and then, just as they were ready to collapse, their second shift began.

There in the dark as the wind chilled them to the bone, they unloaded wagon after wagon filled with building materials—bags of pebbles, stones, and cement. It usually took about three hours before the wagons were all unloaded, while the weight of the heavy bags that they hoisted over their shoulders was nearly the weight of each emaciated man.

Though the men had hoped that over time the guards would be kinder to them, once they got to know them and saw them as fellow men, the opposite proved true. It was as if the more the guards came to know the men, the more emboldened they became to abuse them—perhaps because they had learned that no act, no matter how brutal, would be punished, whereas any kindness they showed would be. Whatever the cause, the captors delighted in their cruelty. When the men were working in the deep wells, the guards would amuse themselves by urinating on them, turning the holes they dug into veritable latrines. Yet the humiliation didn't bother the workers so much because the more they were peed on, the more satisfied the guards were that they'd inflicted sufficient degradation on their charges, thereby lessening the chance of a beating. It was the beatings the men most feared.

As time went on, small graces helped the men to endure the realities of their fate. Ervin learned from Mike's father, who inexplicably was allowed a rare visit and brought news from the outside world, that the guards could be bribed. Though the guards never spoke directly to the men unless it was to deliver orders or rebukes, and never looked them in the eye, through the small acts of bribery, a silent contract had developed. Some young workers received a bit more food, fewer punishments, and even extra clothing. Fortunately, it wasn't long before Ervin learned that his own father had met with the guards, offering free dental treatment for their families, as well as cash, and Ervin received a visit from one of the guards not long after.

"Wolf!" Ervin sprang to attention, ready to withstand whatever was coming. He looked up and saw János, the guard who'd served them sausages at the earlier camp, jerk his head for Ervin to come to him.

Ervin complied, standing at attention before the funny looking man. János had tiny eyes buried in a face so pockmarked that he looked like a burn victim. He was quite hideous, but Ervin concluded it may have been his ugliness that rendered him more sympathetic than the other guards. Still, he was a superior, and Ervin had long since concluded that even the kindest of guards held power over him, and no one holds power without employing it. Thus, when János commanded Ervin to approach, Ervin was as cautious as he was obedient.

"Your parents want you to have this," he said, his voice low and neither kind nor cruel. He handed Ervin a small paper packet as discretely as if he were passing a valet a well-earned tip, then turned and barked orders to a nearby group of men. Ervin used the diversion to sneak back to his bunk and open the packet.

Inside was a chain of gold with a simple four-leaf clover charm, a small ruby embedded in the center. Ervin had never received jewelry from his parents, but this golden four-leaf clover was the most treasured gift he'd ever opened, not for it being gold, but for it being a symbol of their optimism and hope he'd be home soon. He turned the charm over and saw that they'd had it engraved.

In remembrance from your parents. 1943 X 4.

A tear fell from Ervin's face, followed by another, then another. 1943, the year he'd last seen his family. X was the Roman numeral for the month of October, and 4 for the day he'd departed, just a few months earlier. The tears fell heavily now as he realized how momentous that day had been, and how much that date was etched not just upon the golden charm, but also upon his parents' hearts.

Ervin kept the charm around his neck and, though he was not permitted to have jewelry, the guards were well aware of his necklace and no one tried to take it from him. János continued to bring him small gifts of food and words of encouragement from his parents, and Ervin knew that his father had to be continuing to pay the bribes that kept his son safe. While every encounter Ervin had with János made it clear he'd been communicating with his father, Ervin grew more heartbroken that he could not meet with him himself. He yearned to see his family again and wondered how much longer he could bear the miserable life he'd been delivered. He worried even more about how his parents were faring, as there was no way to know what was happening in the outside world other than rumor. As much as his parents worried for his safety, Ervin felt deep in his bones that it was he who was safe and they who were in danger. He didn't know whether his fear for his parents was rational or just his own imagination run wild, given his father's insistence that he memorize hiding places. He only knew that the charm his parents had delivered to him was both auspicious and inauspicious, and one way or another, he had to get back home.

Fortunately, outside the barracks where they slept, the lighting was so poor that they were able to sneak out at night and go to the neighboring fields where the farmers awaited them. The farmers, facing dire economic losses of their own, secretly sold the boys eggs, milk, and bread. If the peasants had been caught, they would have been severely punished, and if the boys were caught, the punishment might prove deadly, but they so hungered for protein and calcium that they risked it regularly. If there were guards who caught on to their nightly escapades, they blessedly said nothing, but Ervin had no doubt that some of the guards would have delighted in beating them badly, torturing them even, having finally had a pretext for doing so.

The nightly visits to the farmers, which Ervin wouldn't dare disclose in his letters even if it would have eased their worries, had another unexpected benefit. They became good friends with the kind peasants, who gave the boys hot water to wash themselves and sometimes even had hot suppers prepared for them. But because the countrymen were so poor themselves, the boys never accepted anything for free and always paid them from what meager sums their families could send, or which they'd received from their paltry wages as compulsory laborers.

The farmers' lives were not much better than those of the boys, as most lived in one room huts with earthen floors made of pressed sand and heated with brick ovens. Chickens, cats, and children ran about unrestrained, yet barely visible in the dim light. While electricity was widely available throughout Hungary, these families were so poor that they could not afford it and instead relied on oil lamps for lighting. The newspapers and radio frequently tried to whip up their rage by suggesting the Jews were the ones responsible for their poverty, as well as the ones who had caused Hungary to lose so much territory after the First World War. While some did come to believe such propaganda, others recognized the age-old trick and didn't fall for it. They understood, instead, that both enslaved Jews and impoverished farmers shared a common struggle brought on by those in power who cared nothing for the poor.

It wasn't escaping to the farms at twilight that so frightened Ervin, however. It was sneaking back to their camp during the deep, dark night while packs of stray dogs followed closely behind. Their savage growls were near demonic and Ervin's fear primordial, as if the hounds had been conjured from his imagination, having taken root as a child when listening to the tales of the Brothers Grimm that his father used to read to him. These hungry, growling beasts could at any moment spring upon him and rip open his throat with a single bite should they so desire. And yet, just as the risk of a beating from the guards didn't dissuade him from the visits to the farms, neither did the vicious bloodlust of the wild dogs that pursued him upon returning. Instead, with every successful nighttime escape to the farms and safe return to their barracks, Ervin's confidence was strengthened. The guards may have been mean and cruel, they may have had power over their captives, but like so many such brutes, they were as lazy as they were mean, as unintelligent as they were cruel, and as foolish as they were powerful.

"You know," Ervin whispered to Frank one evening after they'd snuck out to get some food and were heading back to their beds, "once they've fed us, they seem to forget us."

"Except when they wake us in the night for a beating," Frank said, in not quite a whisper. They were far enough out he wasn't worried about anyone overhearing.

"They never do that until they're good and drunk on the weekends, which is long after we've returned," Ervin said in a voice so low Frank could barely hear him. Unlike Frank, Ervin was still reluctant to speak too loudly, for fear their voices might carry.

"Thanks, Ervin," Frank replied. "It's Friday. Now the whole night's shot just thinking about going back."

"Think about it," Ervin said. "How far away do you think we could get?"

"Uhh, pretty far, I'd guess."

"Yep, pretty far."

They walked the rest of the way back to the barracks in silence, each boy in deep thought, calculating the kilometers they could reach before dawn.

OCCUPATION

Joseph was repairing a patient's cavity when the gendarmes arrived. A wave of activity filled the streets as the officials stepped from their cars and marched from building to building, their ominous footfalls and commands like a fast-approaching storm.

Of course, he'd been preparing for their arrival for some time, and just two days prior, on March 18 of 1944, he had learned from the BBC that Regent Horthy had been summoned to Austria for a dressing down. It seemed that the brutal Horthy had his limits and had refused Hitler's order to deport Jews to Germany. In response, Hitler had given him one last chance. And now, here they were, Hungarian officials acting on behalf of the Nazis to issue their commands to the Jews of Győr.

After finishing his work as quickly as he could, Joseph closed his office. He hid his drill in the place where he'd shown Ervin and quickly concealed anything of value that he could, though there was little time. He had to go to Kamilla who would be terrified, no doubt —and hiding more valuables, as they'd discussed. Even in fear, she knew what to do.

"I pray that Ervin is safe." Kamilla moved through her kitchen, putting away food, cleaning counters, as if preparing to leave for the afternoon. Her hands shaking, a teacup fell to the floor, shattering so loudly she jumped in surprise. Joseph pulled her to him and held her closely.

"Our son is safe, my love. They'll work him hard, but it is better he be under their guard than here with us."

Kamilla's whole body shook, and soon Joseph felt his wife become engulfed in sobs. "What will they do to us, Joseph?" she cried out. "What will they do?"

"I don't know, my love," he answered truthfully. How he wanted to assure his dear wife that he could protect her. Hadn't he vowed to do so when they had married? Yet here he was, after a quarter century together, unable to do anything to save his wife from whatever hellish punishment was in store. How he wished he'd heeded Viktor's advice to flee Hungary and join him in America. He'd so scoffed at Viktor, he was so certain Germany would lose the war, and yet, here they were, sending their Hungarian emissaries to Győr. They were coming for the Jews; Joseph was certain of that much. Still, he would not give up hope. The Allies still might save them. Not today, but soon. They only had to get through the next stage of their ordeal.

"I beg of you, my dear cousin, leave now. I can arrange your exit, but you and Kamilla must leave now with me," Viktor had said. "I leave in two nights' time and I cannot help you once I'm gone. But I must leave. These Nazis shan't win in the end, but I fear they will bring great misery to our people before they are done. They aim to destroy us, and their murderous campaign is already well underway."

"To leave in two days' time would just not be possible," Joseph replied. "Not with my practice and not with Ervin still here. We couldn't possibly leave him."

"He will be fine, at least as fine as he can be given this horrifying state of affairs. But we will not be. They will come for us."

"I doubt that it shall ever come to that," Joseph had laughed at the time. He could not, in 1943, have foreseen this day. Yet now, just a few months later as he held Kamilla in his arms while she sobbed and the gendarmes passed through the streets just outside his door, he could not imagine his foolishness. He had been so certain the Germans would be stopped before it got this far. And yet, day by day the tension had grown greater as they had not been stopped. Day by day the inhumanities and indignities aimed at Jews had grown bolder until they seemed almost natural, as if Jews truly did pose a threat to the Christian world, as if they truly were inferior human beings for no other reason than they had been born Jewish. And day by day, the aggressions of Hitler's Germany had grown greater. Crueler. Bloodier. Now, here they were. Right outside. Hungarians, yes, but under the command of Hitler's Nazis. Would he and Kamilla be enslaved, imprisoned, or merely exiled? Joseph did not know. He hoped that they would not be separated, but he and Kamilla had already prepared for such a consequence and had arranged a means of communication through a few friendly points of contact so that they could be reunited once again. They would face some savage months ahead, undoubtedly, but they'd get through them. He kissed the top of his wife's head, then lifted her chin so they stood face to face. He wiped the tears from her face and said, "*Yevorechecho Hashem Ve'Yishmerecho.*" May God bless and shield you from harm. The same prayer Kamilla had said to Ervin as he prepared to leave for Labor Service. Then Joseph said it again, and again, and again, as he rocked her in his arms.

The next morning the gendarmes arrived on their doorstep. The pounding on the door announced the unmistakable arrival of brute power. Joseph opened it as if welcoming the devil himself, unable to do anything but comply. A short, angry man no older than Ervin pushed his way through the door and demanded all members of the household present themselves. Kamilla stepped into the room. Her tears had long dried and she now stood obediently before the immature officer, as if standing before her own father and awaiting a punishment she knew would be coming for an offense she did not quite understand. As a girl, her transgressions had been so slight, so seemingly inconsequential. A failure to cover her head. A failure to remain focused on her Hebrew lessons. A failure to show respect. Now her failure was beyond her control. She was to be punished by this uniformed man, a mere boy for that matter, for her failure to be born a Christian. Did he not grasp the absurdity of the situation? Did he not understand how contrary to the very principles of Christianity this Nazi aggression against the Jews was by any interpretation of their New Testament? Did he not understand that he had bullied his way into their residence with the same entitled assault of a home invader coming for their money and valuables? Of course, he did not. He was barely old enough to have possessed either money or valuables. He would have been playing hide and seek not long ago, when she was watching Ervin do the same.

He was some mother's child, grown to push his way into their home and summon them to his bidding.

"Anyone else?" he demanded.

"No, there are only the two of us," Joseph said.

"Children?"

"One, in the Labor Service," Joseph replied.

"Your names," he demanded, and Joseph told him.

"Profession."

"Dentist," Joseph said.

The man turned from Joseph and glared at Kamilla, who said, "housewife." Satisfied, he ordered them not to leave Győr.

"We shoot Jews who try to flee," he said, and then departed.

Like a child, Kamilla thought. Like a child playing with a loaded gun.

How she wanted to hold her own child. To know he was safe. To protect him. Somehow. Some way. From whatever horror was ahead of them. Until they could be together again.

The gendarme handed her two large yellow patches in the shape of stars. "You will sew these onto the front of your clothes. You will wear them at all times. If you are seen without them, you will be arrested. Do you understand?"

Kamilla nodded and took the stars in her trembling hands.

In the days that followed, they left the house only when necessary to buy food. What food there was could only be found by waiting in line for hours or purchased on the black market, since the Nazis had plundered the shelves of anything they could get ahold of. The streets were filled with gendarmes, riding on motorcycles or in trucks, patrolling everything and everyone with a level of aggression only found in groups where no one individual can be held accountable. As for the citizens of Győr, everyone wanted to talk to their neighbors and friends about what was happening, yet everyone was afraid to do so. Already they'd enacted the law requiring all Jewish citizens to wear the stigmatizing yellow armbands, and now the yellow stars, which only contributed that much more to the harsh treatment and shunning they endured in public. Even among other Jews, the tension was great. No one could be trusted and nobody was safe. The streets were filled with posters featuring Hitler's face, warnings to be wary of Jews, warnings not to defy the authorities, warnings to report neighbors, friends, even family members, if suspected of anti-German sentiments. A curfew forced everyone in at night and all windows had to be closed and lights shut off so that no allied aircraft might use the lights for navigation.

As for Joseph's business, it was no more. When he returned to his lab, he saw a sign on the door condemning the business as closed. Once he opened the door, he saw that his office and laboratory had been stripped bare. Standing in the wreckage of his life's work, he was devastated but not surprised. He was thankful he had at least hidden his drill, but he made no effort to retrieve it because unlikely as it was, he could not be sure he wasn't being watched. He'd earlier taken steps to safeguard his dental gold, knowing it would have value even in the most treacherous of times. He merely closed the door and walked away, accepting that the practice he'd invested so much money and so many years in building up had been stolen from him in an instant.

Joseph and Kamilla desperately wanted to reach Ervin, but they knew that was not possible. More than anything they wanted to ensure that Ervin would be safe, but with Joseph's practice closed and his equipment and supplies seized, he could no longer provide the guards with free dental care, something he'd been doing for the last few months, when it wasn't money he gave them. But now there was no more money coming in and most of his savings had been left in the care of trusted Christian friends—and he could only pray they could be trusted with such assets. At the very least, however, they wanted to tell Ervin that they loved him and that they would be reunited once again as soon as the war was over. One evening, shortly after the occupation, Joseph sat at his desk and penned a letter, a single tear falling on the page, and then he sealed it. Stepping outside to mail it, he had not even reached the post office before a gendarme had confiscated the letter with a victorious sneer.

Joseph returned home knowing that his son would not receive the letter, nor any other letter that he sent.

ALONE

Just as spring was approaching, everything worsened for Ervin. Although they had no access to radios and were completely cut off from news of the outside world, the triumph of Hitler's army was celebrated by the guards who welcomed the Nazis' command in Hungary. Overnight, their behavior changed drastically, and they did everything they could to make the lives of the Jewish men even more miserable. The men would be yanked from their cold pallets on the floor in the middle of the night, stripped bare, and left outside in the bitter cold while their barracks were searched. Their boots and shoes were inspected nightly and if any were the least bit dirty, the poor man had to report to the guards' quarters where the moment he passed through the door, a blanket was thrown over his head and the guards would kick and beat the man until they tired of the entertainment.

Yet no matter how brutal the beatings, the men never spoke of their ordeal. To return to the barracks beaten and bloody was testimony enough.

At times, however, the injuries suffered were so great that Ervin could not imagine remaining a moment longer. One such beating that impressed upon him the sadistic nature of the guards more so than any beating he himself had suffered—and he suffered enough to endure them with the same stoicism and patience he endured the urination, the hunger, and the constant humiliation—was that of an unfortunate man named Frigyes. Ervin didn't know him well, as the teams changed so often that Ervin had learned not to get too close to anyone other than Frank and Mike, but this man had made an impression on him. Frigyes was a gifted musician who often spoke of his dreams of becoming a professional conductor once he was freed. Ervin had warm memories of enjoying classical music with his family, so he respected Frigyes's talent and dreams.

Unfortunately, Frigyes had done something—Ervin never knew what—to provoke the ire of the guards, who beat him so badly that he lost his hearing. Had he lost his life, Ervin imagined, he would have been more blessed, for his spirit seemed to be wholly crushed from that day forward and he worked as if he were no longer a man, but a mule, despondent, unthinking, unaware of anything but the muffled commands of the guards. Ervin hoped he still heard his beloved music in his mind and had escaped to a safer place inside his now silent world.

With the occupation of Hungary, Ervin knew he would be cut off from his parents. None of the men heard from their parents after it, though all wrote letters, delivering the frantic missives to the guards, who took them with a snicker. While they knew their correspondence was always read, whether sent or received, they now wondered if they would be mailed at all. Nonetheless, whenever he had a scrap of energy left to write, Ervin did so, praying that the letters would reach his parents.

"Have you heard anything from my father?" Ervin asked János one evening, knowing the answer even before he'd asked the question.

"Who?" the guard asked, not looking directly at Ervin.

"My father, Dr. Wolf," he replied.

"Never heard of him," he lied, turning his back on Ervin. From that day forward, any kindness János had ever shown Ervin was past, though he showed no cruelty. He had simply ceased to be bribed, and thus his duties toward Ervin had been concluded, limited as they were. Ervin had been cut off completely from his family.

Within weeks of the occupation, in April, Ervin was sent to the village center of Nagyberezna to obtain supplies, where he noticed a large crowd of Jewish people had gathered in the synagogue's courtyard. They were carrying pillows, baskets, and worn-out luggage held together with rope. Something was going on, though Ervin wasn't sure what. An unmistakable sense of mourning filled the air. The courtyard was packed with people, but they were, to a man, silent. An electrifying fright shot through him, and Ervin hastily wrote a letter to his parents urging them to escape. *"I fear they are being sent somewhere,"* he wrote, *"and it is only a matter of time before they do the same to you, mother and father. Please leave now!"*

With no guards to review his correspondence, he hoped the letter would reach his parents unaltered. The following week, he received a curt, four-line letter suggesting his parents had received it. Though allegedly written by his father, and the handwriting appeared to be his, the words were so uncharacteristic, he feared someone had dictated the response.

Do not worry, they possibly came over illegally and were turned back. Nothing can happen to us. We are solid, well-established citizens of Hungary. I was highly decorated, fighting for my country.

Ervin felt more concerned than relieved, as he could not imagine the author of the letter to be his father.

For the first time in his short life, Ervin realized he was utterly alone.

TWENTY-FIVE KILOS

The Nazis returned in May, this time, through an order from the mayor of Győr, Jeno Koller, for all Jews of the city to relocate to Győrsziget. The gendarmes went door to door, knocking furiously, breaking down doors, ordering everyone inside to step outside. Joseph and Kamilla heard their heavy boots coming up the staircase. They looked at each other, terror in both their eyes. Joseph took Kamilla's hands and had only time to say, "I love you," before the pounding hit their door and seconds later, the door itself flew open with a thunderous crack.

"Get your things," a soldier ordered. "Twenty-five kilos. No more."

Kamilla had no idea what to take. Twenty-five kilos? It was a weight at once too heavy to carry, yet barely more than a few possessions. Would she forever relinquish what she left behind? The broken door was answer enough for her. She was to leave her home unsecured to go to an unknown place.

"Pack your clothes and toiletries," Joseph told her, as he hurried to his office to pack his own small suitcase of belongings. A soldier followed him, watching his every move, making it impossible to retrieve the cyanide he'd saved in the event they were forced to take their own lives. He cursed himself for his foolishness. How could he so carefully plan for the worst, and then not be prepared for it when needed? But of course, it wouldn't come to that. He'd likely be beaten, perhaps even tortured, but he'd endure. He had to for Kamilla. They both had to for Ervin. They would endure whatever was coming. Of course, they'd lose everything. While Joseph had been able to hide some money with Christian friends who he trusted to safeguard it, it was not a great deal, as the costs of providing Ervin with the necessary clothing and supplies had been great, and the bribes to the guards even greater. He and Kamilla would have to begin anew once again, wherever it was they were sent. Hopefully, Ervin would not be subjected too harshly to the brutalities of the guards once Joseph could no longer pay to protect him.

Carrying their heavy suitcases, they leave their home as once friendly Christian neighbors taunt them and cheer the removal of "dirty Jews" from the neighborhood. Along with other Jewish neighbors, Joseph and Kamilla are marched to what the soldiers call the ghetto, a term neither Joseph nor Kamilla had heard before. But they recognized the place. It was Győrsziget, where they'd briefly lived. It had changed dramatically since. They saw that the community, once clean and lively, had been transformed into a mass encampment. Győr's nearly 5,000 Jews were corralled like cattle into the small neighborhood, where Kamilla and Joseph joined several other families in a makeshift shack in the courtyard of some apartment buildings. The apartments themselves were wide open with families crammed inside them. They, like all the buildings in the Jewish community, had been stripped of any furnishings or other valuables. What was left of these buildings, once homes and offices, were mere shells. What would become of their own home, they could only guess, but from the looks of the stripped-down home they now inhabited, the couple assumed that they would have no home to return to.

Joseph and Kamilla introduced themselves to the other families, though everyone was in such a state of shock that names could not be retained. They spoke of their shared predicament, their fears, their optimism. They prayed.

The streets were swarming with gendarmes who patrolled every block. They had established a perimeter beyond which no Jews were allowed. The few who dared breach the perimeter met with vicious beatings, clearly intended to send a message to everyone that they were now captive.

Walking in those streets with Kamilla, Joseph surveilled the situation. As a doctor, he knew he would likely be called upon to treat those who panicked and those who fell ill. If they remained like this for long, he reasoned, many would fall ill for contagion cannot be controlled in such crowded, stifling spaces. The big question, however, was food. Unable to leave Győrsziget, few could work. Even most of those who had originally lived and worked in the community had been forbidden from making a living, their businesses closed. This was an urban environment, not much food was grown or produced in the few small gardens the inhabitants had kept. Any food would have to be brought in, and for that, they were at the mercy of the Nazis.

As the days passed, a black market of sorts emerged and people traded whatever they had for any scrap of food, toilet paper, or clean diapers. There was little to eat, and what came to them reached them through undisclosed networks—guards who had been bribed, perhaps, and occasionally small children would sneak out and bring back what they could pilfer. More and more people arrived and the packed courtyard where Joseph and Kamilla were housed became even more crowded. The cries of young children were near unbearable, and the terror in the eyes of the elderly who looked so frail they might collapse altogether made it clear to the middle-aged couple that they were among the luckier of their lot. Joseph and Kamilla huddled close together, each one thinking, but not saying, how grateful they were that Ervin was no longer a child forced into this hellish world.

How long they would be compelled to live like this was anybody's guess.

"We'll get through this," Joseph assured Kamilla. "They can't manage this many people for very long."

Kamilla was already too weak and shocked to do more than nod. Nothing had prepared her for this moment, to see humans stockpiled like a nest of fishermen's worms. The stench from human waste was already overpowering and no one could properly bathe, other than to wash up, without soap, in the filthy basins they shared with dozens of others. Is this what is meant by the sacrifice of war? Kamilla wondered. Are we to emerge from this hell victorious and proud? Somehow, she doubted this inhumanity was normal even in times of war. She knew only that she had to endure until she could hold her son once again.

The few belongings people had brought were soon gone, bartered away, or stolen, often seized by guards who routinely beat their captives for minor infractions or for no reason at all. People fell ill in the streets, weak from hunger or, as Joseph feared, infectious disease. He, along with the other doctors held captive, treated as many as they could, but with no medicines, supplies, or equipment, there was little that could be done. To be so powerless to help was something Joseph had not known since the First World War and, even then, he had encountered nothing of this sort. No enemy could be this inhumane, but with every passing day it became apparent that this was an enemy unlike any he'd ever known. This was an enemy not to an opposing military, but to humankind itself. This enemy was a force of evil.

By mid-June, Joseph's suspicion that they could not maintain this wretched ghetto much longer proved true. One afternoon they were all ordered to leave Győrsziget and board a train. They were told they were going to work in the vineyards. A collective sense of hope swept through the captive population, and Kamilla felt a profound relief.

"It will be hard work, but we shall be in the open air. We'll get through this," she said, as much to herself as to Joseph.

Joseph merely nodded as he held her gaze. He was not so sure. The couple clung together as never before, praying they'd endure until the war ended.

They marched, along with 5,000 other Jews, to the train station, arriving at dusk. Once there, their few belongings were seized yet again. This time, however, they were given receipts for their valuables so that they could reclaim them later. Joseph and Kamilla turned in their bedclothes, their wedding rings, and Joseph his watch, which he'd somehow managed to hold onto. His pocketknife was long gone, having been exchanged for two tins of fish in the ghetto. Once the gendarmes were satisfied that the two harbored no other valuables, they were pushed and shoved into cattle cars on a train already packed with Jews from other cities. "These are all we have left," the gendarmes barked, "the other trains are all full." The doors to the cattle cars clanged shut and they were packed, body against body, in the pitch-black cars. The only light that shone came through a single barred window.

Where were they going? They would not be sent like this to work in vineyards. Something was wrong. When would they see their son again? It could be months, years even. But Joseph was certain the allies would set them free. They'd be refugees, but they'd get through this. They had to.

Kamilla clung to Joseph, though neither said a word. There was no longer any word to say. They would endure in silence and, though they might be separated, when this horror passed, they'd reunite.

The car was stifling. Designed for cattle, there were no seats, nor anything to hang onto, though there were so many people packed into a single car that it was impossible to fall. Impossible, as well, to breathe, for the only small window was cracked open and people jostled and fought for positions near it. The stench of an open bucket for human waste fouled the air and Kamilla was thankful she'd had so little water she had no need of it.

As the train lurched and commenced its journey in the darkness, the panic began. Those near the window tried desperately to break the bars so that they might leap out, but the bars held tight.

"They're going to kill us!" many wailed, terrified and helpless.

"Shut up!" others cried, "They won't kill us! We'll be sent to a labor camp."

"You don't know that!"

Children wailed for their parents to take them home.

The cries, the arguments, the desperation, the thirst, and the stifling, suffocating heat were unbearable.

Kamilla was, once again, so thankful that Ervin was grown and, she prayed, safe at his camp. How sorry she was for the mothers of young children, for she couldn't imagine how they coped. How could one comfort their child in such a horrific situation? As her body jostled back and forth in the darkness for mile after mile, night after night, as some fought desperately and hopelessly to flee the sealed car, she came to notice through the sliver of moonlight that lit the dark car, a young girl, no more than six or seven, crushed amidst the bodies of adults who towered over her. Her eyes, illuminated as if by God, were as sad as they were large, and the pale skin and dark circles under her eyes spoke of hunger and exhaustion. Kamilla's eyes fixed on hers and after a few moments, the child pushed her way through the mass of bodies toward Kamilla. Once there, she simply took Kamilla's hand and stood in silence.

"Is your *anya* here?" Kamilla asked, using the familiar Hungarian term. She was afraid the small girl had been separated from her parents.

"No," said a small voice in the darkness.

"Your *apu*?"

Again the tiny voice told her, "No."

For the next few nights, they stood together, jostling toward their unknown destination, as Joseph whispered prayers to Kamilla and words of undying love.

Five days later, when the train finally reached its destination, the hordes of prisoners were ordered out, with many beaten mercilessly as they did so. Kamilla, Joseph, and the little girl held tight to each other's hands and, as the crowd was corralled into a massive human queue, Joseph and Kamilla saw with horror thousands upon thousands of men, women, and even children who looked more like skeletons than living people. They were all dressed in red and white striped pajamas and walked with their bare and shaven heads bowed, any trace of spirit long drained from them. Everywhere they looked it was the same, people so fragile they seemed as if they had crawled from the grave, yet carrying or pushing heavy loads, walking as they were beaten with sticks and whips, moving through space as ghosts being driven away. Soldiers walked up and down with snarling dogs, looking for someone or something, as they shouted at the people to keep moving. They had arrived at Auschwitz.

Seeing the multitudes of emaciated prisoners being so cruelly beaten, Kamilla gasped and pulled the little girl closer to her, while turning to Joseph to share her horror.

"We must be strong, my love," he said, though he did not feel strong, not at all. If this was the life ahead of them, it was no life, nor was it even survivable. They would surely be beaten, surely be fed nothing that could sustain them, and the sheer mass of humans, most visibly sick, made it clear that contagion would be impossible to avoid.

"I can't—" Kamilla began, but Joseph interrupted her.

"I love you with all my heart, my dear. I know that I have not always been the man you deserved. But I have tried. I have never stopped loving you or Ervin and—" But it was Kamilla's turn to interrupt.

"You have been a wonderful husband and father, Joseph, more than I ever could have asked for." The words fell from her mouth without thought and she felt her heart burn to hear herself speaking in past tense, as if they were about to part forever. But the horror that surrounded them was so unspeakably ghastly that the words felt as reassuring to say as to hear. Their murmurings continued as they found themselves bidding each other farewell, just as they also assured each other that they'd survive this horror.

"Where are we going?" the small girl asked in a voice so weak and terrified, Kamilla wanted to swoop her into her arms. But she was already too weak to do so.

"I don't know, honey. I don't know." She caressed the child's shoulders and hair as the queue began to move. Exhausted after standing all night in the swaying, lurching cattle car, painfully hungry, and their throats parched, their bodies obeyed the order to keep moving. At long last, they reached what appeared to be the point of registration.

Kamilla gasped yet again when she saw a small, ridiculously attired figure standing at the camp gates as if a doorman, saluting each Nazi who passed by. He appeared to be some sort of comic prop whose very presence heightened the surreal atmosphere.

"Joseph!" Kamilla said, nodding toward him.

"My Lord, what have they done to him?" Joseph asked in shock and horror. "That can't be Zoli, Ervin's clown?"

"But it is," Kamilla said as her voice cracked. But no tears fell for she had no tears left to give.

Poor Zoli, the stage name of Zoltán Hirsch, the Jewish dwarf, had been reduced to the grave humiliation of welcoming the Nazis while dressed as a garish clown—though this time, it was not a dress of his own making, but the perverted costume of an imprisoned clown. Now forced to perform this tragic ritual that transformed him from a respected artist who brought laughter to children and adults alike, he'd become a laughingstock for those who felt no joy.

As they drew closer to him, the men were ordered in one line, the women and children in another. Kamilla turned to Joseph and, as his sad eyes looked into hers with fear and love, Kamilla's eyes slipped from Joseph's far too soon. The human tides pulled them apart, hundreds of women moving in one direction, hundreds of men in another. They were pushing her so quickly, compelling her to move on, move on, as if she were in line for the theater. She'd known that at some point she and Joseph would probably be separated, but it had happened so quickly, so harshly. When would she see him again? What would they do to him? What would they do to her now that she was their captive? Hard labor, yes. Beatings, undoubtedly. Rape? She wouldn't let her mind go there.

Kamilla noticed that the line of women was also splitting, with some women directed to the left, others to the right, though from her vantage point, she couldn't discern what was happening. She could only move along, holding the hand of the small, motherless child who gave Kamilla as much comfort as she gave the child. Soon they reached a slender man of medium height who wore a sneer of a smile as devilish as it was cold. Leaning down and offering a piece of candy, the man spoke to the little girl who gripped Kamilla's hand tightly.

"Hello, little girl, would you like a sweet?"

Kamilla's soul chilled to the bone, as the little girl held out her hand and accepted the sweet—undoubtedly the first thing she'd eaten in days.

"You can go in that line," he told her, his tone turning colder as he nodded toward the line on the right. "I shall see you soon."

"I don't want to go," she said, looking up to Kamilla, wrapping her arms around Kamilla's legs. "Come with me!"

The officer barked at some soldiers to take the girl away and, in an instant, she was pried from Kamilla and taken away crying.

Then he looked Kamilla up and down quickly as if surveying a fish at the market, and with a flick of his hand, motioned for her to go to the left.

Joseph moved ahead in his own procession, eventually reaching the Nazi officer. Speaking in German, the officer demanded to know Joseph's profession. Joseph answered, in fluent German, that he was a medical doctor and dentist. The officer turned to a guard and, in German, said, "He can clean the latrines."

In that moment, Joseph knew that his medical training would not save him. The sickness was everywhere as all about, emaciated men and women passed back and forth, some collapsing, others filthy from their own waste, far too many barely able to put one foot ahead of the other. Many were stripped naked, their skin hanging from their meatless skeletons. Vultures circled overhead awaiting the next corpse to fall. These were terribly sick people. Cleaning their latrines would hasten his own death, for there would be no possibility of surviving the contagion. Dysentery was ubiquitous.

Joseph obediently followed the guard to his destiny, all the while praying for the safety of Kamilla, and for his own miraculous survival.

The little girl. So small, so alone. It broke Kamilla's heart to see them take her away like that. She couldn't imagine what they'd do to her, couldn't imagine her fear. The rage at their inhumanity was so great, but she didn't dare go there, for to even think of it brought her such pain. She had to survive, just get through these next months. She let her thoughts return to Ervin, how small he had once been, how innocent and joyful. How she prayed that he was safe, and how thankful she was that he was not here in this dreadful camp of horrors.

Moving forward, the women all wore the same face of stoic

resolve. At last, they were directed to a barracks where a large woman with cold eyes immediately ordered the women to strip naked.

"After your baths and delousing you can have some coffee," she said, a hint of kindness to her voice. Perhaps here it would be better than the ghetto, Kamilla considered, though still dubious. What delousing would entail, she wasn't sure. All she knew was that it would not matter that she had no lice. They would douse her with their foul chemicals regardless. Slowly, Kamilla peeled her clothing away and, with each piece of fabric that fell from her flesh, she felt the degradation commence. Each woman was similarly humiliated, but there was nothing they could do. They would either comply or their clothes would be stripped off them by others. No doubt they'd be forced to wear some hideous uniform, something ill-fitting and rough. She just had to get through this moment.

Once naked, her arms wrapped around her body to shield herself, they were ordered outside to proceed to the delousing station. They were marched, still naked, across the camp's grounds, humiliated and terrified, to be sprayed for lice. Kamilla had not prepared herself for this subjugation, she had no reference for it. Nothing in her life had been as heartless, as debasing. Had they done this to Ervin? Were they doing the same to that poor little girl? No doubt they'd do the same to Joseph, though he'd hold up, she was sure. Still, she knew he'd be demeaned and she couldn't bear to think it. As the line moved, Kamilla dared look about her at the other women and she realized all were older, some near ancient, others like herself, just 50, but old enough. There were few young women, save for a couple of pregnant women and one poor woman hobbling as if a cripple without her cane. It had been taken from her, no doubt.

Gradually, nearly imperceptibly, the realization came to her. They were the old, the infirm, the useless. The women who didn't matter. Why should they care that the women suffered with lice when they hadn't cared that they starved or were sickened? They were not marching them to the delousing station. No, this degrading march wasn't the beginning of their ordeal. It was the end of it.

As they drew closer to the giant iron doors through which they were to pass, the panic began to swell in the line of women like a wave washing over them. By the time they reached their destination, pure terror had firmly set in. Some screamed, others tried to break free, but the guards drove them onward with clubs and whips slashing their bare skin. As Kamilla was moved by the force of the crowd toward the doors to the concrete chamber, her mind raced with prayers for her soul, prayers for her son, prayers for her husband, prayers for her mother and father. As her naked body reached the doors, the force of hundreds of other naked bodies pushed her inside, the screams now shattering her prayers until she realized her own screams were among them. The heavy metal door clanged shut, with the bare flesh of the screaming women pressed so tightly together that there was barely room even to turn, though they did try as they pushed and clawed their way to the doors, trying desperately, hopelessly, to open them. Wedged tightly among the panicking women, Kamilla tipped her head upward toward a small light that shone into the darkness. There she saw, to her horror, a head concealed in a gas mask peering down at them through an open hatch. The masked man poured something through the hatch and shut it tightly closed.

Joseph hadn't heard the screams, for the concrete chamber muffled much of the terrifying sounds, and the barking dogs and orchestra obscured the rest. He was puzzled by the orchestra, so out of place in this camp of horrors. Yet it had commenced playing not long after he had arrived and played with a fury, growing ever louder by the moment. There was beauty in the sound and, at the same time, a macabre quality, as if those playing were, like the unfortunate Zoli, forced to perform a surreal mimicry of their skills. As the music grew louder, the stench increased—it was a stench he knew well, the stench of burning flesh. He hadn't smelled such a thing since the last war, but it was unmistakable. Bodies were burning.

Ordered to strip, his head and body were shaved and a foul chemical—to kill any lice—rubbed over him. He stood silently, his head high, as he was subjected to the demeaning act. He kept his thoughts on Kamilla, wondering how she was doing. No doubt they were doing the same to her, humiliating his dear wife. They would shave her head, as well, he presumed, for he had seen the emaciated women in the red and white pajamas walking in shame. He understood the shaving. With so many people forced to live and sleep and eat together, lice would spread. Shaving would limit the lice. As well, it would debase the prisoners, and that, after all, was the point.

After being given the requisite red and white striped pajamas, Joseph, now unmistakably a prisoner for the crime of his Jewish birth, was given some burnt coffee and a heel of bread. Then he was shown to the latrines.

It was then that he first noticed great plumes of dark smoke rising from the chimneys and he knew at once that they were the source of the stench of burning bodies. They were cremating the prisoners as they died, he concluded, for they were dying so rapidly, burial wasn't feasible. Would he and Kamilla be among them? He prayed Kamilla could survive, even if he couldn't.

Once presented with the latrines, he could not deny his fate. The toilets were comprised of a long board into which two long rows of holes had been cut, more than 30 in all, and below was a pit no more than six or seven feet deep and already nearly filled. This board was where the sick and exhausted men sat, side by side, back-to-back, eliminating their waste. The stink was near unbearable—these men had diarrhea and dysentery. Their bloodied waste and vomit were everywhere, on the boards, the floors, even the walls. The sun not having yet set on his first day at Auschwitz, Joseph was handed a mop and a bucket and ordered to get to work. Not like a prisoner. Not even like a dog. The doctor, the war hero, the man who'd raised a son and loved a wife, had lived a life of refined elegance and wealth, obediently cleaned the waste of the sick and dying.

The only grace to the humiliation was that the Nazi officers would not enter such a foul and wretched space, so he was spared their presence. But he knew it was only a matter of days before he himself would fall ill, for how could he avoid contagion in such conditions? Tuberculosis, typhoid, rubella. All were rampant. Over the next few days, as he worked without strength, without food, with barely enough water to survive, the other prisoners, safe from the prying eyes of the guards as they defecated in the latrines, discussed the rumors. That the smell was not just from the burning of dead bodies, but from the burning of the living, as well. That the smoke from the chambers was poisonous gas used to kill entire trainloads of people. That even children were being tortured and used in horrifying experiments.

Joseph listened to these rumors, initially rejecting them as impossible to believe. Slowly, however, his disbelief weakened as the unrestrained sadism of their captors showed no limits. Even more troubling was what he didn't see. Passing to and from his barracks and the latrines, he scanned the grounds for any sight of Kamilla. He saw women, mostly young ones, but not his dear wife, nor anyone who even looked like her. Not one older woman. What had they done to her? Where were they keeping her?

When, on his third day, Joseph no longer saw Zoli saluting the Nazis at the gate, he heard that he'd been sent to the chambers to die.

"They arrested him because his star wasn't big enough," one of the captive men explained. "He'd had it made to fit his suit; proportional you know? Well, the Nazis didn't give a damn. They arrested him anyway."

"Yeah, and they killed him because he wasn't a genetic dwarf like the others. They like to put the dwarves on display. You'll see them out here dressed like aristocrats at a picnic one day, naked and standing on stage the next. But poor Zoli, he wasn't born a dwarf, he got rickets as a kid. That's why they had no interest in him. So once they tired of humiliating him, they sent him off to the gas chamber."

Joseph found the rumors beyond credulity. And yet, the sadism of the guards was beyond anything he'd witnessed in war. Could the rumors be true? He wondered if Kamilla had been sent to the chambers, but he didn't allow himself to finish the thought. She was strong. They'd put her to work. Of course they would. She'd one day be freed and find Ervin. The two would live a good life once the Allies came. But he knew he would not be joining them. His medical training had stripped him of that hope, for he was sure the job he'd been assigned was not survivable.

By the end of his first week, when the fever came, he was almost relieved. Death would free him. As he grew sicker, the abuse grew greater, for he was beaten and whipped into continuing the work, scrubbing the latrines as his body failed and his strength waned.

His last thoughts, as he lay dying in the human waste he could no longer clean away, was of his wife and son, as he prayed that they'd survive this hellish cruelty that he could not.

PART II
IT'S BETTER NOT TO KNOW

RETREAT

The brutal winter had passed and in its place came the sweltering heat of the summer. They'd been working on the drainage system for months and now with the job nearly done, that strange mix of relief and dread that came with each pending change permeated the minds of every man. No one knew where the next assignment would take them, whether new and kinder guards would arrive, or new and crueler guards, whether the new assignment would ease their daily misery or intensify it. And it was that uncertainty that lingered like a menacing shadow, upping the anxiety as each day passed.

Added to the anxiety was a sense of hope. Rumors spread from the guards to the men that Romania had turned against Hitler and joined the Allies in their efforts to bring him down. As for Hungary, still under Horthy's rule, hopes were high among the men that he, too, would turn against Hitler, after a couple of the guards had been grumbling that he wanted to surrender to the Soviets—a move that only emboldened the captors to become angrier and more brutal. But the men held out hopes that as much as they distrusted the Soviets, surrendering to the communists had to be better than being a Jew under Nazi rule.

Ervin had been in the Labor Service for close to a year and in that time, he had transformed from a skinny weakling to a muscular, fit man. He could now work with the best of them, and where once he was ridiculed for his laziness, now he was admired for his fortitude and the clever ways he found food. But there were no more baskets from home to share, not from his mother, nor from any man's mother. Their parents had been shut off from contact, probably taken somewhere, that much was clear, but whether that was somewhere in Hungary or somewhere in Germany was anybody's guess. Most likely, they surmised, they'd been sent to a labor camp or prison where they'd remain for the rest of the war. It was painful to contemplate, yet Ervin was confident the war could not continue much longer. The Allies would defeat Germany and Hungary would, with time, return to its former glory. He just prayed that his parents weren't being worked too hard or treated too harshly.

They were laying the cement pipes in an open area when the first of the Russian aircraft opened fire. It was quiet and peaceful one moment, and in the next, the earth exploded as bullets rained down upon them. For a second, Ervin couldn't grasp what was happening, but as his workmates scrambled and screamed for everyone to take cover, he needed no further prompting and dove into the nearest concrete pipe. They were fully exposed in the open field, but thankfully, the concrete pipes were large enough and near enough for everyone to dive into. Whether they would provide protection against the attack, however, only fate would determine.

As they hid, the world shattering all around them, Ervin instinctively reached for the clover pendant his parents had given him, which he still wore around his neck. Holding the charm in his hand, he prayed to live, to see his parents again, to survive this attack. As he prayed, the aircraft flew even lower, machine gunning their area with a vengeance before flying off as suddenly as they'd arrived. A deafening silence settled in the wake of the attack, but it was still another few minutes before anyone dared to crawl out of the pipes. Once standing, Ervin saw that one of his fellow laborers, a hard-working young man who planned to marry his girlfriend once his service was over, lay dead on the ground. He was barely recognizable from the savage trauma he'd suffered. *At least it was quick,* Ervin thought. In this twisted world he was now living in, he had learned to find the kernel of gratitude that lay in every horror, for he knew that no matter how bad things were, they always could and would worsen. Oh, how he couldn't wait to go home. This poor man's parents would never see him again. Ervin couldn't bear to think of his own parents receiving such news. As for news, he wished that he would have some, to be assured his parents were okay. He had no idea where they were or how they were. He knew nothing of their fate.

In the weeks that followed, he noticed an increasing number of Germans in the area. They usually didn't bother the laborers, but for one drunken officer who had shown up at the camp one day running around with a gun threatening to kill everyone in sight. Fortunately, the guards were able to calm him and take him away, but the incident impressed upon Ervin how precarious life was. For so long, it had been the guards he feared, yet now there were these random characters armed with deadly weapons, ignorance, and drink who could, at a moment's whim, end their life for no other reason than that they thought it funny. It was said that survival went to the fittest, but Ervin was beginning to believe that more often than not, survival was a matter of being the luckiest.

Being cut off from news made it even more difficult to make sense of the world, but in some ways, Ervin was relieved. As much as the uncertainty gnawed at him, he feared that if he knew what was happening, he might succumb to even greater anxiety, as his father had by listening to the radio each night, his ear pressed to the speaker like a suction cup. He admired his father's interest in the events of the day, the political acts and shifts, yet he was also concerned that his father was becoming too worried by what he heard. He looked forward to the day when the war was over and the only thing his father listened to on the radio was the classical music he so loved.

Ervin really missed that music himself, as well as the many popular Hungarian numbers. More than news of the outside world, he'd give anything to be able to turn on a radio and listen to the beautiful classical music and opera that his mother had listened to each Sunday afternoon at half-past one. He hadn't always appreciated the melodies, but now that even music was gone from his world, he longed to hear it again. He missed its calming effects and thought how sensible it would be for the guards to allow the laborers some soothing tunes. But sensible wasn't in their vocabulary, for punishment trumped everything. To deprive the men of music was as unquestionable as depriving them of freedom. They were to have neither.

Each Sunday afternoon as he labored in the fields, the trenches, or wherever, Ervin lost himself in memories of those Sunday operatic broadcasts. He imagined his mother's face, so relaxed and lost in the imaginary world the singers conjured up, and knew that the next time he saw her, they would share once again in the entertainment of a peaceful Sunday afternoon.

"Line up!" It was the new commander, Oláh, a malignant, unforgiving man who was always angry. He'd been called out of retirement and so resented his assignment that it was as if he were determined to punish every last man for it. What was worse, his flagrant hostility had influenced the other guards who saw his bullying, punitive approach to command as either permission to unleash their own aggressions or a warning that they ought do so lest they themselves become targets of their commander's anger.

The captive men immediately obeyed Oláh's order, leaving their shovels and pickaxes where they lay and scrambling to line up and stand straight and tall at attention.

"Which one of you animals was talking?" Oláh demanded. "Animals don't speak, so all you animals who were speaking, step forward!"

It was true someone had been talking and any utterance while working was strictly forbidden. Still, it was impossible not to converse, as they were working together and needed to occasionally communicate just to get the job done. They also had to communicate to mentally survive and, for the most part, occasional words exchanged were overlooked. But not by Oláh. Ever since he'd arrived in midsummer, they'd worked in absolute silence. It was now September, the weather cooler but not yet freezing so the work more bearable, but the atmosphere of silence and dread so great that every hour had become more intolerable than the summer's heat or the winter's chill.

"I said," Oláh hissed, barely above a whisper, "which of you animals were speaking?"

Again, absolute silence. No one dare admit guilt.

"Well, what do you know? Now none of the pigs can speak!" Oláh said to the guards, all standing by snickering as if they enjoyed the spectacle of the men's fear and intimidation. "What do you say we punish these cowards properly?" he asked rhetorically, to which the guards all laughed in agreement. Turning to the men, Oláh said, "You know what the punishment for cowards is, don't you?"

Silence hung over the men so heavily that only their breath could be heard.

"You ever hear of decimation?" Oláh strode back and forth in front of the men, lined up at attention but most shaking in fear, Ervin most of all. He was terrified, but knew that to give in to his terror, to let it be noticed in the slight, would be fatal. He drew on his childhood memories of hiding under the table to escape his father's fury, crouched so tightly he felt even smaller than his father's shiny black shoes, so close he could touch them if he dared. Instead, he had learned to accept both his punishment and his survival, to know that if he was indeed pulled out from under that table, he would feel pain, yes, but the pain would pass. If he kept his focus on surviving past the pain, on envisioning a future after that, he knew he could face his fear. Inevitably, his father's shiny black shoes would step away from the table and he could, in time, crawl out. But sometimes, if his father was furious, he'd be found, dragged out sobbing and pleading for mercy, given a good whipping, and then sent to his room. And by morning, the pain would be gone, along with the tears, and his father would once again be the loving father he truly was. It was knowing that safe future lay just beyond the pain that gave Ervin strength in his moments of fear.

And it was envisioning a future past their captivity, past their Labor Service, that Ervin focused on while Oláh marched back and forth, glaring at the men, his nostrils big as a horse's as he breathed in and out like a raging dragon.

"Decimation is a little game we play with cowards," he said, stopping in his tracks and staring straight into Ervin's eyes. Ervin hadn't been the one talking, not that time, but he felt as guilty as if he had, for it was clear the punishment would be inflicted on them all in one way or another. "And here's how we're going to play it. Every tenth one of you Jews is going to be shot dead and left for the vultures. That's what we do with cowards." Then he turned to the guards, nodded, and said, "Start counting them."

One of the guards stepped forward, his grin making clear his sadistic delight, and amidst the dead silence, started counting down the line of men, "One, two, three...." As the numbers grew higher, the fear grew greater and by the time he reached his first number ten, the poor man was near blubbering.

"No, please," he begged, but his cries only brought ridicule as he was ordered to step forward.

"18, 19, 20," and another man pulled from the line.

Ervin was thankful to see that Mike was spared, and a few moments later, Frank, as well. When they finally reached Ervin, he felt both immense relief and guilt as his number, 29, meant he would live. But the man beside him would die.

Is this what my father felt, Ervin wondered, when he spoke of choosing who would live and who would die? Is our fate truly so random as that?

The men were ordered back to work and those selected to die taken away. It was only later, after working the rest of the day in discomforting silence, that it was revealed the men weren't killed after all. Tortured, yes, but shot, no. They had been forced to labor for hours with large blocks of wood shoved in their mouths, a terrible ordeal but preferable to a bullet.

But the punishment had worked. They never spoke to each other while working after that day.

Though cut off from the news, by mid-October, such an unexpected chain of events ensued that the guards were talking openly about the affair and the fate of the nation. After announcing an armistice with the USSR, Horthy met with Soviet officials to negotiate a surrender. During that meeting, the Nazis kidnapped Horthy's son and held him for ransom until Horthy rescinded the armistice. Once he'd done so to spare his son's life, the Nazis removed Horthy from power and put in his place one of the most feared men of the day, Ferenc Szálasi, leader of the savage Arrow Cross. Szálasi then ordered the Hungarian Army to continue the fight against the Soviets.

Szálasi was a notorious and bloodthirsty antisemite who was determined to rid Hungary of its Jewish population through deportation and outright killing, a prospect that seemed to encourage many of the guards, while giving pause to a few. But those few were outnumbered by the more brutish majority as the men were now frequently threatened with deportation or death. The Arrow Cross Party swiftly rose from a marginalized party of misfits and bullies to become the dominant ruling party in the nation. Appealing to the working classes and the unemployed, the Arrow Cross persuaded those who had gained little to nothing from the conservative Horthy government that it was the Jews who were the cause of their poverty and troubles. The Jews were to be emaciated under Szálasi's rule and the guards were, for the most part, all too happy to do their part to make that happen.

By this time, food was scarce in the camp. What little they had they divided into two categories, edible and inedible. The inedible scraps, mostly byproducts of pork, were both forbidden by their religion for most, and included the most revolting parts of the pig—eyes, noses, uncleaned intestines. More common, however, was spoiled meat or moldy bread. To supplement their diets, they secured vegetable scraps from the local peasants—stalks of cabbage and cauliflower or potatoes so soft or bruised not even a poor peasant would eat them.

How Ervin missed his mother's baskets, the smoked meats, cheeses, biscuits, and sweets she would send. How he missed her and worried about her, as well, given the intensifying attacks against the Jews. He couldn't wait to see her again, even if it wasn't in their home, even if they were forced to live in the most wretched apartment in Győr. Wherever they ended up, he was confident she'd cook him the most delicious meal of his life the minute they were reunited once again.

By early November, just over a year since he'd first joined the Labor Service, Ervin began having difficulties with his boots. Though his father had secured for him the most durable footwear he could find, made of the strongest leather and soles and sewn with the heaviest thread, even those fine boots could not withstand a year of hard labor. The soles had cracked, and in both boots, holes had been worn clear through. The stitching was coming apart in one and neither could prevent water, mud, sticks, and stones from finding their way to Ervin's feet. As for socks, he hadn't had a new pair since he last saw his family, so despite the warm footwear he'd arrived with, Ervin's feet were now as unprotected as those of any other man—perhaps more so, as he hadn't developed the thick, calloused soles the others had. Like them, Ervin learned to use white cloths folded into triangular slings in place of socks. They were surprisingly adequate but insufficient for protecting his feet from the repetitive rubbing of the leather. Unsurprisingly, it wasn't long before Ervin's feet were covered in wounds and lacerations that made every step hurt. Soon, an infection had set into one of his toes and become so severe that he could barely walk. He had no choice but to report to medical care, something that was usually punished.

"You should have come here sooner," the doctor said with no hint of compassion. "At this point, there's nothing I can do. You'll have to go to the hospital in Szolnok. I can write the referral, but it will be up to your commander to approve it."

Ervin didn't hold out much hope of Oláh approving anything that might help a Jew, but he also knew that untreated, the infection would reach his blood and sepsis would kill him. A dead Jew would be one less worker, so he banked on the commander's reason, not his compassion, in approving the referral. Still, he knew that the treatment might mean amputation and, while that would get him off hard labor, he had no idea what the alternative might be. It certainly wouldn't be his freedom.

"I don't give a damn if your feet hurt," the commander said when

Ervin gave him the physician's referral. "You think you're the only swine here with bad feet?"

Ervin didn't say anything, for there was nothing to say. Either he'd receive treatment or he wouldn't. After a long minute of silence, during which Oláh merely stared at the referral as if it were a cryptic code, he finally said, "I've got a couple of others who need to go there, so I'll send you all together. You'll be accompanied by an armed guard to and from the hospital. You try anything, he'll spear you with his bayonet like a stuck pig without a second thought. You got that?"

"Yes, sir," Ervin replied, more relieved than insulted. It was no longer possible to insult the men, for they'd been called every imaginable vulgarity so many times that by that point, the insults were mere noise. It was the threats, direct or implicit, that they paid attention to.

As Ervin was packing his things the next morning, the men were called to order. Oláh had an announcement.

"We'll be evacuating camp today. Pack your things and prepare to march in an hour."

As Ervin prepared to evacuate, a guard called him and three other men outside.

Ervin stood at attention. "Yes, sir!"

"When we reach Szolnok, a guard will take you men to the hospital."

Ervin had presumed they would ride in a military jeep to the hospital, but now it appeared he'd be marching. The train station was kilometers away and he couldn't imagine enduring the pain of each step on his infected foot. Again, he fixed his mind on the future beyond his suffering. The pain he would endure, just as his parents were undoubtedly enduring an ordeal of their own, wherever they were. But soon they'd be reunited, a future Ervin awaited with patience and joy. There were rumors that Russia had crossed the Hungarian border and while Hungary was officially at war with the Soviets, for the Jews in captivity, the nation they had loved did not love them back. Now Ervin prayed for the downfall of the government, even if by Russian hands. Thankfully, it was only a matter of time before the Soviet Union would be victorious and free all of Hungary from the death grip of these Nazis. Ervin had to believe in that victory. He had to remember that his captivity and torture wouldn't last his lifetime.

So he marched on. And on. Every step of the way he wanted to burst into tears. As the pain radiated up his foot and into his back, he imagined the relief he'd feel once the foot was amputated. He felt feverish as well, and worried that it might be too late to save his life, much less his foot. Wincing with every step, he saw that Mike, too, was in terrible pain. Unfortunately, the two were separated by several other men marching in queue, so he could only surmise that that the source of Mike's pain was his back, which often flared up. This grueling journey across the most spectacular hills he'd ever seen was too much for either young man—and it wasn't until they felt they couldn't march another hour that Oláh announced their destination—Austria, 965 kilometers away. By the time they reached Ungvár, a small town in Ukraine several hours into their journey, Mike was sent to the local hospital. Ervin wanted so desperately to join him, but his referral was to the hospital in Szolnok, several hours by train, several days of tedious marching.

So he continued the unbearable hike.

The beauty of the Carpathian Mountains was captivating and, to take his mind off his suffering as he marched, Ervin thought about how much he would miss it, how intoxicating it smelled, and how peaceful he felt enveloped by the scenery. At times, he imagined he was in Heaven, but the pain was so acute and the fever so high that he felt he'd been sent to hell. The march was interminable, and at such a high altitude, with so little food, even the strongest among them were weakening.

At long last they reached a train station, where endless trains released an endless stream of German soldiers. Surrounding the train station were many armored tanks and trucks, while hundreds of Ukrainians walking along the road with their dogs and lambs appeared to be following some of the vehicles. Ervin surmised that the Russians were advancing, forcing the Ukrainians to flee. His foot throbbing as if a knife had been thrust through it, his head aching, and his whole body hot with fever, he was comforted by the scene, for it meant it wouldn't be long before he'd be reunited with his parents.

It was here that Ervin and the three other laborers were granted leave to journey the rest of the way to Szolnok by train. As for the other men, they weren't people Ervin knew well, but each was clearly suffering. One man also febrile, one with a ghastly wound to his hand from an accident while working, and the third with probable broken ribs and nose from a guard's beating. As Oláh had said, they were accompanied by an armed soldier with a bayonet at the ready, but Ervin knew he was at last safe. Nonetheless, the train ride was a miserable one as it was so crowded, he had to stand the whole way, all the while just wanting to slump to the floor in misery. Once they'd reached Szolnok late at night, he was even more discouraged to learn they had another long hike to the hospital. By the time they finally reached it, he was certain his foot couldn't be saved. He was even more certain of that fate once he stepped inside the hospital.

The place was crowded and filthy, the waiting room filled with infectious patients, coughing blood, moaning, some delirious, waiting to be seen by a physician. The floor looked as though it hadn't been cleaned in years; the windows were the same. Indeed, there wasn't a square inch of space that looked clean and by the time Ervin was admitted to an examination room, he saw that it was as filthy as the waiting room. He couldn't imagine any of the tools touching his flesh, for they couldn't possibly be sterile.

An attending physician stepped into the room and immediately, Ervin knew the man was no friend of the Jews. He wouldn't look Ervin in the eye and merely glanced at his foot.

"You don't need to worry about it," he said, dropping the foot like a hot coal. "You won't be living long anyway." Then he ordered Ervin admitted to the hospital for treatment and left without so much as a word of concern or compassion for the young man who had just hiked across the mountains to see him.

Ervin's first thought, upon hearing the physician's inhumane prediction, was despair. He was going to die. But his second thought kicked in almost at that exact moment and his rebellious streak took over.

"I'll show him," Ervin declared, as he awaited his transfer to a proper bed—and proper rest. "I'll be damned if I'll give him the satisfaction of dying. Even if it costs me my foot."

Ervin was also motivated by the thought that his parents couldn't bear his death. He had no choice but to live, if not to defy the wretched doctor, then to see his mother and father again. But to live, he had to get out of the Labor Service altogether—no matter what it took.

MARCHING ON

"Your guard's waiting for you," the nurse barked, not even looking at Ervin. He'd been in the hospital for close to a week, a respite he desperately needed and, miraculously, the physicians had managed to save his foot, if only inadvertently. Ervin was astounded at the filth and lack of hygiene in the hospital, though he'd become immune to the cruelty and indifference even healers showed to Jews. Now, however, they'd done all they could for him and his break from the labor brigade had come to an end. He had to meet up with them wherever they were on their long trek to Austria, a trek he couldn't imagine completing on a foot still healing.

"Come on, I haven't got all day. I need this bed for someone who deserves it," the uncaring nurse said, still not looking at him, but clearing away his bedding before he'd even left the bed.

Ervin had long before learned the art of moving fast, and so he did, gathering his things, signing the forms thrust before him, and within minutes of waking, he found himself standing outside the hospital doors, uniformed and obedient.

"We'll meet up with the battalion in Vác," the guard said. He'd been virtually silent the whole way there, but Ervin sensed the soldier had gotten a bit of R&R himself, for his spirits were high and he even looked Ervin in the eyes as he spoke. Ervin felt, if only for a moment, as if he were finally seen. As if he were a colleague, not a captive, of the man with the gun and bayonet.

"Okay," Ervin replied, readying himself for the walk. His foot was still sore, but bandaged and dry and, while he winced with every step, the walk was much easier heading back now that the infection had passed.

Only two of the other men accompanied them back to the battalion, with the man who'd been beaten either dead or still in the hospital. Ervin didn't dare ask which it was, but either way, it was clear that he was only one beating away from death or serious injury. The need to get out was becoming more pressing every day.

As they hiked, the guard pulled a sandwich from his pack and ate it in a few large bites, followed by an apple, then some biscuits. He offered nothing to the hungry men. Ervin envied the simple meal, for he hadn't eaten since the night before, and then all that had been served was a bowl of watery gruel best fed to livestock. He assumed Christians were fed better, but had they not been, it wouldn't have surprised him as it seemed the intent of the hospital staff was to hasten illness and death, not delay it.

It was past noon when a Romani woman approached them. A once-attractive woman worn down by poverty and life, or so she appeared, walked alongside them offering a basket of potatoes so fresh the dirt still clung to them, and some sausages.

"How much?" Ervin asked, pointing to the food. He knew that the Romanies lived on the margins and like all peasants, had little to give.

"A good price," she said in broken Hungarian.

"I have no money," Ervin replied, and the other two men echoed the unfortunate predicament.

She pointed to his throat and, though it took a moment to register, Ervin realized she was pointing to his lucky charm.

"This?" he said, holding the charm in his hand, the gold chain still around his neck.

She smiled broadly and nodded up and down. "For potatoes," she said, then adding, "and sausage." She held out a long-smoked sausage to tempt him.

Ervin was starving, but not that badly. He shook his head

forcefully. "No, no, not this," he said. Then he reached into his pack and pulled out something he knew he'd need but could live without. His ragged pajamas, that he'd somehow managed to hang on to all this time.

She eyed them warily, touching them with care, then snatched them up and thrust them quickly into her basket. She handed Ervin a few potatoes and a small sausage.

"No," he said firmly, "more."

Reluctantly, she handed him a few more potatoes and, seeing that Ervin was not yet satisfied, she handed him another sausage. Ervin nodded in gratitude to the guard for his patience, and then passed the potatoes to the other two men, as well as some chunks of sausage. Munching on the raw potatoes as if they were the sweet apple the guard had been eating, Ervin felt immense relief to finally eat some food. He might regret the deal he'd made when it was time to go to sleep and all he had to sleep in were his day clothes, but for now, at least, he was sated.

Fortunately, the occasional offer of a lift from a passing peasant's horse drawn cart eased their journey. When they'd set out, Ervin had assumed they were heading to the railroad station where they'd catch the train to Vác, but they'd long since passed that station. They were going to have to hike the whole way, more than 100 kilometers. It would take them at least two 12-hour days, with nothing to eat but a few more raw potatoes (the sausage had been eaten quickly), and on a tender foot at that. Ervin considered escaping given a good opportunity, but he had no idea where he was and had no place to go. The realization that hiking over the mountains for 24 hours was his only option in life disheartened him, but again, he kept his focus on the future. This time, however, the future he foresaw was more within reach. He'd get back to the battalion where he and Frank could figure something out. If he was going to end up escaping into the unknown, far better to do it with a friend by his side. Until then, he had no choice but to march. The question was, would he march all the way to Austria?

He knew he would make it to Vác no worse for wear, though his foot wouldn't heal as quickly as it would have had he stayed off it. But the hike, while unpleasant physically, was soothing mentally. The mountain air, pungent with pine and spruce and, at times, a whiff of honeysuckle, the flowing rivers, the vast valley views engaged all his senses and brought him peace. True, his back was aching from the weight of his pack and his foot was still sore but not worsening, and though famished and tired, he'd grown accustomed to hunger and exhaustion. He could do it. But what would it mean to end up in Austria, Germany's close ally? For all he knew, the march was one to their deaths, or at least, a far worse imprisonment. Ervin needed to stay within the borders of Hungary. He and Frank would have to find —or make—an opportunity for escape before they reached their destination. But that was good, he reasoned. The march itself provided opportunity. Even now, just the three men and the guard showed how easily one could fall behind or race ahead of the others, while the guard marched on, confident he had control over his charges. Of course, there would be more guards to contend with up ahead, but they'd oversee far more men. Yes, the march was just the opportunity they would need to slip away. But the situation remained dire. He was in an unfamiliar part of the country, which would be the case throughout the trek. He couldn't just count on opportunity—he needed a plan. Otherwise, he risked capture, which meant certain death—not just for him, but for Frank as well, assuming Frank joined him. What if he wouldn't?

The more Ervin contemplated escape, the more worried he became about the prospects of success. At the same time, with every step forward he felt he was one step closer to doom. Why were they going to Austria? What lay ahead for them there? Ervin's mind raced with possibilities, none of them good. He had to get out, he had to escape. But how? When? Where? Then back to how. He realized that the more he thought about escaping, and the more he thought about not escaping, the more desperate he felt. He needed help, but he had no way to reach his father or mother. He had no idea where they were, or even how they were.

Then it hit him. Captain Kemeny, the man with the shiny sword. His father had told him that if he needed any help he should contact the captain. How ridiculous Ervin had felt his father was at the time to think it would come to this. And yet, here it was. It had come to this. It was time to reach out to the captain.

Night was falling, with another long day of hiking up ahead before they'd reach Vác sometime the following evening. As they settled in to sleep in the open air, Ervin scribbled a quick note to the captain telling him of his predicament, his father's assurance that the captain could be trusted to help, and that all he knew was that his group was heading to Vác where they'd join his battalion before marching on to Austria. And, just in case, Ervin added a word about Frank in hopes that Frank would indeed join him. As for Mike, his back had been so injured that, even with hospital care, Ervin was doubtful he'd be healed in time to make an escape. What's more, to mention three people in need of help might mean no help would be forthcoming, as it would increase the risk to the captain, as well as the risk of the escape itself.

"Get some sleep, Wolf," the guard said. "We're rising early in the morning."

"Just writing a quick letter to my parents," he replied.

"Go ahead. Waste your time," the guard quipped, a note of delight in his cold voice.

Whatever it was the guard knew or thought he knew, Ervin wasn't going to give it much thought. Though unsettling, he knew that everything was a mind game, every word or act intended to frighten, demoralize, or shame the captive men. But one thing the remark made clear; he was right to be reaching out for help.

The next morning, they were up before dawn and on their way, once again on an empty stomach. Fortunately, by noon, they'd reached a town where Ervin was able to post the letter. He was grateful his father had made him memorize the address, and he hoped he'd remembered accurately. Given how many names and addresses he had to recall, he was dubious, but the captain was well known in Győr, so the chances were good that if he were still there, the letter would find its way to him.

As for food, he had no money, nor did the other two men on the march, so he once again bartered for some bread, sausage, and cheese. This time, it was his favorite wool shirt he parted with, but the raw potatoes and sausage long gone, he needed whatever food he could get, even if it meant one less shirt to keep him warm. Though the other men had also bartered what little they had and shared what little they acquired in return, the hike up ahead was going to be a long and rugged one. They'd all hike naked if they had to for the calories and protein to get them through it.

Fortunately, it didn't come to that. The men made it back to Vác by day's end, their feet sore—Ervin's especially—and bellies empty, but all in one piece. Unfortunately, the battalion had already moved beyond Vác and were now 186 kilometers from the Austrian border. After begging some food from some local peasants, the group rested for the night and resumed their journey the next morning.

As they left Vác, Ervin noted endless lines of retreating German armored divisions, their massive tanks leaving the city like unwelcome guests. The sight gave the men hope that their freedom was at hand, but Ervin knew not to be too optimistic. If they were on the brink of losing the war, they were more dangerous. It's when looking defeat in the eye that the last desperate grasp for power is made—which in the case of the soldiers and the captive men meant one last chance to brutalize before the opportunity was gone. It also meant that Austria was more likely to be a poor location should the Soviets liberate all of Hungary. If that possibility was on the horizon, Ervin wanted to be sure he was in Hungary when it happened.

When they met up with their battalion at a makeshift camp by the end of the following day, Ervin was disheartened to be reunited with the new commander, Captain Oláh.

"Oh, you're back. I'm not surprised," he said as he sneered at the exhausted men still healing from their injuries and ailments. "I can smell a Jew a kilometer away and your stench has sickened me all day."

Ervin merely stood at attention, his hand in salute to the superior officer and inferior man. Once dismissed, he was thrilled to see they hadn't missed dinner and never thought he'd be so happy to be fed a bowl of boiled cabbage and potatoes. He was equally thrilled to see Frank.

"Did you hear about Mike?" Frank asked.

"No, is he okay?" From the excited look on Frank's face, Ervin doubted that was the case.

"He's not coming back. His town got liberated by the Russians while he was in the hospital there. He's free!"

Free. Ervin couldn't believe it. He'd thought Mike lucky to have injured his back and imagined him enjoying the respite of a long hospital stay, but never had he imagined that he'd be a free man afterward. Just the prospect of freedom confused Ervin. Should he, too, wait for the Russians? Not risk escape—and the prospect of being caught and killed—or would waiting keep him from ever being freed? If he held off and went on to Austria, what were the chances of the Russians liberating them? Much slimmer than in Hungary, while the chances of being imprisoned, tortured, further brutalized, and even killed only increased once he was beyond the borders of his country. Oh, how he envied Mike. Free at last!

"I can't believe it," Ervin said to Frank and the two chatted a bit about the luck of their good friend. Then, when Ervin was certain that no other man, whether captive or guard, could overhear, he whispered to Frank, "I think it's time we escape."

Frank said nothing and, after a long moment of silence, merely nodded slowly, barely perceptibly. Then he turned to Ervin and whispered, "Yeah, it's time. Whatever's waiting for us in Austria won't be good. We must get out of here."

They said nothing further about the escape that night, but each man fell asleep thinking of a way to make it happen.

Night after night, Ervin and Frank watched the guards, noted their habits, and plotted ways to escape. Ervin kicked himself for not having made the move earlier when they knew where they were. Now in such an unfamiliar terrain, the risk of capture was much greater. Still, rumors that they were about to resume the hike to Austria were swirling, so his determination had never been greater. One way or another, he and Frank had to get out.

"Let's do it tonight," Frank suggested one morning. "There's a full moon, so we'll be able to see better."

"And they'll be able to see us better," Ervin replied. "I think we should wait until we're on the move again. It's easier to fall behind, disappear from the trail. I often fell behind on the hike back, and I could have been gone for hours before the guard noticed."

"I don't know," Frank said. "It's risky in the daylight."

"Maybe you're right," Ervin agreed, his hopes sinking. "Let's wait and see."

Night came and went, but the opportunity never did. One of the men had developed a wretched cough, which Ervin feared might be tuberculosis—a disease that was highly contagious and often deadly. While it spurred him into wanting to leave that much sooner, the man was up all night long and the guards were constantly ordering him to knock it off. Full moon or not, they would have to wait. But they were only four days away from the Austrian border. If they were going to escape, their opportunity to do so would soon be gone.

The next morning, after being in camp for three days, two Hungarian officers rode into their camp on military motorcycles. They immediately sought out the camp's commander, who shortly after summoned Frank and Ervin to his office.

Ervin couldn't imagine what he'd done and, for a moment, wondered if Frank had turned him in for plotting to escape. But Frank wouldn't have done that, not without being tortured, and they had summoned him as well. Could someone have overheard them? No, it wasn't that, as they'd never spoken of the escape when anyone was near—and even that would not have aroused the suspicions of Hungarian officers. Any potential escape would have been dealt with by the commander, Captain Oláh. Then it hit him—all those officers milling around at the train station. He hadn't saluted them. He recalled the time he had got into so much trouble for failing to salute months before and now they had probably discovered his name and this time come to punish him in a way he'd never forget. A beating? No, that would have been handled by the guards. They were going to take him away. Where, he had no idea, but it would be death or imprisonment, that was sure. He hated himself for not listening to Frank and making the break the night before and he knew Frank was feeling the same. But then again, if it was about saluting, why had they called for Frank? No, there was no other possibility. They'd been found out, somehow, some way.

The moment they stepped into the commander's office, however, Ervin's fears left him in an instant. There stood an imposing figure, older than he remembered but just as regal, who he recalled from childhood. The shiny sword was gone but the uniform was not. It was Captain Kemeny. Before Ervin could utter a sound, the captain gave him a quick glance and an even quicker, barely perceptible shake of his head. Ervin was not to acknowledge that he knew him, but suppressing his surprise—his shock, actually—wasn't easy. The captain had received his letter and come to save him. Just as his father had assured him he would.

The relief washed over Ervin like a luxurious shower, but he dared not reveal his emotion. Instead, he and Frank stood at attention as the other man, someone Ervin didn't know, presented them each with a document.

"The Swedish Embassy has issued each of you a Protective Pass," the man said. "Keep this with you at all times."

Ervin looked at the pass. It appeared to be a passport of sorts, printed in blue and yellow with the Swedish emblem of three crowns. It was stamped with a Budapest seal and many other official stamps and appeared to come from the Swedish Embassy there. The pass indicated that Ervin was under the protection of the Swedish nation and was exempt from wearing the yellow star—a new designation Ervin learned civilian Jews had been forced to wear.

Holding the pass in his hands, Ervin glanced at Frank who was equally befuddled. But before he could ask anything more, Captain Kemeny spoke up.

"We request that you release these two men immediately in accordance with the Swedish Embassy's issuance of these documents."

Captain Oláh, who'd been sitting behind his desk all this time, appeared angered and demanded Ervin hand him his document. "Let me see that," he ordered, and Ervin stepped forward and placed the document on his desk.

The captain read the document carefully. All the while, Ervin could barely conceal his excitement. He'd been freed! There was nothing the captain could do now. These documents proved it.

"These Jews can use this paper to wipe their asses," Oláh said, thrusting the paper back toward Ervin. "As long as I'm here, these Jews will be under my guard. They aren't going anywhere."

Following some brief exchanges of mutual respect among the officers, those who had come to save him bid their farewell and departed, leaving Frank and Ervin behind.

As instantly as he'd been saved, Ervin saw that his imprisonment had become even more tightly secured. To have his hopes dashed like that, with the intervention of an embassy no less, was more demoralizing than had he never been called to the commander's office. If official papers and these officers couldn't protect him, what or who could?

After hurling some insults at Frank and Ervin, Oláh sent them back to their battalion to prepare for the march to Austria.

Once there was some distance between the young men and their guards, Ervin said, "There's one consolation."

Frank looked at him quizzically. "Go ahead, what miserable idea do you have that will console me?"

"That officer, the tall one with the big nose?"

"Yeah?"

"That was the guy I wrote to, my dad's friend. Turns out Oláh can't smell a Jew a meter away!"

Happy to see he'd gotten a laugh out of Frank, Ervin added. "At least Oláh had one good idea."

"And what's that?" Frank said, the good humor drained from his voice.

Ervin flourished his protective pass ceremoniously. "Toilet paper *is* hard to come by out here!" Then he folded the pass and tucked it into his shirt pocket.

The young men laughed, a laugh stained with bitter truth and disappointment. Then they rejoined the battalion, the protective passes discretely tucked away, just in case.

ESCAPE

The next morning, the march to Austria began. It was already mid-November, the air biting cold with heavy snows due anytime. Frank and Ervin considered running off before the march began but thought better of it.

"Maybe Oláh didn't respect these papers," Ervin said, referring to the Protective Passes Captain Kemeny had provided, "but that doesn't mean they won't come in handy. If we have these on us, we have a credible excuse for being free."

"But are they even legit?" Frank asked.

"Doesn't matter," Ervin replied. "As long as whoever sees them thinks they are. And they sure look it to me."

"Okay," Frank agreed, taking out a near empty pack of cigarettes he'd been savoring and offering one to Ervin, who declined, as he always did. As much as Ervin envied the pleasure smoking brought to Frank, he had no desire to develop an addiction, especially in the situation they were in where wants and desires were so out of reach.

After savoring the first delicious taste of the nicotine-laced smoke, Frank asked, "So when do we do it? If we don't take off tonight, when? Austria's just a few days away."

"We leave at twilight," Ervin said, feeling confident. "It'll be harder for them to see us in the dark. We just need to get far enough away to hide. We'll watch for the guards to be preoccupied. Maybe when they're eating or someone's taking a leak. But it should be an area with a lot of trees and bushes. Places we can hide."

"But we won't be able to see at night and we don't know this terrain."

"That's why I think twilight's a good time to go. We'll have enough light to see for 20 or 30 minutes. That's about how long it should take them to realize we're gone."

"As long as we move quickly and they really are preoccupied."

"We need to be up front where we can round a bend and not be seen."

"Supposing someone tells?"

"Someone will, they all will once they're threatened. But they won't say anything at first."

"You're sure about that?" Frank wasn't quite as confident as Ervin and knew that one slip-up could mean a punishment he didn't dare think about. It was likely they'd be hung.

"No one ever says anything unless it's their own hide on the line. Turning us in right away won't bring them any rewards. Besides, they'll be inspired. Maybe we'll give them the courage to do the same."

Frank stayed silent for a few long minutes as he finished his cigarette. Once done, he flicked the butt away and asked, "What if twilight comes and the guards are watching? Or we're at some barren place with nothing but birch trees to hide behind?"

"Then we wait another day. We've got three good nights before we reach the border."

Frank nodded but said nothing.

"One more thing," Ervin added.

"What's that, boss?" Frank said, accepting Ervin as the mastermind of this plot they were hatching. As comical as Ervin could be at times, Frank trusted in his friend's clever mind.

"We run in different directions," Ervin said.

"What do you mean, we run in different directions? I don't get it."

"You go one way, I go another."

"Oh, so this is it? To each his own after this?" The tone in Frank's voice showed the first seeds of doubt. Maybe Ervin wasn't such a friend after all, if he would dump Frank the minute he was free.

"We have to. It'll make it harder for them to find us and, if they do, at least they'll only catch one of us and the other will be free. We can meet up in Pest."

Frank agreed it was a good idea and, after some discussion on where to meet up, Frank gave Ervin the name of a relative in Pest where Ervin could leave a message for him. Then they agreed on a signal—Ervin would give it—a subtle countdown to three with his fingers. They were all set. All they had to do was wait for the right time. Then run like hell—and pray they'd survive.

The march started before dawn and, as usual, the food they were provided was barely fit for consumption, much less giving them the energy for the long haul ahead of them. A bit of dry bread, some boiled rotting potatoes, and enough cabbage to give them gas for hours.

The march was miserable. They thought they'd become accustomed to the marches but, for some reason, something had possessed the guards and they were more sadistic than ever. Ervin wondered if they might have sensed—or God forbid overheard—their plans for escape, but he knew that was unlikely as they'd been overly cautious and told not a soul. It was probably just because they were nearing Austria where the men's lives were all the less valued. They were ramping up their brutality because they could.

The guards pushed the men like a herd of slaves, shoving them in the back, beating their backs, bottoms, and the back of their legs with heavy sticks, and cursing them with every imaginable antisemitic slur. If anyone slowed their pace, even for a moment, they were pulled out of line and beaten mercilessly.

Frank and Ervin didn't speak a word to each other. The guards would split them up if they did and beat them both. Meanwhile, they marched on.

Every half hour the guards took a break, ordering the men to keep marching. They marched for two hours, three hours, four hours, still without a break. Five hours, six hours, seven hours, the packs on their back as heavy as rocks. After nearly nine hours, they were told they could rest.

"But don't get too comfortable," one guard—once kind but now not the least so—said. "You've got a long way to go before you'll sleep."

He was true to his word. After a short rest with only more bread and some dried sausage to eat, they were ordered up and moving again. They couldn't have rested more than 15 minutes and every bone and muscle in Ervin's body, as well as his foot, which still hadn't completely healed, were painfully sore. The thought of escape was the only thing that kept him moving, for if he hadn't had freedom to look forward to, he couldn't have imagined continuing. He'd have rather been beaten to death.

As he marched, he thought of the wonderful bed he had at home, of the delicious meals his mother had made. His powers of imagination had become so great that sometimes he felt as if he really had eaten of one of her meals. He imagined every bite of pierogi, chewing her sweet biscuits washed down with tea as if he were really eating them. He couldn't wait to see his parents again, though he knew it would still be some time before they could be reunited. When his mind wandered to the possibilities that something might have happened to them—that some harm might have come to them as his father had feared—he immediately forced himself to think more hopeful thoughts. It was the only thing he could do to keep his spirit alive.

As the sky began to soften from blazing blue to a gentler gray, Ervin surveilled the scene. The soldiers continued taking their breaks every half hour, alternating between them. That meant that there was always a pack of guards behind them, while the other guards would catch up—given the only heavy supplies they carried were their weapons and they were much better fed. There were no guards up front where Frank and Ervin had positioned themselves.

Ervin was so exhausted that it was hard to fathom running ten meters, much less running at breakneck speed through the bushes and trees all night. But his survival depended on escaping. This was a death march, he feared. They were being marched to their deaths, and the gleeful brutality of the guards convinced him he was right. How else to explain it? They were downright giddy over this horrendous ordeal. Yes, he was tired, blood tired, bone tired, and dead tired. But he felt an exhilaration he hadn't felt in ages. He was so excited to think about breaking free, to think about flying through that landscape like a prisoner freed at last. It was just a matter of finding the right moment.

Just as Ervin noted the first glimmer of orange slipping across the sky to mark the setting sun, the guards took another break. The other set of captors was far behind, growing sluggish and tired. They were far from any signs of civilization; they hadn't seen a sign of human life all day. The ground was slippery and the grass wet from the blanket of clouds they were passing through. Ervin knew it would be difficult not to slip as he ran, but the path had been winding through thick brush with plenty of trees, but not so many trees that they couldn't run easily. If ever there was a time to run, this was it.

Ervin felt his heartbeat quicken. He tried to slow it by breathing deeply, but the march itself was putting such a stress on his heart and lungs that the effort to slow his pulse was wasted. Still, he wanted as much control over himself as possible. He was going to have to muster a tremendous amount of energy to outrun the guards.

He glanced at Frank and saw that he, too, was alert, despite the rugged terrain they'd been hiking across since daybreak. In any other context, the hunger and exhaustion would have made running impossible. But now he would be running for his life. As for hunger and exhaustion, he had become so accustomed to laboring like a workhorse through both states that hunger and exhaustion had become his new standard. If anything, he reasoned, he was more likely to find food and rest if he ran than if he marched on. What little food they'd receive at the end of their hike would be barely enough to nourish them, while there would be no rest for another hour or two. Running now would free or kill him. Either option was preferable to waking up another day to march on—toward what doom he could only guess.

Frank had caught Ervin's eye. Their glance held only for an instant, but that was all that was needed. They had both assessed the situation similarly. This was the night. This was the stretch of terrain that best suited them. Just up ahead was another bend in the road, along a steep downhill slope—at the front of the line, they could round the corner and be gone in an instant and only a couple of men would even know what had happened. This was the time to do it. Frank turned his eyes back toward Ervin, nodding discreetly to let him know he was ready.

Ervin took another deep breath and imagined that it was not the mountain terrain he was about to run down, but the swirling waters of the sea he was about to dive into. He imagined the water swallowing him in a shocking gulp, only to kick for his life as he rose and swam as he'd never swum before. He imagined himself a small boy and terrified to dive, but how the first time he did so, he just did it, his parents watching proudly. He didn't think about his fear then, he had just let go, determined to face the water once he was in it. Now, the bend fast approaching, was the time to dive. Now was the time to push away his fears and just do it.

He let his hand fall to his side as he fixed his glance on Frank, his thumb out. One. His index finger. Two. Deep breath. One last finger. Three. They were off!

Ervin dove down the hillside, slipping and nearly falling, but catching himself and running as fast as he could, his pack heavy and hitting the trees, but he just kept running and running and running as fast as he possibly could, through the trees, trampling bushes, slipping and rising, stumbling and getting back up, running for his life. He didn't dare look back, but he could see and hear that Frank had shot from the line just as quickly, the two racing through the mountainside like charging bears, Frank far to his right and lost in the landscape in seconds.

As Ervin ran, the adrenaline pumping through him like never before, he heard someone else running, not far behind him. It couldn't have been Frank, who he'd seen dart away. Someone was trying to catch him. He raced faster and faster, terrified they'd shoot him, but no shots rang out. Something was off. The person behind him was panting not in rage, but in fear, it seemed. No one was cursing him, threatening him, ordering him to stop. He didn't dare slow or turn, knowing that it would take only a second to smash into a tree or trip over a root or a rock and all would be over. He let his head pivot for just an instant in hopes of catching a glimpse of who was in pursuit and saw it was another of the laborers. Just as he and Frank had joked that they'd inspire others to run, that's exactly what had happened. Someone—he couldn't tell who—had seen them break free and just like that, he'd run away, too.

Ervin half hoped that everyone would run, but he knew the situation was dire. The other man couldn't follow him. If he did, they might both be caught. Ervin needed to stay free. He needed the guy to go in a different direction. As he ran, jumping over rocks, bushes, tree roots, thistles, and fallen trees, slipping in the mud and catching his falls with the help of the trees, he caught sight of a wide clearing. Aiming for it, he waved his hand toward one direction as he ran in the other. Thankfully, the fleeing man obliged and ran off in the other direction. Ervin kept running, desperate to get as far from the guards as possible, as far from the other escaping man as possible. As far from Austria as possible. As far from death as possible.

The adrenaline was running out. He was growing weaker. He was so tired. And so scared. What a stupid, stupid thing he'd done. He couldn't outrun them. He would be caught. He slowed his pace and jogged toward some high bushes, diving behind them and letting himself rest, if only for a few moments. He was panting, his heart beating harder than ever before. As he tried to catch his breath, he heard the voices. They seemed a good distance away, but not far enough. They were looking for him. If he didn't catch his breath soon, they'd hear him. He made himself as small as possible, his eyes peering through the thick shrubbery, vigilant for any sign of the guards. He dared not make a sound.

The sun had set as he'd raced through the trees, but it was not completely dark as a full moon illuminated the mountainside. Ervin hadn't even thought about the moon and now he thanked God for the extra bit of light. He prayed that Frank was safe. He prayed they'd both survive.

He had nearly forgotten about the third man when he heard the guards shouting. They'd found someone. Please don't let it be Frank,

Ervin prayed, please let it be the other man. Then he begged forgiveness from God for even praying such a thing, for the other man was as much in need of saving as anyone. But still, he didn't want it to be him or Frank who was caught. Please, not that.

He heard a man cry out—more like a boy, actually—and was relieved it wasn't Frank's voice. They'd captured the third man.

"Where'd they go?" a guard's voice demanded.

In reply, just crying, echoing through the mountains. Then, "I don't know, I don't know!" Then the sounds of beating. Heavy blows. Horrible cries. When they'd finished, he heard them moving again and the sound of something dragging.

Please don't let it be a body, Ervin prayed. Then the crying again. They hadn't killed him. But they were dragging him back. He was in bad shape. The sounds grew more distant. The third man may have saved his life, Ervin realized, as his capture got them off his trail. How he hoped the man would survive.

Ervin didn't know how long he'd hidden in the bushes, but the moon was high, and all he could hear were the sounds of forest life. The nocturnal predators were out. Hopefully none that feasted on humans, Ervin thought. He'd heard there were lynx and wildcats in the mountains, though he hadn't seen any.

That doesn't mean they don't see me. Drained of any strength, he rose, the pack on his back now as heavy as lead and his feet unbearably sore. His right hand was bleeding and pulsating in pain from the long thorns of the acacia trees and, while the wound itself didn't worry him, the trail of blood it left did. If the guards or animals —he wasn't sure which was the greater threat or his greater fear— saw or sensed the blood, they'd find him. He ripped off a piece of his shirt and wrapped it around his hand. That wouldn't fool any wildcat, but at least it would prevent leaving a trail of blood for the guards to find. His throat was parched, his stomach empty, and his back throbbing, but his life was quite literally on the line. He had to keep moving.

He listened intently to be sure the guards were not near. It had turned eerily quiet. Despite the full moon he could barely see as he stumbled around, feeling his way with his painful hand. He hadn't gone more than 50 meters or so when he heard a rustle behind him. Whatever it was, it was big. A wildcat? Bear? There were brown bears in the mountains and, though not usually dangerous, if Ervin had unknowingly approached a mama bear and her cubs, he didn't stand a chance. Then he heard the panting. It was no bear. It was a man. A guard must have stayed on to search.

The terror shot through him like a bullet as the heavy steps closed in on him, a terror extinguished with a single whispered word.

"*Ervin!*"

It was Frank.

Ervin had never felt such relief, never been so surprised. His prayers for his life to be spared, for Frank not to be caught, had been answered. The men fell into each other's arms, hugging, slapping each other on the back, Frank panting from his moonlight run, Ervin from his fear. Neither man could describe his happiness to have found the other in this vast and frightening wilderness. But they had no time for sentimentality. They had to move on, get as far from their battalion as possible, as fast as possible. But they had no idea where they were or what direction to take. And on top of it all, as seasoned as they'd become with hard work and discomfort, they were city boys. Surviving in the wilderness had never been a lesson either boy was taught.

They walked, no longer running, but moving ever forward in the dark, savoring the tranquility of the wilderness, pushing away their fears. This was freedom. No one was watching them. No one could tell them what to do. Only nature ruled over them, no man, no sadistic, brutal man. They were two animals, two primates, trusting their own instincts. Trusting in each other. They were free. The only question was, for how long?

ON THE RUN

They had no idea where they were or where they were going—or even if they were walking further from their battalion or gaining on it. But if they kept walking downhill, they figured they were probably safe. For another hour or so, they walked in silence, each man lost in his own world of fear and pain and exhilarating joy just to be free. At last, the tiny lights of a distant village appeared in the valley below.

"Think it's safe?" Frank asked, his voice still low though nobody else was near, at least not that they could discern.

"Don't know," Ervin answered. "But we need food and water. Let's be careful."

As they neared the village, they saw several military trucks at the foot of the hill.

"Let's circle around this way," Ervin said, and Frank nodded. They made their way around the trucks and hiked beyond the village center. Though dark, it was still early, probably around seven or eight, Ervin estimated. They were so far north that the sun was setting in late afternoon, and it had been three or four hours since sunset. People would still be moving around.

"There's a farmhouse," Frank whispered, pointing toward a lone house surrounded by fields on a road just past the village. "Let's head there. We've had good luck with peasants."

Ervin agreed and they headed toward the farmhouse, sticking to the shadows once they'd left the cover of the trees. As they neared the house, Ervin said, "Let's take off these armbands. We don't know what they think of Jews."

"Good thinking," Frank said, "and good riddance!" He ripped off his armband and was all set to fling it away when Ervin grabbed his arm.

"They see that and they'll know we're here. Shove it in your pack and when we find a place where we can get rid of them forever, we'll dump them."

"Yeah, you're right. Won't be fast enough though."

"That's for sure," Ervin said, tearing his own off his arm. "Besides, according to our Protective Passes, we don't need to wear them." How he hated that marker of his inferiority, that band across his arm that told the world he was to be avoided, mistreated, despised. Once the bands were stashed in their packs and they were standing before the house at last, the pair—looking like they'd just emerged from a volcano, they were so filthy and haggard—looked at each other as if to say, "this is it," then strode up the walk, their aching backs straight and their pounding heads held high. When they reached the porch and were standing under the bright amber glow of the light, Ervin took a deep breath, swallowed, and knocked on the door.

A moment later, the door swung wide open and a small man, his own face weathered and stained by the sun, looked as startled to see the two soldiers as they were to see him.

"Hello," he said in a soft tone. He took in the unexpected spectacle of two bedraggled soldiers, caps in hand, then opening the door wider, he said, "Come in."

Stepping through the door, Frank and Ervin could see a woman and some children seated around a table, a large pot set in the center from which the children were eating with their hands. The scene made a deep impression upon Ervin as it reminded him of Van Gogh's painting, *The Potato Eaters*, and he felt almost as if he'd gone back in time.

"I, I'm, sorry," Ervin began, embarrassed by the bad timing. "It appears we've interrupted your dinner." He had no idea what to say after that, as he hadn't thought that far. For a long, uncomfortable moment, the man looked them up and down—the family watching from the dinner table, their curiosity greater than their appetites. As the man scrutinized them, a thousand thoughts flew through Ervin's mind, none of which were about something he might say to break the awkward silence. Instead, his mind was active with his many worries. Would he realize they were Jews? Would he call the military patrol or throw them out? Was he afraid of them? Maybe he thought they'd come to rob them, or worse. He wished he could read the man's mind, for the man was clearly judging the two soldiers before him and his eyes were intelligent eyes. Ervin knew he would not be easily fooled, which made coming up with a story even harder.

Frank appeared equally ill at ease. His mind was busy wondering what Ervin was doing just standing there saying nothing. This was Ervin's plan and Ervin was the man with the clever mind. Whatever had gotten into Ervin to paralyze his tongue for the first time in his life, it could prove to be the end of them. Frank had no choice but to speak up.

"We've lost our way, I'm afraid, and have found ourselves cut off from our battalion. We have no money, only our good names." Frank immediately regretted that slip, for what if the stranger asked their names? He might then know that they were Jews by their surnames. But in the sliver of silence that followed as he struggled for a way to ask for food and a place to sleep, the peasant spoke up.

"You boys don't know how lucky you are," he said. "I know who you are. I'm not going to turn you in. I'm a communist. You're both welcome to sleep in our loft, but just for one night. Tomorrow morning, you will have to leave the house. There are German soldiers lodged all around the area."

The relief they felt was profound. It was as if they'd been sentenced to die and unexpectedly reprieved, so certain had they each been that they'd knocked on the wrong man's door. Instead, they'd chosen just the right one.

Ervin found it curious that the man had identified himself as a communist. His tone had suggested that because he was a communist, the boys were safe. He had never been impressed by the philosophies of communism that were so popular among many of the educated men and women of Győr who engaged his father in lively—sometimes even heated—discussions. Whether someone at the park, the barbers, or the newsstand, or even at home, it had seemed that many were fervent admirers of the economic equality promoted by the new Soviet Union. Looking about this peasant's humble home and hearth, Ervin could certainly see the appeal of communism. But what struck him was the man's tone—he was proud of being a communist and he presented the information as if that explained his humanity. Ervin had always associated communism with a singular mission to take from people, to rule them, and yet this man was offering quite the opposite—to give to him a night of safety, so that he might not be ruled by the rightwing antisemites who dehumanized and imprisoned him.

"You must be starving. Come, sit down," he said, inviting them to share their family's modest meal. Ervin and Frank thanked them profusely—Ervin finally regaining the gift of speech and babbling his gratitude so repeatedly that the children burst into laughter at the funny soldier. They joined the family in a meal of chicken paprikash, which Ervin found to be one of the best he'd ever had—not because it was perfectly spiced, for indeed, no one could surpass his mother's paprikash—but because he was so terribly hungry and the smell alone had been intoxicating. As they ate, the man asked them where they were from and when he answered Győr, his face darkened.

"Oh, that's not good," he said. "Are your families there?"

"Yes, I mean, they should be. But we haven't heard from them," Ervin said.

"We think they've been arrested or sent to a labor camp," Frank added. "But until the war ends, we probably won't be able to see them."

The man and his wife exchanged glances and Ervin was immediately alarmed.

"What do you mean, it's not good?" he asked. "And what's wrong with Győr?"

The man looked at them with sorrow in his eyes. "The Nazis have occupied the city and they've transported all the Jews to a labor camp in Poland. No one knows for sure what's going on, but the entire city is occupied. They've seized homes, people's belongings. We've never seen anything like it. It wouldn't be safe to return there."

Ervin's heart sank as he reflected on his parents' fate. They would be able to endure a labor camp, of that he was confident. They were both strong and good workers and not yet too old. But he had never considered he'd be unable to return to Győr until the war ended. Of course, he knew they couldn't return to their homes because that's the first place they'd look for the escaped men. But it had never occurred to him that there might not be homes to return to. Was it even possible that the Nazis had stolen their home and all their belongings? Of course it was possible. He knew well their heartlessness and quest for power. And this farmer seemed to be aware of current events. Though a peasant, the little conversation they'd had revealed that he was neither an illiterate nor a foolish one. If he said the Nazis had occupied the city and sent the Jews to Poland, Ervin was pretty sure it was true. His father had been right. He really had needed to hide his valuables. How they'd be heartbroken when they were finally released, especially his mother. He couldn't imagine how sad she would be to lose her lovely home and all the memories it had contained. Just thinking about how they'd feel when they learned they'd lost everything saddened him. Hopefully, as bad as it was, their home would be okay. But he accepted the farmer's judgment that going to Győr wasn't such a good idea right now. They'd need to go elsewhere until the war was over.

Despite the shocking news their host had brought them of their hometown, the meal often fell into silence as Frank and Ervin focused on sopping up every bit of sauce with chunks of bread, too famished to do much talking. Though there was not nearly enough to fill his empty stomach, Ervin was so heartened by the family's warmth and hospitality that he wished he could have stayed for weeks. Alas, they had only one night, but it was a most welcomed night's rest as they were given warm blankets and a soft pallet, along with plenty of bread and coffee in the morning. Though Ervin's mind was filled with worry for his parents, his body was so spent that he quickly fell into a deep sleep. By dawn, as the sun poked its head into the drowsy sky, Frank and Ervin were out the door and back to relying on their wits and providence.

"Where to now?" Frank asked as they walked along the lonely road heading toward the village. "Should we even dare head into town?"

"No, we'd be caught for sure," Ervin said. "And it doesn't sound like a good idea to go to Győr."

"Agreed," Frank said. "I say we head to Budapest. I've got family there and they can help us."

Ervin nodded. "There's the tracks," he said, pointing to a ribbon of train tracks in the near distance. "We just follow them, walking east. What do you say?"

"I like the sound of that," Frank said. "But how do we know which way is east?"

Ervin looked at his dear friend and shook his head. "We follow the rising sun, you dumb ass!" He whacked Frank's butt with his crumpled cap—the cap he hoped he'd never have to wear again but knew the time would come when it would become useful.

Frank grinned, pulled out the last cigarette from a battered pack, and lost his thoughts in his burning tobacco. By the time he'd finished his smoke, they'd reached the railroad tracks and started on their long journey to Budapest.

The trek along the tracks was quiet for the most part, and both men were relieved not to have to deal with humans, since the sentiments of anyone they'd encounter was always a gamble, and neither trusted that they'd run into many like the communist peasant who'd been so kind. For that matter, they didn't trust other communists to be as understanding either, but the man's frankness had impressed upon Ervin a newfound understanding that communism might not be such a terrible thing. Still, he wasn't anxious for the economic trend to take hold in Hungary, but if it did, it had to be preferable to the Nazis. If the Soviets won the war, and they very well still might, a communist government wouldn't be the worst outcome. But his father wouldn't care for such a scenario, that was for sure.

Ervin pushed any thoughts of his father out of his mind. Ever since learning from the peasant what had happened in Győr, he found his mind wandering to worry and he knew that to give in to that worry would do him no good. They had to stay focused and keep their wits about them, because any poor decision could turn out disastrous. All he could do was trust that his father and mother were safe, and know that one way or another, they would rebuild their lives once this dreadful war ended.

The terror of the war continued to menace them with every passing train. Each one was crowded with German and Hungarian soldiers and just the sight of them unnerved both Frank and Ervin.

"Let's switch to the main roads," Ervin suggested as the sun rose higher and their stomachs rumbled once again. How they longed to be eating a warm and tasty dinner, as they had the night before. But it was too risky to beg for food and they didn't have any money to buy anything. They'd worry about nutrition later. For now, they had to concentrate on covering as much ground as possible. "If we hitch a ride to Budapest, we should be there in a couple of hours."

"A bit risky, don't you think?" Frank asked.

"Yeah, but so is hiking. My feet and back just can't take it anymore, and all we have to say is we drank too much and by the time we woke up, our battalion had already left and we need to catch up with it."

"Yeah, that should work," Frank said, "since it was my idea." He smiled to let Ervin know he was just chiding him for the night before.

"But the drinking too much was mine," he added, "which is what will convince them. People only lie about *not* drinking too much."

"It is a good touch," Frank conceded. "Course, I would have come up with that on my own."

"Sure you would, pal," Ervin teased, as the two stuck out their thumbs and readied themselves for their next risky encounter with whoever picked them up.

They were again fortunate in finding a ride with a middle-aged plumbing parts salesman who said very little and asked few questions. Whether he guessed the truth or not, they couldn't tell, but they gave their cover story and he seemed to believe it, saying he was just happy for the company as he spent so much time on the road.

Best of all, he was going close to Budapest, so even if they found no other rides, they'd be in hiking distance of the city once he'd let them off. Along the way, they passed masses of armored trucks and military jeeps, another reminder that the entire nation was under siege by the Nazis. Neither man said anything as they saw the convoys, though occasionally they'd glance over to each other as if to remind themselves of the danger they were in despite their joyous freedom.

They hadn't travelled far before their host and driver turned on the radio, keeping it tuned to a classical station, which brought great comfort to Ervin as he listened to the calming music his mother had so loved. Still, when his worries for her safety crept into his mind, he pushed them away for fear he'd think of nothing else until they saw each other again. He could only trust that she and his father were safe, or as safe as possible, and that he himself would stay that way.

As they reached a town along the river near Budapest, the driver said he had to head south so he let them out near a nice area with stately homes on one side of the river and rows of one-story houses protected by high fences on the other. As he was letting them out, the driver told them it was a good area, a resort town. "Those houses there are owned by a factory here, they're the workers' houses. Those other ones across the river, those are where the factory owners and other fat cats live. You're either rich or poor in this town, so if you stick around, be sure you pick the right side of the river to grow old in." Then he waved them goodbye and drove away.

"Sounds like we didn't fool him," Frank said. "Since he thinks we aren't joining up with our battalion."

"I don't know," Ervin countered. "Sounds to me more like he was just sharing his own dreams of one day ending up on the better side of the river."

"Won't end up there selling plumbing supplies," Frank said.

"For all we know, he was lying to us as much as we were to him."

"In times of war, everyone's someone they aren't," Frank said.

As they reached the town center, the men noticed masses of marching military columns, occasionally interrupted by armored trucks or horse-drawn wagons. The striking difference between the two—one a symbol of power and might and igniting fear in the hearts of the men, the other a symbol of simplicity and self-reliance, invoking peace and safety, if not a world before the war—caused the men to reassess whether they ought to be so bold as to approach anyone at all.

"The alternative is we become thieves just to eat," Ervin said, "and I'd rather bank on people having a good heart than darkening my own."

"I'm with you," Frank said, as he was a man of integrity himself. "But we need to be careful."

"Agreed," Ervin said just as a couple of well-dressed men came out of a building they were passing.

"Good afternoon, soldiers," one of the men said, tipping his hat. The other did the same and no sooner had Ervin and Frank returned the greeting than one of the men asked, "What brings you to our town? We don't have many soldiers out here, other than those trucks and tanks that pass us by."

Ervin gave them their cover story, which promptly brought more questioning. The more he answered their questions—Frank stepping back and keeping conspicuously quiet to not contradict or confuse the explanation—the more nervous Ervin became. What had become a friendly greeting was quickly advancing to a suspicious interrogation.

"Look," the more vocal man said in a lowered tone, stepping away from the street and closer to the building as if it were a safer place to be, away from the passersby. "No one gets lost out here. You're Jews and you've made a run for it."

Ervin's heart raced and Frank's face turned so pale he looked about to drop right there on the sidewalk. But the second man quickly calmed them. "We can help you. You'll be killed if they catch you and no one can miss you in those uniforms."

"Yeah, we saw you a block away and sized you up right away," the first man said. "And if we can, others can. Come home with us. You'll be safe."

While he knew it was a big risk, in all probability a trap even, there was something about the two men that felt safe to Ervin. He had always been good at assessing character, and the characters he discerned here were sincere. Although there'd been every reason to be wary of the men as they quizzed them about where they were from and what they were up to, he had warmed to them as the conversation progressed. He felt safe with them, not frightened.

Ervin turned toward Frank and noted the question in his friend's eyes. Frank was relying on Ervin to make the call. Ervin nodded and before they knew it, they were walking with the two men toward a nearby house.

"You don't know how lucky you are to have run into us," the talkative man said, echoing the peasant's words. Ervin hoped they were indeed lucky again for, while he felt safe, he was still on guard. At any moment they might have to bolt from the men, but he had faith that luck was indeed on their side—for to consider that it wasn't would make surviving a greater challenge. He needed both the confidence that they would succeed as well as the good fortune required.

The house they entered was an impressive, stately one—on the good side of the river, not far from the town center—and the moment they passed through the tall front door, they were greeted with an unexpected and unbelievable sight. The front room was filled with well-dressed men, much like the two men who had brought them there, sitting about reading, playing cards, or just lounging in comfortable armchairs enjoying afternoon drinks. One man was dressed in a military uniform, leisurely reclining on a settee, sipping something from a bottle wrapped in white linen. The whole thing reminded Ervin of his father's many visits with friends, such as the curious Viktor Kroonenberg, who would sit in his father's study discussing the events of the day over a glass of Tokay, brandy, or other intoxicating spirit. But to see a whole roomful of such men, some engaged with each other, others sitting alone lost in thought, was a strange sight, especially at midday.

"These men are all Jewish," their host, who eventually introduced himself as Márk, explained. "All, like you, are hiding from Labor Service. And that man there," he pointed to the uniformed man sipping what was probably champagne, "is their commander. We pay him well and the men are credited with having completed their work. We also pay the warden at the local jail, and he has the prisoners do the work. No one's the wiser—at least, no one who can't be paid off."

Frank and Ervin were both stunned. They couldn't possibly have stumbled into a safe house so quickly, couldn't possibly be safe amidst such open defiance of the military's rules. And yet, these men appeared to be basking in comfort, if not luxury. No one appeared frightened. A few heads popped up, took in the sight of two young and unwashed men in uniform, and merely nodded or just smiled and turned away. There were no signs of hostility. As for the lounging commander, he appeared lost in his white-draped bottle and unaware of their, or anybody's, presence. It was as if they'd stumbled into a surreal piece of heaven in the middle of the afternoon.

Before they could ask any questions, they were ushered into another room where someone was summoned and instructed to prepare lunch for the two hungry men. As the meal was prepared, they were offered tea and biscuits and told they'd soon be shown a place to shower and rest.

"These men are all well off and each has his own false papers and documents," Márk explained. Márk had slipped away into one of the other rooms and they were now alone with the man who had no name. "If anyone asks, they're forest workers. They belong to a tree-cutting unit, but people usually don't ask. It's clear they're wealthy men."

"As we once were," Ervin offered. "But I'm afraid we have no money now and we don't even know where our parents are. We're from Győr and—" but before he could answer, he noted the pain in the man's face at the mention of his hometown.

"No need to explain," he said, as if just saying he was from Győr was explanation enough, an interjection that worried Ervin more than relieved him. What had happened in Győr? What had they done to his parents? "I can see that you need help and that's why I've brought you here."

"We do have papers," Frank said, anxiously pulling out his folded and now tattered Protective Pass. He thrust it before the man, who looked it over, appearing impressed.

"You both have these?" he asked Ervin, who nodded. "This is good, this is very good," he said to the relief of both Frank and Ervin.

"So, these papers are valuable?" Ervin asked.

"Oh, yes, quite so," he said. "Of course, they only have as much worth as those who review them choose to give them, and some will simply ignore them. But they aren't fake papers, they were issued by the Swedish Embassy. A man named Raoul Wallenberg, a wealthy Swedish diplomat, had them printed. Sweden is a neutral country, but they are quite sympathetic to the Jews and quite alarmed by the Nazis' rise to power across Europe. Wallenberg's passes have saved thousands of Jewish lives and you're quite fortunate to have possession of these papers."

Lunch was brought to the young men, an impressive array of smoked meats, cheeses, breads, pickles, and sweets, a meal unlike any they'd had since eating their own mothers' fine cooking. Frank and Ervin marveled at how the man showed around their papers. They were struck by the responses—people seemed to envy them. They had not realized the value of their Protective Passes—especially considering how they were received by their Commander Oláh—and for a moment, both feared the man might not return such valuable documents. After all, to be received with such lavish hospitality and offered safety as they had been seemed so astounding as to be suspicious, and now to have their "valuable" papers, the only valuables they possessed, passed around for all to covet raised whole new concerns.

"You shouldn't have shown them to him," Ervin whispered to Frank. "What if he steals them?"

"He won't do that," Frank insisted, though there was doubt in his voice. "I mean, I don't think he will. He seems nice."

"Almost too nice," Ervin considered.

But his worries proved needless, for the papers were promptly returned just as the men were shown to their new rooms and assured that after they'd washed up and changed, they could join the other men in the front room for drinks.

Still, Ervin kept his pack close by, worried even as he showered that this new turn of events seemed too good to be true. Had they really stumbled into a safe house where they'd be protected despite having nothing to offer? Or had they stumbled into something far darker and more dangerous?

He didn't know the answer. He just knew that it had been an awfully long time since he'd had such a satisfying meal and luxurious shower. If this was a trap, at least he'd go out in style.

HUNTING SEASON

The first week at the safehouse couldn't have been better. Frank and Ervin arranged to pay for their food and lodging—and protection—by doing chores around the house. After the hard labor on empty stomachs that they had become accustomed to, polishing everyone's shoes, cleaning the house, cooking, serving meals, and washing the dishes was a breeze. They joked that they'd become housewives, though they couldn't have been more grateful. They were continually assured that they were welcome to stay if necessary and they could easily have envisioned themselves remaining there until the war's end, had events not taken a sudden and drastic turn.

"Alright, boys, you'll be happy to know you've been promoted from housewives to shipping clerks!" Márk announced one morning. "We need you to transport food to the local troops in the area."

Frank and Ervin were thrilled with the prospect of getting out of the house and, once they were trained in how to drive the open trucks to the fighting units and distribute the food when they got there, they found the work easy enough, though the older men found it quite difficult. Still, everything Ervin did by this point was compared to both the hard tasks he'd endured in the Labor Service and the pathetic efforts that had marked his entry into service. "Poor mother, if only she could see me now," Ervin quipped to Frank. "She'll be stunned when she sees how I work these days!"

"True, you're not such a spoiled boy anymore, Erv," Frank said. "But it won't take you long to get back to it!"

"We're already back to it, my friend. With assignments this easy, we're practically men of leisure!"

They laughed as they worked, both men proving themselves to be the most helpful to the group through their hard work, whether that be cleaning the house or feeding the troops. But it didn't take long before the daily treks to the troops brought the men face to face with the risks they were taking. The activities of the Arrow Cross party had intensified, and as the Soviet Red Army advanced in other parts of Hungary bringing the purges against the Jews to a halt, Arrow Cross soldiers began concentrating their violence in and around Budapest. Dressed in sleek black uniforms, pistols on their belts, the soldiers marched through the streets of the city almost as if in a parade—ten men across, ten times that behind them, demonstrating their heavy numbers. But the marches weren't as intimidating as the wake left behind when they were not marching.

Driving the open truck filled with food and supplies, Frank and Ervin were shocked by what they saw and heard. Incomprehensible tragedies. Gunshots shattered the quiet streets regularly and Jews were routinely rounded up and shot as if they were rodents. Bodies floated along the Danube River, some tied together. Women, children, and the elderly were especially targeted, as if killing the most vulnerable enhanced the terror the Arrow Cross could inflict as they patrolled the city's streets for Jews to shoot. Jews were being hunted and killed openly and lawfully. Ervin had never seen such slaughter, nor had Frank, and they realized that it was only a matter of time before they were apprehended and killed themselves. The prospect of continuing to work out in the open did not sit well with the men, who knew that to do so would put them at risk, but they were not in a position to negotiate their labor. Though free, they had no choice but to do as they were told, even if the streets were fatal for Jews.

Had Ervin known what they were getting into when they'd gone to Budapest, he thought he would have chosen suicide over witnessing such horrors. The magnificent Budapest he'd known and loved while growing up was the Budapest of his mother's world, the big department stores, the fancy restaurants and tearooms, the opera, the plays. Now that he'd returned to the city a grown man, the Budapest he'd recalled with such fond memories had been defiled by evil. He had never seen so many bodies, shot full of holes, beaten into a bloodied pulp of flesh and broken bones, hacked into pieces or, if they were lucky, merely drowned. Worse than the days were the nights when he'd be haunted by the memories of what he'd seen that day, the cries he'd heard from men, women, and children as they were killed. Even in sleep, he couldn't escape the nightmares. In some ways, he had felt safer in the Labor Service where he was brutalized daily, but never made to see such sights that ought not be seen. He began to understand a part of his father that had forever been beyond his reach, that part of him that had never returned from the war, that part that remained haunted. Now it was Ervin's turn to absorb the evils of the world, to exchange his freedom for the price of these horrifying scenes he feared would haunt him through his life. He was only 22 years old, yet he felt so far from his protected childhood, so far from the past when he'd look forward to his father bringing him home a packet of confections. Now he looked forward to his parents simply coming home. Wherever their home might be.

Yet for all the horrors since coming to Budapest, and as frightened as he was working outside, it felt as if some unknown protector was safeguarding him and Frank. The Protective Passes. The unexpected offer of a safehouse. Their new boss, a guy named Kurt, was so impressed with their work that he regularly gave Frank and Ervin extra food. Ervin had never eaten so many sweets, for there seemed to be no end to the treats they received. But not far away was a Catholic nursing home where the elderly tenants were not as fortunate. Many were starving and when Ervin learned of their sad state, he and Frank began bringing them extra food. It brought him great pride to know that for all the extra food poor peasants had offered him when he was hungry, he now had the opportunity to repay the gift in kind. It was a small act and one that he could not have suspected at the time would be repaid with his life when the whole house of cards that had been his safehouse collapsed.

The Soviets were advancing rapidly, and it was apparent that it wouldn't be long before they took Budapest. Rather than cease their brutalities and negotiate a settlement, the Arrow Cross appeared determined to ferret out any Jews who had been hidden in and around Budapest. Tensions were rising in the safehouse, which was just outside the city, and one day, while Frank and Ervin were out working, Kurt called them aside and told them that Márk and several other senior men had been quietly taken away, ostensibly for their own protection.

"What do we do now?" Frank asked Ervin, having long before placing his trust in his friend to come up with a plan.

"We can't stay there, but we need to get our packs. I don't have much, but until I find my parents, their letters are all I have."

"Yeah, me too," Frank said. "Think it's safe?"

"Let's find out!"

"You can't go back there," Kurt said, echoing Frank and Ervin's sentiments. But once they pleaded with him to retrieve their packs, he relented. "I'll wait for you a couple of blocks away. You go in, get the packs, and get out. You understand? No hanging around."

"Got it," Frank said, and Ervin nodded his agreement.

"But first, make sure it's safe to go inside. You see any signs of the Arrow Cross, or even anyone you don't recognize, high tail it out of there. Got it?"

"Got it," Ervin said, and Frank nodded.

There were a few men in the house, but the men's club atmosphere had been replaced with a somber, funereal feel as those few left now faced the ending of a once happy home and the beginning of their uncertain fate. As others packed and a few sat and drank in the darkness, Ervin grabbed his pack while Frank got his and in minutes, they were down the street and in the truck with their boss behind the wheel.

"Now what?" Ervin said aloud, not to anyone in particular. Turning to Kurt, he asked, "Do you have any suggestions about where we should go?"

Kurt, an otherwise quiet man they barely knew, smiled and assured them he'd take care of them. "I know just the place for a couple of young men like you two," he said and from his sudden change in tone, both Frank and Ervin realized they may have made the mistake of their life. Even Ervin, who prided himself on his skills in sizing up people, wondered if he'd made a grave error with the man behind the wheel. He'd seemed so decent, but the entire world had been turned upside down, with decent men doing things they'd never have considered themselves capable of doing. Was he going to turn them in to the Arrow Cross? Or did he have other plans for them?

In reply, he turned up the music, a lively Roma folk tune, and drove out of town singing at the top of his lungs as if the other two men weren't even there. By the time he'd finished with that song and half a dozen others, Ervin saw that he was taking them back to the area where they worked. The music continued to drown out any questions he tried to ask, and it wasn't until he pulled into the nursing home that Ervin began to relax.

"You're taking us here?" he asked once the truck had been parked and the engine—and music—turned off.

"Yep. Feeding those Catholic ladies has saved your souls, my boys!" Then he laughed uproariously. "You should have seen your faces. You kids were more scared than a pig at a party! Thought I was taking you to be slaughtered? No, just taking you to the nursing home a little early in life, but hey, it's a life!" As he continued to laugh at his cruel prank, the boys both thanked and cursed him. But most of all, they thanked him.

Once he brought them inside, however, the joke was on them. Each man was greeted by one of the elderly women they'd given food. Frank was swiftly pulled into the room of one woman, while Ervin was ushered into another. He recognized Ágnes immediately—she was a spitfire of a woman, toothless and frail but with a fiery temperament and wit.

Ágnes had spent her life as a housekeeper to a wealthy Jewish merchant who treated her as one of the family. When her eyesight and arthritis had made it impossible to continue working, the family had continued to provide her room and board until, alas, they were deported. Being Catholic, she was spared, but she was left with no place to live and, with little money of her own, she found herself dependent upon the charity of the church. Given her poor health, she was given a bed in the nursing home, but it was the kindness of strangers—such as Ervin—that kept her fed.

"I never expected at my age that I'd be sleeping with a handsome young man," she teased as Ervin awkwardly thanked her for sharing her room.

He looked around and wondered where, in fact, he would sleep. There were six beds in the room, each occupied by an ancient woman, though none quite as cognitively alert as Ágnes. Three of the other women were fast asleep and the other two sat in their beds, seemingly unaware of his presence.

"Oh, that's Irma," Ágnes said when she saw Ervin staring at a woman who was talking to a visitor only visible to herself. "She thinks her husband visits her every evening, but he's been dead for years. Don't tell her that, it just makes her sad."

Ervin nodded. "Where should I sleep?" he finally asked, to which Ágnes let out a howl of laughter.

"My dear boy, you'll sleep underneath me," she teased.

Ervin was at loss for words. Was he really to sleep with Ágnes?

"Oh, don't worry," she assured him. "You don't have to share a bed with these old bones. You'll have to hide under the bed, I'm afraid. That's the only safe place for you!"

Ervin had woken up in a soft, comfortable bed in a safehouse that morning, never knowing that he'd fall asleep that night underneath the bed of an impoverished 90-year-old devout Catholic with no bladder control.

At least he and Frank were still alive. How long they'd stay that way was anybody's guess.

UNDER THE BED

Living under the bed was as uncomfortable as Ervin had imagined, to the extent he'd had any time at all to imagine his new quarters. There was little to do but sleep and play with the dust bunnies that gathered in the cramped space that became his home. Had he not witnessed the savagery in the streets himself, he would have found the prospect of hiding beneath a bed absurd and humiliating, cruel even, but he knew that to be recognized in public as a Jew would be a death sentence, and that any Christian caught hiding a Jew would be imprisoned or killed. He knew as well that Ágnes was risking her life by letting him stay in her room, as were the others. The elderly residents of the nursing home he had once helped with food were now repaying him the only way they knew how—by saving his life, even if it meant he had to spend his time staring at the black socks and shoes of the visiting priests who would drop by his hostess's room on occasion; far too frequently, Ervin soon concluded. The view from beneath the bed was bad enough, but the weight of the corpulent Father Norbert caused the bed to sag so low, Ervin feared if the good priest ate so much as another pierogi, he'd crush him to death. Fortunately, he could scamper out and stretch when no one was about, but the slightest sound down the hallway meant he had to dive under the bed once again.

I wonder how Frank's doing, Ervin often thought, as he pondered the bewildering life they had found themselves living. Given that Frank was much larger than Ervin, he imagined his good friend was even more miserable than Ervin to be sandwiched between the floorboards and mattress. Considering how miserable Ervin himself was, Frank had to be in absolute agony.

Despite the danger of being caught outside, Ervin knew he had to venture out at some point. He needed money and there wouldn't be any coming his way while he gathered dust under the bed. Reflecting on his father's insistence that he memorize the names of people who could help them—a directive Ervin had found ridiculous at the time, but now appreciated immensely—he remembered that there was one woman in Budapest who his father assured him he could call in case of emergency. Her name was Rebecca and she worked as a cashier at the National Casino, or at least she had when Ervin's father had entrusted her to help them should the need arise. Now the need had arisen. Ervin felt he had no choice but to seek her out. But how to do so without getting caught?

"I know someone who can help you," Ágnes told him when he'd presented his problem to her. "I have a relative who works as a guard for the Arrow Cross—"

"No!" Ervin interjected before she could finish. "They'll kill me in an instant!"

"Not if I tell him not to. He's my niece's husband and she adores me. He's not going to betray her. Let me get in touch with her. Don't you worry."

But Ervin was worried. Was Ágnes turning him over to the Arrow Cross? He could not imagine her doing so, but he could certainly imagine she was naïve enough to think it safe. But she wandered out of the room to make a call so quickly that his only choice was to bolt from the room then and there—where he'd be certain to be apprehended—or wait it out and risk being turned over to a guard who might help him or help get rid of him. He decided his chances were better if he put his trust in Ágnes.

He'd fallen fast asleep beneath the bed by the time she'd

returned. He felt her slippered foot nudging him awake. "Wake up, lazy boy! I can't bend over at my age or I'd yank you out of there."

"Is that my husband?" Irma asked. "Is he bothering you again? He wouldn't pester you so much if you weren't flirting with him every time he came to see me."

"No, it's not your husband," Ágnes said. "Your husband is sitting right in front of you. Can't you see him?"

"He is? Oh, yes, I do see him! Well, it's a good thing you're dressed decently, that's all I can say."

Ervin dragged himself out from under the bed, wondering how much longer he was going to have to listen to such nonsensical conversations.

"I've got good news!" Ágnes told him. She was in high spirits and Ervin realized that for all the risks she was taking, Ágnes was having the time of her life hiding and helping him. Given the dreary life she'd ended up with after all those years of hard work, the excitement of harboring a fugitive was probably the first good time she'd had since she'd lost her own home. It also occurred to him that the violence against Europe's Jewish people was far reaching and affecting nearly everyone in some form or another. For Ágnes, it was hunger and homelessness at the end of her life, a life she was now risking. For Ervin, it was living under her bed listening to her banter with a demented woman and her invisible husband.

"Did you reach your niece?" he asked her, as he brushed off the dust bunnies and sat beside her on the bed.

Ágnes was practically jumping up and down on the bed, she was so excited. "Oh yes, indeed, and she was more than happy to help. She's a good girl, you know, even if her kids are monsters. Especially that little one—he's her fourth and the spawn of the devil if you ask me. Why she has so many kids, I'll never know."

Ervin listened as she prattled on about her family, his mind drifting until he heard her get to the point of interest to him.

"Boris will meet you here and escort you to the casino," she said. "He's got one of those fancy armbands, you know, the official kind. No one will question you. He'll take you there, wait for you, and bring you back. But you'll have to go tomorrow because that's the only day he's got off. And you can bring me back some biscuits, but no nuts, I can't eat those without my teeth."

Her teeth were in a glass beside her bed, as she didn't like wearing them because they were ill-fitting and, Ervin half suspected, she liked to unsettle her guests with the unusual sight.

Ervin agreed to the plan, albeit a bit nervously, but he knew he couldn't go anywhere without money, and this was the only plan he felt might work. And if it didn't, wherever or however he ended up, at least he wouldn't end his life under a bed in a nursing home.

If only my parents could see me now, he thought, as he bid Ágnes goodnight and crawled back under the bed for another night of miserable sleep. He was certain his parents would both pity him and laugh about it for years to come.

The next morning, just as planned, Boris, the Arrow Cross guard, arrived and though not particularly friendly, he was certainly not rude or disrespectful. He appeared a bit put out by the inconvenience, but not by Ervin himself. "Just keep your head low, so to speak," he told Ervin. "And let me do any talking. Anyone asks, I'm escorting you back to your battalion."

It was a sensible plan Ervin had to admit, and he quickly found himself relaxing around Boris. By the time they reached Pest where the National Casino was located, he realized he was far more nervous about asking his father's friend for money than he was about putting his life in the hands of an Arrow Cross guard, an irony that didn't escape him as he noted the mounting ironies in his unexpected young life thus far.

The National Casino had once been one of the most aristocratic and exclusive clubs in all of Hungary, established in the early 19th century for Hungarian nobility. Ervin was aware of its history and felt a bit conspicuous in his street clothes, now worn and tattered, but they were the only clothes he had other than his uniform, stuffed so tightly in his pack he'd be even more conspicuous if he wore it. As they neared the casino, he saw masses of German cars and military vehicles blocking the streets. His heart raced and he felt a rush of heat consume him, as he thought for an instant that Boris had led him into a trap.

"It's always like this," Boris said, noting Ervin's concern. "The headquarters of the German High Command is inside the Astoria Hotel."

Ervin looked about and saw that the hotel and casino shared the same traffic circle. He was relieved, though, when they walked past the military officers with ease and straight into the opulent casino as if they had every right to do so. He'd half expected to be nabbed.

The casino was packed with people. Though it was only the middle of the afternoon, the place was filled with drinkers and diners and the noise level was so high he had to practically shout as he asked for Rebecca. At long last he was escorted to another room, where a tall, red-headed woman who appeared to be about the same age as his mother, but much worse for wear, was exchanging cash with some patrons. When she had finished, Ervin approached and introduced himself.

Rebecca looked to the left and right before saying in a low voice, "you really shouldn't have come here."

"I know that," Ervin whispered back. "But I didn't know where else to go. My father said you could help me and I do need help. I have no money, the Arrow Cross will kill me if they catch me, and I have no idea where my parents are. Have you heard anything?"

Rebecca said nothing as she took care of a couple of other patrons, then signaled for him to follow her to another room. They stepped into a small, empty room where it was much quieter, though she continued to speak in a whisper.

"I don't know where your parents are, I haven't heard anything. No one knows what's going on."

Ervin's heart sunk to hear such news. But he didn't allow himself the luxury of dwelling on his worries. He had come to her with a request.

"I have no money and no way to eat. Is it possible you could help me?"

Her face first flashed annoyance, but quickly shifted to sympathy as she said, "I can give you some money, but you must leave here right away. It isn't safe. You must be very careful. My neighbor," she said as she cocked her head toward the wall to indicate she was referring to someone close by, "is a Nazi sympathizer and if he suspects you're Jewish, he'll report you in an instant—and me, as well." She reached into the pocket of her dress and pressed some bills into Ervin's hands. "Here, take this and go! I pray your parents are safe for they are such good souls. But you must be careful or you'll be deported too!"

Ervin thanked her profusely and hurried away as if the Nazis truly were on his tail. He thought he would have felt safer had he gone straight to the mouth of the dragon—the German headquarters at the Astoria. Once through the doors, he met up with Boris outside the casino. He also seemed to sense the danger, for he got them both out of the area swiftly and silently.

"Wait!" Ervin said as they were almost out of sight of the casino.

"We don't have time to go back," Boris said, his voice stern. "Whatever it is, it's too late now."

"I have to get biscuits for Ágnes," he said, nearly pleading.

Boris nodded. "We'd better not go back without them," he agreed.

By the time he returned to the nursing home, he rewarded Boris with payment for his time and troubles and heaved a sigh of relief that the mission had been accomplished. Then he took a deep breath and crawled back under the bed for another night between the floorboards and the sagging mattress.

After several days in the nursing home, Kurt arrived with urgent orders.

"You boys have to leave at once," he told Ervin, referring to him and Frank. Though no longer boys, they were still so young that in the eyes of their elders they might as well have been teenagers. And though Kurt was no longer their boss, as it was too dangerous to work anymore, after finding them a safe place at the nursing home, he'd gained Ervin's trust. Without a moment to lose, Ervin grabbed his pack. He had learned that when it was time to move, he had to be ready in an instant.

"I'm so sorry," Kurt told him. "I thought this was a safe place, but there are rumors starting, so I've got to get you out of here. I promise I'll get you someplace safe. Let's go!"

Ervin turned toward Ágnes and saw the sadness in her eyes. "Thank you for everything, Ágnes," he said. "I'll always remember your kindness."

"And I yours," she said, taking his hands and pressing them between her own tiny hands. "You be safe and don't let those Nazis get you."

He smiled and bent down, kissing her forehead.

"Are you kissing that hussy?" a voice called out. "I told you to stay away from her! What kind of a husband are you?"

"Sorry, honey," Ervin said, "you know you'll always be my sweetheart!" He gave Irma a flirtatious wink and was gone.

Ervin followed Kurt out to his truck, where Frank was already waiting. After their previous experience with their prankster boss, they now felt secure in his company and found the ride leaving the nursing home much more lighthearted than it had been getting there, when they thought he was taking them to their doom. They laughed about living under the beds and Ervin joked about the black socks of the local priests and how they should wash their feet more often. Kurt laughed along with them as they drove across the streets of Budapest, once again blaring his Roma folk music, with Frank and Ervin occasionally joining in the singing. Though they didn't know where they were going next, they couldn't have been happier to be liberated from under those beds.

They pulled into a campground outside the city and Kurt jumped out of his truck and led the men to a military truck, its driver leaning on the door smoking a cigarette.

"Here you go," Kurt said, smiling broadly, "these guys will take you to a safe place. Don't worry, they know what's going on and they'll take care of you." Turning toward the driver, he added, "You be sure they get there safe and sound, got that?"

The driver nodded, dropped his cigarette to the ground and without a word jumped back in the cab, motioning for Frank and Ervin to get in the back. Happy to be back together and on another adventure, they laughed and swapped stories as the truck drove along the bumpy backroads, transporting them to their next refuge. Ervin told Frank the story of the casino and Frank entertained Ervin with stories of his own. At long last, they pulled into a huge army barracks complex, but before they could even climb out, they were greeted by armed soldiers gesturing with their rifles for the men to get out.

The soldiers weren't smiling. They were with the Arrow Cross. Kurt had turned them in.

CAPTURED

Frank and Ervin were yanked out of the truck and hit a few times with the rifles to get them moving along. They were ushered into a barracks where dozens of other equally frightened young men were housed. It didn't take long to learn that these were other escapees who had been apprehended in what was called "the daily catch." Kurt's betrayal was common, apparently, and each had an equally upsetting tale to tell of how they'd been betrayed and captured by someone they'd trusted.

They were to be taken to a train station in a few days where they would be packed in railcars and deported to Austria. No doubt there were death camps awaiting them there, and Frank and Ervin realized their lives were now down to days.

The room where they'd been taken was a dreadful sight. The scene before them was distressing, for the floor was strewn with personal items. Filthy clothes, leftover food, dirty socks, loose papers, comics, and paperback mystery books were piled knee-high.

"Looks like they were here for some time," Frank said.

"And left suddenly," Ervin added. "Either they all fled or they were all seized."

"Think we're next?" Frank asked.

"Sure looks that way," Ervin said.

They spent the rest of the day amidst the ruins of these strangers' lives and by nightfall, they slept on the dirty floor strewn with trash that had once been people's prized possessions. Though there was no longer a mattress above their heads, much less below them, the men fell to sleep wondering if it would be the last time they ever did so.

The next morning, they were awoken at daybreak by soldiers' orders. "Get up, you lazy pigs!"

The command reached Ervin in the depths of his dreams and as the cacophony of other captives waking to the shouts of the soldiers brought him back to reality, his heart sunk. He was no longer free. He'd been captured. The brutality would not only return to his life—however brief it would be—but the cruelty would also be unlike any he'd known. He was not just a Jew, but now a captured escapee as well. His life had no value. Indeed, his killing would be joyful to these soldiers. How long would they keep him alive? he wondered, as he scrambled to stand at attention.

A broom made of some twigs was thrown at him. "You!" a soldier barked. "Clean up the yard!"

Ervin took the broom and stepped outside, while Frank was ordered to clean up inside. How such a useless broom would clean anything was a mystery, but one way or another, he was going to have to sweep up all the debris that had been scattered about, as well as any loose dirt. He began his task with a heart gone dark, wondering what the purpose was in prolonging his life for the few hours it would take to clean the yard. When he had a chance to look around, he saw a heavy iron gate and on approaching it, he peered through the bars and saw that the area was heavily guarded. There was no way out. *Might as well kill me now,* he thought, though his resignation to his fate was quickly followed by thoughts of his parents. *Whatever it is they've been put through, they will never recover if they find out I've been killed. I have to live.* Thoughts of reuniting with his parents somehow, some way, kept him sweeping the dirt with the pitiful broom, as he awaited the next phase of his punishment.

"If anyone has any reading material, step forward!" It was an odd request, but a booming one in the sullen silence of his work, and Ervin immediately stood to attention. One of the soldiers needed something and he had long since learned that whenever a guard or soldier was in need, there was an opportunity. His instincts kicked in and though he didn't have reading material, he ran straight to the officer who'd called out and saluted him.

"Sir, I have some books, sir!" he lied, while another part of his mind went to work. He envisioned the terrible mess inside, recalling the comic books and mysteries he'd seen. "Permission requested to retrieve them, sir!"

"Permission granted. Don't waste any time."

Ervin hurried inside and saw, to his horror, that much of the mess had been cleaned up by Frank and the other captive escapees. He'd be in so much more trouble than he already was if they discovered he'd been bluffing, so in desperation, he rummaged through the remains of the discarded heaps until at last, he found a tattered book beneath a pile of garbage. *The History of the ABCs*. *They might kill him just for that title*, he thought. But it was all he had, so he ran back to the officer, saluted him again, and presented the book as if it were a sacred text.

"Take it to the front office and deliver it to the officer on duty. He's requested some reading material and he doesn't like to be kept waiting."

Ervin nodded, saluted hastily, and hurried off to the front office, where he saw that the doors of the main entrance were not chained shut as others were. He surmised that the doors would open to the main street and, at least from the inside, they were completely unprotected. He wanted to flee out the door, but then he thought of Frank. He couldn't just leave Frank there to be worked like a horse, then shipped off to Austria to probably be killed. Instead, he returned to his barracks, the ABC book still in his hand, and saw Frank waiting in line for his meal. Ervin went up to him and whispered, "I've found a way out of here."

Frank perked up but said nothing, merely nodded to acknowledge he'd heard him.

"We have to find a reason to get back to the front office. Have you still got some cigarettes on you?"

Frank grinned and tapped his front pocket. As broke as they were, he always managed to find the nicotine to feed his habit.

"Come on," Ervin said, pulling his friend by the arm. Frank dutifully followed, though he wasn't eager to walk away from a meal, however bad that meal would surely be.

They went to the officer on duty and with a new and sudden burst of confidence, Ervin saluted him and said, "Sir, the officer in the main office has requested we bring him this book," he flourished the book, "and a pack of cigarettes, sir. Permission requested to deliver them."

The officer eyed them with suspicion, but seeing Frank produce the nearly full pack of Symposia cigarettes, said, "Permission granted."

As simple as that, they were heading back to the front office. "We have to hurry," Ervin said, "so we can get out while they're still guarding the lunch line."

"Man, Erv," Frank said as quietly as he could, "you always manage to figure out a way to get us out of trouble. Or into it."

"Let's hope it's out of trouble this time!" Ervin said as they reached the main office. "There's the door to Heaven!" Ervin whispered, and Frank looked at him as if he'd shown him the veritable gateway to paradise. There was no one in the foyer and the officer who'd requested the book was behind a closed door. No one could see them.

"What if there are guards outside?" Frank asked.

"We say we're looking for the officer to give him his cigarettes," Ervin replied, having already thought out that scenario. "We're just lost."

"Alright, here's to Heaven," Frank said as they pushed the heavy door open. Seconds later, as if a miracle, they were standing on Lehel Street, the main road.

"Come on!" Ervin said, running across the street as Frank followed. "There's a streetcar!"

They jumped on board the streetcar just in time to look back and see that they had run right past the backs of two guards who hadn't noticed the fleeing men behind them.

Then it hit him. Ervin realized his backpack was still in the barracks—containing the letters from his parents. Now, all he had left were the clothes on his back, the gold watch and gold charm he'd hidden in his pockets, and the ABC book that had set them free.

"We need to split up," Ervin said. He hated the idea of parting from Frank, but realized that the longer they stayed together, the easier they were to spot. Those guards were going to be furious they'd gotten away, and they'd have every soldier in the city looking for them.

"Yeah, I guess so," Frank said. "But I have a relative who might be able to help us. He married a gentile and they've got a shoe store not too far from here." The streetcar was taking them straight into the fashion district and Frank was feeling confident as the area was familiar to him. "I think it's just a few blocks away. Come on!"

They were far enough away by that point that they felt safe leaving the streetcar. Sure enough, just a few blocks later they came to the shoe store where Frank's relative worked. Stepping inside, Frank saw his relative's wife stocking shoes in an empty store. She recognized him right away but appeared as frightened as she was startled to see him.

"Frank, what are you doing here?" she asked him, casting her eyes on Ervin. "Aren't you supposed to be in the service?"

"We've escaped," he confessed. "They're going to kill us. Please help!"

She looked around to be sure no one was there, locked the doors, and hurried them in the back. "I can only help you, Frank," she said. "I can't risk my life for someone I don't know." She continued to eye Ervin with suspicion, but Ervin eased her worries.

"That's okay, I'll find something. You just take care of my friend here, okay?"

She smiled for the first time. "He's safe with me. Here, Frank, get in here." She pulled out a giant hat box, the kind used to store multiple hats, and gestured for him to crawl into the box.

Ervin laughed. "At least you don't have to crawl under the bed, pal!" Then they looked each other in the eyes with a sadness that spoke the unspeakable truth. They might never see each other again. They hugged each other with several pats on the back before the woman broke up their goodbyes. "Hurry! My clerk will be back any minute. Frank, get in the box! And you—" she gestured to Ervin. "Go!"

Ervin flew out the door as Frank crawled into the hatbox, both men thrilled to be set free and heartbroken to say goodbye.

Stepping outside the door, Ervin's confidence rapidly faded. Now where could he go? He was still partially giddy with joy that he had gotten away but leaving Frank in a hatbox at the back of a shoe store didn't exactly fill him with confidence that his friend would be safe. More to the point, now that he didn't have so much as a change of clothes—and had lost his precious letters—he was totally alone in a way he never had felt before. He was a wanted man without any money, and he'd just learned a painful lesson in betrayal. He couldn't risk trusting the wrong person again. He could only rely on the people his father had trusted to keep him safe. Oh, how he longed to see his father again. It was only a matter of time.

PINK ROBE

He didn't know what to do. He felt he had no choice but to return to the casino and ask Rebecca to help him again. After all, she had helped him once, so he knew she had a good heart. And she was a friend of his father's, which meant a great deal. He started walking toward Pest, a rather long walk he calculated, but not more than an hour, which was a whole lot better than walking to Austria for the pleasure of being killed.

He reached the casino by mid-afternoon, hungry but with energy to spare. The walk itself had been invigorating, for he was free again, even free of his heavy backpack, and there was no greater feeling than freedom, he had come to appreciate.

As it had been the first time he'd visited, the casino was alive with activity, despite it being midday. He walked into the establishment feeling conspicuous, but soon saw that he was as anonymous as anyone else, for everyone was focused on their money or their drink. After asking where he could find Rebecca, he was directed to the hotel bar where he found her serving drinks.

"Big surprise, Ervin here!" he said, throwing his arms open wide.

In reply, Rebecca's face made it clear his greeting was poorly chosen. She was clearly not pleased to see him.

In that instant, he felt as small as a grub and wished he'd never escaped. Where once he was popular and well loved, and had never harmed anyone, now he was an escaped Jew—he was a problem for anyone who encountered him, if not a threat to their very lives. He never should have returned to the casino, he thought, but he had. And now he had to scramble to change her view of him.

"I'm so sorry," he said, his tone abruptly shifting from cheerful to serious. "I don't mean to invade your privacy. I just have no other choice or I'll be killed. That's the truth of it. I don't know where to turn and I can only trust the people my father trusts."

Rebecca's face softened, for it was clear he was in a terrible situation.

"Come," she said, handing her bar towel to a waiter and directing him to take over for the next few minutes. Ervin obediently followed as she took him through some back doors and halls and up the service elevator to the fourth floor, not saying a word to him, but smiling and greeting the coworkers she encountered as if he wasn't even beside her. They soon reached the servants' quarters where she used a key to enter a studio apartment with a bed, a reading chair, and a small dining table.

"You can stay here, it's empty," she said, as Ervin scanned the barren room. Though minute and sparse, it was far more generous than he had expected, and he'd be able to sleep in a real bed, not underneath one. "But you have to be quiet. No one can know you're here. These walls are paper thin. You so much as sneeze and they'll throw us both out."

Ervin realized that the favor he'd asked her—even if just a vague request for help—was more than just a favor. He was asking her to risk her life, just as Ágnes and the other women in the nursing home had done, just as Frank's relative had done when stashing him in the ridiculous hatbox, and just as the communist peasant had done when taking them in for the night and sharing their simple but delicious meal.

"Don't worry, Rebecca, I'll be quiet, I know the risk. And I can't tell you how much I appreciate you helping me. I know my parents will really appreciate it as well."

"I just hope your parents are safe," she said, and then added, "and don't open the door for anyone, you understand?"

He nodded, then asked, "Where's the bathroom?"

"Oh, damn, it's down the hall. Hang on." She left, returning ten minutes later with a frilly robe, some makeup, and a shower cap. "You're going to have to wear this," she said, laughing as she handed him the feminine attire. "A little lipstick and some rouge and you'll be prettier than me. But just in case, keep your head down. Don't let anyone see you. You can shave at the table. There's a mirror." She pointed to a small oval makeup mirror, then stepped out the door to return to work, leaving Ervin alone with nothing but time.

For the next two weeks, Ervin stayed in the room, doing nothing but sleeping for the most part. Once a day, Rebecca brought him a hot meal, which she slid through a vent in the window so that no one would see her coming and going from the seemingly empty studio apartment. As instructed, Ervin would don the robe and put on some makeup when heading down the hallway to use the common bathroom, a masquerade that entertained him amidst such tedium. Though free, he was essentially imprisoned, but it was a prison that came without any beatings and included a safe and comfortable room. He had no idea how long his confinement at the casino would last, but the answer came one morning when Rebecca banged on the door, whispering for him to open it.

When he did so, he saw that she was breathless, for she had run up the four flights of stairs in a hurry. "You have to leave right away," she said, not even noting that he was still in lipstick and mascara from his latest trip to the bathroom. "They've just passed an ordinance that we are required to post the names of every tenant of every room on the door. They're going to be inspecting every room—if they find me hiding a Jew, we'll both be killed! I'm so sorry, Ervin, but I just can't risk it, I—" but he cut her off.

"Rebecca, you don't have to apologize. I'm so thankful for all you've done, and I don't want to do anything that could put you at risk. Just let me take off my makeup and I'll be gone."

"You do look rather cute," she said, her face melting into a smile. "Would you like to keep the lipstick?"

Ervin laughed but declined the offer and, after wiping off his face as best he could, he was ready to go. With not even a change of clothes to call his own, he had nothing to pack.

"I have a place for you," she whispered, as they headed down the hallway. "The head chef has a beautiful apartment nearby. Let me introduce you."

Ervin was thrilled and went with her to the busy kitchen where Rebecca introduced him to a tall, handsome man who immediately showed an interest in Ervin. They slipped into a cooler where Rebecca explained the situation to the chef.

"It's no problem," he said, smiling directly at Ervin. "You can stay with me. I'll take you there when my shift ends at three, but I must go now. I've got a soufflé that had to come out of the oven five minutes ago and if I don't pull it out now, I'll be serving a German pancake. Oops, sorry, didn't mean to say German!" Then he winked and disappeared into the busy kitchen.

Ervin couldn't believe his luck and just as he was thanking Rebecca, she said, "Just watch yourself. He's a homosexual and he'll probably put the moves on you, so don't say I didn't warn you!"

As Rebecca laughed at the thought, Ervin's heart sank. He surely didn't want to be in such a situation and if that was the reason the chef was so generous with his apartment, he might well be furious when Ervin declined his overtures.

Sadly, he thanked Rebecca, but told her he'd have to decline.

"Probably a good idea," she agreed. "But too bad you're not a homosexual yourself, because he does know how to cook. Well, whatever you do, Ervin, you just be sure you stay safe, and when you find your parents, God willing, tell them hello for me. And be sure to tell them how cute you looked in that pink robe!"

"Thanks, Rebecca, and I hate to ask, but can you do me one more small favor?"

"Ervin, as much as I love your folks, you aren't exactly a small favor kind of guy. What do you need?"

"I just wonder if you can call a shoe store and see if my friend Frank is still in the hat box," he said, to which Rebecca just shook her head in disbelief, a wry smile on her face.

"Sure, kid, if that's what it will take to get you out of my hair. What's the number?"

After explaining that he didn't know the number but giving her the name of the shoe store and a quick summary of the situation, she disappeared, leaving him sitting in the lobby pondering his next move. When she returned, she had good news.

"He's still there, but his cousin says she can't risk hiding him much longer. He's got to find someplace else. You kids sure have gotten yourselves into a pickle."

"You can say that again," Ervin said, thanking her and giving her a hug goodbye, while Rebecca pressed a few bills into Ervin's hand. Then passing through the front lobby and out the doors for the first time in what felt like ages, Ervin found himself outdoors again. Free again. Alone again. And in need of help, yet again. But thankful as could be that Frank was in the same situation.

By the time Ervin had met up with Frank, it was a pitch dark, silent night. All window shades had been pulled down to keep the streets dark in hope of preventing the Allied bombers from hitting their targets. To add to their predicament, there was a curfew, and they were already violating it. The chances of them being picked up by the police were high.

"We're like a couple of stray dogs," Ervin said.

"Even worse. A couple of stray Jewish dogs," Frank said. "Too bad you didn't bring your makeup bag. I could have dressed you up like my ugly sister and explained you'd run away to join the circus and I was bringing you back home."

Frank found the story of Ervin's dress-up routine to use the bathroom among the funniest things he'd heard in quite a long time, whereas Ervin delighted in reminding Frank he'd just spent the last two weeks stored in a hatbox. Both young men were unhappy to find themselves once again in a miserable state with little food or money and no place to sleep, while doing their best to avoid apprehension. Thus, they gained momentary relief by chiding each other about the absurd lengths they'd gone just to stay alive.

"Well, we don't have the luxury of feeling sorry for ourselves," Ervin said. They had been walking aimlessly through the streets, keeping to the shadows, and speaking in whispers, ducking into unlit doorways and behind cars whenever a police officer or soldier approached. The increased security in the streets and darkness in the homes and businesses put them both on edge. "We need to make a decision. We can't just keep wandering around."

"I say we follow Rákóczi Avenue," Frank suggested. "It's a main street and goes all the way to the National Theater."

"Assuming we aren't taking in a play, why there?" Ervin asked.

"Don't know. But at least it's a main thoroughfare and we'll figure out something along the way."

Ervin shrugged. "I guess it's as good as any plan," he said, and they took a few turns until they ended up on Rákóczi Avenue. After walking some way, Ervin had an idea. "Let's turn right here," he said as they approached an intersection.

"Why here?" Frank asked. "What's down there?"

"Don't know," Ervin admitted, "and I don't know what we'll say if we're stopped. I just have a hunch."

Ervin had always relied on his hunches, though they were usually related to people, which he credited to his keen sense of character. But this time, for no reason he could articulate, he felt he was being guided by some divine force that was telling him to take the side street. Maybe he sensed a soldier or police officer up ahead, or maybe he was just tired and hungry and felt he had to turn somewhere rather than continuing to walk toward a theater he wouldn't be attending. But in making that right turn, both Frank and Ervin stumbled into a situation that wouldn't just change their lives. It would save them.

MATHIASFOLD

They had only walked a few meters down the side street when they caught sight of a sign on the main gate of a building. It was a poster offering temporary shelter to homeless refugees whose quarters had been bombed and destroyed.

"Think we can pass?" Frank asked.

"I don't think we have a choice," said Ervin. "Our luck's been good so far!" He ran up the steps and rang the bell. Moments later, a woman wearing a streetcar conductor uniform opened the door. Before she could say anything, Ervin spoke up.

"Hello, my name's Ervin and this is my friend, Frank. We just saw your poster and I can't tell you how relieved we are. We came to Budapest for work, but it fell through. We were renting a room across town but lost everything when it was bombed. We don't have much money, even our clothes were lost in the attack. We'd sure appreciate it if you could give us shelter."

She looked them up and down, sizing them up.

"Are you Jews? There's a new ordinance that bans us from sheltering Jews, so if you're Jews, I'm afraid I can't help you. Nothing personal."

"No, ma'am," Ervin assured her, while Frank similarly protested. But never one to pass up the chance of telling a good story, Ervin decided to put it on thick. "We're both Catholic. I'm sorry, but the truth is, after what we've been through, losing everything in the bombing attack, it troubles me that you'd doubt us. It's not the sort of thing we'd make up and we sure aren't Jewish. We were raised to be God-fearing followers of Christ and—"

To Frank's relief, she interrupted before he could go any further with his tale. "Alright, get in, it's past curfew and you can't be out on the street. Come on in. I've got a room you can rent. It's not free, but it's cheap."

After negotiating a low price, they paid her for a few nights from the small sums they'd each been given by their previous protectors.

It was a loud and rundown place with Christian messages calling on all who sought refuge to repent of their sins and let Jesus into their lives. From what Ervin could tell, no one there was the least bit Christ-like, as they had no hesitation about denouncing the humanity of Jews, and more than one looked as if he'd slit their throats in the night for the chance to rob them of the clothes on their back. Ervin slept poorly and by morning, he was ready to move on. "I just don't feel safe here and I don't like pretending I'm not who I am," he explained to Frank, who was happy to stay put.

"But we've been pretending to be someone we're not ever since we escaped the first time," Frank pointed out.

"Yes, but this is the first time I've had to deny I'm Jewish. It feels like I'm betraying my family, my history. Even myself."

"I get it, Erv, and I don't like it myself. But I'm so tired of picking up and moving constantly. I don't want to go."

"Then you shouldn't," Ervin assured him. Given that his family had already converted, it was easier for Frank to not be Jewish than it was for Ervin. So, after breakfast, they said their final goodbyes once again, knowing that this time it was even less likely they'd be reunited in the future.

"See you in Győr, buddy," Frank said, slapping Ervin on the back.

"You bet," Ervin said, certain of that fact as he punched his friend in the arm. Ervin could not have known as he left the fate that providence would once again spare him, but he had, by that point, put his trust in God to guide and protect him. Still, leaving Frank behind left him unsettled and disturbed, which he wrote off as the sorrow of parting with the friend who had been by his side during the most horrifying times, the most exciting times, and the most difficult and challenging times. With no pack to grab, he simply walked out the door and found himself back on the streets in need of a plan once again.

There was only one place left to go. Captain Kemeny had saved him once. Chances were, he'd save him again. His address committed to Ervin's memory—as so many names and addresses had been on that last visit to his father—Ervin took a streetcar across town to find the mysterious man who had shown up so quickly with a signed and stamped Protection Pass. When he found him, the esteemed soldier and war hero was dressed in street clothes like a common citizen, a sight that took Ervin a few seconds to grasp, as he had only ever seen the officer in uniform. But after gathering his wits about him, Ervin introduced himself as the young man from Győr whom he had helped with the Protective Passes and Kemeny ushered him inside.

After hearing the story of Ervin's escapes and his present predicament, Captain Kemeny quickly got to work. "We need to get you some papers," he said, sitting down in front of the typewriter, inserting a blank piece of paper into the roll, and tapping the keys quickly. Despite his reticence in contacting the captain, Ervin saw at once that he'd brought a sense of purpose to the retired officer's life. He was every bit as excited as Ervin at the prospect of helping him out, typing away as if electrified with energy.

A moment later, he yanked out the paper with a flourish, stood, and handed it to Ervin. "I'll affix some stamps to give it an official look, and then you take a commuter train to Mathiasfold. It's a suburb outside the city and it shouldn't take you long. Once you get there, ask for the foreman, a man named Wanek. He's hiding several people, including a few from Győr. He'll take care of you. Now go, there's no time to lose. Don't bring any attention to yourself on the way and, son, be brave. These are desperate times. But I can see already that you're a clever boy and if you continue to keep your wits about you, you'll get through this."

Ervin was so thankful, he wanted to hug him, but knowing better, he saluted the officer who once again was coming to his aid.

"One more thing, Mr. Wolf."

"Yes sir?" Ervin asked. He would do anything for this man who was risking so much to help him and giving him so much encouragement at a time when he felt so low.

"Before getting on the train, get yourself a shave and a haircut, young man. You look like an escaped prisoner who hasn't seen a barber in weeks."

Ervin's face flushed, though he was grateful Captain Kemeny had delivered the command with a slight smile. It was true, he couldn't have stood out more with his uncut hair and unkempt beard.

"I'll see a barber right away, sir," he promised and, saluting one last time, was out the door and in search of the nearest barber shop.

He found one just a few blocks away and was pleased that they were able to fit him in right away. As the barber made a few jabs about Ervin's disheveled appearance, he draped an apron around him and, with the eloquence of a dancer, spun the chair around, whipped out a leather strap, and sharpened the straight razor with a well-practiced expertise.

It was such a relief to have a proper shave—it was the first professional shave he'd had in over a year—and Ervin looked forward to finally feeling like a proper man.

"That beard of yours was getting so long I thought for a moment a Jew had walked through the door!" the barber said as he pulled the sharp razor across Ervin's soapy neck. "You aren't a Jew, are you?"

"No, sir," Ervin lied. "I can assure you I'm as much a Christian as you are." That last part Ervin felt was true, as he couldn't imagine any true Christian embracing the hateful sentiments he read in the barber's tone.

"You'd be surprised," the barber said, continuing to pull the razor across Ervin's skin, its newly sharpened edge just centimeters from his carotid artery. "Those filthy pigs are still all over the place, hiding in attics and basements and cupboards like the rats that they are. But they'll come out and dare to show their faces in the streets. Christ killers, they are. Every last one should be shot dead, don't you agree?"

Ervin's heart was beating so hard he feared the barber might hear it. "I sure do," he lied again, this time the lie piercing his heart with what felt like a betrayal to his people, indeed, his betrayal to God. *But what else could he do*, he thought, with the razor so close to his throat and the barber so filled with hatred. All he could do was to keep up the deception to spare his own life. He prayed that his shame would not show on his face, but the barber was so confident in his own ignorance that if it had, he wouldn't have noticed.

"They're all money-grubbing capitalist communist parasites," the barber continued, while Ervin wanted to laugh at the paradox. Clearly this fool didn't know the difference between a capitalist and a communist, much less the definition of either term. "I think Hitler and Szálasi should eliminate them all. Not even waste their bullets, just bury them all alive. Don't you think?"

Ervin mumbled his agreement as the razor slid across his lathered face. Inside he felt his soul dying from the cruelty of the man who didn't even realize he was serving a Jew, a Jew who would pay him for his ability to cut hair, a Jew who had already endured brutalities that would have killed this fool on day one, a Jew who had never done anyone any harm, who only hoped to one day follow in his father's footsteps and go to medical school. A Jew who wanted to heal people, not bury them alive.

"Christ killers," the barber spat, quite literally. His anger was growing greater by the second and he was now spitting out his words. Ervin wondered what any Jew had ever done to him to cause such rage. He thought, as well, that if anyone was killing Christ, it was this man with his hatred toward his fellow man, something so un-Christlike, that even unbelieving Jews could spot the hypocrisy. But Ervin didn't dare say what he really thought.

"I couldn't agree with you more," Ervin said, finding solace in his true sentiments being covertly expressed within the sentence. "It's unbelievable that they even show their faces in public." As he spoke, he admired his freshly shaven face in the mirror as the barber prepared for his haircut.

"You're right about that," the barber said. "And if one should ever walk through my door, I wouldn't think twice about killing him myself!"

Ervin had no doubt he meant it and, tiring of the pretense, he deftly shifted the topic to what a fine shop the barber owned and how proud he must be to run such a business. Taking the bait, the barber rambled on about how a man ought to work for himself and be his own boss, and as Ervin sat still so as not to cause the busy scissors to slip, he listened to the drone of the man so filled with anger and ignorance that he couldn't spot a Jew if he had the head of one in his hands. Once he was done, Ervin paid him and bid him farewell.

"It was such a nice talk," he said, the sarcasm undetectable in his tone, but audible in Ervin's thoughts. "I'll tell all my friends about you."

The barber smiled and thanked him for doing so as Ervin heaved a sigh of relief to be free of such a horrid man. Minutes later and freshly groomed, he hurried to the commuter train, pressing his pockets to be sure he still had the valuable—and very much fake—papers that he'd present to the foreman at Mathiasfold.

He'd no sooner bought his ticket and boarded the train when a jolt of fear shot through him. Onboard there were two terrifying gendarmes—the *csendőrség*—their red rooster plumes affixed to their hats and silver medals hanging from their uniforms to mark their value to the fascists. They had long been feared for their brutality in Hungary, but in recent months, Ervin had heard rumors that they were actively helping round up and deport Jews throughout the country. Had the barber not been the fool Ervin had taken him for? Had he reported him? Even if he hadn't, Jews were not permitted to travel, and they would be all too happy to capture him if they discerned that he was Jewish. He kept his head down, thankful he'd followed Captain Kemeny's advice and gotten a shave and haircut, and walked down the aisle, taking a seat beside a peasant woman who sat with a large basket of noisy chickens. The chickens would be a useful distraction and Ervin wagered that the gendarmes would avoid the area altogether, a wager that proved a wise one as the train took off and the men merely scowled at the peasant and her chickens and kept their distance throughout the ride.

The destination the captain had sent him to turned out to be a massive military service complex. Next to it was a large junkyard of old broken-down cars, trucks, military ambulances, and Ansaldo tanks. Though both were heavily guarded, Ervin had no problem getting past the guards once he showed the papers the captain had fabricated. Explaining he was there to meet with the foreman, Mr. Wanek, he was directed to a small and dirty office where a slim, ordinary-looking working man with a clean-cut face and short blonde hair sat behind a desk filling out a ledger of sorts.

Ervin knocked nervously and asked, "Mr. Wanek?" Except for the communist peasant who'd helped him when he first escaped, and Rebecca who worked at the casino, his experience on the streets had been that common working men, such as this man or the barber, were among the first to demonize the Jews as threats to their livelihoods and way of life. They were the ones who rallied in the streets and cheered as Jews were beaten. The ones who didn't hesitate to curse him when he passed when he'd worn the yellow armband. The ones who were willing to defend Hitler to the death, for no more reason than they'd been persuaded that Jews were the only ones in society beneath them. Looking at this simple man, he saw the face of the barber, the face of all who spat at him and cursed him. But Captain Kemeny wouldn't have betrayed him, would he? No, not him. Ervin was as sure of the retired officer's humanity as he was of Frank's loyalty.

"Yes?" the man said, looking up from his work and taking in the nervous young man who stood before him.

"Might I have a word with you, sir?" Ervin asked, still timid.

"Come in," he said, gesturing for Ervin to have a seat.

Ervin stepped into the office, closing the door behind him, and took a seat across the desk—itself dirty and strewn with papers, coffee cups, and a telephone. He could not imagine how anyone could work, much less think, in such a mess, but beyond the office it was even dirtier and messier. The whole place felt dismal, dirty, and loud.

"What can I do for you?" the man asked. "If you're selling something, you'll have to come back later. I'm in the middle of my accounts and not in the mood to buy anything. I have too much on my mind."

"I'll try not to take up too much of your valuable time, sir, but it's a matter of some urgency. You see," Ervin paused, hoping this man who looked more puritan than brave would prove to have a humanitarian heart once he'd heard his story. "Captain Kemeny sent me to you. He said that you might help me."

Immediately the man's face and posture softened. He nodded, and then asked, "You need a safe place to stay, I take it?"

Ervin nodded, cleared his throat, and said, "Yes, sir. If you can, sir."

"If the Captain sent you, I will help. I can take care of you. I'll give you a place to stay, but I must warn you, it is very crowded. But it's safe. At least for now."

"Oh, thank you, thank you," Ervin said, the relief washing over him like a warm shower. "I can't tell you how much I appreciate your help."

"It's nothing," he said, shaking his head. "I don't have much to offer, but you boys need so much help. I'll give you work. You can assemble bicycles. It's easy labor and no one will notice you as long as you're busy. I can't pay you much, but I can give you room and board."

Ervin couldn't believe his luck and his instincts told him this was a good man. He cursed himself for distrusting him merely based on his appearance, for he saw how readily others had judged him on his appearance. Yet the world had turned into such a frightening, dangerous place that judgments had to be made hastily. Hopefully, Ervin reasoned, this kind and generous man's appearance as a simple, working man would conceal his bravery and generosity to a terrified Jewish escapee.

The next day, Ervin reported for work. There were 15 other boys, including one he recognized from Győr, Ben, the son of a well-known surgeon. They worked in a crowded workshop in an isolated area with little supervision, but all were so thankful to be safe and well fed that no one slacked off. Ervin quickly came to not just be thankful for the work, he also actually enjoyed it. It didn't take him long to learn how to fix and build a bike like a seasoned expert, and before long, he was able to assemble one for himself from spare parts, something Mr. Wanek encouraged of all his men. Having a bicycle could save his life should he need to flee quickly, and though it had only been a month or so since his first escape, so much had happened in that month that Ervin already felt like a cat with a thousand lives. And if there was one thing a cat was always ready to do, it was to flee.

Yet for the first time in his young adult life, Ervin was working as a free man—however limited that freedom was with the Arrow Cross patrolling the area for Jews—and his pride in his work showed in the quality of his bikes. The once lazy young man from the well-to-do family had grown into a hardworking man of character who soon imagined he could be quite satisfied with a future in the bicycle repair business. Get his own shop, be his own boss. That possibility suited him quite well. True, he still dreamed of going to medical school and using his mind and hands to heal people. But the world he'd been born into was a world on fire, and if that meant he had to set aside his dreams, well, Ervin wasn't about to give up on dreams entirely. He'd suffered enough already to know that a dream adjusted to fit his prospects was a dream worth pursuing, however different it was from the future he'd once envisioned for himself.

He was chatting with Ben one morning while repairing a bicycle chain when Wanek appeared and pulled him aside. His new boss spent so little time in the shop, as he was preoccupied with his own work and trusted the young men to keep busy, that Ervin knew something was wrong. Maybe the time had already come for him to jump on that bicycle and get out of town.

"Yes, Mr. Wanek, what's up?" Ervin asked, wiping his oil-stained hands—now perpetually black with grease—on his canvas work apron. It seemed that whenever an authority figure approached him, it wasn't good, so he steeled his nerves.

"Last night some Arrow Cross guards came by," Wanek began as Ervin felt his flesh grow cold. "They were looking for you."

"Okay, I'll leave right now," Ervin said. "I don't want to put anyone at risk, I'll—"

"No, no, you're safe. I assured them I hadn't seen you. I just wanted to alert you. You should stay. They aren't likely to come back anytime soon. I just wanted you to know. Don't worry, I'll take care of you. These guys get ahold of you, and they'll tie you up and toss you in the Danube before you can even get a prayer out."

Ervin couldn't believe his good fortune in finding such a kind man. Of course, he'd been betrayed before, but there was something about Wanek that Ervin trusted implicitly, now more than ever. Ervin thanked him for saving his life, yet again, and went back to work.

A few days later, as Ervin worked on his bikes, his nerves tensed at the sporadic artillery bursts quite some distance away.

"Did you hear that?" Ben asked to no one in particular.

"They're getting closer," one man said. "That's not a good sign."

"Then again, it could mean the Allies are closing in," Ervin said. "They might be coming to save the day."

"You think so?" another asked.

"Seems to me that any combat is a good sign these days," Ervin reasoned. "The fascists are losing this war and as long as we stay out of the line of fire and don't get bombed, the sounds of gunfire are the sounds of hope."

As the men reflected on his perspective, a sense of hope filled the air and, in the days that followed, though cut off from news of the outside world and left to imagine the worst, the men began imagining the best—freedom was up ahead. Though working in the bike shop was the most freedom they could hope for, they were unable to roam freely outside as they were still subject to being discovered by the *csendőrség* at any moment and shot or drowned in the Danube; they were still illegal humans in their own nation. The terrifying sounds of gunshots thus became thundering applause.

Each day that applause grew louder and, as it closed in on them, they could hear the firing of smaller weapons. The battles were escalating and coming so close, they could see the lights from the firing antiaircraft guns. They were nearly in the line of fire, a terrifying yet exhilarating place to be after all each man had endured. Still, they had work to perform, and Ervin did his best to keep his emotions at bay as he worked on the bikes. Whether it was death approaching or liberation, he didn't know, but the only way to keep from going half mad with anxiety was to focus on one bicycle at a time.

In the evenings, the men gathered and speculated on what was happening, each one musing on his life after liberation and each one praying that they'd have a life once the battles ceased. As for Ervin, his hopeful spirits began to erode when the shelling came so close that it wasn't safe to walk outside. He speculated that a Russian attack could be imminent and was convinced that if they remained in the warehouse, they risked being killed.

"I say we stay outside," he said. "It's cold, but if we sleep in the tanks and trucks, we'll survive. It's the buildings they'll target."

"I'm not sleeping outside," said one.

"Me neither," said another.

"Besides, it's against the rules," said yet a third.

But Ervin had long ago given up on following rules. Had he done so, he would have stuck with his unit in the Labor Service and marched straight to his death in Austria. "Forget the rules," he said. "I'm not going to be a sitting duck inside this place. I'm sleeping outside. Anyone else?"

An uncomfortable silence followed, then Ben said, "I'm in." A moment later, another man said the same. But no one else.

The three headed outdoors and looked around in the junkyard until they found an old army ambulance that seemed to have space enough for them to stretch out. They had to huddle together for warmth as they had only their thin blankets and the temperature was below freezing.

"But at least we'll survive," Ervin pronounced, doing his best to inspire the only two who had faith in him.

"I sure hope we don't freeze to death," the other man lamented.

"Better to freeze to death than to be blown up," Ben said, a moment later adding, "hey, Ervin, supposing they blow up the junkyard?"

"Just get some sleep," Ervin said. "This is war."

The building didn't blow up. In the morning, the three men crawled out of the ambulance so cold they could barely unfold their bones. None of them had slept more than a couple of hours, for it was so freezing cold that sleep was impossible. They trudged back into the building to laughter and jeers and Ervin felt so small and embarrassed, and wondered if anyone would ever listen to him again. Ben was certainly unhappy, and the other man lost no time in denouncing Ervin to the others.

"I can't believe I trusted him," he grumbled. "What does he know anyway? He made us sleep in a damn junkyard just because he's a coward!"

The laughter and taunts kept up all morning long and, while Ben didn't join in, he kept his distance from Ervin. Ervin wanted to hide away in that ambulance forever just to escape them. *How I miss Frank,* he thought. Frank never would have turned against him like that. And he never would have avoided him the way Ben was doing. His thoughts began to consume him with shame and anger, but all he could do was continue to work, something that always took him away from the pain of his emotions. If he kept busy, he was free from the demons in his mind.

A week later, in the early morning of New Year's Eve, 1944, they all awoke to heavy artillery as loud, relentless machinegun fire rattled the earth. Looking outside, no soldiers could be seen, but wherever they were, they were close. Ervin knew that it wouldn't be long before they were hit, yet he also knew that no one would listen to him. He had to seek shelter, with or without the other men.

Just as he stepped outside, he saw Wanek running toward him. "Get to the bomb shelter," Wanek shouted.

"Bomb shelter? What bomb shelter?" Ervin asked.

"That big cement building east of the junkyard," Wanek said, pointing in the direction of the junkyard. Ervin knew the building well. It was so small, he'd thought it was just some storage facility. "I've unlocked it. Go!" Then Wanek ran off to alert the other men as Ervin made straight for the shelter, machineguns firing all around him.

He pulled open the heavy metal door and saw that it was indeed a shelter with a spiral staircase taking him far below the ground, where he followed a long, earthen tunnel lined with bunks to a spacious open room. Several other men were already taking refuge and they welcomed Ervin to join them. As others from the bike shop entered, they waited for hours while far above them the landscape exploded with gunfire. Hardly any words were spoken, and the tension was great. At long last, the battle slowed and soon voices could be heard above, though the words themselves were impossible to discern. Some were speaking in German, others in Hungarian, still others in what sounded Slavic. Then, absolute silence.

Whatever had happened above their heads, it had to have been horrifying. They certainly would have been killed had they remained in the repair shop. The question was, would they be killed if they left the shelter? Would they be killed if they remained there, and the enemy gassed or firebombed them? They were sitting ducks. But they were also living ducks.

Ervin assessed the situation. He was wearing only a simple army cap, but no armband. In his pocket were his papers, the ones Captain Kemeny had faked, including the Protective Pass. If there were Germans outside, those papers would reveal that he was a Jew and he'd be killed. For a moment, he thought the best thing would be to destroy the papers or hide them somewhere. Then he realized that if the soldiers outside were Russians, those papers would be quite precious and could save him. He didn't know what to do. But either way, his army cap would raise suspicion from both Germans and Russians, who would recognize him as a hiding soldier. Thinking quickly, he buried his cap in a pile of rubble and waited nervously.

Moments later, as heavy footsteps came down the tunnel, Ervin prayed for his soul. The door swung open, and the large shadow of a caped figure filled the doorway. Holding a machine gun.

AND THEY MARCHED ON

The man in the doorway was neither German nor Hungarian. Nor was he Russian. He was a Romany. But to Ervin, he was Superman.

"You're safe now," he said from the doorway. "We've taken care of the Germans."

A cheer erupted from the men who hugged each other in elation, their cries of joy echoing off the chamber's walls. The thrill that Ervin felt in that moment was immense, as all the fear was washed away by a flood of joy and relief.

"No talking!" the Romany ordered.

The cheering abruptly stopped, and Ervin's spirits came crashing down as the prospect of yet another occupying force hit him like a fist. He saw, for the first time, the suspicious look in the man's eyes and, as he turned to Ervin, those eyes went cold.

"What time is it?" he asked him, pointing to his watch.

Ervin glanced at his watch and just as he was about to answer, he realized the question had been a rhetorical one. Superman's hand was outstretched, waiting for the valuable timepiece just as any mugger on the street might do. Ervin's heart ached as he removed the watch his parents had given him, while he thought himself lucky that the buttoned collar of his uniform obscured the gold charm around his neck.

As he handed the Romany his watch, the latter smiled and said, "You are lucky. You have paid for your freedom."

It was a trade that, as far as Ervin was concerned, was in his favor, for he would have traded nearly anything to be free again. He dearly felt the loss and the injustice as no one else had been compelled to relinquish anything. Still, Ervin knew that he was more fortunate than the others. They likely had no gold watches to trade. He was now as impoverished as any other man, the comforts of wealth he'd arrived with when he'd first joined the Labor Service being gone. He was no less lucky than any of them, he knew. And they were now free, which was all that mattered.

Ervin's first instinct was to grab his bicycle and race off to find his parents. But before he had a chance to do so, the freedom he'd bought with his wristwatch was rapidly curtailed. They were ordered to follow the Romany officer to a nearby building surrounded by Romany soldiers. It appeared to be some sort of command center, where each man would be processed before being permitted to leave.

Once inside, the Romany went up and down the line.

"What is your name?"

Ervin answered.

"Rank?"

"I was in Jewish Labor Service, sir."

The interrogator nodded, then proceeded to the next man.

Once satisfied that all were labor camp survivors, he ordered them to stand aside until everyone had been interrogated. After they had waited several hours, the Romany officer asked the men for their identification papers. Ervin was grateful he'd hung on to the papers Captain Kemeny had prepared for him, hopeful the Romanies wouldn't be any better at spotting fake papers than the Germans or Hungarians. After all the papers had been collected, the men were separated and interrogated individually. When the time came for Ervin to be questioned, he felt confident in his answers for he answered truthfully, telling them of his escape from the death march and his desperation to find his parents. Though showing no sympathy, the officer who interrogated him nodded dutifully, then permitted him to be reunited with the others.

After everyone had been interrogated and their papers processed, the Romany officer appeared again, his eyes and face now softened with compassion.

"Now we shall bless you," he said, and looking into their eyes, he proceeded to pray in Hebrew, his voice gentle as he intoned,

Baruch atah Adonai Elohenu
Melekh ha'olam
Shehecheyanu vekiyman vehigi'anu lazman hazeh.
Blessed are You, Lord, our God, King of the Universe
Who has granted us life, sustained us,
And enabled us to reach this occasion.

Ervin was filled with a sense of pure peace as he joined in the prayer, and he knew for the first time that he was truly safe. Following the prayer, they were all given papers written in Russian, which they were instructed to hang on to at all times. They were warned, however, to be careful, as there were still isolated spots where Germans remained. They were then given loaves of stale bread and bid goodbye. They were free.

The room became filled with activity and excited conversations as everyone imagined where they'd go next, what they would do. Celebrate. Find romance. Eat wonderful food washed down by plenty of drink. For Ervin, though, there was only one thing he wanted to do, find his parents. No, two. There was someone else he wanted to find. Mr. Wanek. The man who had never betrayed him, had given him work and safety. Ervin looked everywhere among the crowds of people, but it was impossible to spot him. There were just too many people. Saddened by his failure to thank and bid goodbye to the man he had once foolishly thought a simpleton but discovered was a courageous humanitarian who had saved countless lives, Ervin joined the others as they left the military command center, each man his own man, each man now set free.

They began in a line, for the military structure they'd been living under had grown instinctual. Despite their eagerness to dance in the streets, the truth was that the country was still at war, and they weren't free of danger. They knew that by sticking together, they would be safer, so they set off to reach the liberated and stable northeastern area of the country, already under Russian control. Their destination was Debrecen, a town about 200 kilometers east of Budapest, which had been liberated by the Russians in November. There they would be able to start their lives anew.

As they hiked, their line gave way to scattered groups, but all marched forward. Ervin found himself in a group of three, with two other men he did not know, each witnessing the devastation of the war with every step. Corpses were scattered like debris along the roads, peasants, soldiers, and gendarmes. Ervin felt nothing for the sight of the fallen gendarmes or German soldiers. While others rejoiced at the sight and some even kicked their bodies, he was surprised that he was so unmoved. They had been living people one moment, dead the next. Born in innocence, loved by their parents, their families, their wives, and children, but corrupted by the politics of the time—if the evil the fascists had carried out could be called "politics." Now their bodies were testament to the cruelty and savagery of war. While others abused their corpses, Ervin prayed for their souls.

The walk was no promenade. It was yet another hike across the hills of Hungary, for there were many areas with no public roads, or zones of danger that they dared not enter. Thankfully, their year or two of Labor Service had strengthened them, enabling them to withstand the long march to freedom.

How many times must I mark my freedom with yet another step? he wondered as he marched on, trying not to consider the prospect of reaching their destination only to discover they were not truly free. To be free in times of war, he knew, was never absolute. Yet now, no one ordered them to do anything, no beatings were threatened, and there was no desire to escape. He trudged on, past the bombed-out buildings, past the tranquil fields of cows and sheep, feeling as if no war had ever been fought, past corpses that knew otherwise, and past villagers turning away, their eyes speaking of the grief they could no longer bear. War's insanity had reached into the most remote corners of the land. And so it was that he continued walking with neither joy nor sorrow across the country that had so betrayed him.

At times they would stop at one of the isolated farms—they had passed hundreds—to ask for food. Most often, the peasants would turn the men away, seeing not newly freed men who'd endured horrific atrocities, but instead three vagrants, unshaven, dirty, and tired. Occasionally, someone would let them sleep in their stable or in an empty stall in a pigsty alongside the swine. The experience was unpleasant, but Ervin had long since stopped dreaming of his comfortable home and bed. Now he sought only sleep, wherever it might be.

They marched on, traveling through unplowed fields and muddy stretches that seemed more like quicksand. Sometimes they were offered food, but most times they would steal it from the fields they passed. Worse than hunger, though, was thirst, and sometimes they would go so long without water that they resorted to drinking from the puddles left in the tracks of carts or cars. This "mud water" was vile, as it was usually mixed with the urine or even feces of whatever animal had pulled the carts or crossed the deep tracks left by heavy trucks.

At times they encountered Russian patrols. The first encounter was the most frightening, for they didn't know if they were truly safe or not, and the officers didn't look Russian but Asian. It turned out they were Mongolians who only wanted to check their papers and what meager belongings they had among them. Only one soldier was combative. He had mistaken a small soap canister for a gun shell, but once he'd inspected the canister and the men's papers, he released them. Despite the fright, Ervin was relieved to have had the encounter, for it demonstrated something he needed to know with certainty. Their papers were authentic.

The march continued and, despite stumbling into a Mongolian patrol trap where they were forced to give to Russian "charity" anything of value—which they lacked—and any loose clothing—which a few gave—they carried on. They were by this point emaciated, weak, and covered in body lice, yet their misery was softened by the certainty that they were heading toward their future —a free future. That certainty grew stronger as they approached more liberated areas, where the peasants were kinder and more generous and even offered them occasional transportation for a few kilometers, along with food and water.

At long last, they reached Debrecen, where they parted. There, a peasant offered Ervin the first real bed he'd slept in in a long while. As he slid in between the soft sheets, freshly bathed, resting his head on a down-filled pillow and covered with a thick, down-filled comforter, Ervin felt, at long last, like a free man.

The first few months of 1945 were viciously cold, but the warmth of freedom was unlike anything Ervin had ever known before. Nonetheless, the road to recovery was not an easy one. He found work as a roofer, but within days was hospitalized with hepatitis, his body so weakened from the infection he feared he might never recover—especially given the conditions of the hospital, which were far from hygienic, with patients stacked two to a bed, windows broken and patched with paper, and a heating system so old it rarely worked. Food was as scarce in the hospital as it had been in the Labor Service. Patients were dying all around him and Ervin knew that if he didn't get out of the hospital, he would surely perish. Thus, he focused all his energy on fighting off the infection and getting better, hour by hour, day by day. It was a survival strategy he'd learned to master.

Once recovered, he discovered that his warm bed had been rented to another tenant, though he was allowed to sleep in the foyer of the building. It was an arrangement that didn't bother him, as nothing could compare to the wretched hospital—much less the life he'd just been freed of. One night he was awakened by a beautiful naked woman passing from her room to the shared bathroom. Though a young man, up until then, Ervin had pushed away any thoughts of women, for they were so beyond his reach. But that night, he fell back to sleep a happy man, dreaming that he could hold that naked woman next to him.

Though such a dream did not come to pass, he learned that she had been a visitor to the room of a Russian officer who took a liking to Ervin and, upon questioning him, learned his story. Győr remained under German occupation and news from the western region of

Hungary was scarce, but the Russian officer offered to help Ervin get to Arad, a city in Romania where Ervin had cousins. Uprooted once again but united with his cousins, he felt safe, loved, and happy. They helped him to resettle, providing him with new clothes, a warm bed, all the food he could eat, and most importantly, love and affection. Still, as the winter passed into the spring with no word of what had happened to his parents, Ervin grew more anxious. Each day, he listened to the radio for any news and he combed every newspaper he could get ahold of. Day after day, there was no news, until finally, on May 15, just two weeks after Adolf Hitler killed himself, Ervin heard the news he'd been awaiting—the Russians had captured Győr. Now was his chance to go back home. Now he would find his parents.

HOMECOMING

Ervin had to get back to Győr. How, however, was the question. Passenger trains were not running from Romania to Hungary, and he no longer had it in him to cross the country on foot. So he climbed atop a pile of lumber being transported by rail to Budapest, reaching the city several days later, sore, tired, and, as always, hungry. As he'd travelled, several other soldiers joining him, he caught his first glimpse of the world that had been shut from his view over the preceding year. At each stop the train made as it lurched along the tracks, passenger trains from other parts of the country arrived, filled with death camp survivors who looked more like corpses than living humans. He had never seen anything like it, and the thought that his own parents might be among them was too much for him to consider.

It was at one of these stops that a small, frail man, not much bigger than a boy, joined them, climbing on top of the lumber. He looked far too weak to manage even the climb and Ervin and another soldier helped pull him to safety. As he settled down and Ervin looked into his eyes, something about the man looked familiar.

"Thank you, thank you," the man said, acknowledging the assistance. "This is good. I only need a small space. Does anyone have any water?"

Ervin offered him some water from a canteen he'd procured and as the emaciated man drank, the sound of his voice lingered in Ervin's memory. He had heard that voice somewhere, seen those eyes.

"Where are you going?" Ervin asked him.

After a moment of silence as he seemed far away in thought, the man said, "Győr. My home."

It was then that Ervin realized who the man was—the Wolf's family physician, the man who had treated Ervin as a boy.

"Dr. Krausz!" he said, and the man's eyes widened.

"Do I know you?" he asked, as he searched Ervin's face for clues.

"I'm Ervin Wolf, the son of Joseph and Kamilla," he said, so eager to speak to this man who might, just might, know what had happened to his parents.

"Ervin! Indeed, I do remember you. You were a sweet, gentle boy, weren't you? A bit soft, but I see this war has toughened you a bit." He chuckled, his eyes and smile warm.

"Indeed, it has," Ervin agreed. "Dr. Krausz, do you know where my parents are? I haven't heard from them in months and I'm so worried. Have you any word?"

Dr. Krausz shook his head, his face turning sad. "I'm afraid not, Ervin, but I fear the news may not be good. All the Jews were deported from Győr, all of us. No one was spared. They sent us to Poland to concentration camps. The horrors…" his voice trailed away, and Ervin's throat went completely dry. He felt his heartbeat quickening and with shaking hands, he lifted the canteen to his own lips, drinking just enough to wet his throat so he could speak.

"Did you see them? My parents?"

Again, the doctor shook his head. "No, not in my camp. I'm sorry, Ervin. I don't know their fate."

Ervin breathed deeply. This was the first he had heard of the fate of the Jews of Győr and in moments, he was bathed in perspiration as the reality began to sink in that his parents may have perished. But that possibility was too horrifying to even consider, so he comforted himself with the knowledge that his mother was a young, healthy woman, quite strong in fact. And his father was most definitely a strong and healthy man. Surely, they had survived.

Dr. Krausz saw the torment in the young man and added, "I know your pain, Ervin. I'm trying to find my own wife and children. I have no idea where they are, but I hope when I reach Győr, I will find them." Again, his voice trailed away, betraying his true fears.

"Where were you in Poland?" Ervin asked, desperate for more information. "What was the name of the camp?"

Dr. Krausz shook his head. "I don't even remember," he said. "The name, it was such an unimportant detail. I don't know that I ever even knew it."

"What happened at the camp? What did they do to you?"

Dr. Krausz looked beyond Ervin toward a distant point in space. "It's unspeakable," he said in barely a whisper. "Unspeakable."

Once they'd reached Budapest, Ervin and Dr. Krausz had hoped to hitchhike to their hometown, but when no one would pick up the two haggard travelers, they set out to walk to Győr on foot, a journey that took two difficult days. Once there, the two were aghast at the site before them. Their once beautiful town looked like a living hell with homes and businesses burned to the ground, some still in flames. The charred empty shells of roofless buildings glowed with burning embers. The buildings still standing had shattered windows, and walls riddled with bullet holes. Telephone and electric wires hung like spaghetti, some live with sparks. Garbage was piled high and strewn about, the stench pungent. Men dressed in rags pushed wheelbarrows and carts with their few remaining possessions. The air was thick with dust and smoke as Russian soldiers patrolled the streets carrying machine guns. There were no women, no children, no birds singing in the trees. Indeed, there were few remaining trees, just smoldering trunks marking their former beauty.

For the first time in his life, Ervin felt he was a stranger, a man with no home. His city had been incinerated and his parents had vanished. He was stunned into silence by the ghostly landscape before him, he could not speak a word.

"Come," he heard someone say, a sound so distant, so foreign, it was only as his arm was gently taken that he realized Dr. Krausz was speaking to him. "Come with me, Ervin." He followed, unable to put into words the horror he felt and, as they walked through the city streets, it mattered nothing to him where they were going. He felt as if he himself was no longer among the living, but among the dead. When at last they walked up the steps to someone's home—friends of Dr. Krausz, he would later learn—he was unmoved by the horror on their faces when the door was opened. The two, who had crossed the country on lumber car and foot, only to move through the city's filth and soot in shocked silence, must have looked ghastly themselves. But in moments, they were pulled into the home and given baths and fresh clothes and slowly, ever so slowly, Ervin felt himself emerging from the shock. As they feasted on a dinner of baked potatoes with lard, Ervin relished every bite as if it was the best meal he'd ever had. His hunger had been so great, his shock so profound, and his grief so painful. To eat of the earth was sublime.

The following morning after breakfast, he ventured outside once again. In the morning light, the hellish streets looked no less shocking as he hurried across the city, passing block by burned out block until he reached his home. He knew, of course, that his parents would not be there, and yet... and yet. How he prayed they would be. Still, if he could only return to his home, establish his roots there once again, he would at least have a base from which to start his search for his mother and father.

And there it was. Unburned, miraculously, in good shape even. The shingle that once hung outside the door to mark his father's practice was gone. Only the rod from which it had hung remained, stabbing the bare wall like a sword. The windows were shuttered, the once beautiful curtains gone, giving him the impression of an abandoned building. Looking upward, he saw the balcony where his mother would sit for hours in the afternoons watching the traffic pass by. She had no car, no telephone, no television. Only this one balcony, which offered her the best view in town. Now empty.

He stepped into the building feeling like a thief. The hallway and staircase were dimly lit, but he knew each step instinctually. As he hurried up the staircase, he noticed the white-tiled wall with the tulips barely discernible in the darkness. The simple sight gave him comfort, as if to acknowledge he had indeed lived there, touched those same tiles so many times as he ran his hand along the wall in his youth. Reaching the first floor, he saw two familiar doors. On the door to his right was a nameplate, Molnár. Mr. Molnár had been a furrier who had been their neighbor for many years. Seeing his name gave him a jolt of hope, for perhaps he was still there. But the jolt passed as instantly as it had hit him, for the Molnárs were gentiles. They would not have faced his parents' fate, whatever it had been. These thoughts and impressions had taken only an instant, but time had become strangely distorted. His gaze turned to the left to the door he longed to pass through. His door.

There it was, the family's door, still looking much the same as it always had, still lacquered white and decorated with a wrought iron panel. The name on the door, however, was out of place. Gulassa. He didn't know anyone by that name. That name did not belong there.

He realized he was shaking. He felt as if he were an intruder, that he was the one who did not belong instead of that name, Gulassa. What if the door flew open, what would he say? How could he explain his presence there, what could he possibly say? "I live here! This is my home! I am Ervin Wolf and this is my parents' home. You must get out right now!"

No, that he could not say. Should he say, "I am a Jew and I just returned from a hard labor camp and now I'm home"? No, no, that would matter little in this world gone mad.

What he wanted to say, what he needed to say, was "Get out! Get out of my house, right now! You have no right to be here! This is my parents' home and it was stolen from them. You dirty bastard, tell me where my parents are, what have you done with them?!"

Should he refuse to leave? Call the Russians and have them arrest the thieving people who had taken up residence in his home? What could he do?

He rang the doorbell. It was all he could do and in the few moments as he waited for the door to open, he steeled himself for whatever he may encounter. He knew he must get himself together, he must be strong. He had endured so much. Surely, he could get through these few moments. And yet.

And yet this was the hardest moment he had ever lived, to stand before his own front door and know that a stranger would open it as naturally as if it was his own. To know, in that moment, that it would not be his mother or his father or their housekeeper, Nora, who would open it wide and usher him over the threshold, wrapping their arms around him. No, that was just a dream, a deep desire, as impossible to attain as flying through the air.

He heard the turning of a key, and then the door opened partially. Ervin strained to see inside, but all that he could discern in the slice of light were unfamiliar furnishings, nothing belonging to his family. Their things must be stored somewhere, he concluded, as his gaze shifted to the man peering at him. He was of medium build with dark brown eyes that regarded Ervin with curiosity. Ervin cleared his throat.

"Hello," he said, as casually as he could, as if he were inquiring about a flat to rent. "My parents used to live here and I was wondering if you might have any information about their new place of residence?"

He heard his own voice as if from a distance, sounding so weak, so feeble, so simple, when what he meant to say—to roar—was *get the hell out of our home!* He both hated and pitied himself in that moment, for he could not say what he so needed to say. He knew that to do so would only worsen an already surreal, horrifying situation.

"I'm sorry," the man said, "I cannot help you. I don't know anything about your parents." The door began to close.

Tears came to Ervin's eyes. "Please, Mr. Gulassa. My father is a dentist. His practice was here. Dr. Joseph Wolf and my mother is Kamilla Wolf. I've been in Labor Service," he began before Gulassa cut him off.

"I don't know anything about your parents," he said. "And this is my home."

The door closed and Ervin heard the turning of the key, locking him outside his family home.

Knocking on the neighbor's door, he was, this time, invited inside. He had known the Molnárs for years and hoped that perhaps they would offer to let him stay with them. After all, his mother had cared for their daughter, Panni, when Mrs. Molnár was ill or had commitments, had often fed her, taken her to school. Surely the Molnárs would help him.

He was wrong. Though they smiled and invited him in, even said how happy they were to see him, their reception of him was notably strained. It was a false enthusiasm, unlike their former warmth and friendliness. Ervin knew at once, as he told them of how much he loved and missed his parents, that he was speaking to an empty room, for they were unmoved.

"I'm sorry, Ervin," Mrs. Molnár said, "but we have no idea what happened to them. I'm sure you'll find them."

They were still standing, had offered him no seat, not so much as a glass of water. Ervin thought of the many times his mother had sent over cakes, cookies, and other treats to the Molnárs, the many times the women had chatted together in the hallway or in each other's homes, drinking tea, discussing their children, exchanging gossip. And now that the Wolfs were missing, the best they could do was permitting him to stand inside their doorway, the tears rolling down his face as they stood side by side before him, squirming with discomfort while offering nothing but false smiles.

"Thank you," Ervin said at last. There was no further point in continuing the conversation. He was speaking to two strangers, never mind how well he'd once known them. "I'd better go. I don't want to bother you any further."

"No bother at all, Ervin," Mr. Molnár replied. "I wish we could help you more, but these are difficult times, I'm sure you know. It was so nice seeing you again. Do keep in touch."

Ervin nodded and stepped out the door, both hurt and disappointed, if not rattled to see how profoundly war had changed even kind and caring people. It was as if their personalities had been replaced with something else entirely, something scripted and unfeeling. Like actors, Ervin thought, pretending to know him, pretending to care. If they had known a fraction of the suffering he and his family had endured, would they not be more compassionate?

There was little point in dwelling on the encounter, he realized, as he wandered up and down the once-familiar streets, wondering where to start his search. He stopped at familiar markets, kiosks, even the gentlemen's club his father once frequented. Many once prosperous businesses were shuttered, and those that remained opened either had new staff who knew nothing or battered and beaten merchants who could only shake their heads in sadness. No one knew a thing.

There was one other stop he had to make. He had to check on Frank's parents. It had been so long since he'd seen Frank. Last he'd seen him, he had been staying in that Christian mission house in Mathiasfold. He hadn't visited Frank's home since he was a teenager and, with the city of Győr so ravaged, it took him a bit of time to recall the right street. When at last he'd found the house, however, he learned from the new residents that Frank's parents had left Győr voluntarily not long before. As converted Christians, they were probably safe, Ervin knew, but still, he worried about Frank.

"Thank you," he said as he turned to leave. Then he stopped and asked, "Their son, Frank. He was in the Labor Service. Did you by any chance hear anything about him?"

"Oh, yes," the woman of the house replied. She was so much friendlier than that awful man Gulassa who was living in Ervin's home. "He did come here looking for his parents. Such a nice boy. They were so worried about him, but they'd had to leave without him. It wasn't safe for them to stay, you know. I'm sure they're back together again by now. He has family nearby who could put them in touch."

"So, you did speak to him? He's okay?"

"Yes, by the grace of God he is. He was staying at a Christian mission house and hadn't been there more than a few days when it was bombed. Absolutely destroyed. He was so lucky he wasn't killed."

"He's okay?" Ervin asked urgently. "Was he injured?" Ervin imagined Frank maimed, imagined himself severely wounded or dead had he not left when he had. If only he'd known he was leaving his dear friend to face such danger, he would have insisted Frank come with him. He had thought him safe there, though, and Frank himself didn't want to leave.

"Nothing serious. It was a miracle he lived, and thank goodness he did, for he saved his landlady. She was terribly injured, he said, and he had to take her to the hospital in a wheelbarrow. She would have died if Frank hadn't been there to save her."

So, there was a bright spot to his leaving Frank there, after all. Ervin was immensely relieved to know that Frank himself was safe and, as eager as he was to find his dear friend, he knew he first had to find his parents. With no place else to look and the sun beginning to set, he returned to the home of Dr. Krausz's friends, people he did not know at all, but who had welcomed them into their home and shared their simple food with him. Theirs was the victory of good and humane behavior, Ervin thought, over the continuously present evil lurking in the background of the world that he'd once known. Their compassion and humanity gave him the courage to carry on when the feigned friendliness of the Molnárs and the unfeigned disinterest of that horrid man Gulassa living in Ervin's home would otherwise have left him bitter and enraged. He kept his focus on the future when he'd be reunited with his family. Even if they were living in a ghetto, Ervin didn't care. He just wanted to find them and live again as a happy family.

In the weeks that followed, as Ervin continued searching the synagogues, markets, neighbors, and family friends to find his parents, he learned more about how his home had come to be occupied by a stranger. When the Jews were deported from Győr, Germanophiles took advantage of their plight, looting homes and businesses and taking up residence in the homes that Jewish families had been forced to leave. No doubt that was how Gulassa had come to reside in the Wolfs' home. This explained his hostile reception. Fortunately, the defeat of the Germans had brought an end to such thievery and the ownership of stolen Jewish property was forbidden by law. Many, fearing arrest—and perhaps, Ervin liked to think, motivated by a sense of shame—returned the stolen property by discarding it in the courtyards of synagogues where household belongings and treasures were piled high. Ervin thought the sight of these discarded stolen items was both heartening and a national shame. There was no point in rummaging through those piles, however. Ervin needed to get back into the family home—even if the furniture was gone, his father had hidden some of their valuables in there and he was determined to get them back. And given Gulassa's animosity, there was only one way to get back in. He went to the police.

Fortunately, a special department had been set up to help restore stolen Jewish property. When Ervin told his story, the police assisted him in securing an order that, while not granting him rights to the entire apartment, did give him the right to live in one room of the apartment—his father's office. He was also given a search warrant to search the premises for one day, as well as rights to some of the stolen furniture that was housed in a warehouse. It wasn't his furniture, and surely belonged to some other unfortunate family, but it was a new beginning at least.

Accompanied by the police, Ervin returned to his home. This time, when Gulassa peaked through the door, it wasn't Ervin who spoke. It was a gendarme.

"We're here with a search warrant, Mr. Gulassa," the police officer said. "Will you please open the door and permit us entry?"

Gulassa reached his hand through the doorway, examined the document, then begrudgingly opened the door. "This is my home," he grumbled. "You have no right to be here."

"These court orders say otherwise, Mr. Gulassa, and I would advise you that you will be best served by cooperating. Mr. Wolf, proceed," the officer directed.

Gulassa glared at Ervin and began to protest, but the presence of the two gendarmes silenced him at last. For Ervin, however, the situation was a tense one. Though his home, he felt as if he didn't belong there, and snooping through someone else's belongings felt wrong, even if those belongings might include his own. Nonetheless, he was determined to inspect the hiding places his father had shown him when they were last together.

The first place he went was the long, recessed panels along each side of the front room's windows where the shutters were housed when open. Joseph had shown Ervin how he'd loosened these panels and hid family photographs, mementos, and jewelry. Ervin pried them open, careful not to do any damage, but the shutter boxes were bare. Had Gulassa found them? Was his father tortured into disclosing them? He couldn't imagine his father removing the items, but whatever had happened to them, they were not there.

Next, he went to the control box where his father had hidden his dental drill beneath a false bottom. Empty. The window shades, where documents had been rolled and stored, again delivered nothing. He inspected every possible hiding place, but none of his family's property remained. In the attic there was nothing but junk and damp clothes. Pulling up the floorboards where his father had hidden other valuables, he found just empty space. In the basement, shared by all tenants and where chopped firewood and coal were stored, Ervin carefully dug up the dirt floor, certain that at least he'd find the heavy box of valuables his father had buried there. But it was not to be. The place, it seemed, had been stripped as bare as if they'd never resided there, never secreted any valuables, never once loved and laughed and lived.

By the end of the day, Ervin's soul was crushed. Nothing had remained, not even a faded photograph. Everything had disappeared.

Though Ervin took up residence in his father's office in the apartment, he felt as much of an outsider as if he'd never lived there. It was Gulassa's home now, rightfully or not, and though he did his best to avoid any confrontation with the man as he came and went, he knew that staying there was not an option as it was eroding all his good memories of the home and replacing them with bad ones. He continued to search for his parents, but these efforts proved futile. At one point, an old woman in the street ran up to him, took his face in her hands and said his name. He had no idea who she was, but she explained that she had been a maid for a judge who lived in the apartment above the Wolfs.

"Your mother was so kind to me," she explained. "Others were not so kind, but Kamilla always treated me like any other woman."

Ervin was touched to hear about his mother. "Do you know where she is?" he asked, his hopes rising.

She shook her head. "No, no, I don't know where they took them."

Ervin's heart fell and he was prepared to wish her well and depart when she grabbed his arm and pulled him toward her.

"No, don't go," she said. "I have been looking for you."

"Looking for me?" he asked. He was bewildered, for as far as he knew he'd never even seen her before.

"After the Nazis took your parents, your apartment was looted by strangers for days," she told him.

The image of strangers ransacking his home sickened him and he realized that he'd been naïve to think that everything had been put in storage somewhere. Everything had been scattered among thieves across the city. Everything.

"After they left, it was empty and silent. The door was wide open, so I went in. Everything was gone, but there was a big pile of photographs in the trash. When I looked at them, I realized they were your family pictures. So, I took them to protect them. I've been saving them for you. Come with me!"

Ervin couldn't believe his good fortune to have run into this woman as he had. He followed her to her new home, where she reached under her pillow and pulled out a satchel filled with photos of his family. At least he had those photos until the time would come when he would, at last, find his family once again. He hugged and kissed the dear sweet woman and left feeling even more excited about finding his parents.

He continued to walk up and down the streets aimlessly, looking for work, looking for his parents, looking for hope. He felt dazed and confused, without money, without anything. He went to all the places his father had had him memorize, but one after the other, all told him that they knew nothing and had nothing—or they themselves were gone. If his father had left anything with anyone, it wasn't there anymore. Occasionally, he would receive Red Cross packages and he could make a bit of money by selling the cigarettes that came in them, but for the most part, he had nothing. Sometimes he ate simple meals in strangers' homes, having learned to strike up conversations with most anyone he encountered. If he could chat with someone, he could keep from dwelling on the sadness of his new, liberated life.

It was from those conversations that he first learned about the death camp at Auschwitz and the rumors that nearly the entire Jewish population of Győr had been sent there to be murdered, burned to death in large ovens. He did not believe the stories. He simply couldn't imagine such uncivilized barbarism, thinking that only mentally deranged people would even think of such a thing. Yet so many people spoke of them that he could only conclude that even rational people could be persuaded of the most absurd rumors. The accounts they related were pure nonsense and the Germans could never have behaved in such a heinous fashion no matter how much they disliked the Jews. And surely no Hungarians would send their own citizens to die in such way. No, it was sheer madness and however many times he heard the rumors, he could not be persuaded that they were anything more than wild speculation borne of not knowing what had actually happened.

Months passed and his life settled into a new, peculiar normal. Each day he awoke with the certainty that he'd find his family and each day ended with the resignation that he had not. One day when he was taking a stroll, he saw a woman across the street who he recognized from his neighborhood. He was struck by how haggard and old she looked, despite not being much more than a decade older than he. Seeing that she had recognized him as well, Ervin crossed to the other side of the road and greeted her.

The sadness in her face spoke of anguish, yet the soft smile brought him comfort. "Ervin Wolf," she said. "*Shalom aleichem,*" she greeted him, blessing him with peace. "It is so good to see you looking so strong and healthy."

Though he did not remember her name, for hers was only a familiar face from the synagogue, he greeted her in kind, then asked, "Where did they take you? I've been looking for my parents for months and no one can tell me anything. Do you have any idea where they are? Could they be in Poland?"

Her kind face darkened, and a look of desolation washed over her. Of all the people he'd encountered and asked about his parents, none had the look of recognition and sheer sorrow he was seeing in her face. "I saw them in Auschwitz," she said. Before she had said another word, Ervin felt a curtain close upon his life. A ringing sound penetrated his ears as if to shut out the words she spoke.

"I was there when they arrived. When your mother got off the train, I saw that she was holding the hand of a little girl."

Ervin was confused. Who was the little girl? "Are you sure it was my mother?" he asked. "I have no sister."

"Yes, I am sure. She was with your father. There were so many orphaned children, she seemed to be comforting her. But yes, it was definitely Kamilla."

"What happened to her? Where is she now?"

He didn't want her to tell him. The sadness in her face told him more than he could handle. The tinnitus grew louder, as if to stop him from hearing the unbearable truth he was about to be told.

"The older women were sent to the chambers as soon as they got off the train," she said, speaking each word as if it was made of glass she was afraid to shatter by speaking too harshly. "Ervin, what they did to those women, so terrible…"

"You must tell me!" Ervin screamed, then realizing his unkindness, added, "please? What do you mean by the chamber? What does that even mean?"

"I'm so sorry, Ervin. They sent her to the gas chamber. They were flooded with poisonous gas. She is gone." The tears were streaming down her face as her words slowly took shape in Ervin's mind. "I am so sorry, Ervin, I thought you knew."

"How could I?" he protested. "I… I… I thought she was somewhere…" his voice trailed away. It couldn't be true. The gas chambers were myths, there could not have been such a thing. But here was a woman saying she had seen his mother go to one. She was gone? Impossible. "But they didn't really have such things," he protested. "That's just a rumor. Did they send her to a prison?"

Her face was filled with sorrow. "It is no rumor. I saw them go. I heard the screams." She was shaking her head at the memory, her eyes tightly closed. "I can't describe it. It's not something I want to remember." She brought her hands to her face and covered it as if to block out the memory. That was when Ervin saw the numbers tattooed on her wrist, that was when he knew that she had been there. Why would she lie about something as horrifying as that? Could it possibly be true? He gathered his wits and asked, "And my father? Where is he?"

She let her hands fall and looked again at Ervin. "I did see your father a few times after that. He was forced to clean the latrines. When I last saw Joseph, they were carrying his body away. He stood no chance. There was so much typhoid, so much dysentery and disease in those camps, in those latrines..."

Ervin didn't remember much of the conversation after that. If only he had never crossed the street, never learned the truth. His parents were gone. Murdered. He would never be reunited with his mother or his father. His entire life, like his home, had simply disappeared.

PART III
FROM YELLOW STAR
TO RED STAR

SHEETS OF GOLD

Ervin was grateful to the Russians for saving his life. But he hadn't been a free man for long before he realized that they too were an occupying force, one which would not single out Jews for abuse, but instead apply their brutality to all citizens. His first realization came early one morning when he was out looking for work and a Russian patrol stopped him. Though he presented his identification papers—written in Russian—and protested that he had just returned from a forced labor camp, his efforts proved futile. He was arrested and sent to a new form of labor camp, one where the conscripts—all men and women who had been picked up on the street in similar fashion—were sent far from their hometowns and put to work without pay. Ervin was pulled into a deep depression as he realized he was still a prisoner. The work was simple enough—taking cows out to pasture. But for a man who had been forced to labor under the Nazis, even a few days of forced labor ordered by an occupying force was an unbearable punishment. What's worse, he was given no food and was forced to milk the cows for nourishment, which made him ill. The illness, however, turned out to be to his good fortune, for he was then allowed to return home where he began to rebuild his life.

Although work was hard to come by, the nation had been ravaged by war, which brought new opportunities. So many physicians had been killed that the Medical School of Budapest was recruiting students. Ervin knew in his heart that his father would have been proud of him pursuing a career in medicine. Climbing on top of a train once again, he rode the rails to Budapest where Captain Kemeny—who had thrown away his Hungarian uniform in disgust at how the nation had treated its Jewish citizens—welcomed Ervin into his home.

He had thought that entrance to medical school would not be a problem given his grades and his family background, but after visiting the school, he was stunned to learn that under the new communist system, students who came from professional families or wealth were given the lowest priority. He was devastated—earlier in life he had been excluded from medical schools because he was Jewish. Now, though impoverished, he was excluded because of his former social status. How could he ever get anywhere if every effort he made to advance himself was met with a door slammed in his face?

Just as he was leaving, a flyer caught his eye. The Jewish Hospital of Budapest, in cooperation with the American Joint Distribution Committee, offered fellowships for up to eight poor Jewish medical students who had lost their parents in the concentration camps. The offer included room and board and a basic monthly stipend. The competition for these coveted positions would be fierce. Ervin knew that his only chance of admission would be if he could find someone to help him gain entry. He looked up the members of the committee, but none were familiar names. He was convinced his dream of medical school was yet another dream dashed. Nonetheless, he wrote down the name of the committee president so that he could at least write to him and make a personal appeal for the scholarship.

That very same night, while dejectedly walking the streets of Budapest, he met a woman, an old acquaintance from Győr. She invited him to her apartment and during their conversation, she asked him about his plans for the future. He told her about his dream of going to medical school, explaining that his only hope was to be selected for one of the eight fellowships. Amazingly, this friendly woman he'd met on the street turned out to be a relative of the committee president, a simply unbelievable coincidence, but then he was discovering that coincidences and random chances were arising so often in his life, it was as though a divine force was somehow watching over him. And she did indeed call the president and recommend Ervin for his personal attention. Soon after, he received the fellowship and his application for medical school was accepted.

Ervin could not believe his luck. So much good fortune was coming his way despite the overwhelming shadow of misfortune that he had known for the last several years. With so many people facing the same fate, it seemed as if everyone had taken to the streets in sorrow and confusion and, as their paths crossed, the shadows were lifted by random encounters with friends and strangers. The world that had been so cruel and barbaric was proving itself caring at long last.

Once he'd enrolled in medical school, Ervin thrived. He relished the opportunity to do something of value, something that called on his mind, not his might. The only drawback was the long walk to the hospital, but that inconvenience was quickly resolved when word of his long daily hike reached the ears of the Director. The Director of the hospital was a kind and brilliant man, Dr. László Benedek, who had been a prisoner of war in Russia and credited for his heroic actions in the war. Dr. Benedek treated all his students equally, regardless of family origin or religion, though he was especially concerned about the Jewish students who had lost family during the war. When he learned that Ervin was walking several kilometers a day to get to work, he provided him with new living quarters in the basement of the hospital.

The room was a modest one with windows at ground level protected by bars, giving the room the feel of a jail cell. One of the windows overlooked the back of an army barracks and that view brought Ervin immense joy as it was the very door that he and Frank had escaped from, ABC book in hand.

"I love it," Ervin told Dr. Benedek's secretary as she showed him the room. "This is perfect."

"Oh, that's wonderful," she said. "I know it's not much, but it's safe."

Safety was important to Ervin. And true, the room was sparse, but far better than many of the accommodations he had had in recent times. There were two simple iron hospital beds with horsehair-stuffed mattresses that smelled of chlorine, two chairs, and a simple table. In the corner of the room was a sink and a two-burner gas range. Down the dimly lit corridor was a shared shower room.

"The Germans used these rooms as stables," the secretary explained. "We've done our best to get rid of the smell, but there's only so much we can do."

"I don't mind, really, it's very nice," Ervin said. Though he could smell the musky odor that lingered, he had slept in enough barns and stables—the animals alongside him—that this room was practically luxurious.

"And I'm afraid you'll have to share it with another student," she said, her tone apologetic. Again, Ervin didn't mind. Where just a few years prior he would have been appalled at the suggestion of sharing a basement room that had once been a stable, now he accepted whatever comforts he was offered, however they came. And a roommate might well be a good thing, for he could use a friend.

Béla was two years younger than Ervin and, like Ervin, had lost his parents in Auschwitz. He had lived for some time in Palestine and earned some money by teaching Hebrew. Despite their shared traumatic loss, however, Béla proved to be no friend. He was irritable and moody, continually accusing Ervin of an endless litany of offenses. It wasn't long before Ervin spent as little time as possible in his room, working long hours so that he might be the best doctor possible and not encounter his mentally unstable roommate. Ervin kept his focus on the future. Doing so had helped him make it through Labor Service. It would easily get him through a bad roommate situation.

As much as he loved the medical environment, there was another aspect to the learning environment he found disturbing and reminiscent of the worst of the days of the Nazi occupation. Many students were members of the Communist Party and unwilling to accept that some, such as Ervin, did not share their political views. Some of these students were fanatical. "Bloody-mouthed agitators,"

Ervin thought, though he feared saying so aloud, for the most extreme among them would not hesitate to report even their own parents over any statements or acts they viewed as "anti-communist." What's worse, many kept their communist sympathies a secret, masquerading as anti-communists so that they could report back to the Communist Party about the activities of those who hadn't joined. Many joined just to avoid problems, but Ervin did his best to avoid any confrontation or interaction outside medicine. Inevitably, some people would be falsely accused of anti-communist activities and disappear. Ervin himself had been approached several times to join the Communist Party and he was careful about how he worded his refusal. "I'm afraid I'm just not politically mature enough to be engaged in any political activities," he would reply, feigning ignorance. At times, he was offered lucrative opportunities for advancement in his career if he were to join—once he was offered a promotion to an assistant teaching position on the hospital's faculty, along with an increase in salary. Others were given free holidays at lavish resorts. The incentives to join the party were great, as were the punishments for speaking against it. But as far as Ervin was concerned, there was no incentive that would persuade him to participate in what he felt was yet another rising state of oppression and persecution. He'd already escaped the Nazis—twice—and lost his parents to a tyrannical government. He was determined that he would not live under another autocratic regime. But until the communists lost power, he had medical school to finish.

It wasn't the most fanatical who were the greatest danger. It was the opportunists, the greedy ones who'd been tempted by the incentives and found that they could continue to receive promotions and raises and join strategic alliances by turning on others. Knocking down their competition was the key to their advancement. To avoid finding himself in the crosshairs of such characters, Ervin made sure he did not speak of politics or make any political jokes. He had learned from the Nazi occupation, and now the communist occupation, not to trust anybody. His sense of people was also still sharp; he had developed almost a sixth sense when it came to assessing people's character. He knew who was reliable and who was not, who could be trusted and who could not, who could be manipulated by more nefarious people and who could not. He chose his friends with care and, for the most part, kept his conversations focused on medicine and schoolwork. By doing so, he avoided trouble with all his heart and mind.

As much as Ervin loved medical school and maintained a friendly rapport with many of his colleagues, he was lonely and restless. Cautious about trusting anyone and especially uncomfortable around his roommate Béla, he spent his free time riding the streetcars back and forth, all day long sometimes. The motion soothed him, allowed him to shut off his mind, make no decisions. Once, while traveling in this manner, he came across the Jewish Community Center at Bethlen Square in Budapest.

It was always a chaotic scene at the Square, which he came to call the Wailing Wall of Budapest. All the trees surrounding the square were covered in small slips of paper pinned to the trunks. The pieces of paper were hastily written notes with the names of lost and loved family members, scribbled by desperate people. The place was a lost-and-found market for human beings. There he saw long lists of people who were arriving daily from different concentration camps. He'd scrutinize the lists weekly, hoping that somehow the news he'd been told of his parents' deaths had been wrong and that their names would appear like magic, announcing their pending arrival. But he never saw their names.

Sometimes while riding the streetcars, Ervin would get off at some random stop and walk through the neighborhood. He was especially drawn to the stately homes where he would peer into the windows, watching the families sitting down to dinner or gathered around the radio. Those moments of voyeurism comforted him as much as they saddened him. He so longed for his family, to return to the life that had been ripped away. He felt like a stray dog that had been thrown out of a good house.

One day Ervin decided to stop by the casino and say hello to Rebecca. She seemed happy to see him and they hadn't been chatting long when she said, "I didn't want to give this to you earlier because I knew it would probably be seized if I did. But now I think you should have it."

Ervin couldn't imagine what she might have, and his thoughts immediately went to family keepsakes—perhaps his father's watch or something his mother had knitted. But when Rebecca returned, she was holding a book.

"Here," she said, handing him a book about the domestic arts. "This is for you."

He looked at her with confusion. What in the world did he want with a book on the domestic arts?

"Go ahead," she said, now laughing. "Open it!"

He opened the book and, as he did so, flashes of gold caught his eye. Turning the pages more carefully, he saw several sheets of paper-thin gold had been pressed between the pages.

"Your father asked me to keep this for him. It's the gold he used in his dental practice."

Ervin didn't know what to say. He was stunned. He had given up hope of ever finding the many things his father had assured him he had hidden, and now, here was one of the best of things his father had concealed. Gold. It may not have sentimental value, but given his poverty, the gift of gold was truly a treasure. All this time Rebecca could have run off with it and he never would have been the wiser. But she hadn't. Instead, she'd protected him by hanging on to it until he was free.

As if reading his mind, she added, "I knew you'd be back. I figured if you got killed, I'd keep it. And if you were free, you'd come back for your pretty pink robe!" Then she laughed loud and long at the memory of Ervin dressed in her frilly pink robe and wearing makeup.

Ervin was so happy he jumped up and hugged her, swinging her round and round in his arms. "Rebecca, I love you! You're the craziest friend I ever had!" he told her. He knew, of course, that it was pure luck that he'd gone back to see her, but whether she had really held on to the gold to protect it or had planned on spending it herself, the bottom line was, she hadn't spent it—at least not all of it—and she'd returned it to him. The only question was, what would he do with it?

Gold had value. In fact, the Hungarian currency had been

devalued so drastically that the only currencies worth anything were the US dollar and gold. But owning any dollars was strictly prohibited and any gold had to be reported and was heavily taxed. Even gold jewelry had to be reported to the communist state.

The entire Hungarian economy had been devastated by the war and as the nation tried to rebuild its infrastructure, the Soviet Union imposed a $300 million charge for reparations, which rapidly doubled in cost as the currency depreciated. Inflation was so out of control that between the time Ervin earned money and the time came to spend it, it had already lost some of its value. Eventually, the pengo became so devalued that it was worthless. Everything, it seemed, was bought and sold on the black market, just as when they were living under fascist rule. Even Ervin made some money in the black market by selling nylon stockings so he could buy medical books. But now he had gold.

Reasoning that his father had bought the gold for his dental work, he found a friendly dentist who agreed to buy it at the latest exchange rate. He was even more grateful for the unexpected gift of gold, as some of his colleagues who had joined the Communist Party were making quite a bit of money by dealing with the Russians, transporting automobiles and other less legal products that enabled them to live rather lavish lifestyles. Ervin envied them their material comforts, their ability to avoid hunger. Now the gold would allow him to buy some food and simple comforts. But he had no need for an extravagant lifestyle. He had been raised in such a lifestyle, true, but wealth had come to his family honestly. Now that he was starting from scratch, Ervin was determined to stay honest. But under Soviet rule, honesty was not rewarded, and a family history of privilege was as suspicious and detested as Jewish heritage had been under the fascists. The snakes may have been banished, but the grizzlies had arrived.

As the first year of Soviet rule passed, the energetic sense of liberation gave way to darkness. There was increasingly less tolerance for contact with the Western world, especially Americans who were viewed as puppets or willing participants in a greedy and oppressive capitalist system that valued nothing but money and power. In its place, Ervin came to feel, the Soviets were offering the Hungarians poverty and no power, no power even over their own movements.

Few Hungarians could get a passport and, while rich communists could travel—those who had been enriched by their willingness to turn in their friends, family, and neighbors, or their less-than-honest dealings in the black market—most Hungarians were forbidden from leaving the country or entering "Forbidden Zones." The Forbidden Zones were 20-kilometer areas that bordered other nations, and these zones were heavily guarded, the fences electrified, with a large network of landmines buried underground. German shepherds, trained to kill, accompanied the guards on patrol, and tall sentinel towers were erected that were enhanced with mirror reflectors so that any movement would be noticed. These borders were the "no man's land" that no Hungarian dared cross. They were effectively caged in their own country. And that fact alone, left many—including Ervin—restless, if not desperate, to escape.

Many did escape. They fled the country with only the clothes on their backs, gaining their freedom through underground agents who worked with Austrian smugglers. These smugglers had established a secret route to Austria via Czechoslovakia. Taking advantage of the communist proclivity for bribery, this smuggling network was able to carry on—most of the time—by bribing communist officials to turn a blind eye.

More students began disappearing, not always those who were falsely accused or otherwise persecuted by the state. Ervin was convinced that they were fleeing the country, a suspicion that was confirmed when one day Béla announced that he was leaving.

"I hate the communists," he said, "they're worse than the Nazis. And I hate this country. I'm leaving Hungary and never coming back."

Given the fact that Béla hated everyone and everything, Ervin felt his roommate's strong convictions reflected as much his ornery personality as his political sentiments. Yet when it came to the communists, Ervin couldn't disagree. The nation he had loved with such pride had betrayed him beyond belief—killed his parents even

—and now, not even liberation meant any sense of freedom. They were prisoners in their own land.

"Where will you go?" Ervin asked.

"Vienna. I'll finish medical school there. Some Zionist organizations cover the costs for those of us who escape. Then I'll go to Israel to practice. I met a girl at the soup kitchen and she's arranging it."

Ervin wasn't so sure that trusting someone he'd only just met was a good idea, but he couldn't help but feel envious. He loved school, but he couldn't bear the communist environment where secret files were kept on everyone working in the hospital or affiliated with the university. Educated people were considered untrustworthy, potential enemies of the state. To be educated and a member of the despised upper middle class under Soviet rule was not much better than being a Jew under the Nazi regime. He'd merely traded his yellow star for a red star.

"What if I want to go, too?" Ervin asked. "Who do I talk to?"

Béla regarded him with suspicion, but knowing Ervin's history, he felt he was sincere. "Here's her mother's number. Call her in a couple of weeks, but act like it's a friendly call and you're just looking for me. She'll tell you how to do it. Just keep your mouth shut. Don't tell anyone, you got that?"

Ervin nodded. The next morning, Béla was gone.

The move was a risky one, that was clear. If caught, Béla would be sent to a labor camp or worse. And the chances of being caught seemed high. Yet Ervin couldn't help but admire his grouchy roommate for daring to escape. After all, Ervin himself had twice risked death or imprisonment for freedom from the Nazis. The prospect of escaping the Soviets was just as tempting. He was becoming so nervous and mistrusting under the constant surveillance and pressure to conform. Though he'd never been a devout or overly religious Jew, he was certainly a committed one. Now that he was "free," he felt no freer to express his Jewish faith than he had under the Nazis. Any religious affiliation was regarded with suspicion under the Soviet system, and those who practiced their faith—any faith, Jewish,

Christian, or otherwise—found themselves blocked from advancement.

For Ervin, friendly, hard-working, and discreet in his faith, opportunities lay ahead. For one, he had a great opportunity to learn medicine. Once he graduated, he would be able to make a modest living and sustain himself financially. Most everyone in the hospital environment treated him well and he kept those he distrusted at a distance. On Saturdays, he was often invited for dinner in the private homes of faculty or other physicians. And even though his room was small, he now had it all to himself. Still, it was such a dark room that the only sunlight that reached his window came after four o'clock and even then, it was just a brief exposure, and only if the sun's rays were at the right angle. The constant darkness and the bars on the windows affected his mood, leaving him feeling imprisoned. Even the welcomed view of the doors to the barracks where he and Frank had found their freedom no longer brought memories of joy, but memories of his captivity. And on top of it all, the corridors were infested with rats. As he lay in bed at night awaiting sleep, their high-pitched, frantic squeaks and chatter gave him nightmares. But he kept thinking that he only had two more years to go before he finished medical school. Surely, he could make it through two years.

He made it two weeks. Two weeks after Béla had left, Ervin made the call.

"I was just wondering how Béla is doing," he said, following his instructions to keep it casual.

"I'm sorry," she said, her tone friendly but unhelpful. "I don't know where he went. I can't help you."

Ervin wondered if Béla had been truthful with him, for she wasn't telling him anything. He decided to be bolder. "He mentioned you might know something about some organizations assisting refugees?"

"No, sorry, I don't. But why don't you leave me your number just in case any travelers want to reach you."

Ervin complied and just as he was about to end the conversation, feeling the call had been pointless, if not ridiculous, she said, "Stay home for a couple of days just in case. Maybe someone knows something about Béla. You wouldn't want to miss their call."

Ervin agreed, but he felt the whole thing was silly. He wasn't concerned about Béla. Had she understood his true intentions, to learn how he too might escape? Her tone was more like that of a friendly cashier than a smuggler's agent. But Béla *had* told him to do what she said, and he did have a couple of days off from the hospital. So, with nothing else to do but ride the streetcars back and forth, he did as directed and stayed in his apartment.

Two days later, the phone rang.

QUICK ESCAPE

"Ervin Wolf?" The voice was deep and strong.

"Yes," Ervin replied, cautious yet curious.

"I understand you are looking for Béla." This voice did not sound like a friendly cashier. This voice sounded like he knew what Ervin wanted.

"Yes," Ervin replied, careful not to say anything too direct. He could hear the unmistakable clicking sounds on the line that indicated someone was listening in. "Can you tell me where he is?"

"No, I'm afraid I can't tell you that. He could be anywhere. But perhaps we could meet. Béla's spoken so highly of you."

The mystery man had not identified himself and Ervin knew better than to ask his name. Though he didn't completely dismiss the possibility that it was a trap, his curiosity was great—as was his desire to get out of Hungary. He could finish medical school in Vienna, like Béla. What he couldn't do was continue to fear that everyone around him was a spy, that any false accusation or minor misstep could lead to his imprisonment. Never again. Never again would he allow himself to be imprisoned by his own country.

They set up a rendezvous for the following day and Ervin arrived early, keeping his eye out for any sign that he'd been followed or any indication the police were waiting. When nothing triggered his alarm, he took a seat and promptly at the agreed upon time, a tall, slender man smoking a pipe approached Ervin and asked if he might join him.

"Yes, yes, of course," Ervin said, any fear gone and replaced with anticipation. He couldn't deny that he was excited. Not just about the opportunity to escape Hungary, but by the sense of espionage the meeting conjured up, reminding him of his prior escapes.

"Everything we discuss here is strictly confidential, do you understand?"

"Absolutely," Ervin agreed.

"Good, then, a few ground rules." As the unsmiling man spoke, he continued to smoke his pipe and Ervin concluded that perhaps the taste of his pipe was the only joy the man knew, for he couldn't imagine him expressing any emotion at all other than a cold anger. But at this moment, while cool and stern, he was angry. He was instructive.

"You are never to ask anything about me, for the less you know the better for both of us."

Ervin nodded.

"And if you happen to see me on the street, you do not know me. You do not recognize me. We have never met, you understand?"

Ervin nodded again. Then he added, "I see that you are a professional, I mean, at what you do." Ervin was referring to the man's clandestine work with the underground network, but the moment he said it, he wished that he hadn't. The man's face clearly showed displeasure.

"You are not to think of me as someone involved in underground activities. All those American spy movies have stoked your imagination, I see." The faintest hint of a smile crossed his face and Ervin relaxed.

"No, no, I didn't mean it that way, I—" but the man waved his hand as if to wave away the conversation.

"Should you decide to go, your assignment will be to escort young Jewish boys and girls across a route, which I will give to you when the time is right. It's the same route that Béla took, and I understand that you're quite the seasoned hiker. You are accustomed to such travels."

Béla had to have told him, or someone, about Ervin's past with the Labor Service, and while he didn't look forward to any more cross-country hikes, he knew that he could walk to India if that was what it took to be free.

Ervin agreed to the assignment and after some further details, the man said, "One more thing. If anything should happen to you during your travels, I will be unable to assist you. Your safety is entirely your own responsibility and you will proceed at your own risk. Is that understood?"

"Yes, yes, of course," Ervin agreed.

"Good, then it is settled. As for the financing of the operation—"

"I haven't much money," Ervin began, preparing to offer him what was left of his sheets of gold.

The man waved his hand again. "I know that. The financing will be our responsibility," he said, referring to his organization. "Don't worry about that. We'll provide you with the funds."

Ervin nodded. "Thank you, thank you very much."

"Alright then," the man said, still smoking his pipe but now rising. "Don't make your decision right now. Think it over. Be sure this is what you want to do and weigh up the risks carefully, for the risks are great. I will call again soon and, should you decide to participate, I'll provide you with the date, time, and railroad station from where you will accompany the youths."

"Thank you," Ervin said. "Thank you for meeting with me. I'm sure I will be ready."

Ervin stood to shake the man's hand, but the man swiftly turned and disappeared into the busy street as if he'd been a dream. As if he'd been a character in one of those American spy movies, Ervin thought.

Days passed, and then weeks, and Ervin didn't hear back from the man. He wondered if he'd done or said something to arouse the man's suspicions, made him feel that he couldn't be trusted. Maybe he came across as too enthusiastic and the man thought him immature. Or perhaps he was a communist spy and had informed the Communist Party of Ervin's interest in defecting. That was a possibility that he didn't want to contemplate but like the squealing rats, the thought kept him up at night. Then finally, after three weeks, the phone rang again and the mystery man's deep voice asked, "Have you had a chance to think about our conversation?"

"Yes, I have," Ervin said, suppressing his excitement. This time he wanted to sound as serious and mature as possible.

"And do you still want to go ahead with it or have you had a change of heart? It would be understandable if you have, so do say so if that is the case. No one will fault you."

"No, I haven't had a change of heart. I want to do this."

"Good," the man said, for the first time sounding pleased. "I think you're making a wise decision." The mystery man then instructed Ervin not to bring any belongings with him and under no circumstances was he to tell anyone of his plans. Ervin wondered if Béla had been instructed similarly, given that he had told Ervin about his plans. Perhaps they were not happy about that, but if so, the man didn't seem upset. If anything, his tone had become if not friendlier, at least more collegial. He told Ervin the date and time and that he would meet the group at the Eastern Station, one of three railroad stations in Budapest.

On that fateful day, Ervin walked away from his room, leaving his medical books and the few possessions he owned—which didn't amount to much, as he'd already lost everything. Still, it pained him to know he wouldn't be returning to medical school, that for all his joy in his education and the sacrifices others had made to ensure that he got that scholarship and education, he would just walk away. But remaining in Hungary under communist control was not an option. He thought back to Viktor Kroonenberg urging his parents to leave Hungary and how his father had wanted to be patient, so convinced that things would get better. Now they weren't getting better, and Ervin didn't want to wait around for them to get worse. The Nazis had murdered his parents. He wasn't going to let the communists murder their son.

He hurried to the train station, his mind whizzing with thoughts about all he was leaving behind, the risks he was taking, his parents' fates for staying, and most of all, the need to not make any mistakes, not do anything to arouse suspicion or put anyone's life in jeopardy. He hoped that he was prepared for the arduous hike up ahead, though he'd been told that clothing and provisions would await them after their journey by train. Still, there were so many things that could go wrong and if caught—well, that was a possibility he didn't dare contemplate. It was a very real possibility, so every minute counted. He didn't dare be late, didn't dare make a mistake.

He made a mistake. In his great excitement, he reached the train station only to find that no group was awaiting him, no one looked as if they were as desperate and nervous and excited as he. He looked up to the sign, yes, the Western Station, where were they? Then it hit him. It was the *Eastern* Station he'd been instructed to go to.

Ervin couldn't believe he'd do something as stupid as going to the wrong station. How had he made such a mistake? What would they think of him now? Surely, he stood no chance of ever receiving their help again. He had no choice but to rush across the city to the Eastern Station. He'd be late, but hopefully not too late. He jumped on a streetcar and raced across the city only to get there minutes after the train had left. He was so disappointed he wanted to cry. The tears welled up in his face, but he forced them down. No, he wouldn't cry. He was no longer a boy, but a man. What an unfortunate man he was! How could he have made such a foolish mistake? He returned to his room, miserable, hating himself, and feeling so sorry for himself that he yearned for his mother to hold him. But she would never again hold him in her arms and comfort him. Now he was grown and alone. And he had to get to the hospital, late for work on top of it all.

It took him a couple of days to find the courage to call the number he'd originally called with his feigned inquiry about Béla. He knew he had to explain what had happened and pray that they would understand and give him a second chance, however unlikely that was. After leaving his message in code, ("I missed Béla, I'm afraid, and wondered if your friend might know another way I could reach him") he waited in hopeful expectation for the mystery man to call. The following day, he did so.

Ervin told him of his foolish mistake and implored the man to give him one more chance. As the clicking on the phone again made clear, every word had to be chosen with care for the communists were obvious in their surveillance. The man agreed to meet with Ervin as he had news of Béla, and once again, Ervin found himself meeting with the mystery man, smoking his pipe with a keen concentration that reminded Ervin of his father in his study pondering serious matters.

"You are a most fortunate young man," the secretive stranger informed him. Ervin looked at him quizzically, confused as to how such a mistake could be to his good fortune. "Everyone was caught when they reached Czechoslovakia and thrown in jail. It turned out that one of the travelers was more foolish than you. She told her boyfriend, and he relayed the information to authorities. An organization from Vienna was able to bail them out, claiming they were refugees, but I'm afraid your friend Béla wasn't so lucky."

"What happened to Béla?" Ervin asked, astounded at the news, both of Béla and the capture of the refugees. If he'd been on that train, he'd be one of them and his medical career would be over. As for Béla, while he hadn't cared a lick about what might happen to him when they were roommates, he certainly didn't wish him any real harm.

"I'm afraid he was also caught by the Czech border guards. He was traveling with another group, and they were apprehended as well," the mystery man answered, then drew on his pipe, if not in thought, at least from desire for its warmth and taste. Exhaling, he said, "He'll be spending some time in prison, I'm afraid."

Ervin couldn't believe the news he was hearing. The mystery man was certainly correct. Ervin was a fortunate man after all. If ever he had sensed that God was watching over him, now he was certain of it, for his mistake was not only incredibly lucky, but it was also so uncharacteristic of him to become so confused as to go to the wrong station. What he'd previously concluded was evidence of his foolishness, he now felt was evidence that God had guided him to the Western Station for his own protection. Providence was on his side once again.

After thanking the mystery man and bidding him a cordial good evening, Ervin returned to his room and studies and let any thought of escaping leave his mind. He had no desire to take such risks anytime soon. He had a medical degree to finish. But with one phone call, he'd discover that his will to finish his studies was no match for his determination to be free.

UNDER THE DARK SKIES

"How would you feel about leaving the country again?" The mystery man was once again sitting across from Ervin in an outdoor café, smoking his pipe with amusement.

Ervin had been surprised by his call, but pleasantly so. The truth was, in the back of his mind he kept imagining himself somehow escaping—reaching the train on time, getting across the border, somehow, some way. His daydreams had become so constant that they rivaled even those he'd had when he was in Labor Service, for now he had no family keeping him in Hungary. While he was no longer a prisoner in any physical sense, he'd become a prisoner in his mind as the pressure grew greater to join the Communist Party and never speak ill of it.

Mátyás Rákóczi, the General Secretary of the Communist Party, ruled Hungary and had dropped any pretense of democratic governance. Anyone suspected of the slightest deviation from party loyalty was purged from power and exiled. Though Rákóczi was Jewish by birth, he had renounced religion. Adopting the Soviet strategy, religious schools were nationalized and in place of religious doctrine, communist ideology and allegiance to the party became the central focus. Russian language study was compulsory in all primary schools and universities, and to enrich the state, property—whether a home, building, art collection, or household goods—was seized with every arrest. All agriculture was nationalized, as farms and vineyards were seized. As the fear and suppression of individual thought intensified, Rákóczi rose in influence and popularity. Though most of the population detested the autocrat, a sizeable and vocal minority celebrated his condemnation of any dissent, any questioning of his authority, and any suggestion that the needs and views of others might be considered. They loved him for his aggression and his might. Ervin loathed him for the same, while knowing he was surrounded, at work and in the street, by those who relished living in a nation so divided—so long as they loved Rákóczi.

No one could be trusted, and fear had taken hold of the country, as anyone, at any time, could be accused of political crimes and apprehended and exiled. Careers could only advance through loyalty to the party and careers were routinely destroyed for failure to demonstrate that loyalty. And it all played out in medical school and in the hospital, where Ervin watched as students and staff disappeared or seemed to have personality changes overnight, becoming secretive and furtive, paranoid or self-serving in ways they never had been before. No one knew from one day to the next if the person beside him had struck a deal with the party and might do or say anything to advance, if they might be gone the following morning having fled or been exiled, or if they harbored suspicions of their own that made working with them risky. The only thing that was certain was that the political climate wasn't improving. It was growing darker by the hour.

So now, as Ervin sat with the mystery man who'd broached the topic of escaping as casually as if he were asking if Ervin had plans to vacation anytime soon, the question had only one answer. "Yes."

The man smiled ever so slightly. "We've made some changes," he said, "which should prevent any further problems. We've reorganized and now work with some reliable Austrians who are skilled at this sort of thing." He took a puff of his pipe. "And we've tested everything out. You should have no trouble, though as I'm sure you understand, there's no guarantee of success."

"No, of course not," Ervin said, relieved to hear they'd made some improvements. It was clear he was dealing with professionals and his confidence in this next attempt was much higher than it had been after the aborted first attempt.

"Our organization will take care of any expenses," the man continued, being careful not to reveal to Ervin just what or who the organization was—information Ervin was relieved not to know in the event he was captured. "But if there is any trouble at all, I must warn you that I cannot help you. As far as anyone is concerned, we have never had this conversation." He removed the pipe from his mouth and looked directly into Ervin's eyes.

"Of course not," Ervin assured him, nodding. "I understand."

"Good then. Here's how it will work. Pay close attention, and don't write anything down."

Ervin was grateful for his medical education, which had demanded that he memorize everything he was taught, though clearly this had not stopped him from going to the wrong train station. His skills would prove useful as he listened intently to the man's instructions.

The man instructed Ervin to furtively obtain—and forge—an official paper from his hospital that would allow him to enter the dangerous, forbidden border area, the so-called "no man's land." The task demanded of Ervin made him uncomfortable, as it was a betrayal of the trust the hospital had placed in him and, if caught—which could easily happen if someone saw him—it would cost him his medical career. Yet Ervin had developed a taste for adventure and the prospect of pulling it off excited him—he knew he could do it.

One night, after administering some controlled medications, he excused himself to record the medication he'd used. After doing so, he snuck into the adjoining office where the secretaries kept stacks of letterhead in the unlocked drawers of their desks. Switching on a desk lamp, he worked quickly and confidently as he typed out a document indicating that Dr. Ervin Wolf had been assigned by his clinic to travel to the hospital in Moson to repair a machine in their radiology department. He liked calling himself a doctor, though he hadn't yet achieved that status. Smiling, he found the official seals and blue ink pad tossed like junk in the top drawer of the secretary's desk. Stamping the paper with the seals, he admired his work in the dim light of the lamp, then carefully folded the document, slipped it into an envelope branded with the hospital's name and address, switched off the light, and returned to his patients. The entire task had taken just 12 minutes, but in that brief time, Ervin felt an excitement he hadn't known since he and Frank had slipped out the door of the army barracks and freed themselves from the fascists. Now he would free himself from the communists—if all went as planned.

Once he had the document, he was to leave a message for the mystery man that he would like to get together for coffee. He did so, calling the mystery woman's mystery mother who would relay the message to the mystery man, an intrigue that had initially annoyed Ervin, but now only added to his sense of thrill. He felt like a character in an Alfred Hitchcock movie as every step became fraught with danger. And he loved it.

"Good, good," the mystery man said as he admired the document. He was not smoking his pipe and with his mouth empty, Ervin had a good look at his face for the first time. His features wouldn't strike anyone as strong, Ervin thought. He looked more like an unassuming accountant than a smuggling mastermind. Ervin noted how the pipe had yellowed his teeth and thought that his father would have shaken his head at such poor dental care. But the man's brown eyes were intelligent ones and Ervin had no doubt that whatever this man's story was, it was a fascinating one.

"Now you'll need to prepare another one and no time can be wasted. We need it as soon as possible. In this document—"

As he spoke, Ervin wondered if he'd been made a dupe. Were they just using him for his access to the hospital? Was there any plan at all to help Ervin himself escape or was he just to assist others in escaping? As the thoughts ran through his head, he realized he hadn't been paying attention. "I'm sorry," he said, shaking his head as if to wake himself up. "Can you repeat that?"

The man gazed at him with his penetrating eyes. "I was explaining that she's a prisoner and that her life is in danger as long as she's incarcerated. You're to state that she is pregnant and for the health of herself and her unborn child, she must be released. Do you understand?"

"Yes, yes," Ervin said, embarrassed by his lapsed attention. He must not allow his mind to wander, he reminded himself. This was serious business.

"Once you've prepared that document, take it to our central command at number six Nefelejcs Utca, where you will knock three times at Office 12. Remember that address."

"I won't forget," Ervin said. How could he forget? he thought. The street name translated to "forgotten street." He was beginning to think the whole thing might be one elaborate prank. How much more baroque and absurd would the instructions become? he wondered.

After some more discussion, he bid the mystery man goodbye and returned to work. That same evening, he slipped into the admitting office and from there into the secretary's office once again, where he hurriedly typed out the requisite document. This time, however, as he hammered away at the typewriter's keyboard, he froze. There were footsteps approaching and the sound of late-night typing would attract attention, for it was unmistakable. The steps were heavy and fast. A man's steps. A security guard? Another doctor?

He switched off the desk lamp just as he heard the door to the adjoining office open. He listened, his heart hammering nearly as loudly as typewriter keys. He saw through the gap at the bottom of the door frame that the light had been turned on in the outer office. Then the walkie talkie. It was a guard. How could he possibly explain being in the secretary's office? As the guard spoke into the walkie talkie, indicating that no one was in the office, carefully, ever so quietly, Ervin unrolled the document from the typewriter then slipped from the secretary's chair and tucked himself beneath her desk. There would be no explaining his position if caught, but the guard would have to step behind the desk to find him. His breath was so heavy, he feared his breathing could be heard in the next room, so as the door opened, he held his breath. The light switched on and stayed on. Ervin didn't dare exhale and thanked God for his years of swimming that had helped him to develop strong lungs. Just as he thought he couldn't bear another moment, the light switched off, the door closed, and the steps receded.

Ervin exhaled, as quietly as he could, until the light in the outer office switched off and the door closed tightly once again. Unfolding himself from the cramped space under the desk, he heard and felt his heart pound. He could even smell the stench of fear that had come with the veil of sweat now seeping from his skin. Despite his fear, or perhaps because of it, the smile that cracked across Ervin's face was unlike any other.

He knew he was safer now that the room had been checked. He could relax, though he had to return to the floor soon lest his absence be noted. Confident the guard had left, he switched the light back on, inspected his document, and noted that all he had left to add was the signature line and stamps. He quietly rolled the paper back into the typewriter and typed a signature line and name quickly. He knew if anyone was passing by, they might hear the keys again and return, but he'd been emboldened by the close call rather than scared off. He was enjoying this new game.

The document finished, stamped, and the light turned off, Ervin opened the door to the admissions office, leaving only the most imperceptible crack. He didn't dare fling it open in case anyone was passing in the hall. A cluster of aides and orderlies were discussing something at one end, but their backs were facing him, so he slipped out the door and returned to work as if he'd merely stopped in the restroom for a moment.

The "forgotten street" was aptly named, for it was a short, neglected street near the Eastern Railroad Station. The address took him to a nondescript six-story building. Opening the outer doors, he stepped into a sunny cobblestone courtyard where the strong aroma of fresh coffee wafted from a nearby coffee roasting factory. He looked for the office marked number 12, which he found up the first staircase on the first floor. As he'd been instructed, he knocked three times. The door opened a few centimeters and a face, obscured in darkness, peaked through the small gap.

"I have a document," he said. As he spoke, he wondered if there had there been a password. If so, he had forgotten it and hoped his cryptic but honest statement would suffice.

It did. A hand reached out for the document, then the door opened and he was invited inside. The room was dark though the day was bright. The curtains were closed and three men and one woman sat around a coffee table littered with cigarettes, half empty teacups, and nearly full wine glasses. Ribbons of smoke hung in the air and Ervin noted the haste with which their cheap hand-rolled cigarettes had been put out. Despite the somber atmosphere, the four strangers welcomed him warmly.

"Sit, have a drink," one of the men said, motioning for the woman to bring Ervin a glass. She complied as Ervin protested that he had to get going. He was on call at the hospital and needed to return to his room in case the phone rang. The woman returned and placed a wine glass on the table before him as another man poured some amber Tokay into it.

"Just one glass for all you have done. You don't know how much we appreciate your efforts. You are saving a woman's life, you know."

Ervin waved his hand to indicate no more wine. "Thank you, I'm happy to help," he said. "I'm so sorry. I do wish I could stay, but I must get back to my room. I'm on call and I'm supposed to stay by the phone in case I need to return to the hospital. I don't want to arouse any suspicions."

"Then you must go," the first man agreed. "But you leave with our eternal gratitude."

The man shook his hand and Ervin hurried from the room, half relieved to be out of there and half disappointed he could not have lingered and learned more about the group tucked away in the darkened room in the middle of a sunny day.

Soon afterward, when he was enjoying a couple of days off work, he received a phone call from the mystery man instructing him to go to the Eastern Railroad Station early that afternoon and walk to the ticket office carrying only a briefcase.

"A woman will approach you wearing the smile of a good friend," the man said. Ervin noted that there was no clicking on the phone line, which told him the man was indeed correct about the success of the recent changes, changes that no doubt included a different telephone line for such communications. He was relieved, as well, that there was no clicking on his end of the line, which told him they were not yet onto him.

"Follow her directions," the man said, "and I wish you good fortune in the life ahead of you."

So this was it. His reward for producing the document for the imprisoned woman was to be his own freedom. That very afternoon, he would leave forever the only country he'd ever known. The country he had so loved, had sworn his allegiance to. The country that had sent his parents to their deaths, imprisoned him, and seized all his family's property. The country that was educating him to become a physician and had given him respite and a new start in life. The country that demanded he now pledge allegiance to the Communist Party and its leader Joseph Stalin.

Ervin hung up the phone and reflected on all he was leaving behind, the good and the bad. He emptied his briefcase of his medical school papers and replaced them with a razor and toothbrush, some fresh underwear and socks, and a change of shirt. A few hours later, he closed his apartment door and left everything behind.

This time, he made sure to go to the correct train station. The Eastern Station. As well, he arrived punctually—not so early as to arouse suspicion, but not one second late. Not sure what to do, he approached the ticket office and just as he did so, a nice-looking woman wearing a black broad-brimmed hat and a friendly smile approached, locking arms with him.

"So happy you made it," she said as if they were old friends. "I'll take care of everything."

"Uh, okay," Ervin said. He found the situation a bit comical, but he felt his pulse quicken as he realized it was really happening. He was fleeing the communists and risking imprisonment and ruin to do so, and yet he delighted in the espionage. *I'm really getting good at this,* he thought. This was his fourth escape, only one of which had failed—and yet it hadn't, for he had been spared the misfortune of those who'd boarded that fateful train. And now he was escaping on the arm of a good-looking woman. *Just like in the movies,* he thought once again, imagining himself a Hitchcockian hero daring everything for the cause.

"One ticket to Moson," she said, referring to the town near the Austro-Hungarian border about 160 kilometers northeast of Budapest, where his forged document indicated his clinic was sending him. It would be about a two-and-a-half-hour ride Ervin noted, as the woman turned and handed him the newly purchased ticket.

"You'll have to switch trains in Győr," she said. "Stay put until your connecting train comes, then you'll go straight to Moson." Again taking him by the arm, she accompanied him to the platform, walking slowly and discreetly pointing out his upcoming entourage one by one. "And that man right there," she whispered, leaning closer, "he's in charge. You'll all follow his lead. Don't let him out of your sight."

"I won't," Ervin whispered back, delighting in their feigned romantic whisperings in the busy train station, which only heightened the excitement. He half wished this pretty woman would cling to his arm all through the train ride, though he knew she'd only bought the one ticket. Still, he could dream.

"Memorize all their faces, but whatever you do, don't show any sign of recognition, or do anything to suggest you're connected to anybody here. As far as the world knows, you and I are the only friends here. You've got that?"

Ervin nodded as he took in the faces and figures of his fellow escapees. One was an older man toting a heavy piece of luggage. Another was a woman who looked to be in her mid- to late thirties and accompanied by two younger men. The last was a single man carrying a light load of luggage. Ervin wondered why he alone could only bring a briefcase but, given how little he owned, he decided not to dwell on it. He would look like a proper businessman, a role he thought suited him well.

"This is where I leave you," the woman said, releasing her hold on Ervin's arm. She leaned close to him, and he could feel her warm breath and smell her floral perfume as she whispered into his ear amidst the cacophony of the train. "Take any seat on the first train, but when you switch trains in Győr, sit quietly in the last compartment. Do not talk to any of the other travelers. When you reach Moson, watch your lead. He'll jump from the back of the train. Follow him closely under the dark skies."

Then, pulling herself away from Ervin, she said in a clear and loud voice, "Have a wonderful trip, sweetheart, and I'll see you when you get back!" She kissed him on both cheeks and disappeared into the crowd, leaving Ervin feeling as if he'd just said goodbye to a woman he loved and whose arms he couldn't wait to return to.

Of course, he knew there'd be no returning, nor any arms to hold him for that matter. But for just that short moment, he'd felt so alive. Now it was time to shake off the fantasy and focus on the reality. He was embarking on a dangerous mission and his mind had to be crystal clear.

Imagining himself a proper businessman, Ervin boarded the train and chose a random seat in the third car. The ride was uneventful, but his mind was active with thoughts about his future. Where was he going, ultimately? Would he be able to go to medical school? What if they got caught? Would he ever see that beautiful woman again?

When the train reached Győr, he yearned to get off and run to his home, yet there was no home to run to, no family awaiting him. Győr was now a memory belonging to his childhood and nothing more. A stop on the way to Moson. He grabbed a sandwich while waiting for the next train, and later, some fruit, for it was a long wait, but he didn't dare risk walking through the streets of his hometown. He would only arouse suspicion, if not put the entire operation in jeopardy.

By late afternoon, the train to Moson arrived and as directed, he boarded the last car, doing his best to not so much as glance at his partners in crime. He wondered what their own stories were and who and what they were leaving behind. Had they lost family as he had? He figured they probably had. Not many people would dare such an escape without having already lost a great deal.

The train reached the border late at night and despite the long day and late hour, Ervin had never felt more alert. He kept his eyes on "his" man, the lead smuggler, who appeared to be half asleep. Does he even realize we're here? Ervin wondered. He half feared the man had given up or was so inept he would miss the opportunity to escape altogether. Then, suddenly, and silently, the man got up, hurried down the aisle, and jumped from the train and ran off. Ervin did the same, following his shadow into the dark, as did the others. He'd run after the group for about 60 or 70 meters, fearing he'd lose sight of them, when he heard a sharp command behind him.

"*Állj!*" Stop!" a voice ordered, just as a strong hand roughly grabbed hold of Ervin's arm.

He turned to see a mean-looking border guard holding a machine gun. The sight alone nearly knocked the wind out of him, but Ervin reminded himself of one lesson he'd learned in Labor Service. Beneath the uniform, they're merely men.

"Wait here," the guard ordered as he rounded up the others one by one. As for the lead smuggler, he had disappeared into the darkness. Once he was confident he had everyone and they couldn't slip away, the guard returned to Ervin. "You were trying to cross the border illegally," he said. "All of you. You were following that man who was running away. We'll catch him, don't worry."

Ervin had never been so cool in his lifetime. He didn't like to lie or manipulate anyone, but he'd learned to do both in the Labor Service. The guards had trained him for this moment. "I don't know what you're talking about," he protested, as if he was genuinely stunned by the accusation. "I'm a doctor. My hospital in Budapest has sent me here to examine the radiology equipment at the Moson hospital. I've no idea where anything is here. This place is completely unfamiliar to me. I was just following everybody else. It's pitch black out here, you know. I have no idea which direction the hospital is, much less the border. Here, I'll prove it to you."

Ervin reached into his pocket and produced the document he'd forged, the one indicating he was to repair a broken machine in the radiology department. As the guard inspected it, Ervin noticed a local commuter bus was parked nearby, its motor running. The bus would be taking the train passengers into town and was ready to depart. Ervin had to get on that bus.

"I don't believe your story for one minute," the soldier said. "Stay right here. The only place you're going is the border guard station."

As the guard turned to leave, Ervin shouted after him, "You do that and you can expect a great deal of trouble, because the only reason they've sent me to this God-forsaken place in the middle of the night is that there's an emergency and I need to fix that machine. If I'm not there by morning, their patient could die, and while I can't tell you who that patient is, I don't think you'll be so happy if he doesn't make it due to you keeping me from getting there in time."

The guard hesitated and Ervin played his last card. "If you don't believe me, call the hospital right now to confirm it. Go on, I'll wait. But you might want to be sure that bus waits, as well."

God forbid he make that call, Ervin thought. That had been his last chance at convincing the guard of his outlandish lie.

"Alright, doctor," the guard finally said, "I'm sorry, but it looked like you were with this group here. Hurry up, that bus will be leaving any minute." He handed Ervin his forged document and apologized one more time.

"Apology accepted," Ervin said. "You're just doing your job." Then he ran for the bus as if his life depended on it. Because it did.

As he took his seat, he thanked God for getting him on the bus in time, for if he hadn't made it, even with the guard letting him go, he would have ended up having to walk a long distance in the dark in unknown and dangerous territory. Once again, he'd been spared a horrid fate. Once again, God was on his side.

The ride into town was a bumpy, horrible one, the bus stopping every few kilometers to let new passengers on and old passengers off. Ervin was tired and hungry and the further away he got from the border guard, the more anxious he became at such a close call. He looked about him in the darkness of the bus and noted there were few passengers aboard. Closing his eyes for a moment, he imagined he was sinking into quicksand, which he thought would be more comfortable than the lurching ride he was enduring. When he reopened his eyes, to his great surprise, he saw the old man with the heavy piece of luggage sitting beside him. The man's eyes indicated that he recognized Ervin, though neither man said a word. Eventually, the bus reached the town center and stopped in front of a local inn. They both got off the bus and Ervin looked around. The streets were completely empty and the entire place felt like a ghost town. *For that matter,* Ervin thought, *perhaps we're the ghosts.*

"Let's take a drink at the bar," the man said, speaking to Ervin for the first time. "They should be able to direct us to a place to stay for the night."

Ervin felt relieved. Now someone was in charge again and he was no longer flying by the seat of his pants. He followed the elder man into the crowded inn where they ordered a couple of beers. The bar was loud and border guards in uniform were openly drinking heavily, laughing uproariously, and showcasing their belligerence by goading and one upping each other with every emptied glass.

"Can you recommend any lodging nearby?" Ervin asked a guard, as if he were just another traveler in search of a bed for the night rather than a failed escapee trying to erase the entire night from his mind and get back to Budapest as fast as he possibly could. "Some place not too expensive?"

"A place to stay, you say?" said the drunken soldier. "Hey, this kid is looking for a place to sleep tonight," he hollered over the crowd to his drunken colleagues. "Anyone know a place?"

"The Farkas place rents out rooms," one of the men said. "It's just down the road. Let's buy the kid a few drinks for the road!" The room erupted in cheers as calls for joining their reverie grew louder.

"Thanks, but we've got to get going," Ervin said, gesturing to his traveling companion. "But I appreciate the tip. How do we get there?"

The guards gave a series of contradictory directions, but it was enough for the men to know they need only wander down the road a bit and follow a few signs. Bidding the drunken guards goodnight, they set out.

It wasn't long before they found the home and inquired about a nice, clean room for the night. The lady of the house confirmed she did rent rooms, but cautiously asked the men the purpose of their trip as she knew they were on a popular escape route. "You can't be too careful," she said. "All kinds of bad news come through here, rich people trying to leave the country because they can't bear change and don't want to do their fair share. Disloyal is what they are, if you ask me. I don't want no trouble."

"You're safe with us," Ervin assured her. "We're here on business only and just want to rest our heads. I'm a doctor and this gentleman is my traveling companion. I have an appointment at the hospital in the morning and just need to get some rest."

The hostess responded with a pleasant smile. "Wonderful! I work at the hospital. I can take you there in the morning!"

Ervin felt his heart stop. He'd come so close. But now he may have reached the end of the line. If she took him to the hospital, his ruse would be blown. Just as he was struggling to think up something to say, the old man interjected.

"I'm afraid I have to complicate the good doctor's morning," he said. "You see, I'm a salesman and I must get these sculptures of Lenin and Stalin to the party offices first thing in the morning, and I promised them I'd bring the doctor with me before he does his business at the hospital. I've got a client there with a terrible case of eczema and the only way I could get him to agree to the sale was if I brought the best doctor in Budapest to personally attend to him."

"Yes," Ervin improvised, "ridiculous, but true. I specialize in dermatology, so when my uncle asked for my help, we figured we'd schedule our trips to kill two birds with one stone. Otherwise, I'd love to take you up on your kind offer for ride. But we must leave at the crack of dawn."

He wasn't sure any fool would fall for such a story, but as fortune would have it, she was such a fool. "A dermatologist, you say?"

For the next half hour, Ervin listened to her carry on about her rashes, moles, and skin tags, inspecting this concern and that, until any talk of his trip to the hospital was long forgotten.

As expected, both men suffered through a restless night, both waking early the next morning and slipping out the door before their host or hostess awoke. After reaching the inn and having breakfast, still not discussing their aborted escape at all, the elder man bid Ervin farewell. Ervin wanted to get to the train station as soon as possible so he walked as quickly as he could back to the station, reaching his destination by mid-morning. Once there, he purchased a newspaper and continued holding it in front of his face as if reading it keenly, again and again, until that afternoon when the first train for Budapest departed. The long wait was a living hell, for he feared that at any moment he would be apprehended. Given that they had caught the other travelers attempting escape and perhaps tortured or threatened them, the chances were high that at least one or more of them would have revealed that he had lied the night before. The authorities could be looking for him and the older man as well. *We shouldn't have gone anywhere together,* he cursed himself. They had only increased the odds that they'd be caught. He could feel his rapidly beating heart in his throat and felt enormous relief when the train finally arrived. He looked around with keen attention, realizing nobody had followed him. The coast clear, he boarded the train. Once the train started moving, seemingly out of nowhere, the old man appeared, tossing his luggage up on the rack as if it were light as a feather. Then he sat in the seat across from Ervin.

"I had a lovely walk around town," the elder man said. "And I was fortunate to be able to sell all my sculptures."

Ervin had no idea what it was he really had unloaded, and he didn't want to know. But one thing was clear, it wasn't the authorities who had their eye on Ervin. It was the organization.

By nightfall, he was back in Budapest and sleeping in his own room, the room he'd thought he'd never see again. The next morning, he was once again on call, as if nothing had ever happened.

JUDIT

Several weeks had passed since Ervin's second effort to escape. Though those failed attempts had convinced him that he oughtn't try a third time, he felt he should contact the organization. He didn't feel right just walking away, and his curiosity had only intensified as he'd ruminated on the aborted escape attempt. Who was the old man and what had he been carrying in that case? What had happened to the others? Were they unhappy with Ervin? After all, the mystery man hadn't contacted him. He had tried calling the number he'd called in the past, but that number had been disconnected. Thus, he did the only thing he could think of doing. He returned to the headquarters —or whatever they called it—on the "forgotten street."

There was no answer. And the mystery man never called Ervin again. It was as if he'd never existed, and as if Ervin had never done anything to flee the communist country. His life resumed.

As time passed, he tried to forget the whole matter. His goal was to earn his medical degree, and he considered his failure at escape to be a sign that he had to keep his focus on his studies. It was a mixed blessing, for if he was to fulfill his dream of becoming a physician— after he'd learned of his parents' fate, he wanted more than anything to live a life they would have been proud of—then he was going to have to remain in the vast prison known as Hungary. He knew that if he kept his mouth shut and never uttered a word against the regime, he'd make it through the medical program. He reminded himself that he might even make a comfortable life once he'd adjusted to remaining silent on matters of the state or religion. Yet the daily beatings the police inflicted on people on the street, the disappearances, the injustices, the long lines for basic food items and clothing while others grew fabulously wealthy from the black market or betrayals, all contributed to a sense of hopelessness. Ervin felt defeated, resigned to the somber atmosphere of this new Hungary. And there was no sign of anything improving. If anything, the dreadful military might of the Soviet Union proved that the communists had the potential to conquer the entire world. There was no safe place to flee to. He did his best to find refuge in his work, where he could devote himself to healing in a world that was so badly hurting.

Not long after his aborted escape, a young woman sought him out at the hospital. It took a moment for him to recognize her, but when he did, he realized she was Director Benedek's niece. He'd first met her in his early months at medical school. She was visiting a patient at the hospital, a former prisoner of war, and had she not been his boss's niece, he wouldn't have given her a second thought as she was just a teenager at the time. Later, he saw her spending time with Béla and as she was older and lovelier by then, he presumed she was his girlfriend. Despite his curiosity—what was Béla doing with Dr. Benedek's niece?—his relationship with Béla had been so strained that he didn't ask about it. And now, here she was. She introduced herself as Judit Vas.

"I'm looking for my Hebrew teacher, Béla," she said. "My Uncle Laci said you might know where he's gone."

"I've no idea," Ervin lied, noticing for the first time her enigmatic brown eyes and infectious smile. "He left a few weeks ago. I don't know where he went." He knew otherwise, however. He knew that Béla was in prison for having tried to escape, but he didn't dare reveal this knowledge. As far as he was supposed to know, Béla had merely disappeared. Like the others.

"That's funny," she said. "He didn't say anything about leaving and he just stopped coming for our lessons."

"So, you're not his girl?" Ervin asked. He had to admit, with Béla out of the picture and this young lady a couple of years older and that much prettier, he wasn't anxious to end the conversation.

Her laughter enchanted him. It was both innocent and wise. "Béla? Heavens no! He was my Hebrew teacher, that's all. Though I can't say he didn't make me uncomfortable. He knew how to teach Hebrew, but I didn't always appreciate some of the comments he made. I don't think he was a happy man."

"I never found him happy either," Ervin said, thinking that was quite the understatement. "But he's had his share of losses."

"Yes, I suppose he has," she agreed. "As have we all. I do hope he was able to escape and didn't end up arrested for his views." Just as the words had slipped from her mouth, she blushed and stopped herself from continuing. "I mean, he did have some strong views. I'm not suggesting he should have tried to escape."

Ervin was touched by her boldness and naiveté. Within a year or two, he thought, such slips of her personal views would no longer threaten her social interactions. Yet he was grateful that she had expressed herself, for it demonstrated to him that she shared his own sentiments. He wasn't surprised. She was Dr. Benedek's niece and during their Saturday dinners at his home, where Ervin delighted in chatting like family with Helen, Dr. Benedek's wife, and their little girl, Susie, the esteemed Director had expressed many times that he, too, could not bear the oppressive Communist Party. In fact, Dr. Benedek was the only person Ervin truly trusted in the hospital, because even though he knew he was not alone in his sentiments, he was wary of trusting too easily. He knew how quickly and completely so many turned, when incentives for doing so were great and penalties for not doing so even greater. And once they did turn, they erased any former sensibilities, becoming the most loyal of the loyalists. But Dr. Benedek hadn't turned. He despised the communists, of that Ervin was certain. And now, here was his niece, saying she hoped Béla had escaped the communists.

"Would you like to go for coffee?" Ervin asked her. "There's a lovely café nearby and I'd welcome the company."

"I'd be delighted," she replied.

Ervin began seeing Judit regularly and with each visit, he grew more charmed. Judit was as intelligent as she was kind, as good humored as she was beautiful. And while she was young, so was he. Being with Judit made him realize how the war had robbed him not just of his family and home, but of his own youth. In her company, he felt that youthful joy and humor return. For the first time in his 27 years, he felt the stirrings of romantic love. Each time the two were together, he learned more about this fascinating young woman.

Though she hadn't suffered the grievous loss he had during the war, she was not without her scars. Her father had abandoned the family when she was a child, fleeing to the United States. Though he had promised to send for Judit and her mother, Violet, he never did so. Being Jewish, she and her mother had hidden at a farm during the Nazi occupation, but her maternal grandfather, a rabbi, had been pulled off a streetcar and sent to Auschwitz where he died at the age of 70. When the war ended, her mother divorced her father and married a former prisoner of war, Albert Liebermann, who was appointed the first commercial attaché of Hungary in the new state of Israel. Given his diplomatic status and assurances that they'd return, Judit's mother and stepfather were granted permission to go to Israel. Judit was not. Consequently, she remained in Hungary with her widowed grandmother who became her guardian while she finished school. It seemed the war had left nothing but splintered and devastated families in its wake and Judit's was no exception.

And like in so many families, not only were lives lost or family separated, but political alliances also forged even deeper chasms among once-close relations. While Judit's family was strongly anti-communist, her maternal uncle, Zoltán, had become a loyal communist with a high-ranking position in the Communist Party. His socialist leanings had taken root at a young age and, after being caught at a secret meeting arranged by Mátyás Rákóczi, then a rising star in the Communist Party, Zoltán had been sentenced to 16 years in prison by the Hungarian government. His freedom was bartered, however, when the Soviets returned some 1849 Hungarian flags they had seized in exchange for Zoltán and Rákóczi's freedom. Once settled in the Soviet Union, Judit's uncle rose rapidly in the party ranks. His loyalty to the Communist Party only deepened after he was freed by the Soviets, further distancing him from the family—but not entirely, as his position would prove to be protective.

Still, Judit missed her mother and longed to leave the new Hungary, for she found the communist government a stifling one. The pressure was great for her to join the party, as it was for all young people fresh out of high school, but she was adamant that would not happen. Like Ervin, she dreamed of a career in medicine and wanted to go to medical school. Her plan, she explained to Ervin, was to visit her mother in Israel for a few months, and then decide what she wanted to do with her life.

The thought of her leaving devastated him, for he knew the temptation not to return would be great. Would he ever see her again once she was set free from Hungary? But he knew she hadn't seen her mother in a very long time, and he had no right to protest. She had to go. After telling Judit of his strong feelings for her, he was thrilled when she revealed that she felt the same and vowed to return. Still, Ervin knew that not even love could temper the desire to be free.

After she left, Béla returned to Budapest. He had spent six months in a Czech prison and once freed, he found that he had been expelled from medical school and because of his escape, he could not be readmitted. Eventually, he found work with the national ambulance company as an emergency care attendant. He would never become a doctor. If the man was miserable before, he was even more so now and, as much as Ervin wanted to help, he had no desire to entwine his life with his former roommate's. Thankful that he hadn't met the same fate as Béla despite coming precariously close, his thoughts now were on Judit as he prayed for her return.

She wrote him often and the letters touched his heart and gave him hope. With every letter, she assured him of her return, but he could not count on such assurances. Would he have returned for her if he had been able to leave? He doubted he would have done so, as much as he cared for her. The taste of freedom lingered in his memory and he so longed to have it back—even if his only memory of freedom had been as a small boy. Having known imprisonment and the killing of his parents, freedom had become an obsession for Ervin. He would never take it for granted. And he would never miss an opportunity to seize it.

When Judit did return, he learned that it had been more than just her love for him that had brought her back. Her Uncle Zoltán, who since his release had served as Mayor of Budapest and a member of Parliament, had been appointed Chief of the National Planning Commission and had written to tell her that if she failed to return, her family faced dire consequences for her betrayal of her country.

This threat wasn't purely based on his allegiance to the Communist Party, Judit would later discover. Zoltán himself was facing intense pressure inside the party for his devotion to the Hungarian people. Despite his decades of commitment to the ideals of communism, as a compassionate human being concerned with the fate of his people, he was still regarded as suspect. Had Judit failed to return, he would have been branded disloyal and, like other Hungarian party members similarly distrusted, his family would have faced exile while he himself would have seen a return to prison.

Ervin was thrilled to have Judit back but upon hearing the details of Zoltán's warnings and predicament, he became even more distressed at the prospect of remaining in Hungary. But he was in no position to do anything about it. Escape was now out of the question. His only solace was his work at the hospital, his growing love for Judit, and her growing love for him. His love for medicine and a woman who loved him in return would, he hoped, see him through the troubling years ahead.

Ervin thrived in his work and in 1950, at the age of 28, he graduated with his medical degree. He wished more than anything that his parents had been alive to see him receive his degree, but he was more than comforted to have Judit and her family in attendance. Her grandmother, Karolin, had become like a second mother to him and her Uncle Laci—Ervin's Director, Dr. Benedek—had become like a second father. They took the place of his parents as he walked in the procession to receive the degree that conferred upon him the title of Doctor. At long last, he had fulfilled his dream. Now he had only two more dreams to attain. To marry Judit and to one day escape the horrors of Hungary.

Judit continued to pursue her plans to study medicine and was accepted into medical school where she excelled. Ervin secured a residency where he would specialize in obstetrics and gynecology—having witnessed so much violence and death, devoting his career to bringing life into the world seemed to be a healing path for the young man. He worked long hours and even established a national blood bank. Any spare time he had was spent with Judit. But the life beyond their love was a dark one. Although medical knowledge was advancing rapidly, the Communist Party seized all new equipment and technology for private hospitals available only to the privileged party elites. For all their talk of equality, there was no mistaking the wealth and access to resources that was available only to a select few. For most, poverty and neglect were the best they could hope for.

Ervin noted, however, that an American organization was delivering equipment to the hospital, and he came to see that Americans cared more for the fate of Hungary than the Soviets in charge. A future in America took root in his mind as every donation brought to him a reminder of all that was possible in another world, a world free of the oppressive atmosphere that grew greater by the day. The disappearances continued and rumors were that the communists were killing "disloyalists" as readily as the Nazis had killed Jews. If one person was found to be disloyal, their whole family was punished. Writers, artists, educators, and dissidents were sent to frigid gulags where they were forced to labor breaking and hauling rocks. Listening devices had been planted everywhere and no one felt safe expressing their true feelings, even in the privacy of their own home. Not even party members were safe. If anything, they were less secure than anyone else, for they were constantly watched for signs of disloyalty. When Uncle Zoltán came to visit his mother, usually unexpectedly, he would arrive surrounded by guards in plainclothes who would monitor their conversations. And when Judit's mother and stepfather announced that they would not be returning to Hungary after all, Zoltán made it clear that the party could count on him, even in matters involving his own sister and mother.

Ervin and Judit were visiting Karolin shortly after Judit's mother had communicated her decision when Uncle Zoltán arrived, accompanied as always by his bodyguards. He was visibly nervous. After taking a seat in the front room with the formality of a guest the family barely knew, he told Judit, "One of these days, your mother and stepfather will be hanged because they did not follow the instruction of the party to come home."

Karolin gasped. Her own son was threatening her daughter with hanging. "Zoltán," she said, her maternal voice firm and unwavering, "You will not speak like this in my home, and you will not threaten your sister's life. I expect you to take that back."

Zoltán turned his gaze to his mother and, visibly shaken but determined in the presence of the party guards who had accompanied him, he replied, "It is not up to me, Mother. I am simply stating a fact. The party will not tolerate disloyalty and whether she returns home to see you, Judit, or attend your funeral, she will be apprehended and hanged. That is not my decision. It is hers."

Karolin left the room as furious as she was powerless. As for Ervin, he had no idea what to do. As Judit scolded her uncle for his disrespect toward his family, Zoltán bid her and Ervin goodbye and left with his guardians. For the rest of the visit, the fear and fury among the three lingered, but no one dared discuss the conversation that had just taken place. Throughout the visit, Ervin couldn't shake his fear that given Zoltán's high position in the party and Judit's mother's position as the wife of a diplomat—and now a defector—there was every chance that a bug had been planted in Karolin's home. Listening devices were everywhere, in businesses, offices, and even private homes. A dinnertime conversation about a party member—even if that party member was someone's son and uncle—or a defector who would not return—was as dangerous as any escape Ervin had ever attempted or achieved.

The right to free speech and free thought was gone. Political freedoms had been essentially eliminated as only one party existed and no dissent from its tenets was permitted. Citizens dared not discuss politics with anyone, but politics was all anyone had on their mind. That and hunger. For everyone was hungry. Despite the long lines for basic food items, the Communist Party warned its citizens to not accumulate food, so Ervin, like other doctors, kept butter, flour, and sugar in his hospital locker, in case his apartment was raided. The fear of raids in private homes was great, perhaps even greater than it had been during the Nazi years. Though no one was killed for their Jewish beliefs anymore, being caught with an extra sack of potatoes or a pair of stockings might be all it took to end up in jail. As for practicing the Jewish faith, the Communist Party had effectively established a state religion everyone was expected to embrace—the religion of atheism. Those who embraced religion of any other kind were viewed as giving their loyalties to another institution and hence were disloyal. No one was imprisoned for their faith, but organized religion was banned and the social pressure great to abandon any pretense of belief, especially for those who swore their allegiance to the party.

Ervin learned just how great the pressure was on party members when he fell ill with hepatitis again. While hospitalized, he shared a room with another physician, one who was known as a hard-core communist and suffering the same illness. Given those political views, Ervin made a point to not discuss politics, but his hospital mate would not relent on preaching the Communist Party line every chance he got. Eventually, Ervin avoided discussing any topic whatsoever.

Then came the Jewish high holiday, Yom Kippur, when even secular Jews traditionally fast. Though there is an exception made for those who are sick, Ervin wanted to observe the holiday, especially considering his parents had given their lives for their faith. When it came time to order food for dinner—to be served after sundown when the fast began—Ervin declined, while his Jewish hospital mate requested the largest meal available, demonstrating that he rejected any religious observance. The following day when the dinner arrived Ervin left the room, so as not to be tempted by the food he could not enjoy.

When he returned, the food was gone and all that was left were the dirty dishes, which the staff took away.

"Looks like you've cleaned your plate this time," the nursing aide said in good humor as she cleared away the dishes.

"And every last bite was delicious," he said. "I could eat twice as much if you'd let me!"

She laughed, scolded him for his greed, and left.

A few minutes later Ervin excused himself to use the bathroom. There, in the toilet, were the last remnants of the meal that had been flushed away. Though vocally an atheist who had no need for religious observance, the man was at heart a more devout Jew than he dared let on.

Ervin reflected on the incident. The man's beliefs were apparently the same as his own and though an educated physician, he felt compelled to play the communist game by lying—possibly even to himself—and living an alternative reality. Such behavior, Ervin thought, was typical for so many people in Hungary at the time. The purported communist doctor was not as bad as he had acted. And that little episode on Yom Kippur was a simple reflection of their daily lives, existing alongside daily terror, where one had to be constantly vigilant. So much had changed since the defeat of the Nazis. And so little had changed.

For Ervin, it was no way to live. He had no idea how he'd get out, but one thing was certain—he wasn't going to leave without Judit. He was determined to spend the rest of his life with her and create a new family for himself.

TWO WEDDINGS

In 1953, Ervin married Judit. He was making very little money at the time, as physicians were paid just enough to survive, and he had to donate his salary from the first two months in exchange for a five-year commitment to employ him. He loved his work as an obstetrician, especially as he was working for Judit's Uncle Laci, whom Ervin admired a great deal. Still, just getting by was a struggle and to make a bit of extra money, he saw patients secretly on the side, a practice prohibited by the communist state. Judit's mother also sent the couple money secretly, and if Zoltán found out about the payments, Ervin's work and freedom would come to a swift end. It seemed to Ervin that the communists would rather physicians were hungry and homeless than paid enough to raise a family. Having already lost one family to the Nazis, he was not about to forego starting a new one, so the risk was one he gladly accepted.

Risk had become his way of life. He thrived on challenging the odds and proving himself capable of outsmarting those with lesser wits but greater power. He had failed just enough to know when to restrain himself and when to trust his instinct and abilities. Fortunately, those very qualities proved valued in obstetrics where Ervin was among the first called on for high-risk pregnancies and deliveries. His reputation as a skilled physician was rapidly increasing, even if his income wasn't. But none of that mattered. What mattered was sharing his life with Judit.

Their wedding, however, proved to be yet another risk the two had to take. It was important to them both that they be married by a rabbi, but if they did that, Judit risked being expelled from medical school. Allegiance to atheism was expected of all patriots, and patriotic allegiance to the communist state was expected of all students. So they not only arranged a civil ceremony for the afternoon with a city councilman officiating but also a secret ceremony at Dr. Benedek's home that same morning.

The home was beautifully decorated with fresh flowers, though the window shades were drawn so no one would report them. Judit's paternal grandfather, Grandpa Simsovits, who was the head of the Jewish Burial Society, the Chevra Kadisha, performed the ceremony, as he had his rabbinical license. For a wedding canopy, the *chuppah,* a prayer shawl known as a *tallith* was held over the couple's heads, as was the Jewish tradition.

As the couple stood under the makeshift *chuppah,* Grandpa Simsovits recited the traditional wedding prayers while wearing his own prayer shawl. Judit and Ervin exchanged wedding rings and as was the custom, Ervin stomped on a wine glass, shattering it. Finally, a blessing over wine was recited. Everyone wished the Wolfs a *Mazel Tov* and Grandpa Simsovits signed the *ketubah,* the Jewish marriage contract stipulating Ervin's obligations to his bride, and tucked it away in a linen closet. The two young lovers couldn't have been happier, and the few guests were joyous, for the ceremony was even more sacred for having been clandestine.

When the ceremony was finished, the couple and their guests broke their fast, enjoying a kosher wedding feast of sardines, bread, and fruit. And then it was time to be married all over again, this time in the public civil ceremony at City Hall—a gray block of a building lacking any personality or architectural style. It was a building more suited to be a mausoleum than a space for celebrating the union of two people, but it was fitting for the cold hearts of the communists as far as Ervin was concerned.

And cold hearted it was, for the wedding guests were forced to wait outside, even though it was a nasty, rainy January afternoon. There was a long line of guests, for not only was this public ceremony sanctioned by the state, and thus more friends, colleagues and family could be invited, it also conformed with the communist spirit. Not surprisingly, their ceremony would be communal. Several couples would marry in unison in the public space outfitted for that purpose.

Once admitted inside, the guests and the wedding couple were sent to a special room on the third floor where a Persian carpet covered the floor and a large chandelier hung from the ceiling, a rare elegance permitted by the communists. A long table covered with red cloth stood at the front of the room, while in the back, rows of folding metal chairs had been lined up for the guests.

The state florist had provided the brides with identical floral bouquets and the grooms wore single stems of a seasonal flower. Because it was January, the flowers were simple ones, but Ervin had imported red Russian roses from Crimea for the event. When everyone had gathered, the couples all stood as a recording of the "Bridal Chorus" from Wagner's *Lohengrin,* followed by Mendelssohn's "Wedding March", played. As the music ended, the City Councilman appeared with a wide white ribbon draped on his right shoulder like a sash, looking like a circus clown. Ervin half expected the flower in his lapel to squirt water.

As the master of ceremonies launched into a speech, Ervin let his mind wander, thinking that as tasteless and corny as the whole thing was, this was his happy ending. He was married in the eyes of God to a beautiful woman he loved. He would, one way or another, break free of Hungary and he and Judit would start their family in another land where they would live freely. His only sadness was that his parents weren't there to witness his marriage, yet he felt that they were there in spirit watching over them and blessing his marriage.

Ervin barely remembered the ceremony, his thoughts were so far away. As far as he was concerned, the state ceremony was an intrusion on his wedding vows, not a confirmation of them. He and Judit had truly been married in the home of Uncle Laci and he couldn't wait to start his new life with his bride.

The reception began at five o'clock, again at the Benedeks' fine home, with at least 150 guests in attendance. Judit's grandparents had generously paid for the lavish event and under the circumstances, Ervin felt they could not have enjoyed a more elegant wedding party, which included hot and cold hors d'oeuvres and endless champagne. The hospital's pastry chef had prepared all the desserts and each was perfectly executed—walnut cookies, delicate cakes, and gingerbread. He was an especially gifted confectioner, having owned a well-known confectionery in downtown Budapest for many years, which he was forced to relinquish to the state government when private businesses were nationalized. After that, he worked as an employee in his own shop and in later years was forced to work for the hospital as his "retirement." If anyone was as happy as the wedding couple, it was the pastry chef who delighted in the opportunity to display his skills once again.

The couple were given many beautiful gifts, despite the humble circumstances of most guests, and for just that one night, Ervin and Judit were almost able to forget the wretched existence they lived under communist rule. They so enjoyed the company and support of so many family members and friends and Ervin felt warmly welcomed into Judit's family. Laci was especially supportive and remained in a jovial mood all evening, or so it appeared, and Ervin felt a particular debt to his good friend and supervising Director for having made it possible for the couple to have a true Jewish wedding —even if it was performed with the shades drawn.

But for all the loving friends and family that joined in the celebration, there was one conspicuous in his absence. Uncle Zoltán. Despite his decades of commitment to the Communist Party, Zoltán had fallen from grace as untrustworthy, given his sister's defection to Israel. His penalty for his alleged disloyalty—a disloyalty neither Ervin nor Judit had ever discerned—was banishment to the remote countryside where he was assigned to run a coal mine. With few resources and no support from the party he so loved, Zoltán was struggling for his own survival.

As much compassion as Ervin felt for his new in-law's fall from grace, and he certainly did empathize given his own experience in forced labor, he had to admit he didn't miss him at his wedding. Had he been there, Ervin had no doubt every detail would have been reported to the communists and for just this one night, Ervin wanted only joy.

After a couple of hours of festivities, the Benedeks' chauffeur, Oscar, arrived to take Ervin and Judit to the small village of Mátrafüred where there was a government-run resort where they would spend their honeymoon. After a long and happy drive, they arrived at the resort late at night eager to start their honeymoon. Coincidentally, another couple, also newly married, arrived just as they did.

Taking in the scene of the two men and two women, the desk clerk checked them into two separate rooms.

The two men were appointed to one room, the two women to another.

When the husbands protested, the desk clerk dug in his heels, and even when his supervisor was called, rather than resolve the problem, he only further defended the action. The women would stay in one room and the men in another, and any alternative was unacceptable. After much dispute, the desk clerk was finally persuaded to admit that he'd made a mistake—something bureaucrats were loath to do, Ervin noted. Exhausted, Ervin and Judit were finally assigned a room together.

"Let me help you," Oscar, the chauffeur offered, as he took their luggage to their room. Once inside, Oscar lit a fire in the fireplace and with a smile, bid the couple goodnight.

And a good night it was, after all. It wasn't until the next morning when Judit called to thank her aunt and uncle for their gracious generosity in hosting the wedding and reception that the consequence of the Benedeks' kindness was revealed.

Uncle Laci had been arrested.

DARK AND GETTING DARKER

Once Judit and Ervin had departed and the guests had gone home, her aunt explained, Uncle Laci broke down. He had been suppressing his apprehensions amidst the tension of the clandestine ceremony for so long that with the bridal party gone and a few glasses of wine in his blood, the stoic doctor had crumbled. He had lived under fascist and communist rule long enough that he had recognized the plain-clothed secret police, the infamous AVO—the State Protection Authority—mixed in among the guests. Once alone with only his wife by his side, Laci sobbed, for he knew what their presence meant. As the elder couple prepared for bed that evening, putting out lights before climbing the stairs to their bedroom at 11 p.m., an urgent pounding on the door told them the time had come.

The AVO agents burst into the home and announced that the house had been under surveillance by secret agents since the early morning. They were aware of the illegal wedding and would find the evidence to prove it. As the Benedeks watched powerlessly and in horror, the agents ransacked their home, the home that just hours before had been the site of such festivities and happiness. Eventually, they found the *ketubah* that had been hidden in the linen closet. They also produced a letter forged by the secret police, which allegedly proved that Dr. Benedek was involved in espionage for the American

Joint Distribution Committee. Though the document falsely claimed that Uncle Laci was working for someone who had long ago departed Budapest, it mattered little. Just as Ervin and Judit had been settling into their firelit room for the first night of their honeymoon, Dr. Benedek was arrested and taken away.

When the couple returned a week later, they felt as though they'd stepped into the eye of a hurricane. Everyone was in a state of panic. They had no idea where Laci had been taken and Zoltán—the only person who could have helped them—could offer nothing. And without the good doctor's income, Aunt Helen feared she'd lose her home. As for Ervin, he feared for Laci's life. The communists thought nothing of killing their own; doing so only cemented their power as everyone lived in fear and obedience. For someone like Laci, who had never been a friend to the Communist Party, his life was even more disposable. With both Laci and Zoltán gone, Ervin was now the eldest male. Though only 30, he was responsible not just for Judit, but for her entire family as well.

He returned to work to find the hospital staff in deep silence for weeks. No one dared ask any questions about what had happened to their director. Dr. Benedek's first assistant ran the obstetrics department, but the atmosphere was dark and rumors swirled. For his part, Ervin didn't speak of the wedding or arrest. He knew that even the most innocuous or well-intended comment could lead to harsh repercussions, if not for him or his colleagues, then for Laci himself. Instead, he kept his head down, focused on his work, and went home each evening to his new bride where at least he felt loved, supported, and inspired to break free of the oppressive weight they lived under.

Within three months, Dr. Benedek's wife was terminated from her job in the hospital, where she worked in the laboratory. Her daughter just starting kindergarten, Helen found herself without means to support her child and was forced to send little Susie to live with her mother to ensure her education. Ervin was stunned at how rapidly such a fine and upstanding family could be toppled, and for such a small reason—hosting a wedding ceremony.

Ervin and Judit did their best to offer their moral support to the family, though Ervin was hardly making enough to support his wife, much less the whole family. As the weeks passed into months following Laci's arrest, the stress became nearly unbearable. Helen could not afford to hire an attorney and her efforts to find out where her husband had been taken went nowhere. The inquiries she, Ervin, and others made, however, revealed that the Benedek household had been under surveillance for some time. The telephone was bugged, and recording devices hidden in the home. But perhaps the most difficult discovery was that once Laci had been arrested, the Benedeks had few friends. Nearly every friend they had abandoned them, spread rumors about them, or treated them with contempt. It was that reality that most wounded Helen, but for Ervin, who had seen what fascism had done to turn kind people into inhumane ones, it was no surprise. But surprise or not, he realized that his future with Judit would never be secure if they remained in Hungary. They had to get out. Unfortunately, the iron grip of the Communist Party clamped down on Ervin as well and, before he knew it, he was once again forced into servitude for a ruling power he detested.

He was ordered into military service, assigned to quality control for the nutrition of the soldiers. In other words, he was a food taster, required to sample the food prior to serving each meal. Like something out of a Shakespearean drama, Ervin thought, where his job was to die for those targeted for murder. He didn't suppose anyone would poison the soldiers, but the work was humiliating and kept him away from his obstetric responsibilities and from Judit. What he hadn't imagined was just how dangerous the position would prove to be.

After he tasted the food and declared it safe, the soldiers were fed, and the leftovers put in an unrefrigerated locker to serve the next day. Only Ervin had the key to the lockers, above which a sign warned of not letting the food get into "the hands of the enemies." The paranoia of the communist government was great under Stalin and a persistent belief that people sought to poison the soldiers prevailed. Ervin quickly realized the danger of the job—in the heat of the hot Hungarian summer, the unrefrigerated food would quickly spoil. His fears were compounded when he learned of previous doctors who had been appointed to the post being imprisoned, a few even sentenced to death after serving leftovers which gave the soldiers food poisoning. Ervin knew his fate should the leftovers be served. Eventually they would sicken the troops. He had only one option. All leftovers went to the dogs.

"They've got big appetites," Ervin said of the soldiers when the Chief Commander asked why there were never any leftovers. "They're hard working and big eating."

He was dismissed and he thought that was the end of the matter. He'd dodged another bullet.

Shortly after, however, the party secretary approached Ervin and invited him to his room. Though not reflected in rank, the party secretary had greater power than the chief commander, given his close affiliation with the top leadership in the Communist Party. Ervin wanted more than ever to turn down the invitation, but he dared not. He knew that it was forbidden to refuse any request issued by party leadership, no matter how seemingly benign.

Ervin followed the secretary to his office, which was in another building and behind heavy double iron doors. *Like a private fortress,* Ervin thought, imagining the horrors that might await him once he was on the other side of those doors.

"Have a seat," the secretary said, motioning for Ervin to sit across the desk from him. Ervin complied and as he waited for the secretary to step around the massive desk and take his own chair, he noted the large maps that adorned the walls of the office and the many telephones that sat on his desk. This was a man whose sole focus was safeguarding the Communist Party, a powerful man with powerful friends, despite his small stature and friendly smile. Did he suspect Ervin had been purposefully disposing of the leftovers? If so, the punishment would be brutal. A feeling of horror seized Ervin as he realized he could disappear without a trace. He might never even be seen leaving this office, noting two other doors leading to closets, other rooms, and back corridors. He had no idea. He knew only that he might join the tens of thousands of other Hungarians whose lives had been extinguished by the very nation they had loved. He was thinking of Judit and how she might never know his fate, nor he hers, when he realized he hadn't been paying any attention at all to the words of the secretary.

"And that is why I've called you here today," he heard him say, suddenly coming to his senses.

What is why? What a fool I am for letting my mind wander, he thought. *How might I rewind this conversation?*

"I'm sorry," Ervin said as he wiggled his finger in his ear and shook his head, "I've been having some problems with my hearing lately. An old injury from the Labor Service. Could you please say that again?"

The secretary looked at him with compassion. "You must get that checked out. I'm so sorry for what you've been through. I've heard many such stories from you men in the Labor Service. So many beatings."

"Yes, yes, I will," Ervin assured him, wondering if his comment about beatings was genuine empathy or a threat of more to come.

The secretary continued. "I was just saying, there are so few men of your intellect out here, it is refreshing to encounter a man as clever and quick witted as you."

Ervin felt his heart race and his flesh turn cold. Throughout the country, wherever people congregated or worked closely together, informants for the Communist Party infiltrated the groups and reported back to the party every detail, every suspicion, every name and address. This man was privy to what Ervin had done with the leftovers and aware, as well, of all his social connections throughout the hospital and through Judit and her family. He'd been called to the secretary's office to be recruited as an informant. His choice would be to accept and survive—at the cost of those he loved and respected—or decline and disappear without a trace.

"Thank you," Ervin heard himself say and his mind was ten paces ahead of his mouth, scrambling to get out of another horrid fate. "But I—"

"Oh, no need to be modest," the secretary said, interrupting him and relaxing into his chair. "You know you're smarter than most of the men you answer to and I'm no exception. That's why it's such a pleasure to get away from this wretched madness and talk about something besides politics. It's lonely as hell in this office, as I'm sure you can imagine. As I'm sure you feel yourself in your position. Why, just the other day..."

As the secretary launched into a discussion of his isolated existence and his intellectual frustrations with his job, Ervin came to realize he wasn't being recruited as an informant after all. He had summoned the frightened doctor for nothing more than a friendly chat with a bored loner who was seeking company during his deep isolation. After an hour or so of discussing existential topics related to growing older in the modern world, shifting to Hollywood movies, the difficulty of finding a decent *gulyás,* and their favorite Greek philosophers, the secretary bid him good afternoon with a hearty smile and a thank you and Ervin returned to his barracks.

Still, he feared the visit may have been to groom him for the big ask, but it never came. His further encounters with the secretary were friendly hellos, but he wasn't asked back to the man's office. Shortly after, Ervin was discharged.

His service had only lasted a few weeks, and he was thankful to return home and get back to work. He did so just in time to learn that an AVO agent had visited the Benedeks' home. It had been six months since Laci's arrest and there had been no news of him. Thinking the agent was there to inform her of her husband's death, Helen was immensely relieved to learn that he was only there to pick up the doctor's glasses. They had some documents they wanted him to sign, and he had indicated he could not do so without his glasses. Ervin knew that any documents they wanted him to sign were being put before him under coercion—and he didn't dare think of what that might entail—but it also meant that Laci was alive. That was all that mattered.

The visit proved hopeful in another respect, for the AVO reported that a defense attorney had been appointed to represent Dr. Benedek. Though such attorneys were usually employed by the police and the process a pretense at best, even the false formality gave the family a sense of hope. Still, nothing happened for several more months.

Then, on March 5, 1953, Joseph Stalin died. The family hoped that Laci would be released with the death of the genocidal madman who ruled the Soviet Union, but like so often, their hopes remained unfulfilled as month after month passed with no word. For the free Hungarian citizens, however, the quality of life improved somewhat as Khrushchev assumed power and openly admitted the terrors of the Stalinist era—thereby disposing of any possible competition from old Stalinists. A new, more humanitarian approach to communist rule ensued and the stringent surveillance in the satellite states lessened. But the omnipresent darkness had not entirely lifted and periodic reminders that no one was free made it clear that the Communist Party may have changed its spots, but not its bite.

Old black, mysterious cars belonging to the secret police and looking like carbon copies of those their Nazi counterparts would drive passed slowly by homes and businesses, keeping watch. Sometimes they would stop in the middle of the night, the drivers, dressed in full-length leather coats, knocking on people's doors at two or three in the morning. The unfortunate residents of those homes would disappear, kidnapped by the secret police just as Laci had been under the guise of an "arrest."

Some were merely evicted and relocated to remote, rural areas where they were forced to survive as farmworkers. They were never told how long they would toil or live in the dilapidated, unsafe structures that housed them. The punishment was presented as the purification of the intellectual and bourgeois class, their crimes being nothing more than teaching, writing, or merely thinking out loud in the company of others. To be "elite," to be an intellectual, those were the intolerable sins that merited their exile—and those sins came at the expense of their home and belongings, their property seized by the state, rendering these people homeless and penniless upon their release.

Tempora mutantur, nos et mutamur in illis, Ervin thought. Times are changed, we are also changed with them. He had been so changed by time. And so, he soon discovered, had his dear friend and mentor, Dr. Benedek.

A BROKEN MAN

Uncle Laci remained imprisoned by the Hungarian secret police for over a year. When he was at long last released, he was a changed and broken man. Ervin was stunned at his transformation from a strong and joyful, sharp-witted man, to a frail and frightened one. He had lost half his body weight and was severely malnourished. He had difficulty walking and talking. He stuttered, which he never had done before, and barely spoke to anyone. He requested that lights be kept off, as he could barely tolerate light. But perhaps the most heartbreaking of all was the crying. He frequently cried, often quietly and to himself, lost in his painful memories of those cruel and tortuous times.

His interrogators had used blinding lights to coerce confessions from the doctor. They had burned his fingers with cigarettes, deprived him of sleep, beaten him for no reason. This abuse would happen at random hours, often in the middle of the night when he'd be awakened from sleep and subjected to physical and mental tortures. As part of the mental torture, they would repeatedly play tape recordings that sounded like his daughter's voice pleading, "Daddy, please confess! If you will not, they will kill us!"

What they wanted him to confess to was a range of offenses, from conspiring with friends and family to leave the country, overthrow the government, or organize anti-communist activities, to assassinating the Swedish diplomat, Raoul Wallenberg. Wallenberg was renowned for saving thousands of Hungarian Jews through his Protective Passes—the very ones that had served Ervin so well. In 1945 when the war ended, Wallenberg vanished and was believed to have been killed in prison in Moscow two years later. A confession from a Jew that he had murdered the Swedish hero would have gone far to mitigate suspicions against the Communist Party.

In their efforts to force Dr. Benedek to confess to this and other crimes, the Hungarian secret police produced a series of documents detailing false confessions and tried to make him sign them. The more he defied their efforts, the greater the brutalities became. By the time they gave up and released him, this man who had survived a forced labor camp in Russia during the war and had marched for thousands of kilometers with frostbitten legs had transformed into a man barely able to speak.

One year after his release, the communists deemed him a rehabilitated man. Though forbidden to return to his former position as Director, he was assigned a subordinate position at a suburban medical clinic. All for hosting a Jewish wedding.

As Judit advanced in medical school, Ervin passed his examinations to qualify as a specialist in obstetrics and gynecology, becoming Assistant Professor of Obstetrics and Gynecology in 1955. His position with the Budapest Hospital was secured. He and Judit settled into a relatively easy life. Each Wednesday, on his day off, he would take Judit out for a late lunch and sometimes they'd visit the thermal bathhouse at the Hotel Gellert. The relaxed outings reminded Ervin of the many lunches and spa visits he had enjoyed with his mother, and he savored the opportunity to relive them with Judit. But money remained tight and his pay low. What little he did earn was further reduced by obligatory deductions the state imposed to finance industrial investment, as the nation rebuilt its infrastructure following the war. As well, all wage earners were required to invest in state bonds, further reducing income. What was left was not enough for the couple to live on.

Given their limited income and the uncontrolled inflation, the couple gladly accepted the generosity of Judit's mother, who continued to secretly send them extra money. On Judit's part, the extra income from her mother served as her contribution to the household income, given how little physicians were paid. But to Ervin, the money wasn't always as exciting as the mission required to obtain it.

Sending money through the mail was impossible. All mail was monitored. Nor was there any way to go to the telegraph company to collect the funds, as receiving money was prohibited. His only option was to go to the Israeli Embassy, but there was one problem. Entering foreign embassies was strictly forbidden. Making it even more difficult, the Hungarian government had these embassies under close surveillance. The entrance to the Israeli Embassy was under surveillance by cameras and all the buildings surrounding it were heavily guarded by the Hungarians.

On his first attempt, Ervin studied the location closely, trying to learn every possible opportunity for escaping attention as he entered and exited and disappeared into the streets without being recognized. Once he figured out his plan, he put it into motion, a complex series of dangerous steps that turned each mission into an adrenaline-pumping act of espionage.

When the Consul arrived from Vienna, he would place a call to Ervin from a public telephone and tell him the day and time to meet. To avoid being followed, Ervin would board a streetcar and when he neared his destination, rather than getting off at the scheduled stop, he would jump from the moving streetcar and run straight through the gate into the building, his head hidden in a brimmed hat in order that the cameras would not capture his face.

Once in the building, a radio would be cranked up to full volume as the Israeli diplomats knew the Consulate was bugged. Any conversation had to be obscured. It was then that Ervin would be told any news that Judit's mother had wanted to convey, and he would be handed a care package, which usually included money, a written letter, and sometimes coffee or other precious treats unavailable to common people in the socialist paradise. He would then watch from the window as a collaborator outside would give him the signal that the streetcar was approaching. When the signal came, Ervin would run from the building and jump onto the moving streetcar with the same dexterity he'd jumped from it. After two stations, he'd jump off the streetcar and run into a building that had double doors—one he could run into and another on the opposite side he could run out of. If anyone was following him, he'd know it. Once safely exited, he would walk calmly home.

The entire escapade was made in complete secrecy, not even Judit knew how he managed to pick up the care packages and she knew better than to ask. Ervin knew, however, that he was playing with fire every time he did so, but he did not think much about the risks involved, for risk had become his way of life and they needed the extra money—and he needed the extra adventure.

It was not just the constant surveillance and threat of disappearance that weighed on Ervin and Judit's minds. The grip of the Iron Curtain had loosened with Stalin's death, and they were thankful Uncle Laci was home, however beaten and broken he was. But the scarcity of such basic things as coffee, flour, sugar, oil, much less luxuries like stockings, made daily living more difficult and challenging. Even basic hardware was near impossible to obtain. Once when an egg slicer broke, not only could the slicer not be replaced to Judit's disappointment, but the wire to repair it was unavailable. Wanting to please his wife, Ervin had an idea. Wire was not available, but zither strings were. He went to a store that sold musical instruments and asked for a zither string.

"Sure thing," the merchant replied. "Which string would you like?"

"It doesn't matter," Ervin shrugged. "Any will do."

The shopkeeper looked at him incredulously, and then chuckling, he said, "Oh, so you're just learning, are you? I'm sure I can help you out. Which instrument do you play?"

"Egg cutter," Ervin replied.

That evening, he proudly presented Judit with a freshly repaired egg slicer.

Despite the scarcities, things were relaxing. The government allowed a bit more travel abroad if one had a passport—another scarcity—but the only currency worth anything was foreign currency and little of that was available. Meanwhile, the early morning visits from the KGB continued, though they no longer searched through people's garbage cans unless they were looking for something specific. And much to Ervin's relief, physicians could accept money from their patients without fear of retribution, which enabled Ervin to not only receive tips—something patients often offered, knowing physicians were paid less than waiters—but he could also see private patients.

Thus, the Wolfs adapted as best they could to the new way of life. Ervin loved his work as a physician and felt he had accomplished a dream that just a few years before had seemed impossible. No matter how poor the system became, the government could not take from him his achievement, nor the love that he and Judit had for each other. There was even a sense of hope in the air in the summer of 1956 as Rákóczi was forced to step down. Though he'd proved himself among the most loyal of world leaders to the Communist Party, if not one of the most feared and repressive, with Stalin gone and the extent of the genocidal Soviet leader's atrocities becoming known, Khrushchev made it clear that Rákóczi had to go. Yet just one year earlier, the Warsaw Pact had been put in place and Hungary, along with the other Soviet Bloc countries, had pledged their support to any of the member nations if they were attacked. Thus, Rákóczi's exit did little to lessen the tight reins the Soviets held over Hungary, and his replacement, another communist, Ernő Gerő, was every bit as sadistic. Nonetheless, social tides were compelling even Gerő to temper his authoritarianism. The landmines were cleared, some of the electric fences were disconnected, and much of the barbed wire was coming down. Most citizens were still not free to travel, not having the necessary passports that were so hard to come by, but compared to the lives they'd been living, these small changes had a big psychological impact.

Yet Ervin and Judit dared not fool themselves into thinking they were safe. Still, they rationalized to each other that their life was good and that things would improve as time passed. Rather than dwell on the hardships of life under communist rule, they focused on what pleasures and joys they did have. Then, in 1956, the world as they knew it changed in an instant—and with it, their destiny.

REVOLUTION

As the social climate of communist Hungary brightened ever so slightly, so too did the spirits of the youthful intellectuals, artists, writers, and others who had not lived long enough to become embittered, nor briefly enough that they were easily swayed to the party's ideology. While Ervin and Judit were still young themselves, the trauma the couple had endured through the brutal reign of the Nazis—Ervin especially—along with their promising careers as physicians—had tempered any dreams of rebellion. For Ervin, his monthly adventures to the Israeli Embassy were rebellion enough. But for others, the time was ripe to call for greater change. Through a series of open discussions in public forums called Petőfi Circles, after the 19th century Hungarian poet and revolutionary, Sándor Petőfi, these idealistic artists and intellectuals—mostly students—called for a free press, free speech, and the right to free assembly. They also called for new leadership, singling out Imre Nagy, who had briefly been the leader of Chairman of the Council of Ministers—a high ranking office that determined how multiple branches of the government were run—to be reinstated. Though considered a "Moscow Communist" loyal to Stalin, Nagy was known for his humanity and commitment to a humane socialism and a free society. The daring defiance of Soviet suppression the activists called for, and their open criticism of the Rákosi cult that had persisted in the wake of Rákosi's exile, inspired Hungarians throughout the nation—including Judit and Ervin—who felt for the first time that change might truly come to Hungary.

Their optimism was bolstered by the recent uprising of workers in Poland. Though the uprising was violently suppressed with many killed and thousands arrested, the event forced Poland's communist leadership to make several concessions, including raising workers' wages. Hungarians, for too long forced to live in poverty while working long hours, became inspired to make similar demands.

To show their solidarity with Poland, the students organized a march to the statue of Polish General József Bem, a 19th century national hero of Poland and Hungary who had been among the Hungarian freedom fighters during the struggles against the monarchy.

The march began peacefully as the university students, both men and women, marched in an orderly fashion to General Bem's statue. They were carrying the red, white, and green flags of Hungary, but altered by cutting out the hammer-and-sickle symbol of the Communist Party.

"They're David fighting Goliath," Ervin observed to Judit when the first stirrings of the movement came to light. "But I hope they're victorious."

"As do I," Judit agreed, "but I fear the consequences may be far greater than the rewards. If they fail, we'll suffer even more."

"Something tells me they won't fail, not this time," Ervin said, a smile curling his lips upward as he wished he were free to join them. At 34, Ervin felt both young and old. It seemed as if it was just yesterday that he and Frank had escaped the Nazis, and his memories of hiding under the bed, sleeping in lofts, riding on lumber trucks, and working in secret in Mr. Wanek's bicycle repair shop were so clear and sharp in his mind that he could still smell the hay in the lofts, the dirty socks of the visiting priest, and the oil that perpetually stained his hands in the bicycle shop. At the same time, those exciting memories were buried amidst such a rubble of pain that he felt he'd lived a dozen lifetimes in what was barely more than a decade. His burning desire for the students to triumph was matched by his fear that they wouldn't—and his knowledge that the punishment for seeking freedom was inevitably barbaric, cruel, and beyond all comprehension.

On 23 October, Ervin kissed Judit goodbye and with a happy heart, went across town to pick up a mobile serving cart from a local cabinet maker. It was a heavy piece of furniture, but beautifully made with exquisite inlay work, hand-polished, and one of a kind. He and Judit had saved up for some time for the luxurious piece. After making his final payment, he left with it—wheeling it more than six kilometers across town as he had no other means of transporting the costly jalopy. While wheeling his new treasure, he observed a large, peaceful crowd of young people chanting, singing, and marching in the streets carrying Hungarian flags. Flags were also hanging from nearly every window of nearly every building and home and the sight filled him with a sense of patriotic pride and the joy that comes of people united in a common mission. Despite Judit's concerns that their efforts might lead to greater oppression, the youthful exuberance, joy, and peaceful unity persuaded Ervin that he was witnessing a spark of the human spirit that had been missing for so long in Hungary. Though unconvinced they'd be victorious in their ultimate goals, it never occurred to him that this same crowd would soon become the target of a terrifying moment in history, one which he would soon find himself a part of.

The march, for Ervin, was nothing more than that. A march, as if witnessing a passing parade on his way home to his wife. What was pressing on his mind had nothing to do with politics or social movements. All he could think of was how heavy the damned cart was and how ridiculous he must look pushing it like a common peddler selling his wares. At long last, he reached his building and couldn't wait to present the cart to Judit. He knew she'd be thrilled. But just as he was getting off the elevator, one of the wheels got stuck in the elevator door and as he struggled to free it, the wheel came off and fell into the elevator shaft, from where it would be impossible to retrieve it. By the time Ervin presented the cart to Judit, it was missing a wheel, and he was drenched in sweat and in such an ill temper that he completely forgot to mention to Judit the massive march he had witnessed. He had to shower, for they had tickets to the theater that evening and he was not about to let that broken wheel spoil one of their rare evenings out.

Meanwhile, as Ervin showered and Judit fashioned a makeshift prosthesis for her new cart, outside the crowd swelled to nearly 200,000 when workers left their posts to join in the demonstration. Once the massive river of chanting reformists reached Bem's statue on the Buda side of the city, they were energized. They marched on, this time moving toward Pest where their destination was the Central Radio Station building where communist propaganda was regularly broadcast. As some seized the microphones at the radio station, others marched on to the Communist Press headquarters where the communist newspaper, ironically named *Szabad Nép* (Free People), was published. As the students announced their demands for a freer humanistic socialism at both destinations, others split from the group and rushed to the massive bronze statue of Stalin near the city park. There, they used torches to destroy the sculpture of the tyrant and, once toppled and dismantled, they scattered the pieces across the city as if dismembering Stalin himself.

But it was at the radio station that the demonstration transformed as the AVO opened fire on the protestors. In an instant, all hell broke loose and things careened out of control. The Hungarian Revolution had started.

Judit and Ervin were in high spirits by the time they reached their favorite place, the Political Cabaret. Within certain limits, the cabaret was a place where they had felt free to openly laugh at the system that oppressed them. But that night, the laughter was stilted and restrained. The tension was palpable and mid-performance, the actors aborted their production to recite patriotic poems and sing the national anthem. It was then that Ervin realized he hadn't even mentioned to Judit what he'd witnessed that afternoon and made a mental note to tell her when they left the theater.

As they did so, he had no time to say a word for everyone on the street was talking about what had happened at the radio station.

"Be careful," strangers warned, "a fight broke out there and tempers are hot!" How hot, the couple had no idea, and it wasn't until they were riding home on the streetcar that they heard gunshots in the distance and felt that maybe they were indeed in danger walking in the streets. They hurried home and went straight to bed, both unnerved, as well as happy to have enjoyed a night at the cabaret, however odd the performance.

At two a.m. the phone rang. As an obstetrician, Ervin had become accustomed to being woken in the middle of the night for an emergency delivery. But this time, he wasn't summoned to deliver a baby. It was the surgical department in desperate need of emergency assistance.

The first sign that something terrible had happened were the lights. The hospital was brightly lit through every corridor. In communist Hungary, electricity was yet another resource one learned to do without. Lights were used where they were most essential, turned off or low where they were not. But now, every light was on.

Because the Wolfs' apartment was in the hospital, Ervin had reached the emergency room just as the first of the ambulances arrived. The first contained two young women and a young man lying in pools of their own blood, their faces lacerated, their clothing torn. They had been sitting inside the cab of a semitruck when the bullets from a sniper's machine gun shattered the front windshield and riddled their bodies. Ervin couldn't imagine what they had done to deserve such a fate, yet he knew. They may have participated in the demand for free speech. Just the possibility of their involvement was enough to justify killing them in the eyes of the communists. Ervin seethed to live in such a society, a society that regarded itself as so righteous that any act it carried out, at any cost, was regarded as justified.

But he had no time to reflect on the communist state, no time to reflect on the lives of those who began pouring in through the hospital doors in numbers beyond anyone's comprehension. All were in critical condition or dying, all were riddled with bullets or sliced open from flying glass and metal. Brains spilled from skulls, and guts were split open. Blood flowed everywhere.

Ervin sterilized his hands and joined the surgical team, his task becoming ever more serious and strained as the gunshot victims were rushed into surgery throughout the night, many dying before they could even be treated. The team worked on their patients into the next day, not finishing until late afternoon. Even then, their work was unfinished as so many were in critical states, needing more surgery and round-the-clock care. As they urgently fought off death, births continued. Ervin had never been so busy and, as women continued to give birth, he was sent back and forth from the surgical ward to his own OB/GYN department. As much as he truly loved bringing new life into the world, he couldn't help but wonder with every birth what kind of world he was bringing these innocent babies into.

As the night turned to day, gunfire continued to shatter the city, while every able-bodied person on the hospital's staff was recruited to work around the clock attending to the trauma patients. Judit joined the team, arranging the blood transfusions that so many patients needed, while Ervin worked between surgery and obstetrics.

Whenever he had a free moment, he listened to the radio to get a sense of what was going on, but what little information was reported by the Soviet controlled stations was inconsistent and untrustworthy. The only credible news came from the gunshot victims themselves, as survivors recounted the sudden attack that turned an inspiring, peaceful protest into a bloodied battlefield. The initial shots were fired at the radio station, under heavy guard by the AVO, when a small group split from the massive crowd of protestors and attempted to gain control of the airwaves to broadcast their demands. Before they could do so, they were apprehended, and rumors quickly spread like forest fire through the crowd that they had been killed. As the mood transformed from one of jubilance to fury, tear gas was thrown into the crowd and the AVO agents, under orders from Gerő, opened fire on the young protestors. As bullets flew and bodies fell, chaos erupted and the once-organized peaceful demonstrators fought back by surrounding and overturning police cars, smashing windows, throwing rocks, and fleeing in terror. Angered for years as their freedoms, rights, and resources were tightly controlled by the Soviets, inspired that fresh change was on the horizon, then in the height of that emotion, to be fired on indiscriminately by a government that did not hesitate to kill them, the joyous crowd of 200,000 turned in an instant into an angry mob. Tear gas and bullets rained down upon them. Within hours, Budapest had been transformed into the battleground of a civil war that was anything but civil.

Eventually, the AVO ran out of ammunition and hid in ambulances, but they were quickly found and attacked by the enraged protestors. Soon soldiers were called in to control the crowd, but once they arrived and saw the streets strewn with the bodies of young people—some just children—they tore the red stars from their caps and joined in the protests. In response, Soviet tanks came rolling in, their turrets constantly rotating 360 degrees, making it clear that at any moment, anyone could be killed.

Despite the terror of the Soviets, it was clear that not even their mighty tanks could eradicate the social tides that now, like a tsunami, could not be turned back. The power of the movement forced Ernő Gerő, just a few months into his rule, to step down the next day and communist officials appointed Imre Nagy as Prime Minister. Despite this acquiescence, the violence only escalated. The Soviets were intent on crushing the movement with as much brute force as possible, killing and arresting protestors en masse, sending more and more dying and critically injured young people to the hospital where Ervin and his team worked in a constant state of shock.

As they worked, the rural peasants got busy delivering food to the city to supply the freedom fighters and the hospitals, which boosted morale and further challenged the Soviet machinery as it became clear the protest was no longer a protest but had become a revolution. Even Nagy, the new Prime Minister, shared the goal of ending Soviet rule, calling on the Soviets to leave Hungary and for free elections to commence. The Soviets had no intention of relinquishing control for just as Hitler had used autocratic means to expand his global empire, so did the Soviets. But the Hungarians were determined. By October 25, two days after the slaughter of citizens had begun, the violence reached a crescendo.

In the heat of the revolution, as protestors were shot, the spirit of change was in the air. As Soviet tanks moved in, 10,000 to 20,000 people gathered at Budapest's Kossuth Square establishing a perimeter around the troops, ostensibly to protect them. At the same time, many communist officials were urging the protestors to flee, suggesting it wasn't safe to remain. Yet the drivers of the tanks were nonthreatening, so much so that many protestors began chatting with them and the friendly tone of the Soviets implied that their presence was solely to ensure their safety given the volatility of the past few days. The atmosphere of the gathering was more joyful than angry as the protestors had no clear demands. Unlike the first day of the protest and the storming of the radio station where specific demands were made, this gathering had no aim, being more spontaneous and festive than strategic, a moment's calm amidst the carnage of the past two days and nights.

Then, suddenly and without warning, the tanks opened fire and machine guns fired from nearby buildings, including the Ministry of Agriculture, while Soviet guards shot from ground level, showering the crowd with fire from every possible direction. Some of the tanks and armored cars aimed their shots at the buildings from where the shots were firing, defending the crowd as they'd assured them they would. Some Soviet soldiers even came to their defense, being shot and killed themselves. For the next quarter hour, Kossuth Square was a battlefield as the bloodbath continued. Everybody fell to the ground, covering each other in human pyramids. Then, as suddenly as it had started, the firing stopped. In the silence of the aftermath, the injured and dying staggered and crawled away as others ran toward them to help. Then the firing resumed, as the injured and those who came to their aid were targeted for murder. For another 15 minutes, the firing continued, and then the guns fell silent again.

After some time, a dozen trucks arrived. They stacked the dead like firewood and took them away. No one knows the exact number who died on that day, which came to be known as Bloody Thursday, but most estimate that between 800 and 1,000 were killed in the two showers of bullets, and thousands more injured.

As the wounded arrived in the hospital, one after another after another, Ervin's heart broke. He thought he was seeing the last of the carnage, but now, here came a new procession of shooting victims, some so savagely injured he knew nothing they did could save them.

Some were paralyzed, others blinded, some had lost limbs, others their insides. All he could do was join the medical team and treat them to the best of their ability.

Many of those they attended to were Soviet soldiers, most of them of Mongolian origin. They were young, naïve, and totally unaware that they were in Hungary. They had been told they were going to combat in the Suez Canal and all they knew is they had traveled for days to reach their battlefield and presumed they were in Egypt to fight in the Sinai War. They believed they were firing upon a deserving enemy. They were treated in the same wards as the freedom fighters, sleeping beside them as their bodies healed.

By nightfall, some of angriest of the freedom fighters, who sought vengeance, snuck out of their beds and tried to suffocate the soldiers, forcing the staff, already overwhelmed, to not only treat their patients, but to protect them as well. As they did so, gunfire sounded through the night and long into the day, while Soviet tanks patrolled the city.

Several days later, a menacing Soviet tank was stationed next to Ervin and Judit's apartment on the hospital campus. On the other side of the campus were the freedom fighters. A volley of sniper shots from the fighters and the tanks turned the hospital campus into another war zone, making it deadly just to get from one building to another. To block out the sight, the Wolfs would pull down their shade, but the old wooden roller shades made such a noise that each time they did so, the Soviets were startled and started shooting again.

By the week's end, 2,500 people had been killed, including 700 Soviet soldiers, and thousands more injured.

If this was what it meant to be liberated by the Soviets, Ervin wanted no part of it. Either the Soviets would leave, or he and Judit would.

NOT A REAL ENEMY

The battle continued through the end of the month and amidst the chaos, the OB/GYN office had been ransacked. Equipment was smashed, lights, chairs, and tables knocked over, and files were strewn throughout the room. The secretary had fled in terror, her office now empty. Ervin stood alone in the office, exhausted from the constant surgeries and the fear that at any moment a bullet could end his or Judit's lives as they walked home. Only 34 years old, he felt as if his entire life had been lived on a battlefield. How far away was that childhood of comfort and peace where he'd delighted in afternoons by the river with his mother and father. Then his only source of stress was having to go home too soon.

As he'd consistently discovered, with every loss came opportunity, and as he stood amidst the papers strewn across the floor, he realized that among them were the confidential files the Communist Party kept on all employees, the notorious "cadre report." Like everywhere else within the Communist regime, their hospital housed a party secretary and employed secret agents to work among the staff, keeping everyone under constant surveillance. All the information these agents accumulated would be delivered to this secretary who would record whatever was reported. She was probably the most powerful person in the entire hospital, even if her position was formally a lowly one. If someone had an argument with her or she simply disliked a staff member, she could easily record false information about someone, which not only determined whether one advanced professionally, but could be used to condemn the unfortunate soul to prison or exile. Should that happen, they would never even know the reason why, as they would never know the contents of their file nor have a chance to defend themselves. The files were extensive, as the communists wanted to know all they could about every Hungarian citizen, from their living standards to their social connections and, of course, their political views. And now here they were, all scattered on the floor. Ervin's own file would be among them.

He closed the office door and crouched down. He recognized many of the names of his colleagues. He wasn't interested in them. He wanted only to know what might be contained in his own file—not from any concerns about his employment, but because he wanted to know what the communist party might have on him. Experience had taught him that one could live a noble, ethical life in communist society, yet be branded with any number of secret accusations, accusations that would arise when there came a need to silence or disappear someone. And having seen firsthand what they'd done to Uncle Laci, as well as Zoltán Vas—a true loyalist to the communist party—he knew his own future might well be precarious.

It wasn't long before he found the file bearing his own name. "Politically immature, not a real enemy, but untrustworthy, unreliable. He does not express political opinions. He has mixed with reactionary elements and had an illegal private practice. Professionally alert and shows humane understanding toward poor party members." A relieved Ervin thought, *this is it?* Yet another part of him felt slighted. *If only they knew the lengths I've gone in order to escape them. If only they knew the depths of my hatred for their rule. If only they knew I am a real enemy of their authoritarianism.*

Ervin returned home that night and he and Judit laughed over the file's characterization of him. While it was true that he did his best to avoid discussing politics or involving himself in any way with political matters, what wasn't noted was that he was a man of action when circumstances called for it. But he was also wise enough to know that sometimes it was best not to act. This was one of those times. In the weeks following the revolution, he and Judit felt there was no need for action. The Soviets had backed off and Nagy had announced, more than once, that the Soviets would soon be leaving the country. The Wolfs were ecstatic to hear such news—and even more so when Judit's uncle Zoltán, who was working closely with Nagy—confirmed it. Despite the years of neglect, treachery, and betrayal the Hungarian government had inflicted upon its people—even despite the cruelty of sending its Jewish citizens to their deaths—the couple loved their country. Their desire was not to leave it, but to return to it—to return to the nation it had been before outsiders had occupied its streets, its offices, its national spirit. Now, at last, it looked as if those days were up ahead.

But on the first of November, Nikita Khrushchev announced that the Soviets had no intention of going away. Instead, as he visited the Eastern Bloc countries, he warned that he would be invading Hungary. In response, on the third of November, Nagy formed his own government, one that included Communist Party members, but they were a minority. Hungary would henceforth be self-ruled. Early the next morning, the Soviets launched "Operation Whirlwind," and a whirlwind it was as they attacked Budapest and Nagy, realizing his own militia was no match for the mighty Soviets, ordered his military not to resist. He and some of his close associates, including Zoltán, fled to the Yugoslavian Embassy and begged for asylum. The embassy granted their request, but just three weeks later, when Nagy and Zoltán stepped out of the embassy for fresh air, they were arrested by the Soviets. Nagy was sentenced to death by hanging and Uncle Zoltán was imprisoned again. The revolution had brought hope to Hungary, but it was a hope soon quashed and the pressing weight of communism—offered as a liberating form of governance that would uplift all citizens, but instead bringing oppression and impoverishment—would squeeze the spirit and life from anyone who dared challenge its right to do so.

By the time Ervin and Judit could leave their work and home safely, they were stunned by the ravaged city. It looked as it had in the wake of the war, with windows smashed, concrete broken into bits, signposts twisted and beaten down. Nearly everything had been riddled with bullets. With every step, they saw terrible destruction. Bonfires remained ablaze and crumpled trucks, debris, wires, and cables alive with electricity that sparked ominously in the ruins of the ravaged streets testified to the horrors of a revolution suppressed.

"It's worse than Győr right after the last war," Ervin said, shaking his head in disbelief.

"It is the war," Judit observed as a truck carrying refugees rolled past them. There was no other transportation as the streets were effectively blocked off by the multitude of overturned trucks, disabled or abandoned tanks, and streetcars. As for people, most everyone the couple saw appeared to be as shocked as they were. Many wore shabby clothes and wheeled their belongings in wheelbarrows or pulled them in carts, their homes having been destroyed.

The couple walked along the Danube for kilometers before returning home, defeated but determined. Ervin saw that his beloved city had collapsed like a castle made of sand, and with it, the hope he and Judit had had for a new and free society. Though Judit had already started her internship and was only nine months short of graduating from medical school, the future they saw before them was a gloomy one. As physicians in a communist country, they would forever be struggling. But much worse was the constancy of surveillance, whether monitored phone calls or apparent "friends" who were, in fact, communist agents. Colleagues, neighbors, or friends seeking promotions or avoiding their own imprisonment would be enticed to make up any accusation for their own gain, for the pressure to turn in those closest to you was ever present. And for Judit, whose mother had fled, and thus betrayed, the country, and whose uncle was an increasingly disillusioned key player in the Communist Party, there would forever be a target on her and her family. As for Ervin, he had already lost one family to fascists. He was not going to risk losing another. The couple refused to wait any longer. The time had come to escape their living hell. But how? Ervin dared not reach out to the mystery man, for he had proven to be a danger himself given how each of his plans had turned out to be disastrous. For all Ervin knew, he was still in prison. He had to find another way.

Ervin had heard from a reliable source that thousands of people had already fled the country, crossing the Austrian border.

He broached the possibility of their doing the same to Judit.

"If we do this, there's no knowing if you'll be able to return to medical school, so if you want to stay and finish, we can do that."

"I'm not waiting any longer, Ervin. It's too risky. They've already arrested Uncle Zoltán again and we know what that means. We saw what they did to Uncle Laci, and they'll do the same to Zoltán. They still want to get back at my mother and the best way to do that is through me. Or you. Now that you're established at the hospital, there'll be pressure on you to turn against your colleagues. Who knows what they'll do?"

Tears were running down Judit's face and her usual calm demeanor had cracked. Ervin held her hands tightly in his, but he could still feel them shaking. There was another reason Judit was anxious to leave. At the height of the revolution, she had received word that her mother was gravely ill. She not only wanted to flee the hell they were living in Hungary, but she also wanted to be with her mother.

"I just can't sit here and wait for a letter telling me she has died," Judit said. "I need to be with her and if that means giving up school, then that's what I want to do."

Ervin reached over and drew her close to him, calming her with words of love and assurances that he was sure she'd see her mother again. He would have given anything to see his own mother again and couldn't bear the thought of Judit suffering as he had. It may not have been the Hungarian government that was killing her mother, but he'd be damned if he'd let the Hungarian government keep her from seeing her mother as she lay dying.

"Then it's settled. There's nothing we have here that we can't lose. If I leave with only my parents' photos, my lucky charm, and my beautiful wife, then I'll be a happy man." Ervin kissed Judit and they both smiled.

"I don't suppose we can take that serving cart with us?" Judit teased, referring to the heavy inlaid cart Ervin had pushed across town as the revolution began.

"Only if you push it!" he replied, and the two laughed and cried together as they discussed their final days in Hungary, preparing to risk their lives for the chance of freedom.

They knew that if they were caught, at best, they would lose everything. Most likely, they'd be imprisoned, probably sent to hard labor camps, perhaps for years. And leaving meant settling in a new country, learning a new language. The thought of venturing out to an unknown world and adjusting to a new life petrified Ervin. There was something different about this decision to leave, something he hadn't felt before when he'd made his aborted efforts to defect. Now he had Judit to think about. It wasn't only his own life he'd be risking. Her life would be at risk too, possibly more so given her relationship to Zoltán. They'd surely torture her and that was a thought he could not bear. Nor could he risk losing her after having lost his parents. He was confident he could survive nearly any torture the communists inflicted upon him, except losing his dear wife.

Even if they succeeded in crossing the border, he would no longer be a respected physician with a comfortable apartment and wide circle of friends. He and Judit would be penniless refugees speaking in a foreign tongue. But if there was one thing Ervin had learned from his time in Labor Service, it was that he could never allow fear to be his master. He would master his fear. He and Judit would break free of Hungary and all the horrors it had inflicted upon its people.

There was another difference about this escape. With his last two attempts, he'd made sure not a soul he knew was aware of his plan. But in the days and weeks following the revolution, escaping was on everybody's mind. And as head of an important medical department, Ervin had come to know many illustrious citizens of Budapest; hospital directors, other physicians, and department chiefs. They all spoke of their own determination to flee and within days of the violence coming to an end, the Wolfs' apartment had become the center for their discussions, where prominent men gathered for the latest information as they listened to the news on Ervin's radio. Pressing his ear to his contraband radio, like his father before him, desperate to know what was happening in the corridors of power, Ervin sat in a circle of serious men. The radio was turned low. Though this radio was not banned and the news it reported could not be trusted as the truth, what was reported provided at least a guide for where the country was headed. And what they were learning was that the Communist Party had not been humbled by the revolution but emboldened by it. They were arresting people left and right. Even the men who gathered in his apartment could not be entirely trusted because each lived in fear of their own arrest.

Ervin was cautious to keep his plans to himself as much as possible, but as others spoke of their desire to escape, he confided in the chief of his department about his desire to leave.

"You should go," the chief told him. "I'd do the same if I were in your shoes, but I have family here. It would mean leaving my children and grandchildren and my wife, and I can't do that. But you can. If something happens and you don't make it, you'll always have work at the hospital."

Ervin thanked him and was comforted by the support, though he knew the chief's benevolence would not be shared by others. There would be no place for him or Judit in Hungarian society if they failed, even if they miraculously weren't imprisoned. Yet having that support, being able to share his desire to leave with someone else and hear others speak of their own dreams of defecting, gave him a confidence he now realized he had missed in his previous efforts. He wasn't just a dissatisfied man unappreciative of his country, unwilling to put up with a bit of political restraint for the good of the masses. No, he was a reasonable man, a man who like so many others knew the future was bleak, the determination to break the will and spirits of the people was not just a consequence of communist rule, but an objective of it. No longer alone in his unease and dreams of a better life, Ervin was surrounded by like-minded men and supported by a loving and equally determined wife as he strategized their exit.

They had little time to plan that exit. A new Soviet tank division had taken over a part of the western border's defense. Added to their presence, in the wake of the revolution, the country was in chaos. A nationwide strike had commenced, and businesses were shut down.

Desperate Hungarians were fleeing the country day and night, abandoning—as Ervin and Judit would—everything they owned.

The gatherings at their apartment brought not just support, but information. They learned that there were escape routes to the Austrian border that could be secretly arranged for a fee. They would be transported in dilapidated, canvas-covered, stolen factory trucks packed with refugees. Ervin imagined that traveling in the trucks, as wretched as it might be, had to be far better than the train his parents had taken to their deaths, so no matter how uncomfortable, he was prepared for the long journey.

As limited as their income was, the Wolfs had managed their money well. Kamilla's many lessons in thrift had imprinted on Ervin the importance of saving and Judit had similarly learned not to waste money. Though they enjoyed the occasional luxury of dining out or going to the theater, they lived modestly and as a result, had been able to stash away enough American dollars to finance their exit—though just barely. As for other valuables—Ervin's medical school diploma, the few family photos that had been safeguarded for him, and even some hidden family jewels that had unexpectedly and fortuitously been delivered to him by a family friend just before the revolution—those Ervin smuggled to the Israeli Embassy, taking the same comical and risky route via streetcar that he'd employed to retrieve the gifts from Judit's mother. Once there, he arranged for the valuables to be sent to Judit's mother and stepfather in Israel via the diplomatic courier service. All that was left to do was walk out the door and start the journey.

SECOND THOUGHTS

The decision to leave had been made and not a day could be wasted. The next morning, after depositing their valuables with the Israeli Embassy, the Wolfs each packed a single bag. As Ervin selected his change of clothes, his toiletries, and his reading material, he reflected on his parents' departure. He had learned from neighbors and survivors how that departure had been forced upon them and imagined their anxiety and fear as they did just what he was doing now—choosing what to take and what to leave behind forever. He also had no idea what fate awaited them once they walked out their door, but surely nothing as horrific as what his parents had suffered. No, Ervin was leaving comfort behind for certain discomfort and exile. That was something he was prepared for. To be captured was indeed a risk, but it, too, was survivable. He unconsciously placed his hand upon the gold clover hanging from his neck, the charm he had worn since his parents had had it delivered to him in the labor camp. The tears rolled down his face as he realized he was reliving his parents' final days as he prepared to leave the only country he'd ever known for a future home entirely unknown.

Their first stop was the home of Judit's friend Maya, who had established connections with people organizing escapes. "The truck will stop here," she'd assured them, "as if they're just stopping for coffee. We won't have much time, but you'll be able to jump into the back and they'll take you to the Austrian border. It's all set."

Ervin and Judit waited all day for the truck, but it never arrived. Disappointed, they returned to the home they'd left behind.

"I don't think we should rely on Maya," Ervin said. "I think this was a sign that we shouldn't get on that truck. She's taking too big a risk as it is. Let's not put her in jeopardy."

"I'm relieved to hear you say that," Judit agreed. "I was afraid of the same thing. I feared if the truck did arrive, she'd be arrested. I just can't let her take that risk for us."

"Don't worry," Ervin said. "We'll find another way."

The next day, he got in touch with some people he'd heard could be of help and, though he was given a tip of a pending organized escape, nothing came of it. He returned to the hospital and continued working while Judit resumed her studies as if nothing had happened. Yet again and again, they were offered tips and promises, none of which materialized. At one point, someone suggested there was a train that would stop near the Austrian border for technical repairs and if they were in one of the cars, it could be disconnected and rolled over the border.

"Why doesn't someone just offer to fly us to Austria in a balloon or disguise us as giant rocks and cantilever us over the border?" Ervin suggested. "These ideas are becoming more preposterous every day. I fear we'll never get out at this rate."

Now it was Judit's turn to be optimistic. "I know it's discouraging," she said, "but you've escaped more hopeless situations. We'll get out. We just need to be patient."

Ervin smiled. She was right, he had escaped more hopeless situations. Her confidence was exactly what he needed.

Still, they were running out of time. It was mid-November and with each passing day it would be more difficult to get across the mountain pass. The snow was already falling, and it would be even worse in the mountains where visibility would quickly worsen in the brutal terrain. Hiking through deep snow would not only make an already challenging trek more difficult but leaving footprints would increase the possibility that they'd be caught. There was no time to waste. One way or another, they had to decide. They either got out or they stayed until spring.

They agreed upon November 25, just a few days away, as their self-imposed deadline. If they couldn't get out by then, they would stay in Hungary through the winter and Judit would finish her studies. They risked Judit not reaching her mother before she passed, as well as remaining in an already volatile and dangerous country under intensifying political control. Either choice was a risk, but one other factor played heavily in their decision—both Ervin and Judit had no desire to spend another season under communist rule.

As discreet as their plans to exit had been, the desperation to flee the country after the revolution had grown so great that tens of thousands of people had already left. Thus, the topic was on everybody's mind and on everybody's tongue. The open secret of anyone's plans to leave brought with it two things—one, information, and two, unexpected traveling companions. Ervin and Judit hadn't made up their minds long before both came their way.

Rumors spread that the most practical way to get out was to take the "dissident train"—the train to Győr, where they would then catch the train to Sopron, the closest town to the Austrian border. There was only one train leaving each day to Győr and it was watched closely by the secret police, but that leg of the journey wasn't a concern for the young couple, given that it was Ervin's hometown. He had every reason to travel there if questioned. But he would have to be careful about boarding the train to Sopron, as that move could arouse suspicion. And once they disembarked, the real journey would begin—crossing over the mountains.

Once their plan had been made, a visitor arrived on the Wolfs' doorstep with a plea for help. It was Ervin's former roommate and Judit's former Hebrew teacher, Béla. He was barely recognizable as he stood in the doorway, hat in hand, his once cocky smile now a trembling stretch of lips across his face.

"Ervin, it's been a long time," he said, as Ervin slowly came to recognize the man he'd once detested. His shoulders were now stooped, his frame thin and weak. Ervin was shocked to see what prison and the social shunning that came of it had done to Béla. For an instant, Ervin wondered if this apparition on his doorstep was a sign of what became of men who tried—and failed—to cross the border.

"May I come in?" Béla asked as Ervin greeted him with caution.

"Yes, yes, of course," Ervin said, inviting him in. He noted that Béla looked over his shoulder toward the shadows and immediately he sensed that the Wolfs might be being led straight into a trap.

Judit came to the doorway and gasped to see her former Hebrew teacher both in her home and looking so drastically diminished in spirit and in stature.

"Let me take your coat and get you some tea," she offered after exchanging greetings. She cast a look toward Ervin as if to say, "Where are your manners?" but he knew that Judit didn't know Béla as he did, so he maintained his caution as he awaited the reason for the visit.

"I have heard that you are planning on leaving soon," Béla began before Ervin cut him off.

"I don't know why anyone would say that," Ervin responded, but Béla held up his hand to stop him.

"I know, I know, you haven't seen me in some time and the last time you saw me I was trying to escape myself. And I got caught. And you know the penalty I paid. You were a lucky man, Ervin, to have missed that train. Some even said that you gave us up, but I know that's not the kind of man you are. You're a good man."

Ervin was growing impatient with the man's story and his flattery. He wanted him to get to the point. "What do you want, Béla?"

"I want to go with you. I want to get the hell out of here and never come back."

"Béla, I can't help you," Ervin said, growing increasingly convinced that the visit was an ominous one and that Béla couldn't be trusted.

"It's not just for me," Béla said. "My friends need to get out as well." Then he turned, opened the door, and motioned with his head for whoever had been hiding in the dark to come in. As Ervin waited for—for who? The police? A gang of ex-prisoners?—to emerge from the darkness, he saw the forms of two people take shape. It was a young couple and in the woman's arms was a sleeping baby.

Béla motioned for them to hurry inside, then he closed the door and introduced them. "This is Thaddeus and his wife, Greta." The couple nodded, murmuring their greetings. Ervin could see that they were frightened and any fear that he was being set up quickly vanished.

"How old is your baby?" he asked Greta, guessing the child to be about six months old.

Her proud smile warmed his heart as she answered, "He is eight months old and already crawling," she told him.

Ervin wasn't surprised to learn the baby was older than he'd guessed, as food was so scarce that many mothers had little to feed their babies once their breast milk was no longer sufficient. No wonder they were eager to leave.

"Béla told us you are a good man, a doctor, and that you can help us get to Austria," Thaddeus said. Ervin noted that all three of his adult visitors were growing taller and more confident as they gained the courage to speak up. And while he was not prone to respond to their flattery, he could now see that these were fellow citizens looking for the same thing he and Judit were seeking—freedom.

"Come in, won't you?" he invited them at long last, gesturing to the comfortable chairs in their living room. "Let's have some tea."

By the time they left, the couple planning to leave on their journey toward the unknown had become a team of five adults and one lively infant. It certainly was not the exodus they had anticipated, but nothing in Ervin's life had been anticipated.

Two days later, on their last day at home, both Ervin and Judit found themselves in a state of great anxiety unlike any Ervin had experienced in his prior attempts to flee. This time, the loss felt much greater, as did the stakes. He had long before learned not to become too attached to possessions, yet this time, walking away from those possessions hit harder than he'd thought. He looked at the silly hostess cart he'd pushed across the city only to break it in the elevator and thought of how much it had meant to Judit. Judit's pretty dresses, his fine suits, their good china, his books. Nothing they couldn't replace, yet these *were* the replacements—the replacements for the life the Nazis had seized from him and his family. He had had nothing just over a decade earlier and had worked so hard to rebuild his home and create a family with Judit. And now, once again, he was losing it all.

Yet it wasn't the possessions that were making it difficult to leave. He'd miss a few things, but he'd replace them all in time. It wasn't things he cared about. There was something else, something gnawing at him so relentlessly, so insidiously, that he had barely noticed it—he'd become a coward. All that frantic hustling that had distracted him as he and Judit prepared to leave had come to an end and now that it was time to step out the door, he realized that he had lost both his nerve and his self-esteem. His once spirited determination to risk anything for freedom had been replaced with an apathy he didn't quite understand.

Was it simply that he just did not care anymore what his fate would be if he remained in Hungary? As much as he'd thought he would give anything to escape, now that the time had come to do so, he realized he'd been lying to himself—and consequently, to Judit, as well. His reluctance to give up what he had strived so hard for over the past 12 years now overpowered his dream to flee.

Despite his previous lone efforts to leave, this time he knew that had Judit not pushed him to abandon their motherland, he would not have done so. He would have remained, a devoted doctor and citizen, one who loathed the communists, but they were right—he was not a real enemy, for he no longer had the fire inside him to be one. Like nearly everyone in Hungary, they'd beaten him into subservience. He railed against the communists in private and true, he had been meeting with others in his home, encouraging everyone to leave. But the truth he hadn't dared speak was that he would have been content to endure, just as he'd learned to endure the hard labor and inhumane conditions of the Labor Service. No longer an optimist, nor a pessimist despite all he'd survived through the Holocaust and the persecution that followed, now his only thought was that he didn't want to leave if it meant leaving behind his respected position as Director of the OB/GYN department. If it meant leaving behind his title of doctor. And in some comical way, if it meant leaving behind the absurdly heavy hostess cart he'd pushed through the streets of Budapest as the revolution began.

"Ervin?" Judit had finished combing her hair and fixing her face and was ready to go. "Are you ready?"

"What?" Ervin asked, looking up. He realized she'd been talking to him, and he hadn't heard a word. He was just finishing his coffee, sitting at their table, letting his gaze fall upon the simple objects that had never before meant much to him. Now it seemed that each piece held meaning. The coffee pot Judit would polish with pride, the apron she wore when cooking breakfast that brightened every morning, the egg slicer he'd repaired with a zither string. Such simple, unimportant things.

"We have to get going. Come on, dear, I know it's hard. But you've done harder things. Let's just step out the door." Judit walked over to her husband and touched his shoulder with the tenderness of a mother. She bent down and kissed his mouth and said, "It's going to be okay. We can do this."

He appreciated her intuition. He knew she sensed all the thoughts, fears, and memories going through him in that moment. How powerful his love for her was, he thought, as he pushed away his ambivalence about leaving. He knew that for all his reluctance, for all his fear, he would brave anything for her. He knew she missed her mother and wanted to see her again and if for no other reason, they'd say goodbye to Hungary so that she could do what Ervin hadn't been able to do—say goodbye to her mother.

"Come," Judit said, taking Ervin's hand and pulling him close. She walked him not to the door, but across the living room to their most cherished treasure, a Czech record player they had been gifted by a patient's family. Owning such a luxury was a great privilege, as few people could afford, much less access, one. Judit pulled out a Sarah Vaughan album and set the player's arm to their favorite song, "Tenderly." As the jazz singer sang, *the evening breeze, caressed the trees, tenderly...* the couple danced slowly together, swaying to the rhythm of the song about two lovers embracing, which they had come to think of as their own.

"And now for something to get us out the door!" Judit teased, pulling out another album, this one by Ervin's favorite English vocalist, Alma Cogan. As she set the needle onto "Mambo Italiano" and the mambo beat turned their melancholy to joy, they danced like two young teens, jumping and bumping, shaking their hips until they were both laughing with love and joy.

The music over, Ervin turned to the hostess cart and saluting it, he said, "You are now relieved of your duty!" Then without a word, they turned off all the faucets, made sure the gas was off, and walked out the door forever. Ervin felt like a tramp, dressed in three shirts, three sets of underwear, and wearing a heavy canvas raincoat over it all. He was grateful it was early winter, for he couldn't have suffered through the heat of a summer dressed as he was. He carried with him his medical bag, which he had packed with the best available supplies in the event there were any illnesses or injuries on the trip. He also carried a canvas bag containing three bottles of rum and four wristwatches in case he needed to bribe any Russian soldiers or other border guards along the way. For themselves, he brought chocolate waffles and Neapolitan ice cream, which would hold up well in the freezing temperatures. He had reasoned that the sugar, dairy, and carbohydrates would give them the much-needed energy to survive the journey. Judit, also dressed in layers of undergarments and skirts, carried only her handbag, but that, too, was packed with feminine necessities and a bag of nuts for protein. The two looked like any ordinary doctor and his wife leaving for a daytrip.

They walked for hours to reach Judit's grandmother Karolin's apartment where they would rendezvous with Béla and the young family who'd be joining them. Karolin lived quite near the Eastern Railroad Station where they would catch the only train to Győr, scheduled to leave in the early morning hours. As they walked along the streets of Budapest, they passed horrifying scenes of bombed buildings, closed businesses, and broken windows. The scars of war and revolution, Ervin thought, feeling an overwhelming sadness, outrage, and relief to be leaving it all. They spoke of ordinary matters, careful not to be overheard by any passersby, commenting at times on the tragedy that had transformed such a glorious city to such a ruin. Most of the walk, however, was made in gentle silence, as each thought of what they were leaving—Ervin his respected position, Judit her future career, both, the land of their birth, the only home they'd ever known—and what the possibilities might be for their future.

They reached Karolin's apartment in the late afternoon and though they knew that she would not be there—for she was recovering from an illness in the hospital—they could not believe their eyes when they stepped inside. Bullet holes peppered an arc above her bed with more bullet holes peppering the windows. There'd been sniper fire and if Karolin had been sleeping in that bed, she might well have been killed.

If Ervin harbored any residue of reluctance regarding their departure, that image wiped it away in an instant. He could not raise his family in such a world. Fleeing was their only option, even if it meant never seeing Karolin or any of their other friends or family again.

They telephoned Karolin at the hospital to say their goodbyes. They hadn't told her of their plans, but she had known it was coming. "We're going for a little vacation," Judit said, speaking in a coded language so that her grandmother would understand, again presuming the calls were monitored. "We aren't sure when we'll be back, but we've locked up the apartment. We'll stop by and see mother, of course."

There was a heavy sigh on the other end, but a wise and selfless woman, Karolin didn't conceal her joy as she encouraged her granddaughter to be careful. "You have a safe trip, and your mother will be so happy to see you," she said. "Oh, how I wish I could join you!"

"We'll miss you," Judit said, trying hard not to let her voice crack, which would alert anyone listening in that this was no short vacation.

"I'll miss you, too, but don't worry about me. I'll be safe. My brother and his wife are sharing my apartment now, you know, and they're awfully good to me."

After Karolin had asked God's blessings for Judit and Ervin, they said goodbye and hung up the phone. Then they dialed the Benedeks and said much the same, adding that they hoped the couple could soon join them.

By evening, Béla had arrived. Thaddeus and Greta would be meeting them at the train station the next morning. After a simple dinner, everyone was in bed early, prepared for their journey to commence at the crack of dawn.

At two a.m., the phone startled the household awake. Ervin's first thought was that they'd been found out. A secret agent, perhaps, calling to set them up? Or warn them? "Hello?" he said, coming to his senses quickly. As an obstetrician, he was accustomed to shifting from deep sleep to an alert state within seconds, but this time, along with adrenaline, there was fear pumping through his bloodstream with every thundering heartbeat.

"Ervin? It's me, Berci," a familiar voice said through the crackling of the long-distance line. It was Judit's stepfather, Albert Liebermann. Ervin's first thought was that Judit's mother had taken a turn for the worse, perhaps even died. But within moments, that worry was replaced by another. "Why are you still there? I've come to Vienna to meet you. When are you leaving?"

The fear shot through Ervin like a bullet. What was Berci thinking? After everything that had happened with Uncle Laci and Zoltán, didn't he realize the secret police could well be recording their conversation? Now if he flat out denied any knowledge of going to Austria, Berci would likely reveal even more in an effort to establish that he'd come to Vienna for good reason. The best he could do was say as little as possible.

"We're going to Győr in the morning," he said, hoping Berci would take the hint. He didn't. He was so eager to help that he said even more. "Good, good. Now listen carefully. When you get to Győr, look for Uncle Gyula. He can help you."

"Okay, Berci," Ervin said, trying to wrap up the call. "We've got to get some sleep now."

"Of course you do, but write this down. I'm staying at..." As Berci gave Ervin the name and address of the hotel he was staying at, Ervin committed it to memory, something he'd learned since his father had compelled him to remember so many names and addresses when he was in Labor Service—and a skill his profession as a physician had only honed.

Ervin hung up and turned to Judit. "I hope to God he didn't just get us killed."

Neither slept well for the rest of the night, terrified the secret police would burst through the door at any moment. They woke at dawn, both feeling the need for more sleep, both feeling the need to decide once again about their fate.

"We can just go to Győr as if that was the plan all along," Judit said, her gaze drifting from Ervin to the bullet holes above her grandmother's bed where they'd slept and now lay together in the golden morning light, "and then go home. If that's what you'd rather do. We don't have to go through with it."

Ervin wanted nothing more than to do just that but he, too, turned his gaze upward to the wall riddled with bullet holes and knew that Judit wanted to take the risk. He also knew that if they were listening in on the phone, there was just as good a chance that there were recording devices in the apartment itself.

"Even if we go back, if they've been listening to us, we're as good as dead. They'll exile us to Outer Mongolia. They'll doubtless split us up. It's a risk either way, so we might as well risk it for freedom."

Judit smiled softly and looked into her husband's eyes with tender love. The risk was indeed now greater, but just knowing that their telephone conversations, even her grandmother's own apartment, could be bugged, that bullets could fly through the window at any moment, was reason enough to flee.

After sharing their concerns with Béla, he also agreed that despite the escalated risk, they'd continue as planned. Ervin still didn't entirely trust Béla and worried that the young couple whom Béla himself hardly knew probably shouldn't have been invited, but he couldn't turn them away at this point. If there was one thing the Nazis and communists had taught him, it was that no one could be trusted, but there came times when trust was all you had. This was one of those times. The young couple had put their trust in Ervin to help them escape and Béla, despite his unpleasant personality, had become a broken man. As worried as he was about them, Ervin knew his own parents had once been a young couple themselves, but they had not been able to escape. Heightened risk or not, they'd make the flight together.

STRANGER ON A TRAIN

It was a cool, clear morning with no snow in the forecast. Each was dressed in several layers of clothing which, while uncomfortable, helped to warm them in the winter weather. The three started out silently, each considering the magnitude of their act and the risks they were facing with every step. For Ervin, however, another escape brought a wave of familiar emotions. He felt like a child preparing for mischief and it wasn't long before he realized that his anxiety had turned to excitement, as the thrill of the risk creeped up on him, a thrill he'd thought long gone.

He didn't dare reveal to Judit or Béla the current of joy he was feeling, despite his own fear. Fear had become Ervin's fuel. Though he was frightened, knowing from experience how easily a good plan could go bad, with every step he became more confident that he was in his element. The game, as Sherlock Holmes would say, was afoot!

By the time they reached the railroad station, Thaddeus and Greta were waiting, their baby boy fussing in Greta's arms. The train to Győr was also waiting, filled with passengers peering out the windows. As they bought their tickets, they chatted as if they were old friends heading off to a picnic, but when they boarded the train, the festive atmosphere darkened. The compartments were full of tense, chatting men, women, and children, all talking loudly about their plans for a day journey, while their faces and body language suggested few among them planned to return. Nervous laughter, voices a bit too loud, busy hands, and shaking legs, sheer terror in their darting eyes. Ervin noted the many feet tapping anxiously and realized that they were traveling with a train full of fellow defectors, each probing one another's eyes. How the secret police would miss these signs he couldn't imagine but, then again, he was always surprised at what they missed. They saw in the most innocent gestures and words a certain guilt and in the most obvious deceptions trustworthy souls. Their judgment was so obscured by their prejudice and bias that they were as easily deceived as they were flattered, so long as one confidently communicated that one shared the same views. As he and Judit took their seats, he noted one sign that stood out above all others—everyone was dressed like an American football player, wearing layers of clothing three sizes too large. This train ride was going to be the experience of a lifetime, Ervin realized, concluding this train of desperate refugees dressed so ridiculously was at the same time the train of the wise.

As the departure time approached, the fear intensified. The nervous chatter settled into a disquieting silence, a silence that turned thundering as the time for departure passed and the ever-punctual train stood still. Even the routine safety tests were neglected. Minutes passed, each minute more nerve wracking than the last. The nervous chatter returned, the joy replaced by irritation and then anger as the children wailed, the mothers snapped, and the men broadcast their views on everything they resented, from the government that couldn't run a train on time to a wife who couldn't calm a tearful child. Béla grumbled, but having served a prison sentence, said nothing about the Hungarian government. Judit chatted calmly with Thaddeus and Greta, helping them to keep their baby calm, while Ervin stayed quiet, knowing that the delay spelled trouble, trouble he was not about to compound by complaining.

An hour passed, and then another. Finally, just as Ervin feared a riot might erupt, the overcrowded train began to move and a collective sigh of relief broke the tension. For Ervin, however, the movement of the train was no assurance they were safe. The delay may have been caused by a minor railway issue of no importance to the passengers. The delay may also have been due to a more pressing concern of the secret police who were setting a trap for the passengers upon their arrival. The only thing that was certain was that the trip had already grown riskier, and Ervin's instincts told him to watch everyone carefully. Ervin had spent the last decade in relative comfort and safety—were his instincts as sharp as they had once been? Was his luck as great? He turned his gaze from the faces of the strangers whose fate he would share and let it settle upon the face of his wife. Judit seemed to sense him, for she turned toward him, as well. They locked eyes and, in that moment, Ervin knew luck and instinct were all they had. And his instincts told him this just might be his riskiest escape yet. He prayed in silence for luck to see them through.

After a few hours, they reached Győr. A stab of pain shot through Ervin as the familiar skyline of his hometown came into view and with it, the painfully sweet memories of the parents and life he had lost. Yet the setting was fitting, for what better place to serve as the start of their journey toward a new life.

The chaos at the railway station shook Ervin from his thoughts. People were shouting like noisy birds and as the passengers spilled from the train, their numbers swelled as they met up with their friends and family.

"Uncle Gyula!" Ervin shouted, calling the name of their connection who Judit's stepfather had provided them in his latenight call. Judit joined in as well and as the two called out, again and again, Ervin prayed that by calling the name, he wasn't invoking the secret police who may have been listening to the call. As their calls went unanswered, Ervin noticed—perhaps only in his imagination—that the crowd around them grew uneasy. Glares, confused faces, people swarming them like beggars seeking help. Slowly it occurred to him what was happening. These fellow defectors, far less seasoned than he, had mistakenly thought that it was he, Ervin, who would be smuggling them out of the country. For some reason, they'd been led to believe that he was in charge. Now Ervin's worries intensified, for if they believed him to be a smuggler, they might well call attention to him and Judit and their small entourage. Attention was the last thing he wanted in that moment.

"Looks like Uncle Gyula won't be joining us," he said loudly, gazing one last time across the crowd. Time was running out. They still had a connecting train to catch and if he waited any longer for their mysterious aide, they'd miss it. "Come, let's leave without him," he said, motioning for Judit, Béla, and the young family to follow and with a friendly wave to the fellow passengers, he turned and walked away, hoping they wouldn't follow.

Fortunately, they didn't. It seemed they'd turned their sights on another man, the entire train full of defectors bewildered and confused. If there was one thing risk and escape had taught Ervin, it was that he must never appear confused—unless confronted by an official whose interest in Ervin's movements he must appear not to understand. Conveying confidence in his behavior and movements was essential, no matter how much of it he lacked.

As they made their way to the connecting train, Ervin kept his eyes moving across the crowds, watching for any sign of Russian soldiers. The busy train station evoked vivid memories for Ervin of his aborted escape seven years earlier. That one had nearly ended in disaster. This one could end much worse. But he didn't spot any guards, just an occasional off-duty Hungarian soldier passing through the station. Nonetheless, anyone, at any time, could turn out to be a secret agent.

Once aboard the new train and settled into their seats, Ervin felt the passengers relax. It was the same group who had been on the train from Budapest, mixed in with a few new locals, though now they were laughing and smiling, greeting each other like old friends.

"It's like a shipwreck," Ervin whispered to Judit. "Everyone's just relieved to be alive."

Judit smiled. "Let's hope it stays that way," she whispered in reply.

The train was taking them to the village of Sopron, an ancient village about 70 kilometers southeast of Vienna. The hike over the mountains would take about 12 to 15 hours, depending on the weather and the strength of the travelers.

Ervin opened a map, spreading it across his lap and inviting Béla and Thaddeus to join him.

"Here's where we'll get off," he said, tapping his finger at Sopron. Lowering his voice to a whisper, he said, "we don't know where the Russian patrols are or the strength of the border's defense. We must prepare for the worst."

Béla nodded, while Thaddeus appeared nervous. "What do you mean?" Thaddeus asked, clearly frightened.

Ervin had feared this would happen. He wasn't saying anything he hadn't already made clear before they left, but Thaddeus was young and inexperienced and clearly concerned for his family. Worse, he was unable to conceal his nerves. His upper lip was beaded with sweat, and he couldn't stop fidgeting. Even the most oblivious officer was bound to note that something was up. Ervin glanced at Greta and the baby and saw that Greta was equally nervous. He never should have agreed to bring them along, he realized, but there wasn't much he could do at this point other than try to calm them.

"Don't worry," he said. "You're in good hands. Relax." He cast a warm smile toward Thaddeus and received a grateful smile in return, but no less a nervous one.

It was while discussing their next step after Sopron that a man wearing a long, black overcoat and broad-brimmed hat sat down behind them. Ervin changed the topic, not wanting to be overheard. "The weather should be crisp but clear," he said, "just right for an afternoon in the mountains."

"There's a village near the border called Nemeskér," the stranger offered in a warm, caring voice. "It's just south of Vienna and is a safe place for crossing."

Ervin turned to take a closer look at the man. He could not see his face clearly because his hat was pulled down to his eyes, giving him a rather sinister look. Ervin's instincts came to life. He could not be too careful. Before he could say a word, the man continued.

"There were no Russian commando positions this morning. It's your safest bet."

Béla was the first to respond. "How far is it from Sopron?"

"About 30 kilometers south," the stranger said.

"How can we get there?" Thaddeus asked.

"You'll have help."

Ervin and Judit glanced at each other ever so briefly. This must be the man her stepfather had sent, Uncle Gyula.

"Who do we ask for?" Judit asked.

"Look for the village priest," he answered.

"Who is this priest?" she asked, suspicion in her voice.

"I am," he answered.

A long, quiet moment followed, when at long last, Ervin risked asking a question himself. "Would you mind staying with us for the rest of the journey?" They were approaching the train station at Sopron and he knew that without assistance, he would be the one everyone would look to as the leader of the group. But he had never, not successfully at least, crossed a border illegally. He felt more like the teenager he'd once been, relying upon his parents to protect him, than the grown man he had since become.

"I'm sincerely sorry, but I must meet with the Bishop of Sopron early tomorrow morning. But if you're able to wait here overnight, I'll be happy to accompany you on another train to the village."

"Thank you," Ervin said, trusting in this stranger for no reason he could name other than that he had no idea what else to do.

The stranger opened a paper and with a friendly nod, sunk his concealed face into the day's news as the train slowly moved westward.

It was late in the evening by the time they reached Sopron. The stranger bade them farewell, promising to return the next morning. Ervin still wasn't sure why he was trusting in him, but he felt no fear, and it was that absence of fear that he had long relied on as an indicator of safety. Still, he knew to be cautious.

Refugees filled the railroad station like an airport after all flights had been cancelled. Men, women, and children sat and waited on the floors or the long wooden benches, everything they had left stuffed into duffle bags, backpacks, and battered suitcases held together with belts and ropes. The Wolf party—Ervin, Judit, Béla, and the young family—settled in a corner of the station for the night, hoping they'd get enough rest for the strenuous journey ahead. Even the baby had settled in, sleeping like a tiny angel nestled in his mother's arms.

Despite the number of refugees, the station was surprisingly free of any signs of Russian or Hungarian soldiers, though Ervin knew that the secret police were likely scattered among the swarm of travelers. The smell of cheap tobacco fowled the air and litter was strewn everywhere—scraps of food, papers, tickets, and political flyers that blew across the dirty floor like fallen leaves, even trampled clothing that had spilled from bags. Every so often, a few shabby-looking local peasants dressed in homespun wool sweaters would approach, offering to smuggle people across the border. Ervin got the impression that these peasants weren't secret agents and likely knew the mountains well, as well as the locations of destroyed barbed wire fences and the undestroyed underground mine systems that could be used for clandestine escapes. But he had no doubt they were amateurs when it came to the risks of defecting. Having already escaped the Nazis twice and tried, unsuccessfully, to escape the communists as often, Ervin knew that the consequences of failure could be dire. He also knew that wherever there were opportunities for profit, there were opportunists. Most of these smugglers would be honest. But a minority would not be. And distinguishing between them wasn't always easy. With every eager group of refugees disappearing into the crowd with one of these peasant "smugglers," Ervin prayed that they'd be safe, while shaking his head in certainty that many of them would not be.

Later, these smugglers would return, looking for more refugees to recruit, leaving Ervin to wonder of their fate. He had to admit, however, that the temptation to accept one of their offers was great. That stranger on the train, the so-called priest, could be anyone. He had no assurance that he was in fact Uncle Gyula. He hadn't mentioned Judit's stepfather. He could just as easily have overheard them and spun a tale. On the other hand, he hadn't asked for any money and if he had been a con artist, he wouldn't have risked leaving them there in the station to run off with someone else without at least securing a "deposit." And a secret agent or police officer would not leave without making the arrest. So, Ervin waited, watching as the station gradually grew emptier, quieter, and slower. Eventually, they all fell asleep, huddled together on the cold station floor.

The morning arrived with a startling blast of sound and activity as the baby wailed and all awoke to the cacophony of a busy train station. Standing over them was the priest. He had returned just as promised.

"Are you ready?" he asked, his voice and smile warm and inviting.

Ervin felt an immediate sense of relief and his trust in the stranger grew. The priest, if he was in fact a priest, appeared calm and confident, which Ervin found reassuring. "Yes, yes, we are," Ervin said as Judit hurried to gather their belongings. As the others scattered to wash up and get ready to depart, the priest explained the journey to Ervin.

"Buy tickets for the next train to Nemeskér," he said. "My village. It's not far. You can stay with me there until it's safe to cross. I'll surveil the area myself tonight with my altar boy. He's got a sharp eye. I won't let you cross until I'm confident it's safe."

Before Ervin could ask him any further questions, the priest was lost in the morning crowd, leaving Ervin as bewildered as if he'd been conversing with a phantom. Had it not been for Judit and the others having listened in on the conversation, he likely would have convinced himself the man had not even been real, but knowing how critical the journey and how great the risks, the strange priest's clandestine movements impressed Ervin. He did as instructed, purchasing tickets for him and Judit as the others followed suit and before they'd had so much as a cup of coffee, the Wolf party was once again aboard a train.

The train moved slowly, but the trip was short, consisting only of a couple of stops. Along the way, Ervin noted several isolated spots where Russians patrolled, alert to any signs of "hikers" slipping across the border. His greatest worry was that some of these soldiers would appear on the train, checking papers. Though still in Hungary, they were close enough to the border that anyone who did not reside in one of the local villages was considered suspicious. And the last thing Ervin wanted was to arouse suspicion.

The priest reappeared at the third stop in the tiny border village of Nemeskér, jumping off the train with the step of a young man, motioning for Ervin and his group to follow. They did so, walking with the good priest to his home next to the parish church. Ervin was half surprised to see that the stranger really was a priest, as he'd expected the priestly garb to be a ruse. Seeing that it was not, any suspicions he'd harbored quickly vanished for he did not find it likely that any man of God would go to such lengths to lay a trap for an unsuspecting doctor and his family.

Once inside his home, the priest introduced them to his parents, a nice old couple who welcomed the group with kindness as if accustomed to such transitory visitors. They were friendly and inviting, treating everyone like genuine houseguests, and they were especially delighted to enjoy the company of a baby. While the priest disappeared to investigate the route they would be taking that night, the hosts offered Ervin and Judit their own duvet-covered beds with down pillows so that they could have some proper sleep before their strenuous journey, giving Béla and the young family similar comfortable beds on which to nap. Ervin thought their hosts were the most gracious he had known and concluded that they were either off to a most auspicious start to their journey or this was one final rest before they faced the reckoning for their crime.

They awoke to the aroma of chicken and paprika. The priest's mother had prepared a generous meal of chicken paprikash served over homemade spaetzle. As she set down bowls of sauteed cabbage cooked with onions, laced with caraway, an assortment of pickled vegetables, and warm bowls of stewed plums, Ervin knew before tasting a bite that this would be a marvelous meal, every bit as delicious as any his mother had made.

As the group gathered around the table laden with food, everyone rose to say grace and their hosts crossed themselves in the Catholic manner, though their guests did not. Their hosts, including the priest who had returned from his mission, noticed the omission of the customary gesture but said nothing, showing no sign of judgment. Ervin saw that though they realized their guests were Jewish, to his great relief they treated them no differently.

The meal was unforgettable and left Ervin nearly in tears as he recalled the marvelous dinners his mother had so often prepared. Leaving Hungary meant leaving a past he feared relinquishing, as if once across the border there would no longer be such splendid, aromatic meals that filled him with such pleasure. Yet he knew that was nonsense, for Judit herself was quite a decent cook and there was no reason he would not have a lifetime of comforting meals ahead of him—indeed, more comforting since food would be easier to come by and the fear of socializing with the "wrong" people—friends turned secret agents, political targets, or just those too naïve to even realize their homes were bugged—would be gone. He and Judit would be free to host as many dinners as they desired. Once they were no longer homeless, that was.

As they ate, the priest revealed that he had been imprisoned for many years. Ervin was astounded to hear such news.

"But you're a priest," he said, expressing his surprise that a man of the cloth would be imprisoned.

"Yes, a priest who worked for Cardinal József Mindszenty, the Prince-Primate, Archbishop of Esztergom. The Cardinal was strongly opposed to fascism and communism in our country and given a life sentence for his opposition. Fortunately, the Hungarian Revolution brought us both our release."

"And that is why you are helping us?" Judit asked. "Because you've suffered under their rule yourself?"

"Precisely. We cannot leave," he said, gesturing to his parents who remained quiet through the discussion. "But we can help others to do so. The Arrow Cross are cruel tyrants. God gave me the gift of survival and I repay that gift by helping others."

Ervin was in awe of this kind and courageous man who was helping them flee. His ordeal could be Ervin's own if they did not escape. Knowing this kind man's story made Ervin even more grateful to have been blessed with meeting him.

After dinner, they gathered in the front room where the priest told them of his findings. "The route looks good. We didn't spot any signs of trouble, nothing out of the ordinary. It's a new moon tonight, so it's going to be dark, but clear. It's harder to see where you're going, but harder for anyone to spot you. Are you ready?"

They were ready. There was no turning back at this point. They all nodded and voiced their eagerness to go, indeed, the excitement of the group made things seem nearly festive. Only the baby seemed unmoved as he slept peacefully, oblivious to the momentous journey he was about to undertake. Ervin marveled at how good he had been up to that point, though he was doubtful any baby, no matter how well behaved, could restrain himself from fussing and wailing once the discomfort of the cold set in.

"Alright then, let's get going," the priest declared. As if on cue, the sounds of creaking wheels and horse hooves outside drew everyone's attention.

"It's my altar boy," said the priest, a broad smile lighting up his face. "Your carriage awaits. Shall we go?"

The door opened and there sat a horse-drawn cart, its open wagon filled with hay. The altar boy sitting up front with the reins in his hands tipped his hat and with an expansive wave of his arm, gestured for his passengers to hop on board.

FREEDOM

The priest had been right. It was as dark a night as Ervin had ever known. Luckily, there was no snowfall, for as romantic as falling snow might be, this was no romantic journey. It was life or death. The ride, bitter cold and uncomfortable, was quiet, the only noise the creaking of the cart's wheels and the rhythmic percussion of the horse's hooves hitting the frozen soil.

After about an hour, Ervin guessed that they were only three to five kilometers out when the wagon abruptly stopped. The road was blocked by some huge trees that appeared to have been deliberately placed across it. In the distance, small lights flashed, a sight familiar to Ervin from his days in Labor Service. Someone was smoking, no doubt guards.

The priest, who had been riding up front with the altar boy, said in the softest voice, "We mustn't take any unnecessary risks. We'll have to call it off for the night. We can try again tomorrow." The wagon made a wide U-turn, and they rode back in the cold night air, this time drained of any excitement. In its place was disappointment and foreboding.

We'll never make it, Ervin thought, though he heard himself speak otherwise to the disappointed travelers. "He's right, we can't take the risk. Tomorrow might be better."

Early the next morning, the good priest again departed for another reconnaissance trip. Ervin hoped that this time he'd go further along the route to ensure that there were no roadblocks. He was grateful, though, that the roadblock had been established, for what if it hadn't? They would have proceeded, only to be apprehended by the guards. Would they be there again this night? The chances were high that they would. Would they take another route? Ervin hoped so.

By noon, the priest returned with good news. "I met with a friend and he's planning to smuggle several people across the border tomorrow night. He's agreed to let the five of you join him," the priest paused, then smiling toward the baby boy, he added, "and of course, the baby."

"Has he ever done this sort of thing before?" Ervin asked.

"Oh, yes, there's nothing to worry about. He has quite a bit of experience getting freedom fighters across the border. Don't worry, you'll be in good hands. He knows every route of the border area. You'll be much safer with him."

Ervin wasn't sure what to make of that last statement. Was the priest suggesting they hadn't been safe in his hands the previous night? But he knew his options at this point were limited. They could return to Budapest and live out their lives under communist rule or they could try once more to escape. "We've come this far," he said aloud, as much to himself as the priest. "We've no choice but to trust your judgment."

"Good decision," the priest said, slapping him on the back. "Now let's see what my mother's been cooking for us. It smells like sauerkraut and sausage, one of her best!"

Later that afternoon, this time in broad daylight, they took another hayride. After about half an hour, the wagon stopped in front of a hayfield. The priest, again sitting up front, turned and whispered, "This is where we get out. On the other side of this field, there's a house." He pointed in the direction he wanted them to run. "Make absolutely no sound and use those haystacks for cover. Follow me. Good luck and," he paused, then said in a most serious tone, "may God bless."

Ervin climbed out of the wagon first and helped the women down, with Greta holding her baby close. Béla and Thaddeus followed, and they all scattered across the field, silently running and ducking behind haystacks, trying to catch their breath in silence. When they reached the small farmhouse, a man was waiting in the doorway. He quietly motioned for the travelers to come in quickly. One by one they were whisked through the doorway until all were reunited. The man looked tough, the way Ervin had imagined a smuggler would look, and he was glad the man was on their side for he wouldn't have wanted him as an enemy. He was all muscle.

The priest introduced him as their guide, not revealing his name. "We're old friends from school. You're in good hands."

"We've got a couple dozen more coming," the man said, and Ervin realized that their small party, which he felt was already rather large at five adults and one baby, was about to quadruple in size. He hoped they all had their wits about them and that such a large group passing over the mountains wouldn't draw any attention.

As the hours passed, more people came running across the field and were hurried inside to wait for darkness to descend once again before they could make the dangerous crossing. While they waited, the smuggler made several nasty antisemitic remarks about "dirty Jews" causing all this trouble in his homeland.

"They should just leave the country rather than forcing good Hungarian patriots to flee," he said, going on and on about how dangerous the Jews were to everyone's well-being. As he said such things, the priest remained calm, but Ervin could see that the kind and understanding cleric felt uncomfortable with the comments, for he would glance at his companions with tenderness in his eyes, and he periodically put his finger to his lips and winked, signaling for everyone to ignore the fool. Ervin was glad he had done so, for there was always a hothead in every group and they couldn't afford an angry madcap mouthing back, no matter how understandable it might be to do so. There would be no purpose in calling out the antisemite for his cruel ignorance as their fate was in his hands.

As the afternoon turned to evening and the sun began to set, the tensions brought on by the smuggler's remarks lightened as excitement—and a good deal of anxiety—took over. The sky was darkening, and the group was growing restless when a loud wail shattered the silence. The baby wouldn't stop crying as Greta anxiously tried to settle him down, but her infant was no doubt picking up on her own stress and the strain in the room. Judit tried to calm the baby, as did several others in the group, but nothing could stop his wailing.

"You'd better shut up that kid," the smuggler said, "for he could get us all killed. We can't have him crying once we start to cross."

"I'm trying!" she cried in response, clearly at her wit's end as to how to settle her sobbing child. "He's a good baby, he'll settle down, just give him a minute."

"I can help," Ervin said, "if it's agreeable to Greta and Thaddeus. I've brought my medical bag. I can administer a low-dose sedative, nothing too strong, just enough to calm him. Would you like me to do that?" Ervin was looking directly at Greta and saw her face soften in relief.

"Oh, yes, yes, please, if you're sure it won't hurt him."

"I'm sure, I've done this many times in the hospital when we've had infants in need of medical intervention. It won't be too strong."

Ervin prepared the shot with the whole group watching his every move. He felt apprehensive being on stage, so to speak, for he hadn't been watched so closely since medical school. But once he administered the shot, the baby quieted right down, and a huge collective sigh of relief seemed to sedate the tense group just as the sedative had calmed the baby.

But just ten minutes later, the baby woke up crying even more violently than before. Greta herself was near tears, feeling helpless.

"I'm sorry," the smuggler said, "but I can't risk taking you across with him. You'll have to stay behind."

The small family who Ervin and Judit had grown close to over the last few days of sharing their common ordeal were heartbroken and Ervin felt their sadness as his own. He knew how desperately they wanted to leave Hungary, and he also knew the crushing disappointment of an unsuccessful escape. But he realized the smuggler was right. They couldn't risk the trip with the baby in such a state and Ervin didn't dare administer any more sedatives.

"Please," Thaddeus implored. "If we can just wait a bit longer until he's asleep."

The smuggler shook his head. "Nope. Not doing it. But if you'll come back tomorrow night and he's good, we can try again."

They accepted that option with relief and the priest accompanied them back to his house. By nightfall, the time had come for the rest of the group to set out once again. It was a cool, clear night, but unfortunately, that very day, the fields had been plowed. The once easy terrain had become so muddy that every step was heavy and felt as if they were climbing stairs. The trek was filled with quiet tension. The smuggler led the pack with Judit close behind him and the others scattered. Ervin, weighed down by his medical bag and briefcase, was soon far behind Judit. He was wearing a heavy canvas raincoat that made a whooshing sound with every step as his arms moved back and forth.

"Can you take that thing off?" the smuggler hissed. "It's making an awful racket."

"It's too cold," Ervin protested, "and it's my only coat. And my hands are already full." Ervin knew the guide was unhappy with him, but the temperature was falling quickly, and he couldn't risk walking without it. He did his best to keep his arms as still as possible and in time the guide stopped complaining. Ervin didn't much care for the smuggler, but he was grateful for his assistance and especially pleased to see the smuggler occasionally help Judit by holding her arm when they traversed the muddy fields, at times reaching deep ditches they had to scamper down and out of in the dark.

As the trek continued, Ervin was surprised that there were no farmhouses around, not even many trees. Above them the starless sky, thick with a blanket of clouds, felt heavy and ominous. Every step was treacherous as they walked further into the darkness, and the smell of the fresh manure the farmers used to fertilize their fields was the only reminder that the vast terrain held any life at all. The monotony of the emptiness combined with the risky journey added to the suspense, as if at any moment something would happen to shock them from the nerve-racking tranquility, while the barely muffled breathing of the other refugees advancing in the darkness gave the entire atmosphere a menacing feel. And yet, every step brought greater hope.

Ervin was lost in his thoughts of foreboding when suddenly a stream of Soviet planes burst through the silence, illuminating the fields with a searing light as if daylight had burst through the darkness.

"Get down!" the smuggler ordered, dropping to the ground. Everyone did as ordered, running to the nearest ditch and lying down for several minutes. Ervin felt his heart pounding as if it would burst while he waited in the mud for the bullets to rain down upon them. When the planes had passed and darkness returned, they slowly rose and resumed their hike, now muddied from head to toe. The scene repeated several times through the night as the planes surveilled the area, each time feeling as if it were the last moments of life before the shooting started.

After walking a few hours, Ervin and Judit now traveling side by side, both exhausted, a faint green light appeared in the distance as if a beacon urging them ever closer. They hiked another 13 kilometers toward the mysterious light until, through the silence, the smuggler announced, "There's one more ravine and once you climb over it, you'll be on Austrian soil."

Ervin couldn't believe what he was hearing and with a few steps forward, he saw that there was indeed another ravine, as if the earth itself had cracked open to separate the worlds of fascism and freedom. He and Judit leapt across, and each fell upon the ground and kissed the soil, as one by one the other travelers did the same. Ervin and Judit hugged and kissed each other, delirious to enjoy their first moments of freedom. Yet no sooner had they done so than several strange spotlights, like tiny fireflies on a hot summer night, flickered and glittered in the distance, clearly aimed in their direction. Within seconds, the lights grew bigger as they came closer, and Ervin's heart froze. Had the smuggler tricked them?

"Welcome!" the guards, invisible behind the bright lights, called out. "You have made it to the free world! Good luck with your destinies!" They were surrounded by Austrian guards, all welcoming them to this new land as if they had been awaiting their guests all evening.

With tears streaming down his face, Ervin thanked the smuggler for risking his life for their freedom and rewarded him with nearly all that he had remaining from his Hungarian savings. Turning, he was instantly bathed in bright lights and surrounded by armed guards, yet none had their guns drawn, none threatened them in any way. Ervin felt no fear, no danger, only joy as the guards continued to welcome them like long-lost friends. Now free at last, he and Judit were near penniless, but so much richer than ever before.

They were taken to a nearby school and given a warm meal of soup and bread. Ervin was fascinated by all the colorful plastic flowers that decorated each table, as if these simple decorations symbolized the bright future ahead of them. Once fed, they were taken to the border guard Command Center where the guards, speaking in German, told them they could catch a bus early the next morning that would take them to Vienna, where Judit's stepfather would be waiting for them.

"Alas," Ervin said, "we've no Austrian schillings. Would you be able to loan us enough to get to the capital? I can assure you that my father-in-law will repay you right away."

The guards shook their heads and one explained, "I'm sorry, but we can't do that. We get this same request each night and we just can't provide every refugee with money. When we've done so in the past no one has repaid us, no matter how sincere their assurance. I'm afraid you'll have to find another way to pay."

"I assure you," Ervin protested, "we are honest doctors and we know that how we treat you now will determine how others are received in the future. We owe our lives to the good souls who've helped us reach your country. I beg of you, trust one more refugee couple and we shall restore your faith in humanity."

The guards looked at each other, shrugged, and collected the shillings to see the Wolfs safely to Vienna.

The guards also let Ervin and Judit use their telephone to call Berci, who was overjoyed to hear they'd reached Austria. "This is such wonderful news!" he said. "Judit's mother is quite ill, but this news will do more for her spirits than any medicine! When you get to the bus station, take the streetcar to the Hotel Mozart. I'm staying there and I'll arrange for you two to have your own room when you arrive." They further explained about the need to repay the guards and Berci arranged their repayment. When they hung up, Ervin reached into his bag and pulled out a few bottles of rum he had smuggled out and gave them to the kind guards who were delighted to receive them. As the guards drank, their mood turned jovial and before long, Ervin and Judit were stunned to hear them praising Adolf Hitler.

"We were all in the SS," one explained. "Hitler wasn't as bad as they say."

"No, he was a nice man," another said. "It was Heinrich Himmler who was a piece of work. Nasty one, that man!"

Several others agreed, while Judit and Ervin merely smiled and nodded, careful not to express a word of disagreement. Ervin surmised that they were dupes and had no real idea of the atrocities Hitler had orchestrated, and Ervin wasn't about to tell them of his own tragic loss for it would serve no purpose.

As dawn approached, the couple, exhausted but accustomed to such sleepless nights from their many years working in the hospital, bid the drunken guards goodnight as they walked through the last of the darkness toward a new dawn.

The fluorescent lights of the bus station seared their eyes, but having never seen such bright lights before, Ervin found them fascinating. They bought their tickets, boarded the bus, and slept leaning against each other through the brief but bumpy ride. Their bus reached Vienna just as the business hours were starting and the streets were buzzing with Austrians on their way to work.

They stepped off the bus, both covered in dried mud, their hair matted and messy. They looked horrible, like bums or homeless vagrants, but neither had ever been happier. Ervin looked about at the crowded bus station, noting the well-dressed businessmen hurrying to work, and young women and their children dressed neatly for school. Everything appeared to be moving so smoothly and efficiently, as if by magic they had arrived in this new and vibrant world. Despite his exhaustion, he felt intoxicated with joy.

"We must find a streetcar," Judit said, looking around for a stop. "We need to figure out which one goes to the Hotel Mozart."

"Okay, but first, there's something else I want to do." He had saved his American dollars for many years and now, having saved up five of them—the last of all his money in the world—there was something special he wanted to use them for.

"And what's that?" Judit asked, curious but just as deliriously happy as Ervin.

"First, let's find a confectionary!" he said, as delighted as if he were once again six years old.

Judit smiled. "Candy? The first thing you want is candy?"

"Yes, it is," Ervin said, taking his dear wife by the arm and escorting her down the street, behaving like they were dressed in royal finery. They walked along the streets of Vienna inhaling every sight with their eyes. It was like they'd never seen a city street before. The Wolfs were enchanted and within minutes, the two mud-splattered refugees were standing in front of a display case filled with candy. Ervin stepped up to the counter, reached into his pocket, and placed his long-saved dollars on the counter. Moments later, they were outside the shop enjoying a bag of chocolate pastilles, or "cat tongues" as they were called. Walking the streets of Vienna, Ervin's memories of his childhood rekindled as if the years had never passed, each small chocolate sating him with his father's love, a love that would be with him forever, and now a love he shared with his wife.

When the chocolates were gone, they stopped at a street cart where they bought an exotic fruit that Ervin and Judit had never tasted—a banana. Tasting the sweet and wondrous fruit, they walked arm in arm, not believing their good fortune and all they had overcome to reach this miraculous city. At long last, they took a streetcar to the Hotel Mozart where a concierge notified Berci of their arrival.

Seconds later, Berci stood at the top of the stairs dressed in a dark blue silk robe, looking like a baron, his smile wide and radiating love and joy as he descended the stairs, his arms open wide. He hugged and kissed the happy couple. Overcome with emotion, he sat down on the steps and cried.

Rising, Berci wiped away his tears and, when accompanying the couple up the stairs, he asked, "What is your first desire? Anything, and I shall provide it!"

"First, call my mother. And then, a hot bath!" Judit declared.

"Ah, yes, a bath would be wonderful. And one other thing," Ervin added. "Is there any chance you have that drink I've heard so much about? The one they call Coca-Cola?"

Berci smiled. "I do indeed," he said, ushering them into his room. "I do indeed..."

EPILOGUE

The Wolfs spent three weeks in Vienna, strolling the streets, enjoying the delicious food, and listening to the music they'd so long missed. Much to the disappointment of Berci and Violet, the couple chose not to move to Israel since the Sinai War had erupted between Israel and Egypt, and they could not bear to endure further conflict. Judit's father, Harry, had emigrated to America, so at his invitation and with the help of the Hebrew Immigrant Aid Society and the Joint Distribution Committee, the couple emigrated to the United States. "We were intoxicated with happiness," Ervin said of their journey to the free world. As they sailed across the Atlantic Ocean, the salty breeze like a soothing balm, Ervin recalled sitting on the edge of his bed as his mother read to him a favorite fairytale, *Óperentzia*, referring to the ocean. "Once upon a time, somewhere, nowhere," his mother would read to him, "it was so beautiful, maybe it wouldn't even be true at all, over the large sea, far, far away over the *óperentzia*, was a big, shiny kingdom." After a turbulent and cold voyage over the North Atlantic Ocean (even by the captain's standards, they were told), the US military transport ship filled with refugees reached New York on January 7, 1957, the city's lights glittering like the most magnificent kingdom he'd ever imagined. Ervin realized that his childhood fairytale had come true.

The couple settled in Mt. Clemens, Michigan, a suburb of Detroit, where after struggling to learn English, Ervin became a beloved obstetrician, delivering more than 10,000 babies during his long career. He and Judit soon had a son of their own, Robert, who also grew up to become a physician.

Over the years, the couple made several trips back to Israel and Hungary, and became active in their community, especially by helping to document the stories of Holocaust survivors and those enduring communist repression and persecution.

As time passed, Ervin had the opportunity to piece together more stray threads of the story of his life in Hungary and his efforts to escape. He learned early on that Greta and Thaddeus had been able to escape Hungary with their baby shortly after Ervin and Judit made their escape. Ervin saw his friend Frank one last time and was thrilled to hear that Frank had survived the communists, though he remained in Hungary. Years later, Ervin met the mysterious pipe-smoking man who had arranged his early, aborted, efforts to escape. His name, Ervin learned, was also Laci and he was married to the mysterious woman from the train station, the one with the "smile of a friend" who had appeared from nowhere and advised him what to do. Her name was Ilonka. The couple had been arrested and jailed, which was why Ervin could never reach the mystery man again. The false papers Ervin had prepared at Laci's request to help rescue the incarcerated pregnant woman had been sitting on the table when the gendarmes burst in. Fortunately, there was just enough time for Ilonka to stuff the documents inside a cookie jar. Had they been found, Ervin would surely have been arrested and imprisoned himself.

He also learned that the group of people from the dark apartment who had suddenly disappeared had also been arrested. Fortunately, none of them revealed Ervin's name nor his efforts to escape.

Laci Benedek emigrated to Sweden with his family, while Zoltán Vas, Judit's uncle, no longer banished to the remote countryside, returned to Budapest to help organize the country's economic reforms.

To express his gratitude for the priest's unforgettable sacrifice in helping them to escape, the Wolfs donated money to the Catholic Church of Nemeskér. Each year during the Christmas season, Ervin sent a package including a gift of money to his pastor friend and his family, until one year, their annual gift was returned accompanied by a sad note that read, "Unable to deliver, addressee deceased."

Of the over 800,000 Jews living in Hungary before the war, only about 255,000 are believed to have survived. Between late April and August 1944, up to 440,000 Jews were deported from Hungary to concentration camps. Like Joseph and Kamilla, 320,000 died upon arrival or shortly after. Many died in the Labor Service, though for some, such as Ervin, the Labor Service spared their lives because it kept them from being deported to the death camps. Győr was among the most decimated of communities, with almost all of the city's 4,700 Jews, comprising 8% of its population, deported to the death camps. Despite this horrific loss of lives, the history of Hungary during the Holocaust remains unknown to most Americans. Ervin and Judit were determined that this history would not be forgotten.

After living a long and happy life, Ervin died in 1997 at the age of 74 and Judit died in 2016 at the age of 83. Before his death, Ervin related this story of his and his family's lives in Hungary to his son, Robert, who now carries on his parents' mission to never let the past be forgotten.

ACKNOWLEDGMENTS

This work and exciting journey became possible because of the help and support from many people. Kim Parr, a long-standing family friend and historian from our hometown in suburban Detroit, Michigan, handed the author a CD-ROM of Ervin Wolf's autobiography, originally written by hand in the 1970s, after his wife Judit passed away in 2016. Book coach, author, marketing advisor, website designer, and friend Mark Cahill has been an amazing guide throughout this path and continues to offer his advice.

Editors Deborah Larsen, Keidi Keating, Melisa Carter, and Kellie Morin-Araujo have all been invaluable. Keidi is also an author and book coach. Tara Serafin, a talented artist, has helped with book cover design ideas. Historian Peter Black verified the events that occurred behind the stories included in this biography. Author Lisa Tener recommended the work of my current co-author, book coach, advisor, and friend, Janice Harper. Janice's tenacity, integrity, hard work, pragmatism, strategies, and advice are unmatched. This collaboration was the turning point in transforming the stories into something special to share with the world.

The support of extended family and many friends will never be forgotten and has been a true motivator, especially when needed the most. I wish to thank author Jill Grimes, MD, Rob Sawyer, MD, Andy Sheufelt, Anne Sebestyen, John Oggiono, Mark Hughes, Rick Jellesma, the Morton family—and a special thanks to the patient Dawn Morton Wolf—the Schlanger family, and of course my stepsister Darlene Zietz and her son Jonathan, an excellent producer/director who filmed and integrated our high quality and valuable marketing video blogs. Longtime family friend Amy Weber led us to Henry Greenspan, co-author of a Holocaust memoir with Amy's late mom, Agi Rubin. Henry participated in a critical Beta read. Their work together is inspirational. The feedback and touching testimonials by Professors Michael Berenbaum, Ed Westermann, and Monty Penkower are deeply appreciated.

Our assembled team also includes author Natasha Link and Maddie Davis, both so helpful with social media and other marketing strategies, website assistance, SEO, developing professional business pages, and public relations in general.

Most of all, we need to thank the main characters who endured these often-harrowing experiences, Ervin and Judit Wolf, dad and mom. Without your love, wisdom, guidance, perseverance, interest, knowledge, ambition, integrity, due diligence, righteousness, sense of team play, and care for God and His people, the content in this book would not be available to be shared with interested readers. Your message is strong and poignant. Your voice means as much in today's world as it ever has. May the good Lord bless you both and may you permanently rest in peace.

AMSTERDAM PUBLISHERS HOLOCAUST LIBRARY

The series **Holocaust Survivor Memoirs World War II** consists of the following autobiographies of survivors:

Outcry. Holocaust Memoirs, by Manny Steinberg

Hank Brodt Holocaust Memoirs. A Candle and a Promise, by Deborah Donnelly

The Dead Years. Holocaust Memoirs, by Joseph Schupack

Rescued from the Ashes. The Diary of Leokadia Schmidt, Survivor of the Warsaw Ghetto, by Leokadia Schmidt

My Lvov. Holocaust Memoir of a twelve-year-old Girl, by Janina Hescheles

Remembering Ravensbrück. From Holocaust to Healing, by Natalie Hess

Wolf. A Story of Hate, by Zeev Scheinwald with Ella Scheinwald

Save my Children. An Astonishing Tale of Survival and its Unlikely Hero, by Leon Kleiner with Edwin Stepp

Holocaust Memoirs of a Bergen-Belsen Survivor & Classmate of Anne Frank, by Nanette Blitz Konig

Defiant German - Defiant Jew. A Holocaust Memoir from inside the Third Reich, by Walter Leopold with Les Leopold

In a Land of Forest and Darkness. The Holocaust Story of two Jewish Partisans, by Sara Lustigman Omelinski

Holocaust Memories. Annihilation and Survival in Slovakia, by Paul Davidovits

From Auschwitz with Love. The Inspiring Memoir of Two Sisters' Survival, Devotion and Triumph Told by Manci Grunberger Beran & Ruth Grunberger Mermelstein, by Daniel Seymour

Remetz. Resistance Fighter and Survivor of the Warsaw Ghetto, by Jan Yohay Remetz

My March Through Hell. A Young Girl's Terrifying Journey to Survival, by Halina Kleiner with Edwin Stepp

Roman's Journey, by Roman Halter

Beyond Borders. Escaping the Holocaust and Fighting the Nazis. 1938-1948, by Rudi Haymann

The Engineers, by Henry Reiss

Memoirs by Elmar Rivosh, Sculptor (1906-1967). Riga Ghetto and Beyond, by Elmar Rivosh

The series **Holocaust Survivor True Stories** consists of the following biographies:

Among the Reeds. The true story of how a family survived the Holocaust, by Tammy Bottner

A Holocaust Memoir of Love & Resilience. Mama's Survival from Lithuania to America, by Ettie Zilber

Living among the Dead. My Grandmother's Holocaust Survival Story of Love and Strength, by Adena Bernstein Astrowsky

Heart Songs. A Holocaust Memoir, by Barbara Gilford

Shoes of the Shoah. The Tomorrow of Yesterday, by Dorothy Pierce

Hidden in Berlin. A Holocaust Memoir, by Evelyn Joseph Grossman

Separated Together. The Incredible True WWII Story of Soulmates Stranded an Ocean Apart, by Kenneth P. Price, Ph.D.

The Man Across the River. The incredible story of one man's will to survive the Holocaust, by Zvi Wiesenfeld

If Anyone Calls, Tell Them I Died. A Memoir, by Emanuel (Manu) Rosen

The House on Thrömerstrasse. A Story of Rebirth and Renewal in the Wake of the Holocaust, by Ron Vincent

Dancing with my Father. His hidden past. Her quest for truth. How Nazi Vienna shaped a family's identity, by Jo Sorochinsky

The Story Keeper. Weaving the Threads of Time and Memory - A Memoir, by Fred Feldman

Krisia's Silence. The Girl who was not on Schindler's List, by Ronny Hein

Defying Death on the Danube. A Holocaust Survival Story, by Debbie J. Callahan with Henry Stern

A Doorway to Heroism. A decorated German-Jewish Soldier who became an American Hero, by Rabbi W. Jack Romberg

The Shoemaker's Son. The Life of a Holocaust Resister, by Laura Beth Bakst

The Redhead of Auschwitz. A True Story, by Nechama Birnbaum

Land of Many Bridges. My Father's Story, by Bela Ruth Samuel Tenenholtz

Creating Beauty from the Abyss. The Amazing Story of Sam Herciger, Auschwitz Survivor and Artist, by Lesley Ann Richardson

On Sunny Days We Sang. A Holocaust Story of Survival and Resilience, by Jeannette Grunhaus de Gelman

Painful Joy. A Holocaust Family Memoir, by Max J. Friedman

I Give You My Heart. A True Story of Courage and Survival, by Wendy Holden

In the Time of Madmen, by Mark A. Prelas

Monsters and Miracles. Horror, Heroes and the Holocaust, by Ira Wesley Kitmacher

Flower of Vlora. Growing up Jewish in Communist Albania, by Anna Kohen

Aftermath: Coming of Age on Three Continents. A Memoir, by Annette Libeskind Berkovits

Not a real Enemy. The True Story of a Hungarian Jewish Man's Fight for Freedom, by Robert Wolf

Zaidy's War. Four Armies, Three Continents, Two Brothers. One Man's Impossible Story of Endurance, by Martin Bodek

The Glassmaker's Son. Looking for the World my Father left behind in Nazi Germany, by Peter Kupfer

The Apprentice of Buchenwald. The True Story of the Teenage Boy Who Sabotaged Hitler's War Machine, by Oren Schneider

Good for a Single Journey, by Helen Joyce

Burying the Ghosts. She escaped Nazi Germany only to have her life torn apart by the woman she saved from the camps: her mother, by Sonia Case

American Wolf. From Nazi Refugee to American Spy. A True Story, by Audrey Birnbaum

Bipolar Refugee. A Saga of Survival and Resilience, by Peter Wiesner

Before the Beginning and After the End, by Hymie Anisman

The series **Jewish Children in the Holocaust** consists of the following autobiographies of Jewish children hidden during WWII in the Netherlands:

Searching for Home. The Impact of WWII on a Hidden Child, by Joseph Gosler

See You Tonight and Promise to be a Good Boy! War memories, by Salo Muller

Sounds from Silence. Reflections of a Child Holocaust Survivor, Psychiatrist and Teacher, by Robert Krell

Sabine's Odyssey. A Hidden Child and her Dutch Rescuers, by Agnes Schipper

The Journey of a Hidden Child, by Harry Pila and Robin Black

The series **New Jewish Fiction** consists of the following novels, written by Jewish authors. All novels are set in the time during or after the Holocaust.

The Corset Maker. A Novel, by Annette Libeskind Berkovits

Escaping the Whale. The Holocaust is over. But is it ever over for the next generation? by Ruth Rotkowitz

When the Music Stopped. Willy Rosen's Holocaust, by Casey Hayes

Hands of Gold. One Man's Quest to Find the Silver Lining in Misfortune, by Roni Robbins

The Girl Who Counted Numbers. A Novel, by Roslyn Bernstein

There was a garden in Nuremberg. A Novel, by Navina Michal Clemerson

The Butterfly and the Axe, by Omer Bartov

To Live Another Day. A Novel, Elizabeth Rosenberg

A Worthy Life. Based on a True Story, by Dahlia Moore

The series **Holocaust Heritage** consists of the following memoirs by 2G:

The Cello Still Sings. A Generational Story of the Holocaust and of the Transformative Power of Music, by Janet Horvath

The Fire and the Bonfire. A Journey into Memory, by Ardyn Halter

The Silk Factory: Finding Threads of My Family's True Holocaust Story, by Michael Hickins

The series **Holocaust Books for Young Adults** consists of the following novels, based on true stories:

The Boy behind the Door. How Salomon Kool Escaped the Nazis. Inspired by a True Story, by David Tabatsky

Running for Shelter. A True Story, by Suzette Sheft

The Precious Few. An Inspirational Saga of Courage based on True Stories, by David Twain with Art Twain

The series **WWII Historical Fiction** consists of the following novels, some of which are based on true stories:

Mendelevski's Box. A Heartwarming and Heartbreaking Jewish Survivor's Story, by Roger Swindells

A Quiet Genocide. The Untold Holocaust of Disabled Children in WWII Germany, by Glenn Bryant

The Knife-Edge Path, by Patrick T. Leahy

Brave Face. The Inspiring WWII Memoir of a Dutch/German Child, by I. Caroline Crocker and Meta A. Evenbly

When We Had Wings. The Gripping Story of an Orphan in Janusz Korczak's Orphanage. A Historical Novel, by Tami Shem-Tov

Jacob's Courage. Romance and Survival amidst the Horrors of War, by Charles S. Weinblatt

Want to be an AP book reviewer?

Reviews are very important in a world dominated by the social media and social proof. Please drop us a line if you want to join the *AP review team* and show us at least one review already posted on Amazon for one of our books.

info@amsterdampublishers.com

www.ingramcontent.com/pod-product-compliance
Lightning Source LLC
LaVergne TN
LVHW091548070526
838199LV00024B/583/J